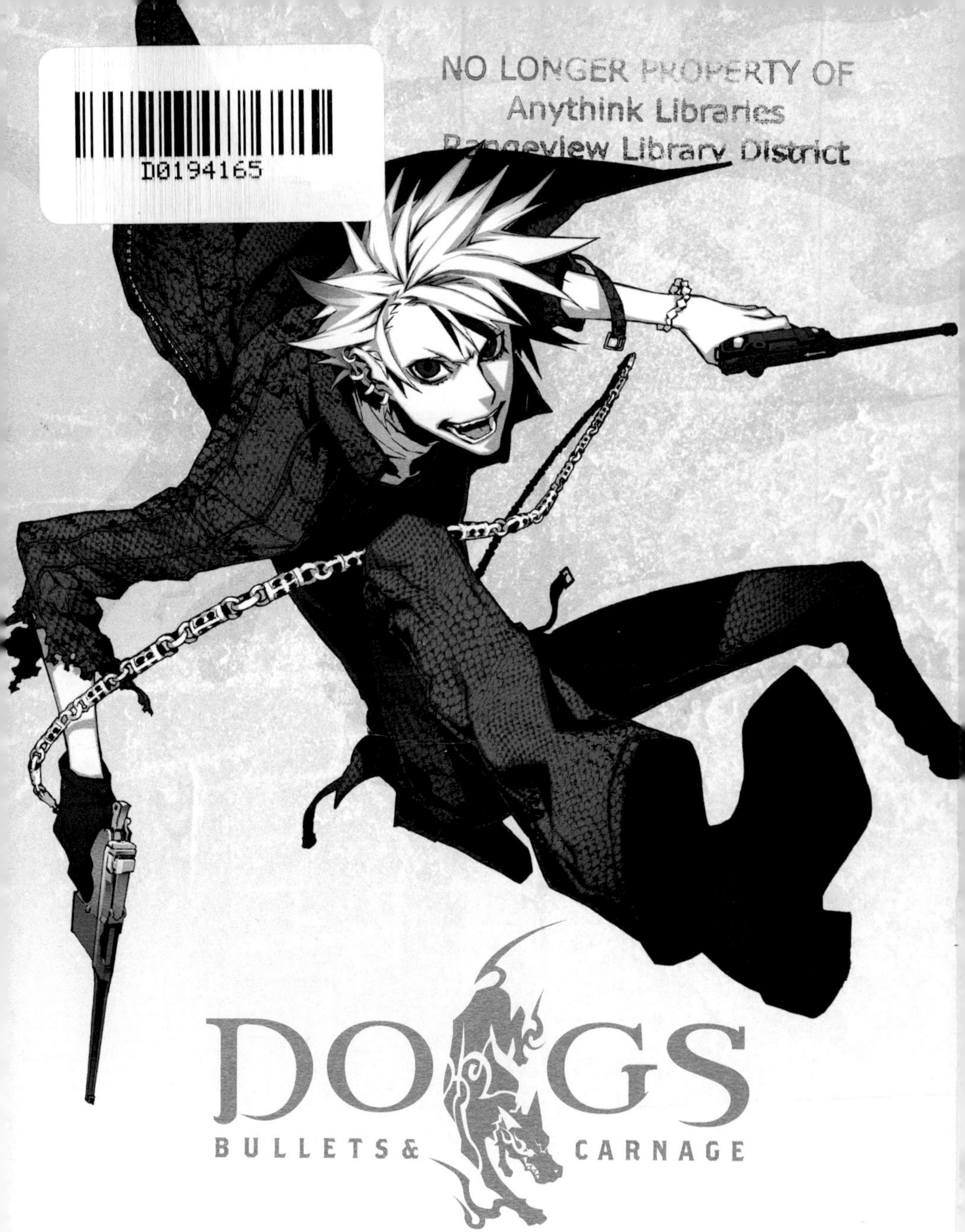

DOGS

BULLETS & CARNAGE

4

SHIROW MIWA

DOGS
BULLETS & CARNAGE

4

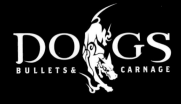

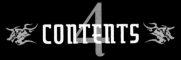

CONTENTS

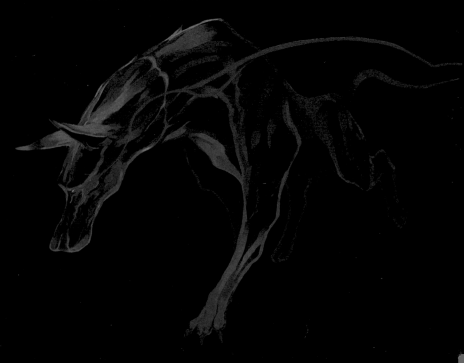

#29 Clutter & Foreboding Ⅰ

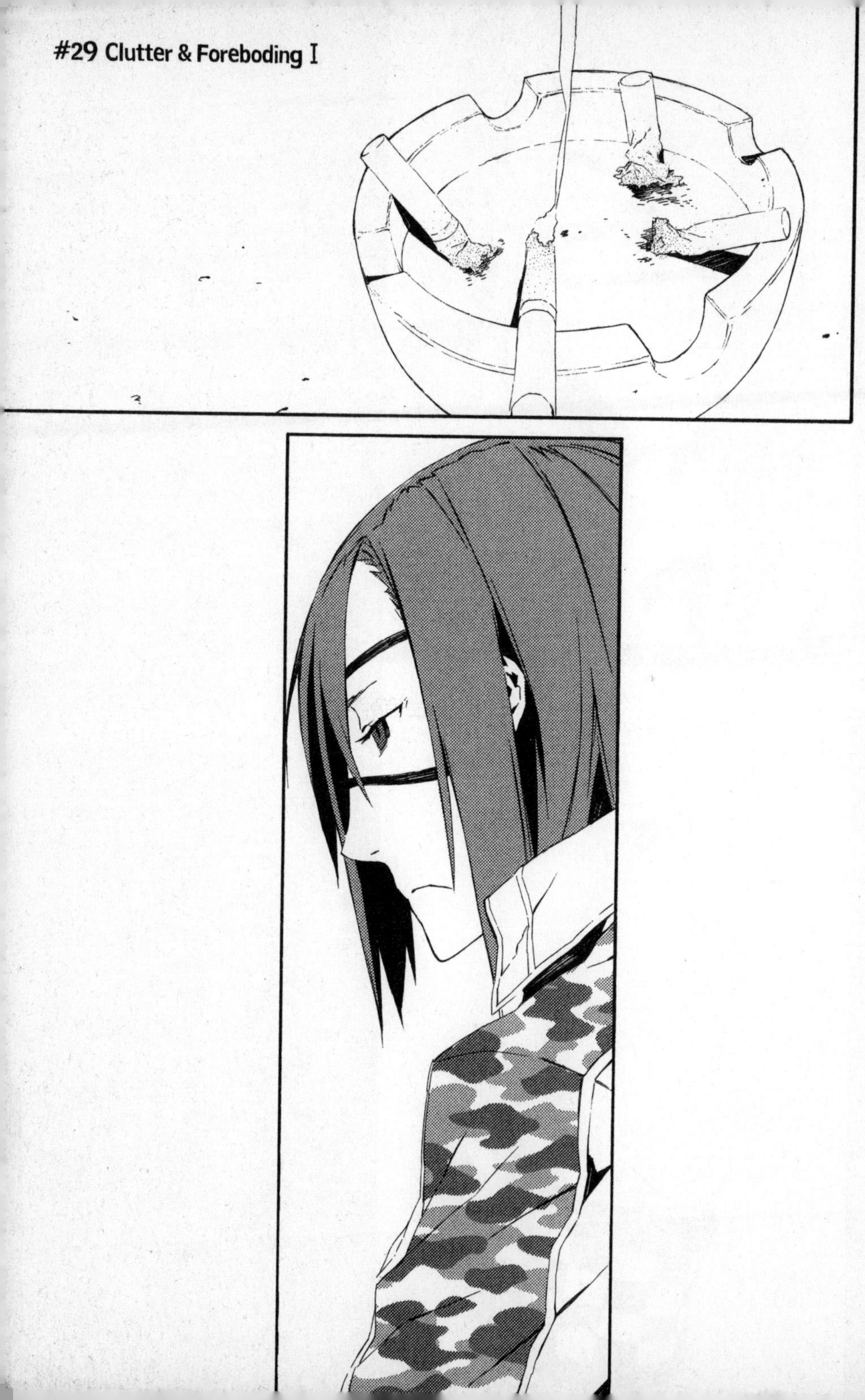

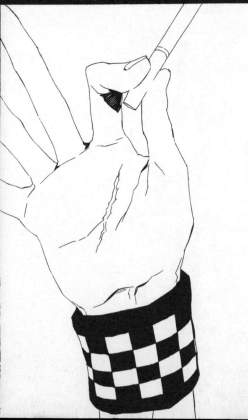

#29 Clutter &
Foreboding I

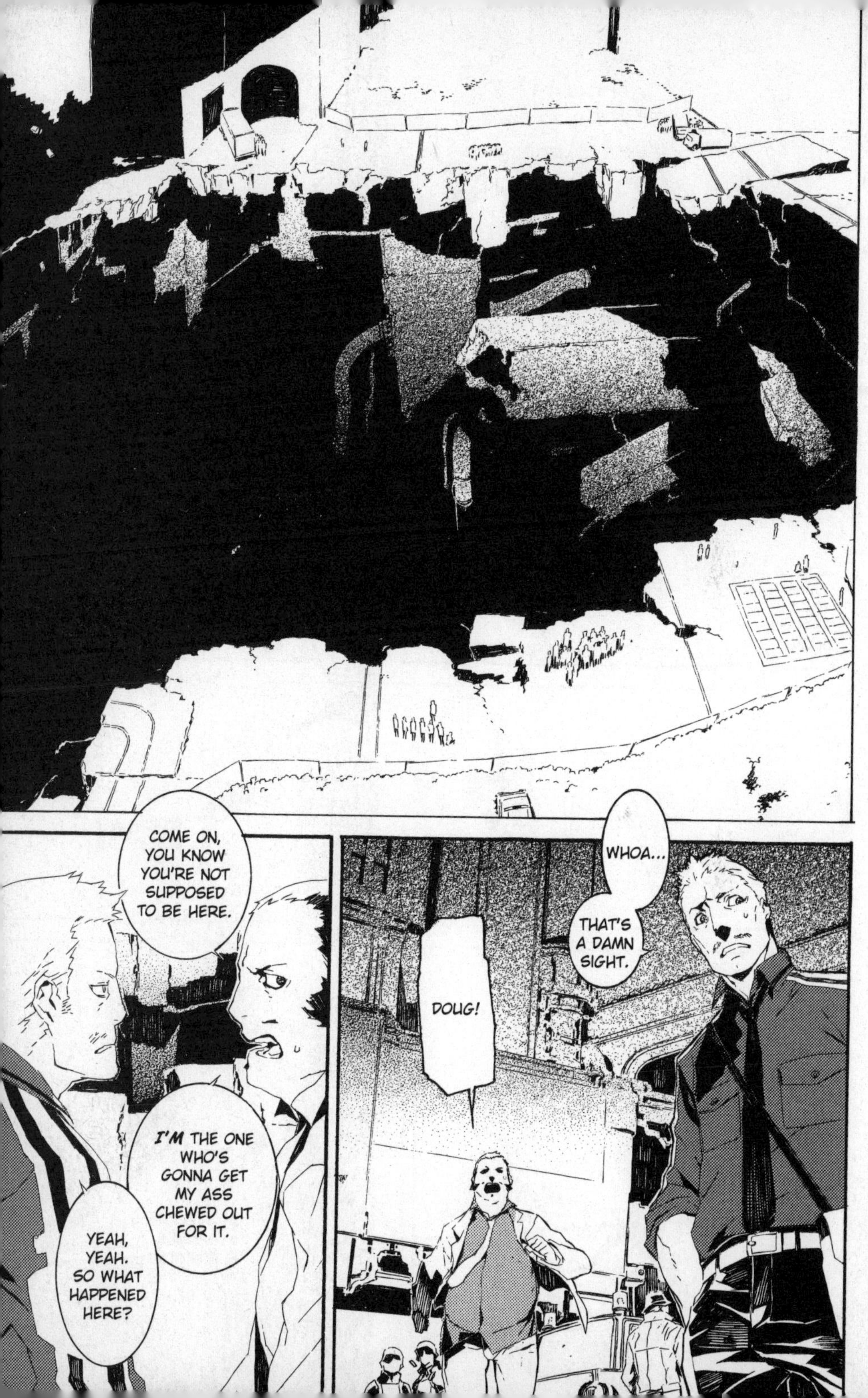
WHOA...
THAT'S A DAMN SIGHT.
DOUG!
COME ON, YOU KNOW YOU'RE NOT SUPPOSED TO BE HERE.
I'M THE ONE WHO'S GONNA GET MY ASS CHEWED OUT FOR IT.
YEAH, YEAH. SO WHAT HAPPENED HERE?

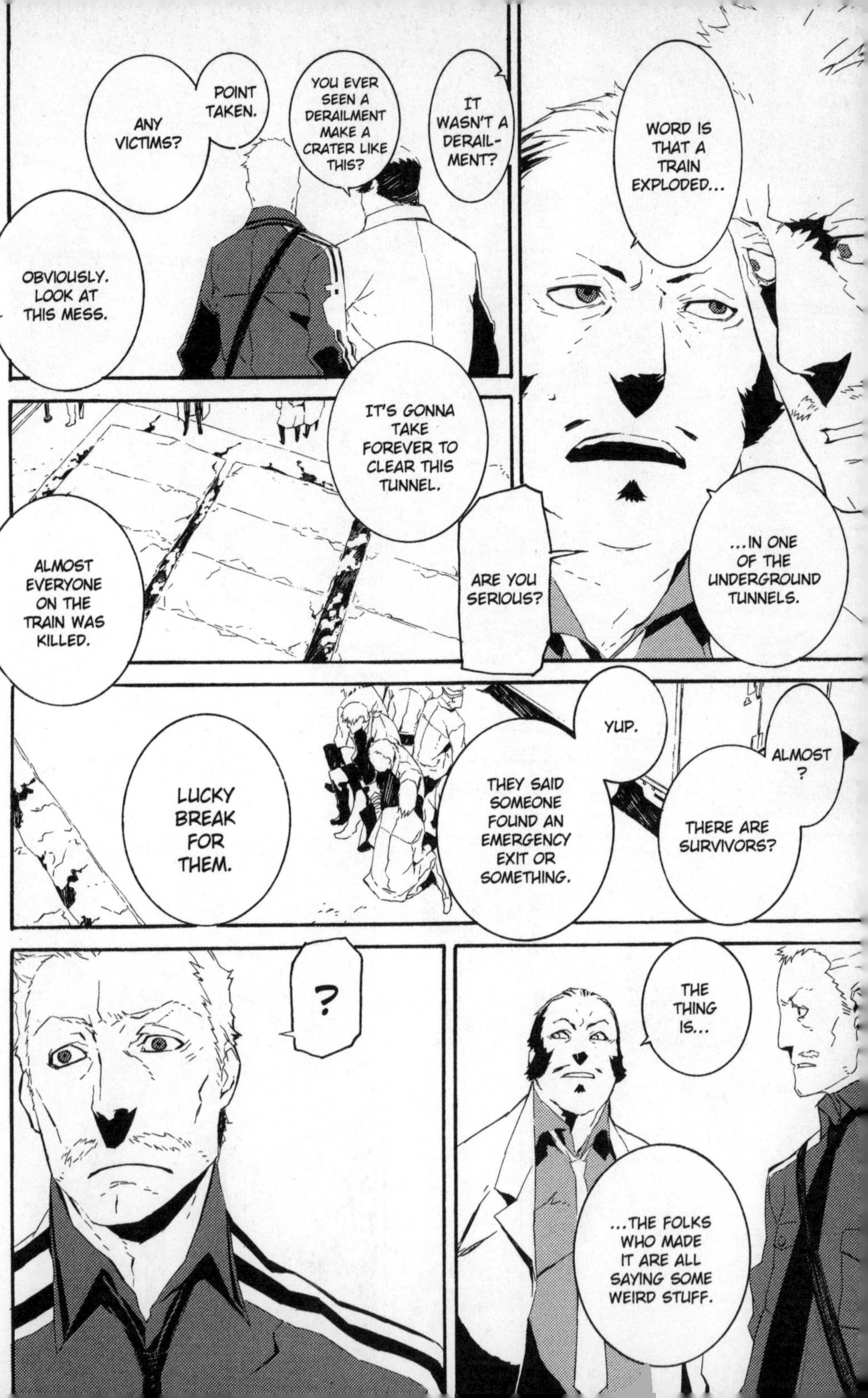
WORD IS THAT A TRAIN EXPLODED...
...IN ONE OF THE UNDERGROUND TUNNELS.
ARE YOU SERIOUS?
IT WASN'T A DERAIL-MENT?
YOU EVER SEEN A DERAILMENT MAKE A CRATER LIKE THIS?
POINT TAKEN.
ANY VICTIMS?
OBVIOUSLY. LOOK AT THIS MESS.
IT'S GONNA TAKE FOREVER TO CLEAR THIS TUNNEL.
ALMOST EVERYONE ON THE TRAIN WAS KILLED.
ALMOST?
THERE ARE SURVIVORS?
YUP.
THEY SAID SOMEONE FOUND AN EMERGENCY EXIT OR SOMETHING.
LUCKY BREAK FOR THEM.
THE THING IS...
...THE FOLKS WHO MADE IT ARE ALL SAYING SOME WEIRD STUFF.
?

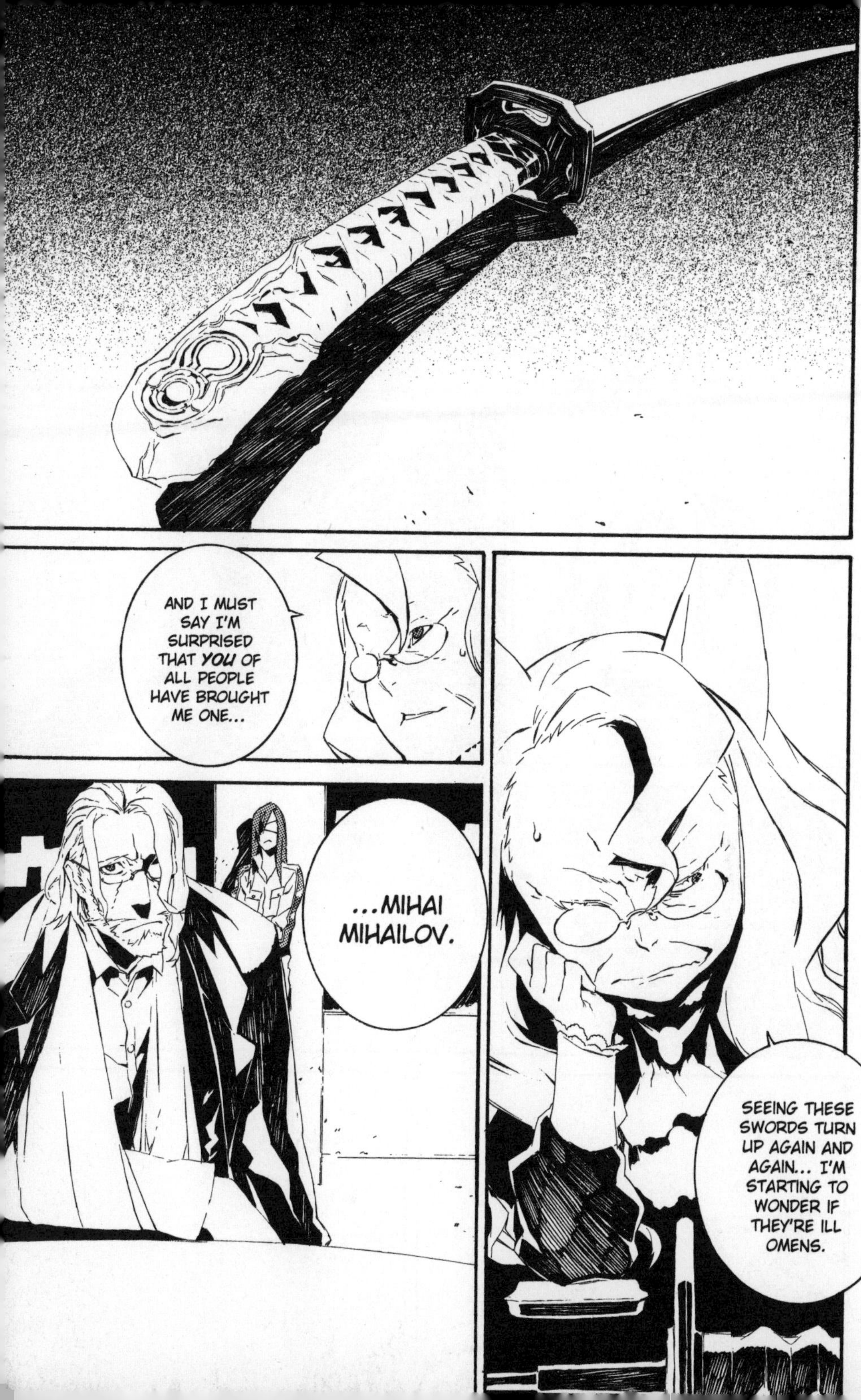
SEEING THESE SWORDS TURN UP AGAIN AND AGAIN... I'M STARTING TO WONDER IF THEY'RE ILL OMENS.
AND I MUST SAY I'M SURPRISED THAT *YOU* OF ALL PEOPLE HAVE BROUGHT ME ONE...
...MIHAI MIHAILOV.

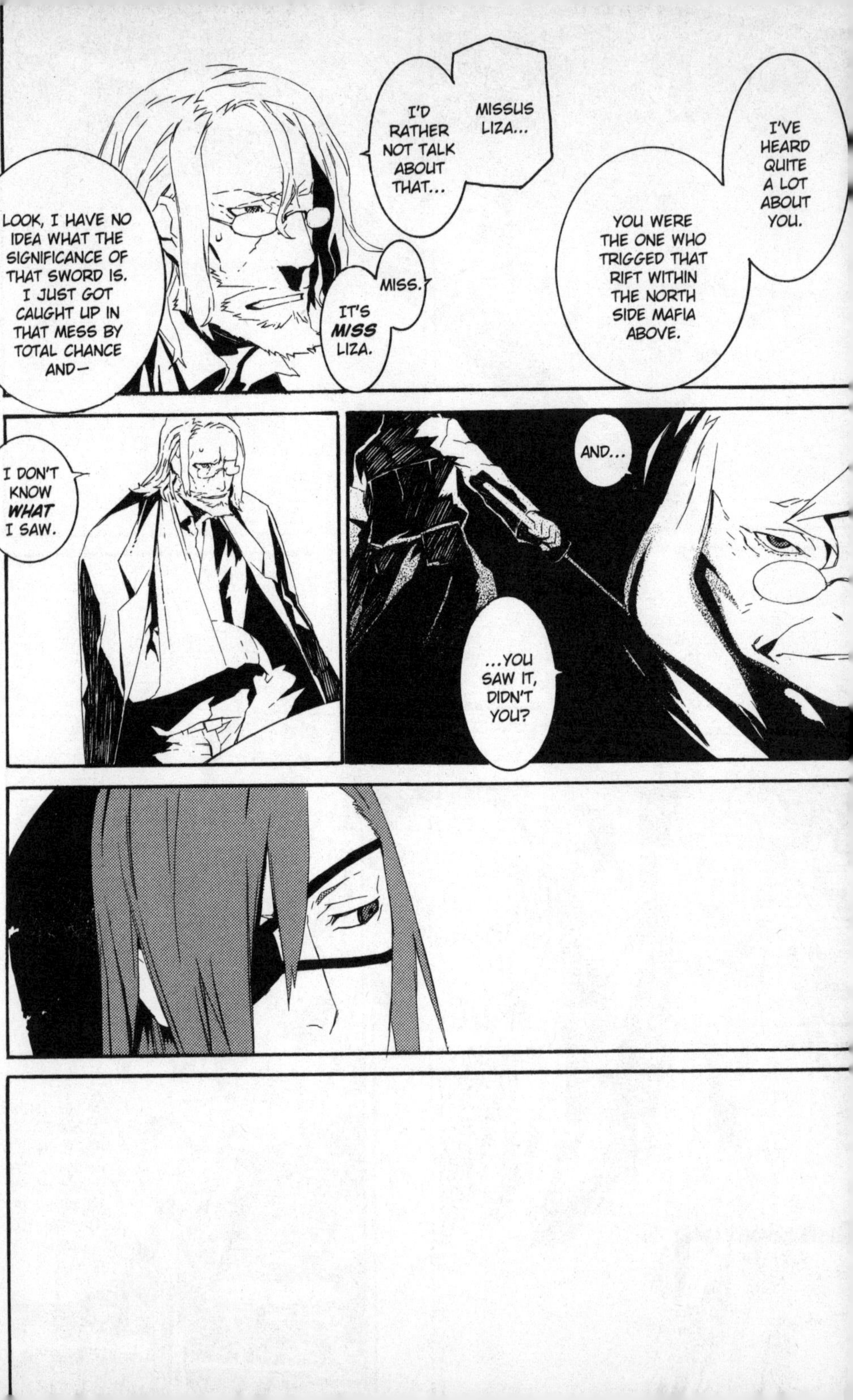
I'VE HEARD QUITE A LOT ABOUT YOU.
YOU WERE THE ONE WHO TRIGGED THAT RIFT WITHIN THE NORTH SIDE MAFIA ABOVE.
MISSUS LIZA...
I'D RATHER NOT TALK ABOUT THAT...
MISS.
IT'S *MISS* LIZA.
LOOK, I HAVE NO IDEA WHAT THE SIGNIFICANCE OF THAT SWORD IS. I JUST GOT CAUGHT UP IN THAT MESS BY TOTAL CHANCE AND—
AND...
...YOU SAW IT, DIDN'T YOU?
I DON'T KNOW *WHAT* I SAW.

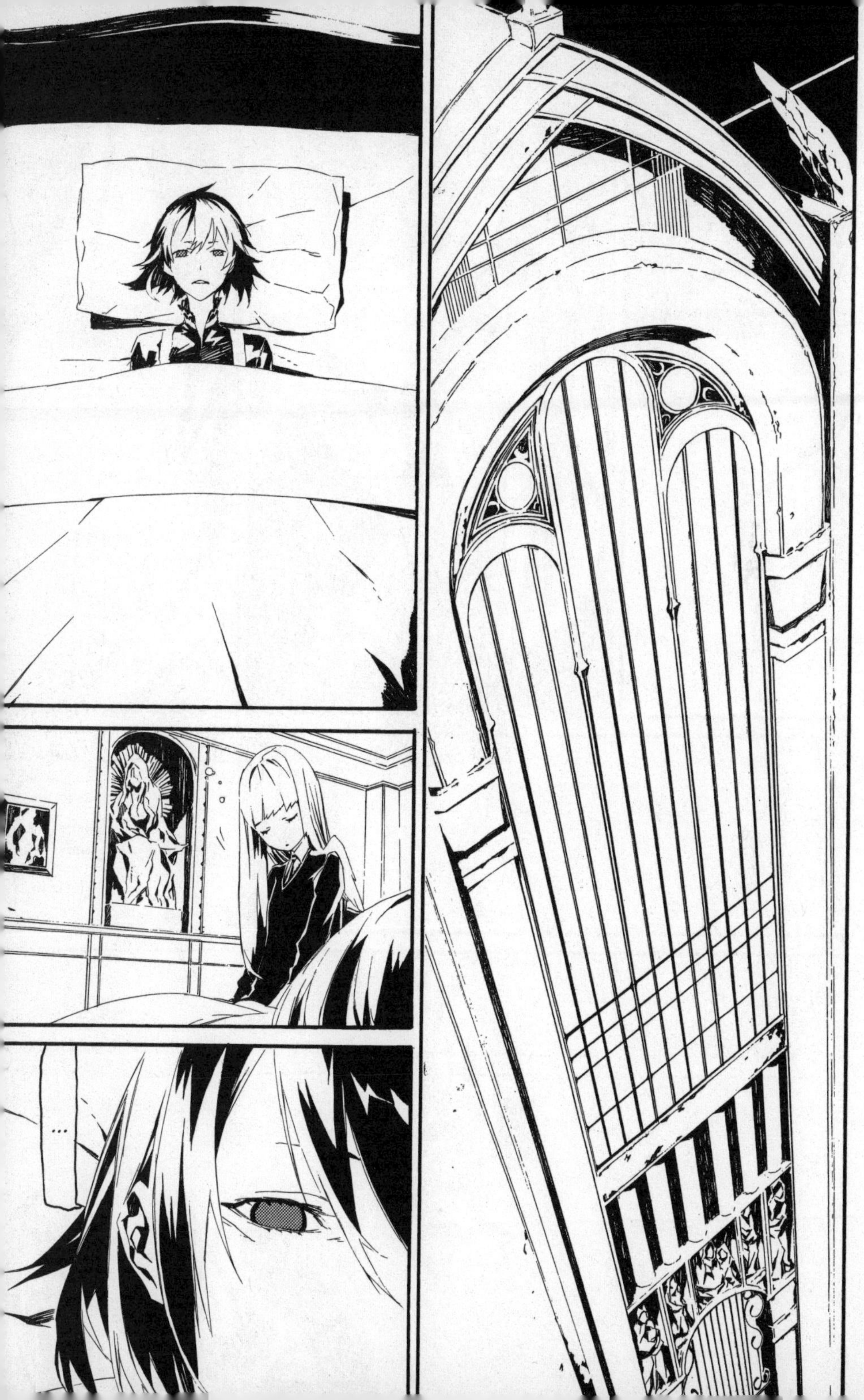
...

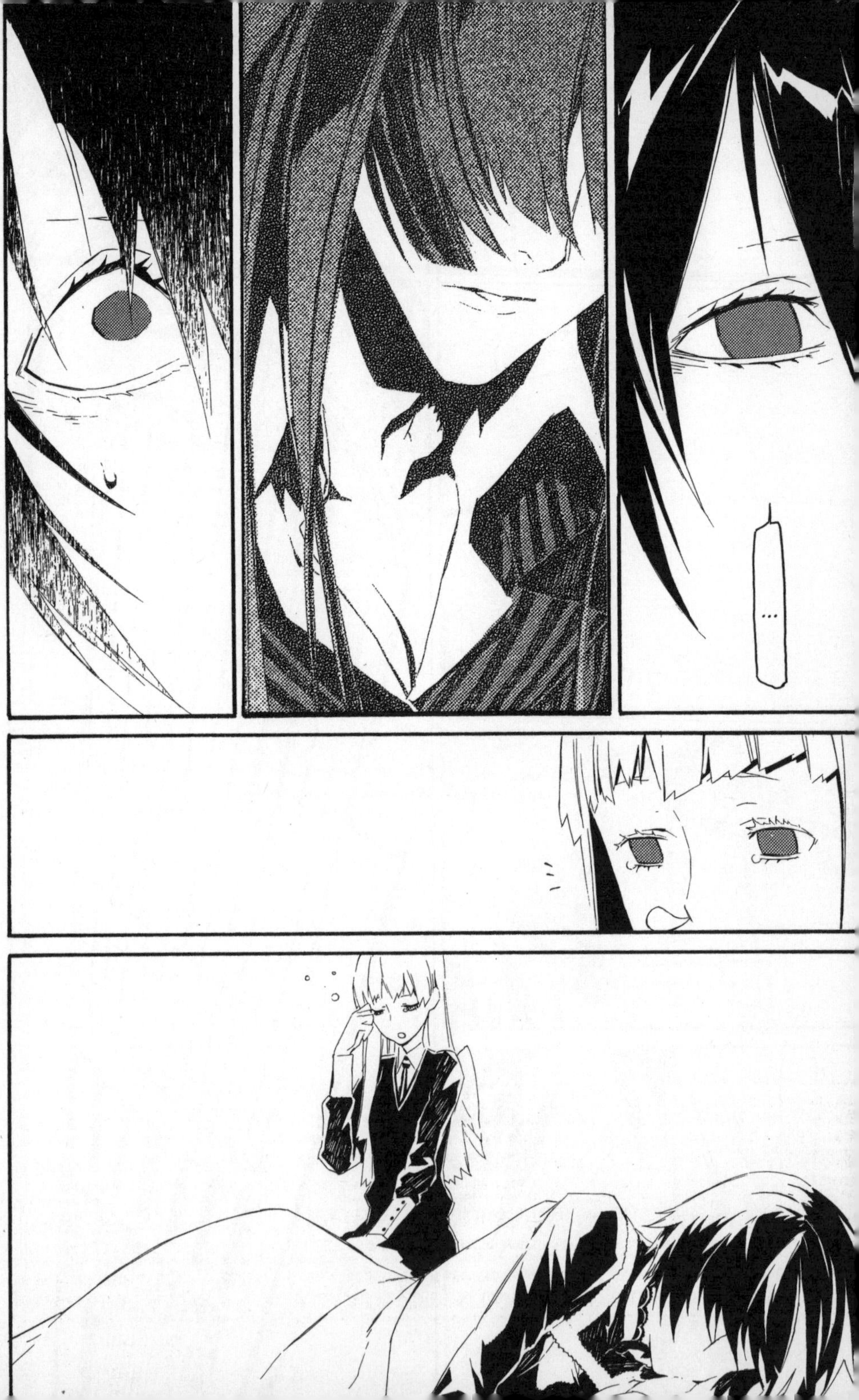
...

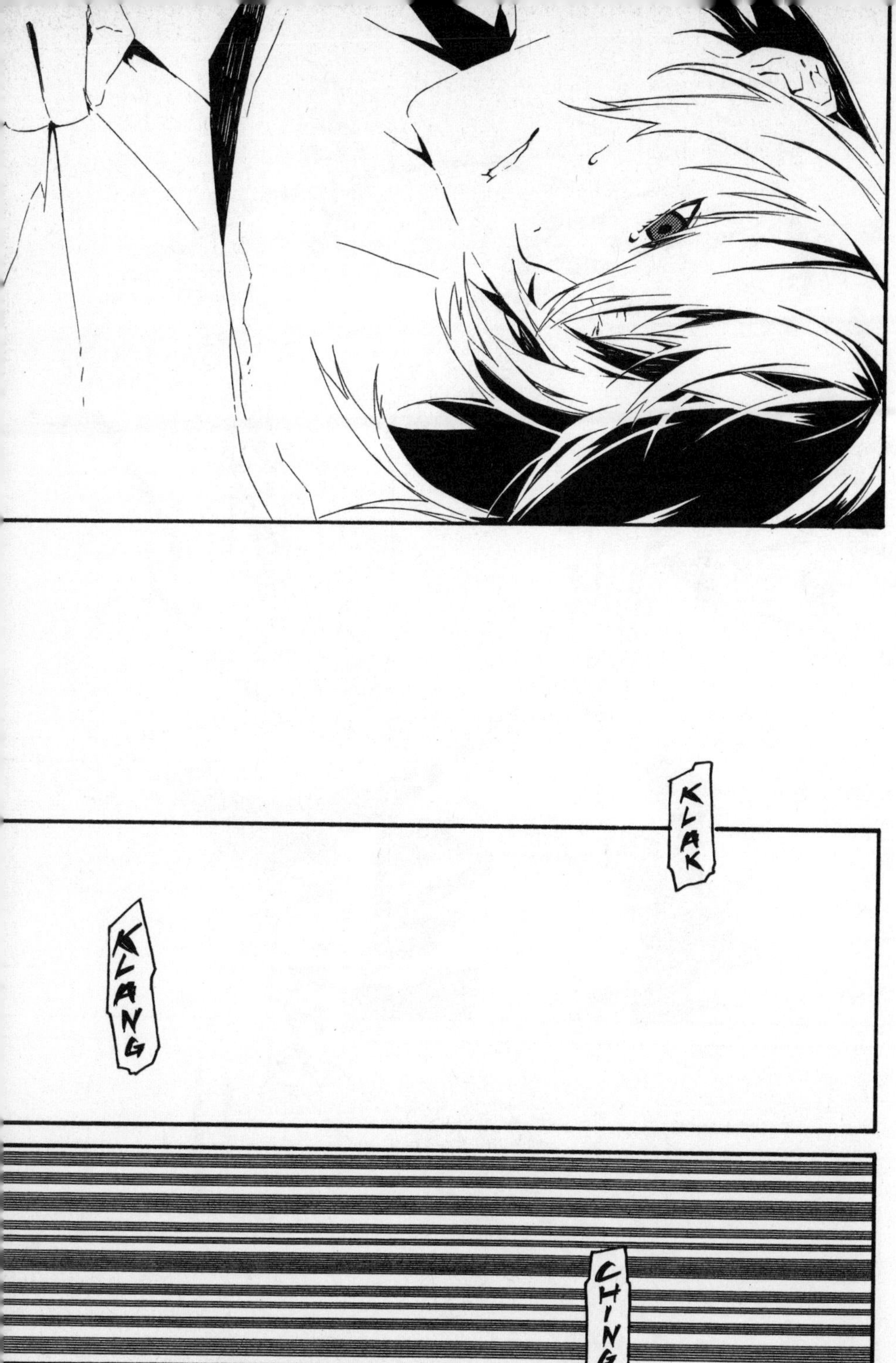
KLAK
KLANG
CHING

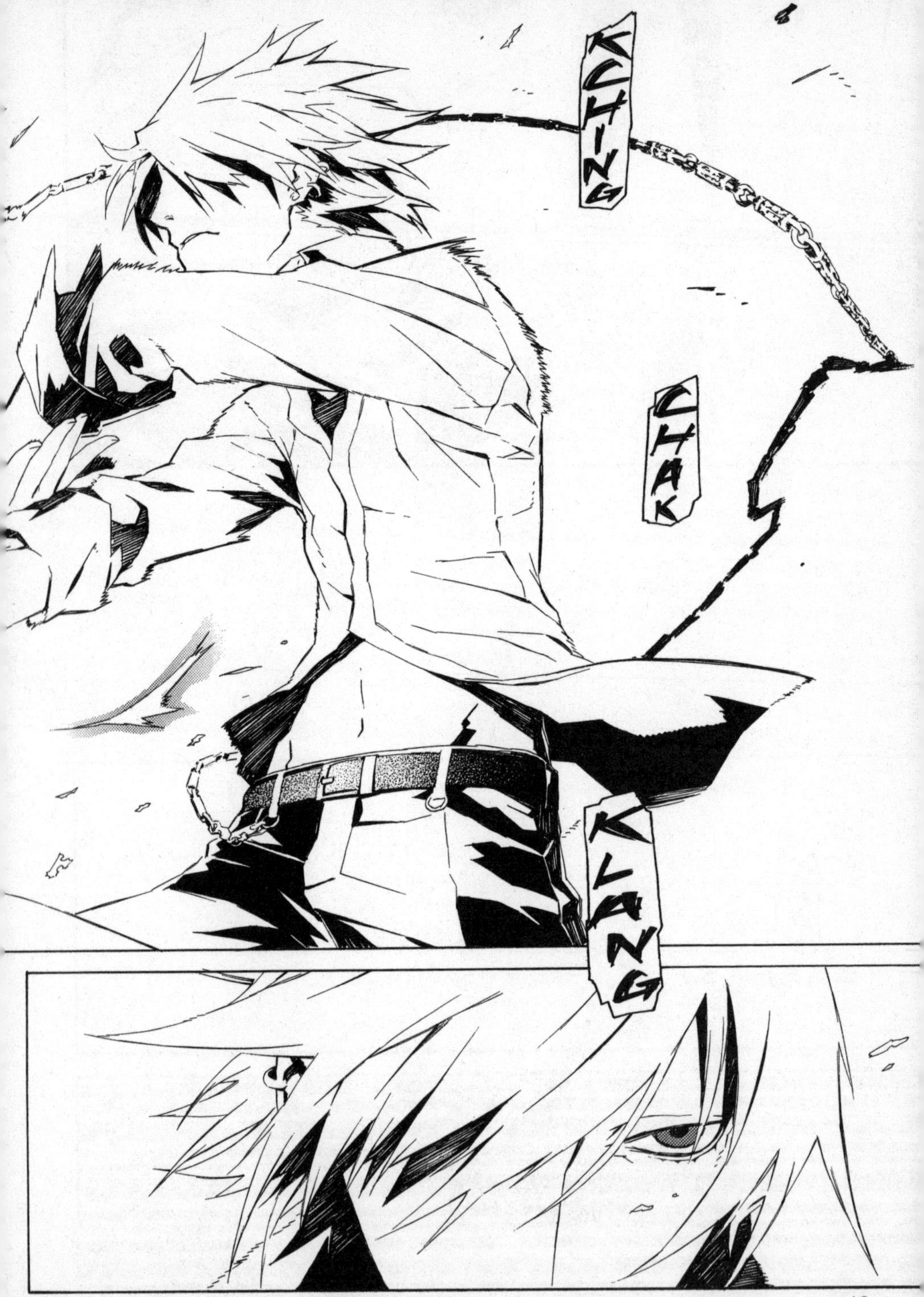
KCHING
CHAK
KLANG

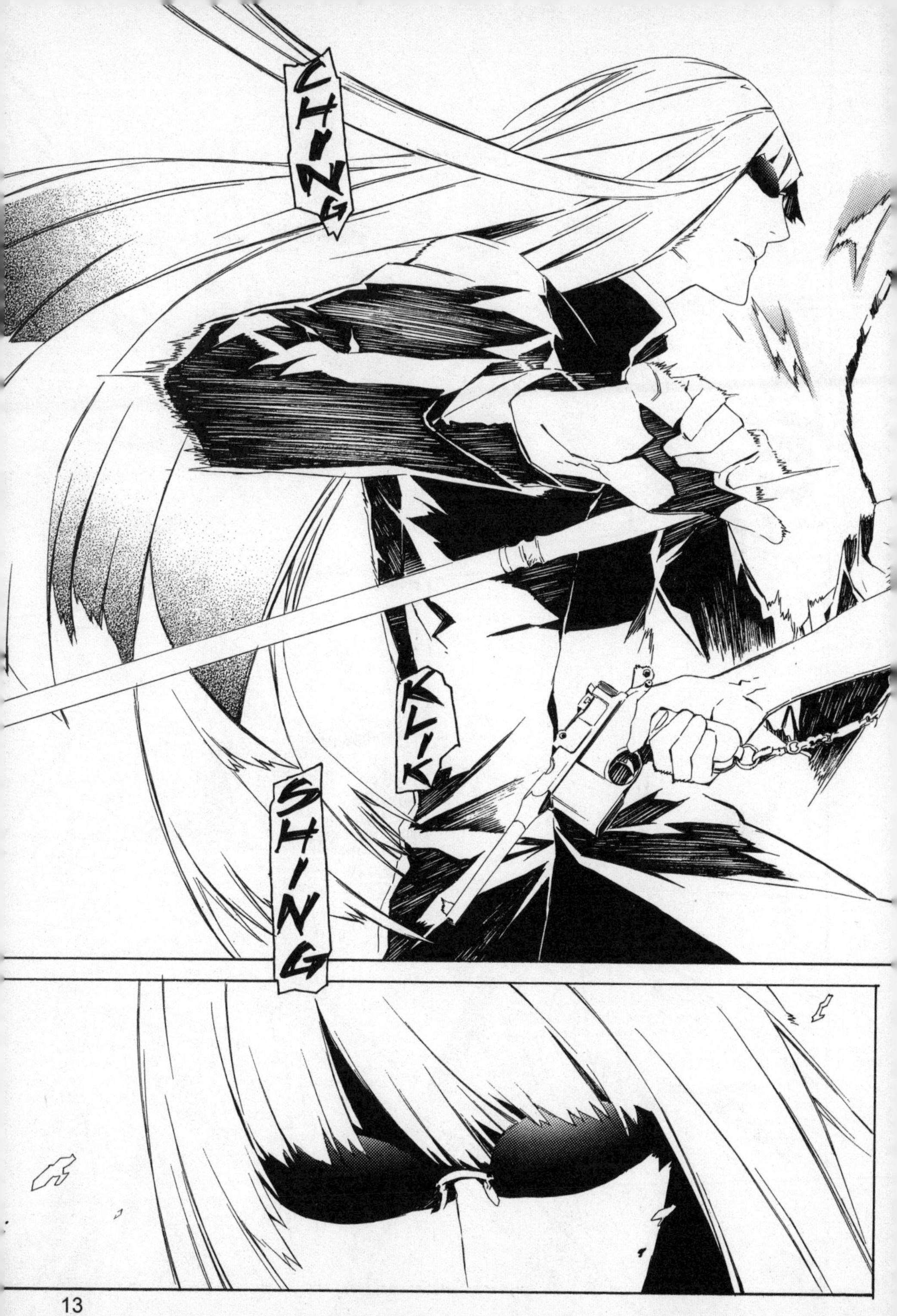
CHING
KLIK
SHING

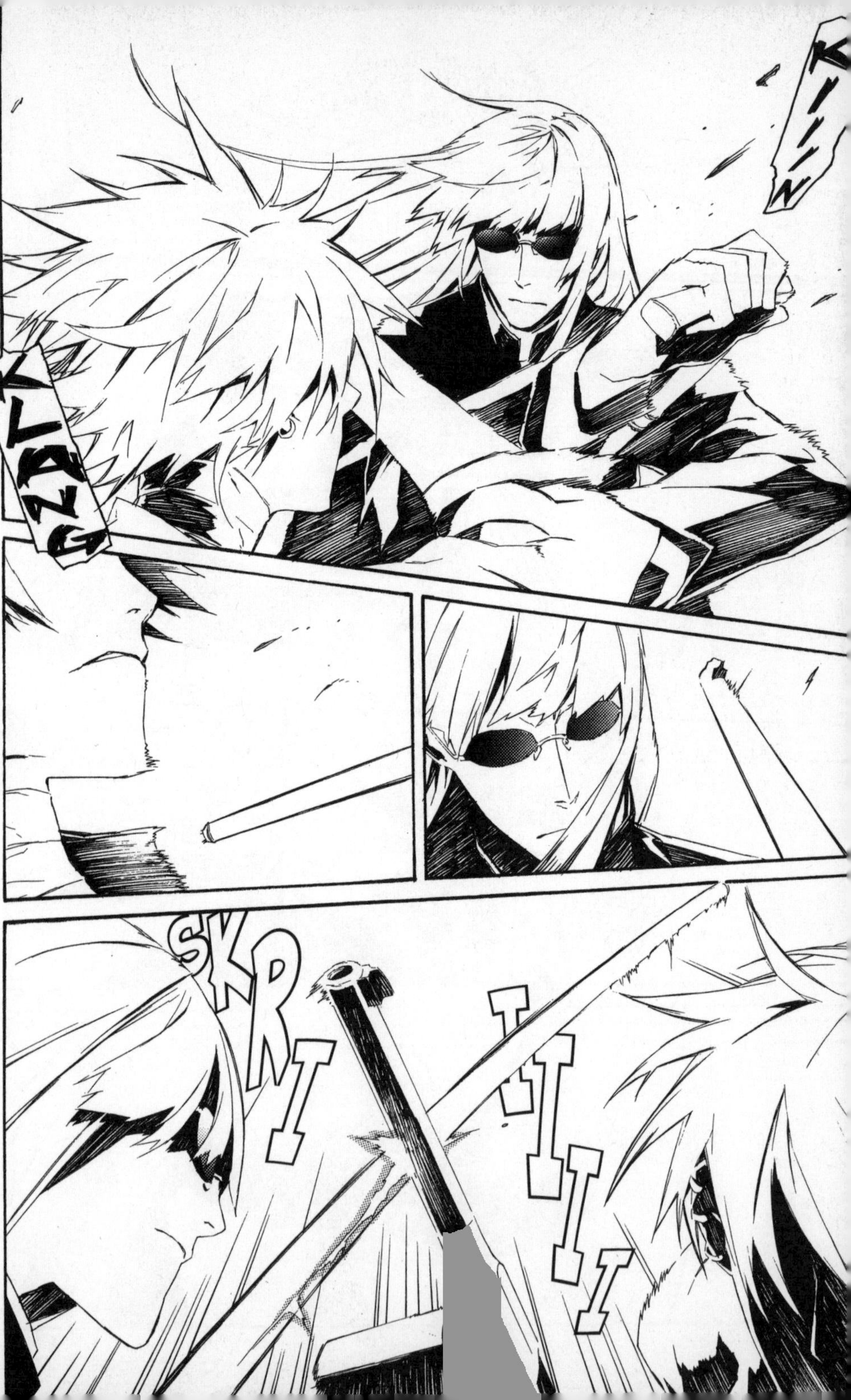
KRIIIN
KLANG
SKRIII

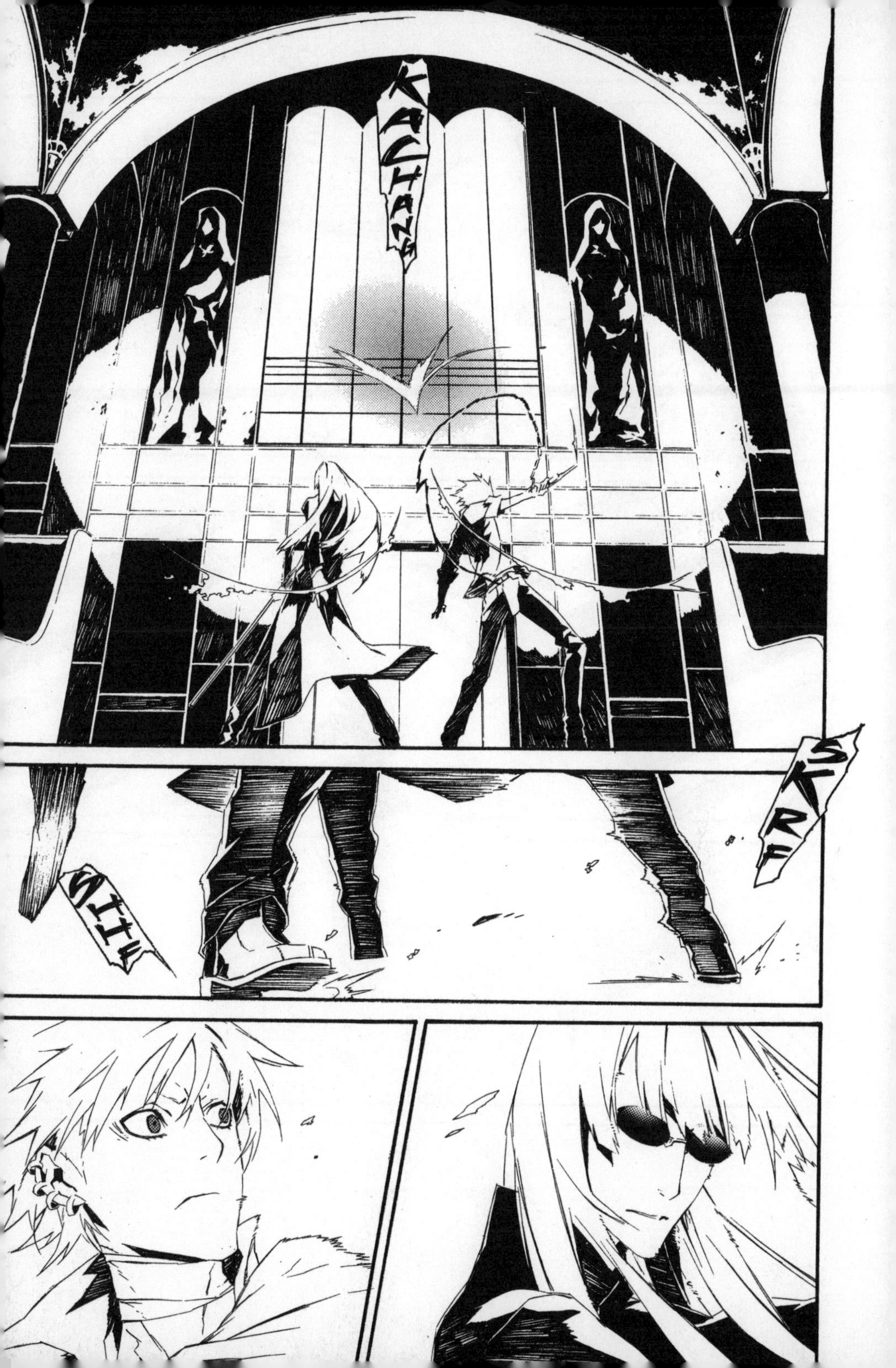
KACHANG
SKRF
SHFF

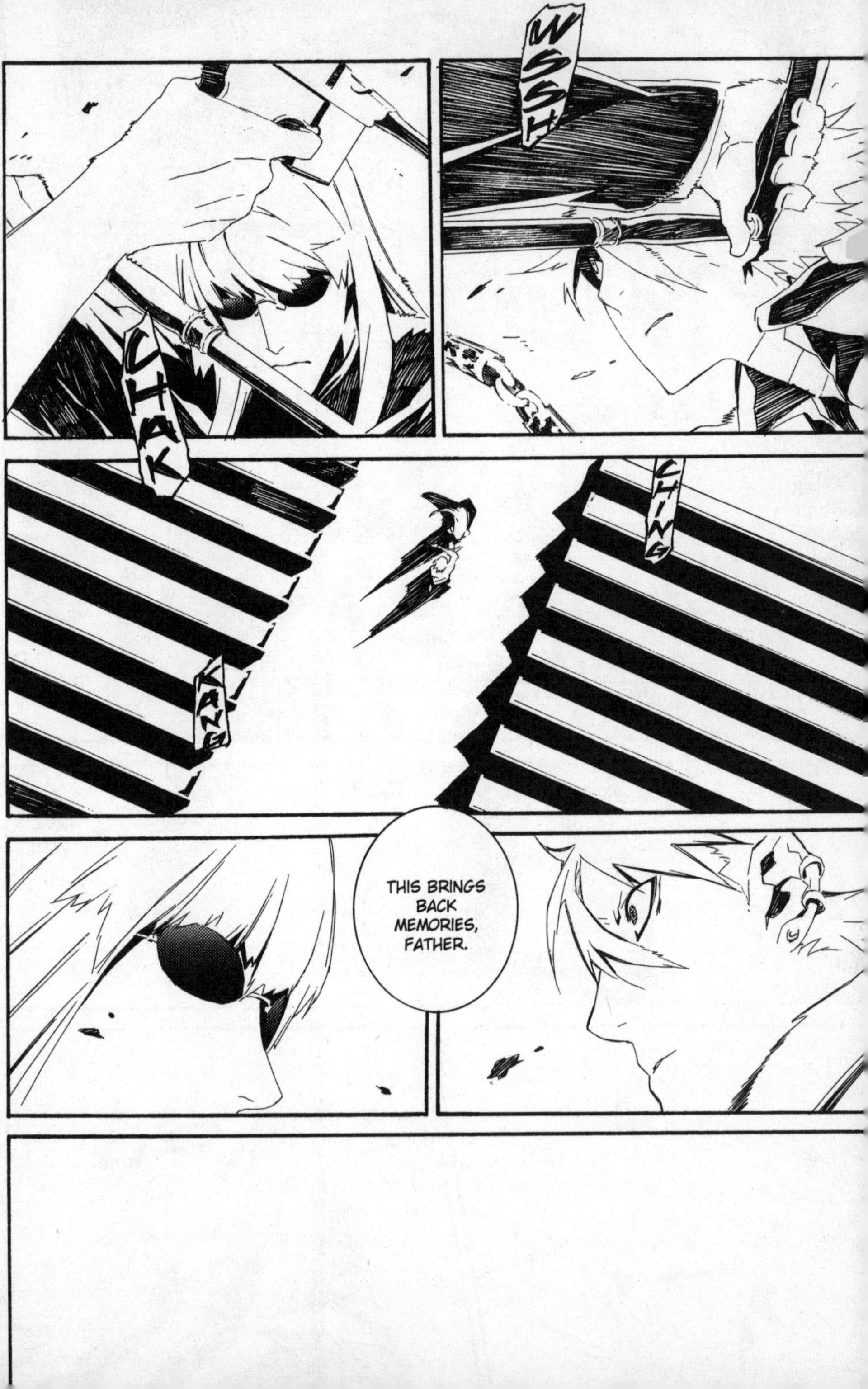
WSSH
CHAK
CHING
KANG
THIS BRINGS BACK MEMORIES, FATHER.

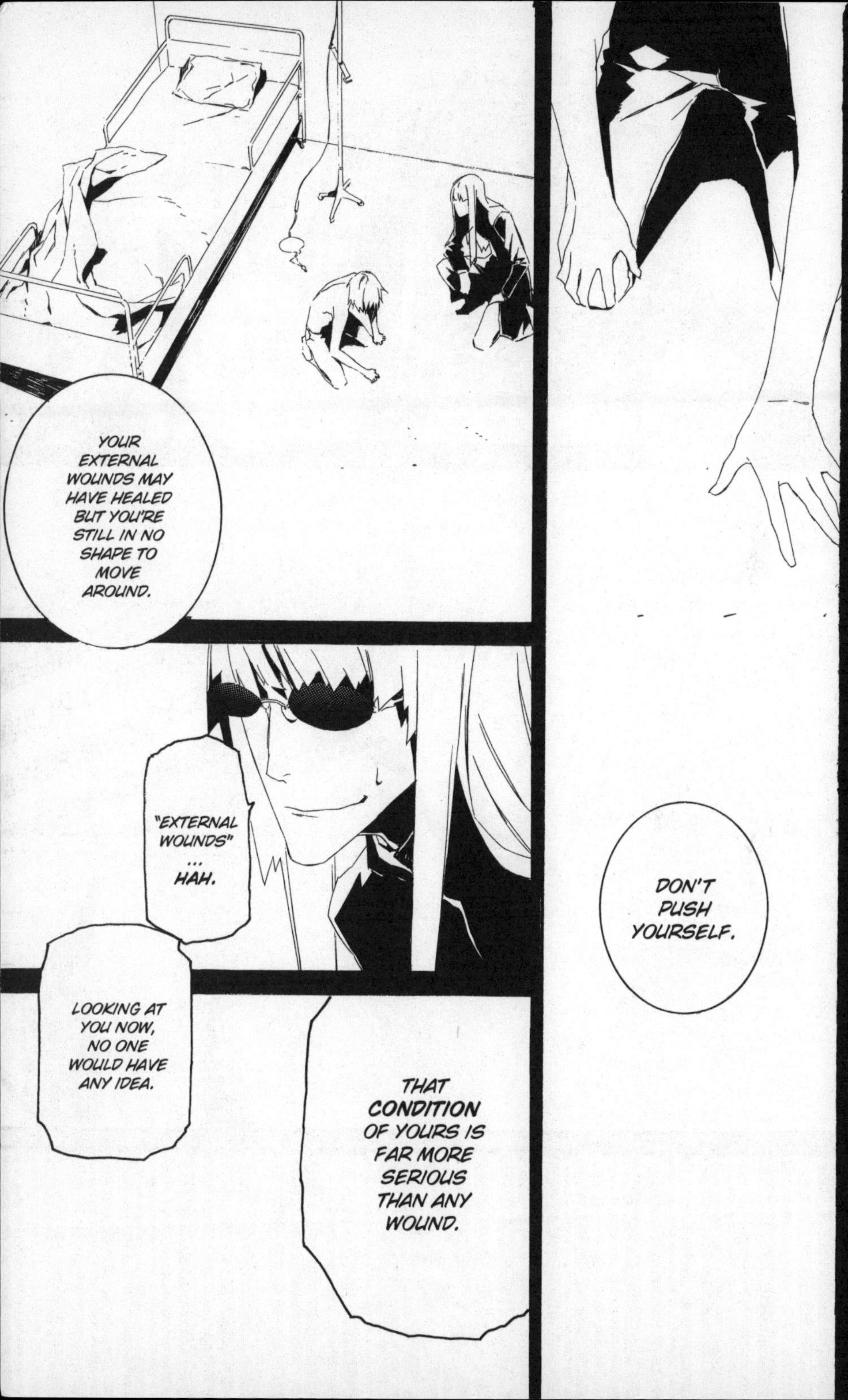

DON'T PUSH YOURSELF.
YOUR EXTERNAL WOUNDS MAY HAVE HEALED BUT YOU'RE STILL IN NO SHAPE TO MOVE AROUND.
"EXTERNAL WOUNDS" ... HAH.
LOOKING AT YOU NOW, NO ONE WOULD HAVE ANY IDEA.
THAT CONDITION OF YOURS IS FAR MORE SERIOUS THAN ANY WOUND.

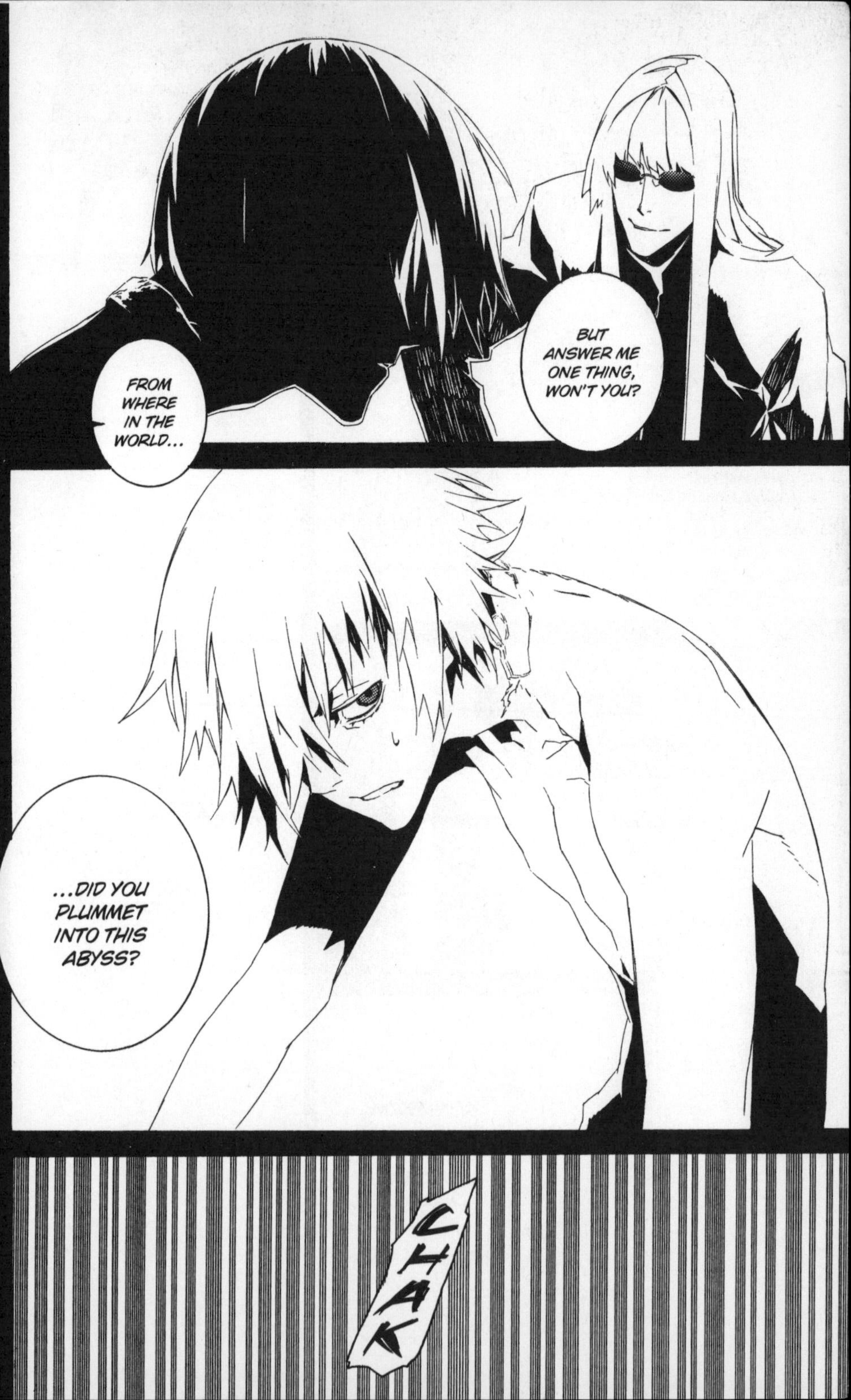
BUT ANSWER ME ONE THING, WON'T YOU?
FROM WHERE IN THE WORLD...
...DID YOU PLUMMET INTO THIS ABYSS?
CHAK

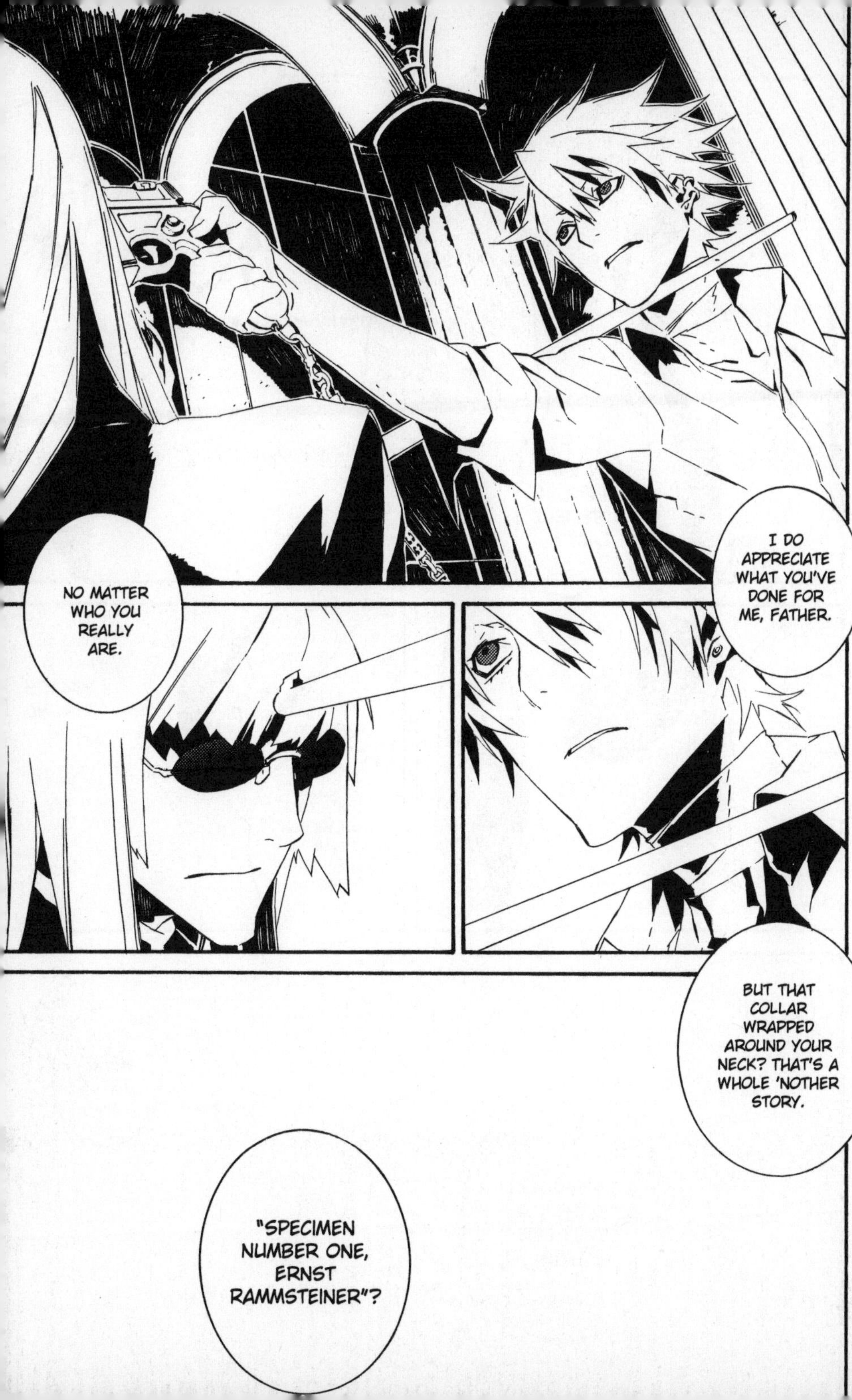
I DO APPRECIATE WHAT YOU'VE DONE FOR ME, FATHER.
NO MATTER WHO YOU REALLY ARE.
BUT THAT COLLAR WRAPPED AROUND YOUR NECK? THAT'S A WHOLE 'NOTHER STORY.
"SPECIMEN NUMBER ONE, ERNST RAMMSTEINER"?

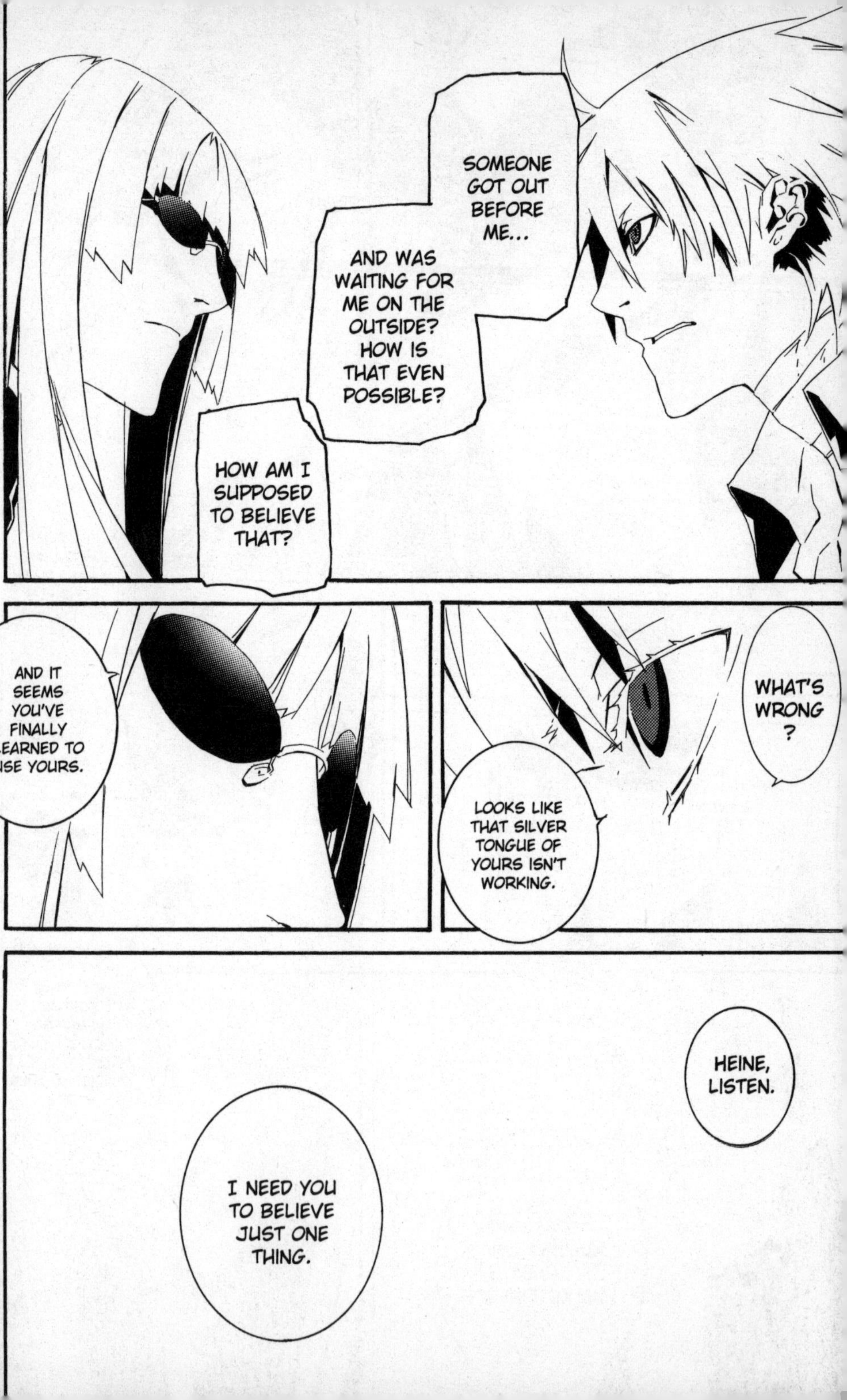
SOMEONE GOT OUT BEFORE ME...
AND WAS WAITING FOR ME ON THE OUTSIDE? HOW IS THAT EVEN POSSIBLE?
HOW AM I SUPPOSED TO BELIEVE THAT?
WHAT'S WRONG?
LOOKS LIKE THAT SILVER TONGUE OF YOURS ISN'T WORKING.
AND IT SEEMS YOU'VE FINALLY LEARNED TO USE YOURS.
HEINE, LISTEN.
I NEED YOU TO BELIEVE JUST ONE THING.

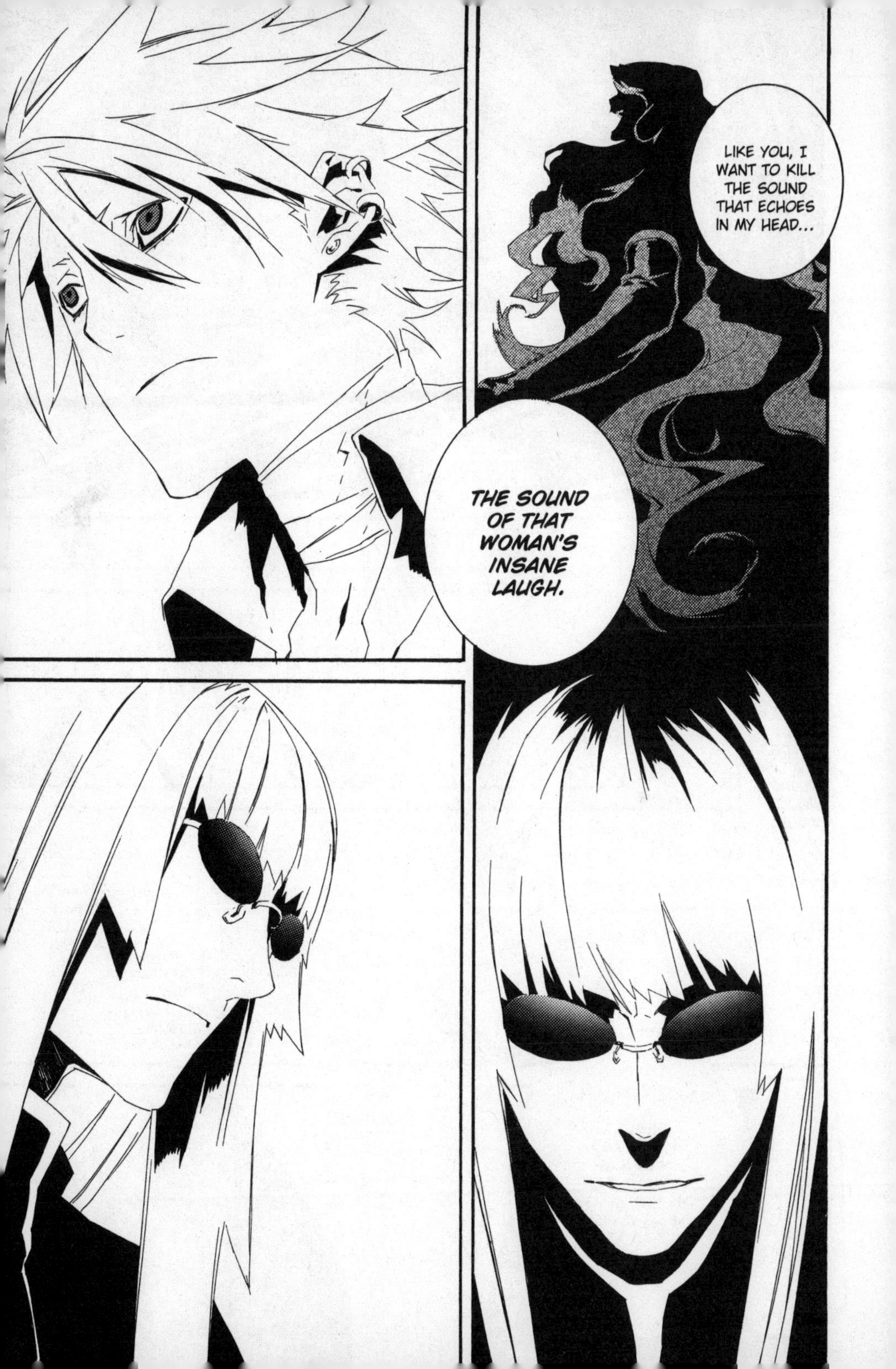
LIKE YOU, I WANT TO KILL THE SOUND THAT ECHOES IN MY HEAD...
THE SOUND OF THAT WOMAN'S INSANE LAUGH.

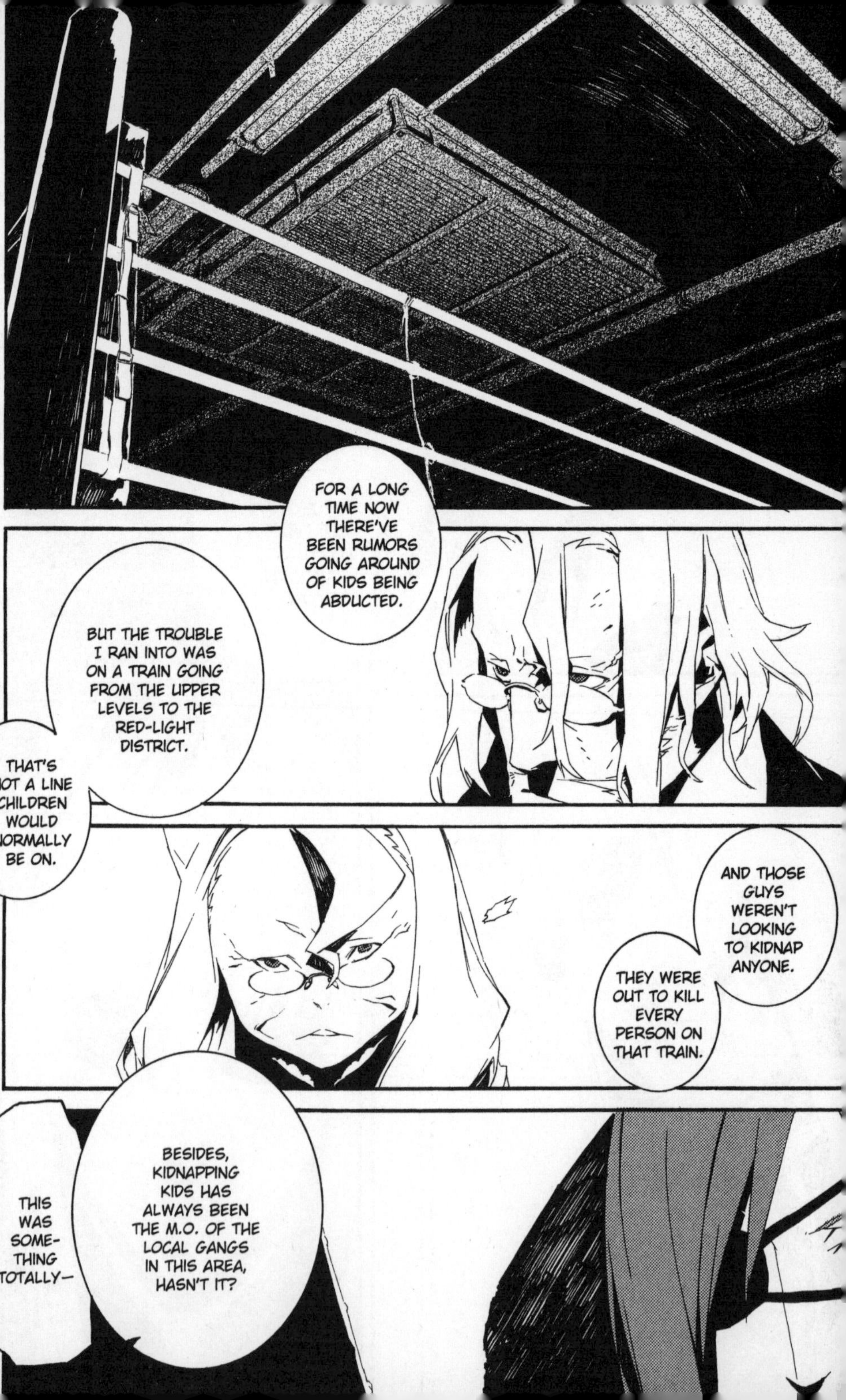
FOR A LONG TIME NOW THERE'VE BEEN RUMORS GOING AROUND OF KIDS BEING ABDUCTED.
BUT THE TROUBLE I RAN INTO WAS ON A TRAIN GOING FROM THE UPPER LEVELS TO THE RED-LIGHT DISTRICT.
THAT'S NOT A LINE CHILDREN WOULD NORMALLY BE ON.
AND THOSE GUYS WEREN'T LOOKING TO KIDNAP ANYONE.
THEY WERE OUT TO KILL EVERY PERSON ON THAT TRAIN.
BESIDES, KIDNAPPING KIDS HAS ALWAYS BEEN THE M.O. OF THE LOCAL GANGS IN THIS AREA, HASN'T IT?
THIS WAS SOME-THING TOTALLY—

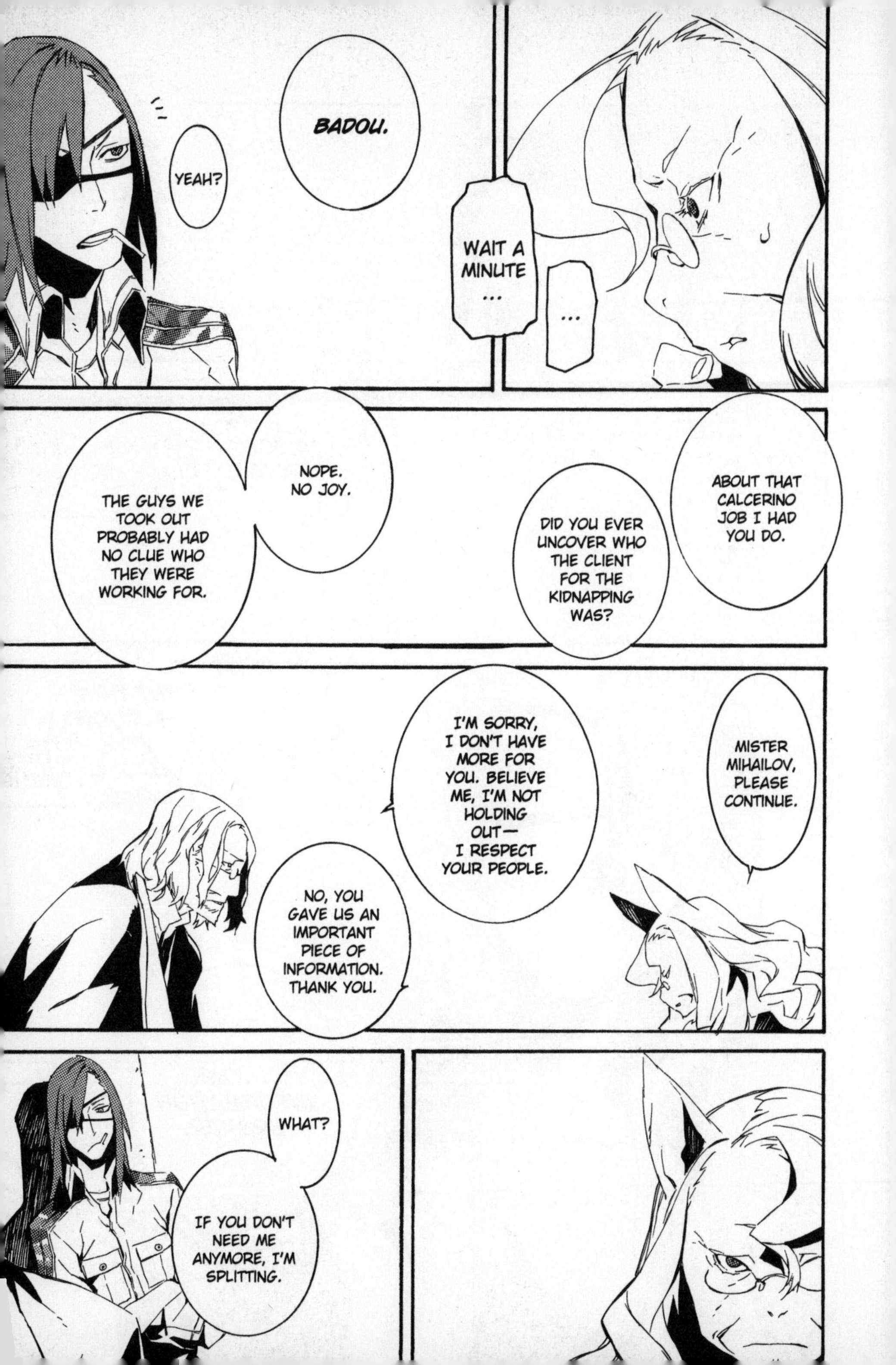
WAIT A MINUTE ...
...
BADOU.
YEAH?
ABOUT THAT CALCERINO JOB I HAD YOU DO.
DID YOU EVER UNCOVER WHO THE CLIENT FOR THE KIDNAPPING WAS?
NOPE. NO JOY.
THE GUYS WE TOOK OUT PROBABLY HAD NO CLUE WHO THEY WERE WORKING FOR.
MISTER MIHAILOV, PLEASE CONTINUE.
I'M SORRY, I DON'T HAVE MORE FOR YOU. BELIEVE ME, I'M NOT HOLDING OUT— I RESPECT YOUR PEOPLE.
NO, YOU GAVE US AN IMPORTANT PIECE OF INFORMATION. THANK YOU.
WHAT?
IF YOU DON'T NEED ME ANYMORE, I'M SPLITTING.

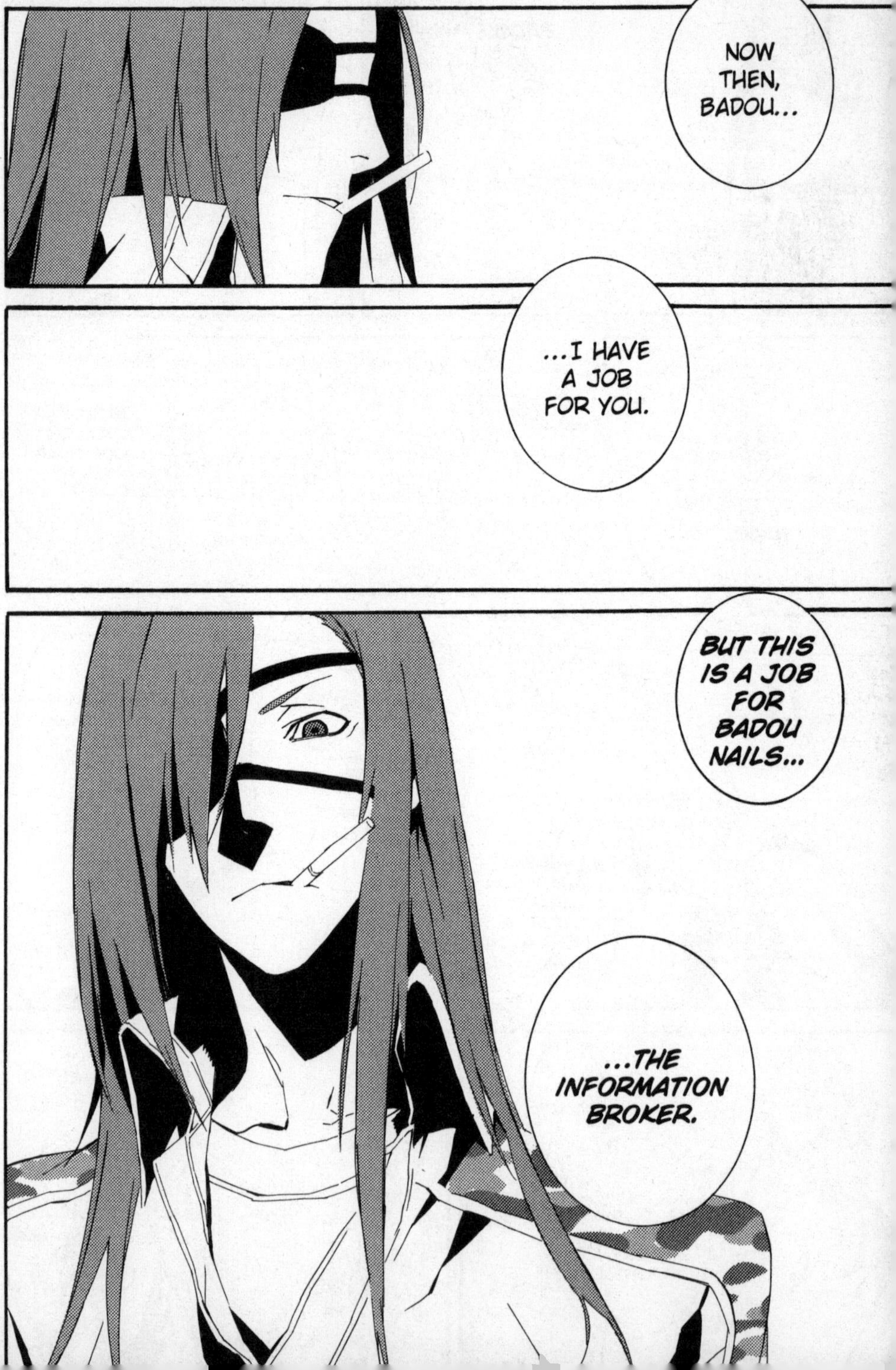
NOW THEN, BADOU...
...I HAVE A JOB FOR YOU.
BUT THIS IS A JOB FOR BADOU NAILS...
...THE INFORMATION BROKER.

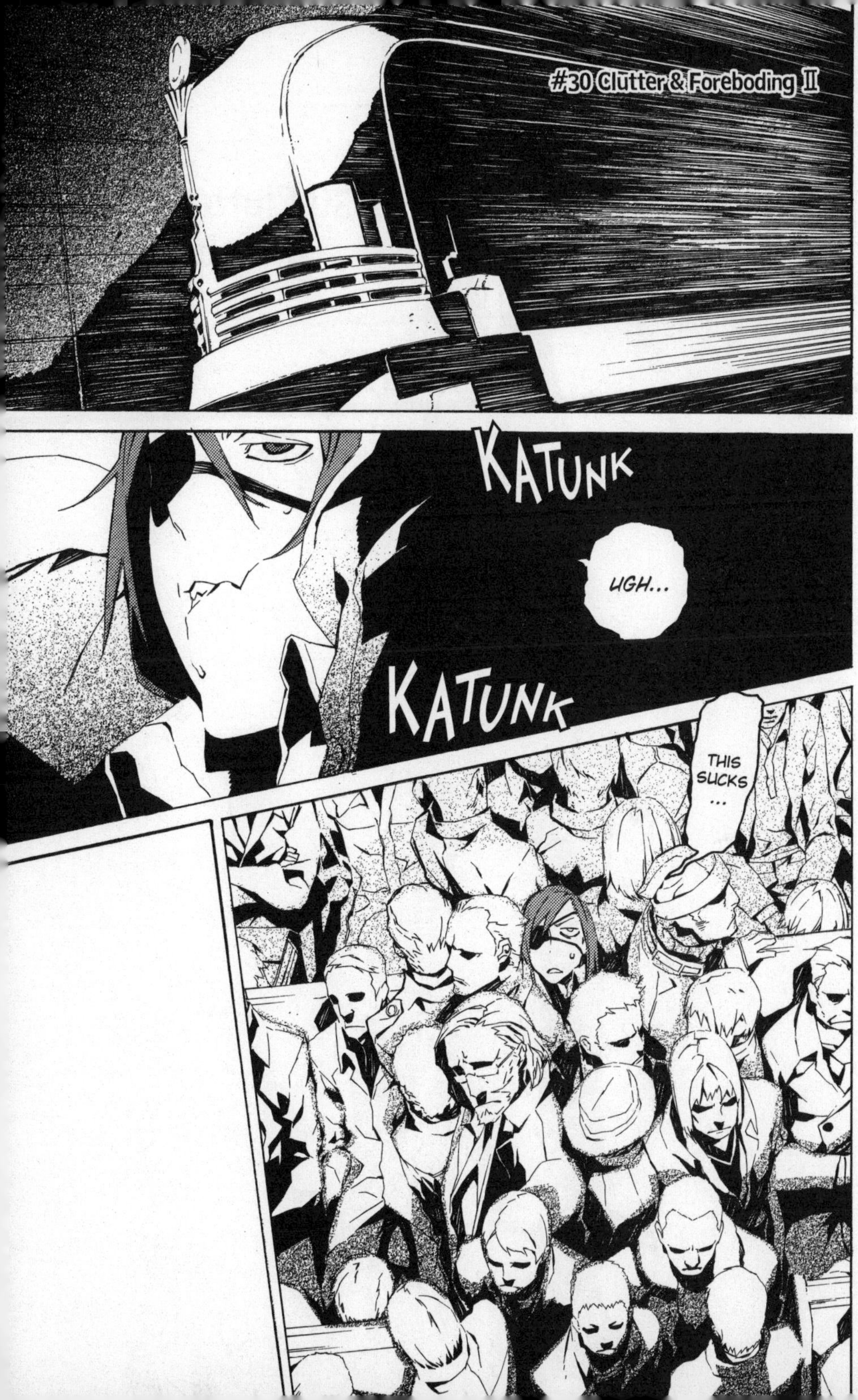
#30 Clutter & Foreboding II
KATUNK
UGH...
KATUNK
THIS SUCKS ...

#30 Clutter & Foreboding Ⅱ

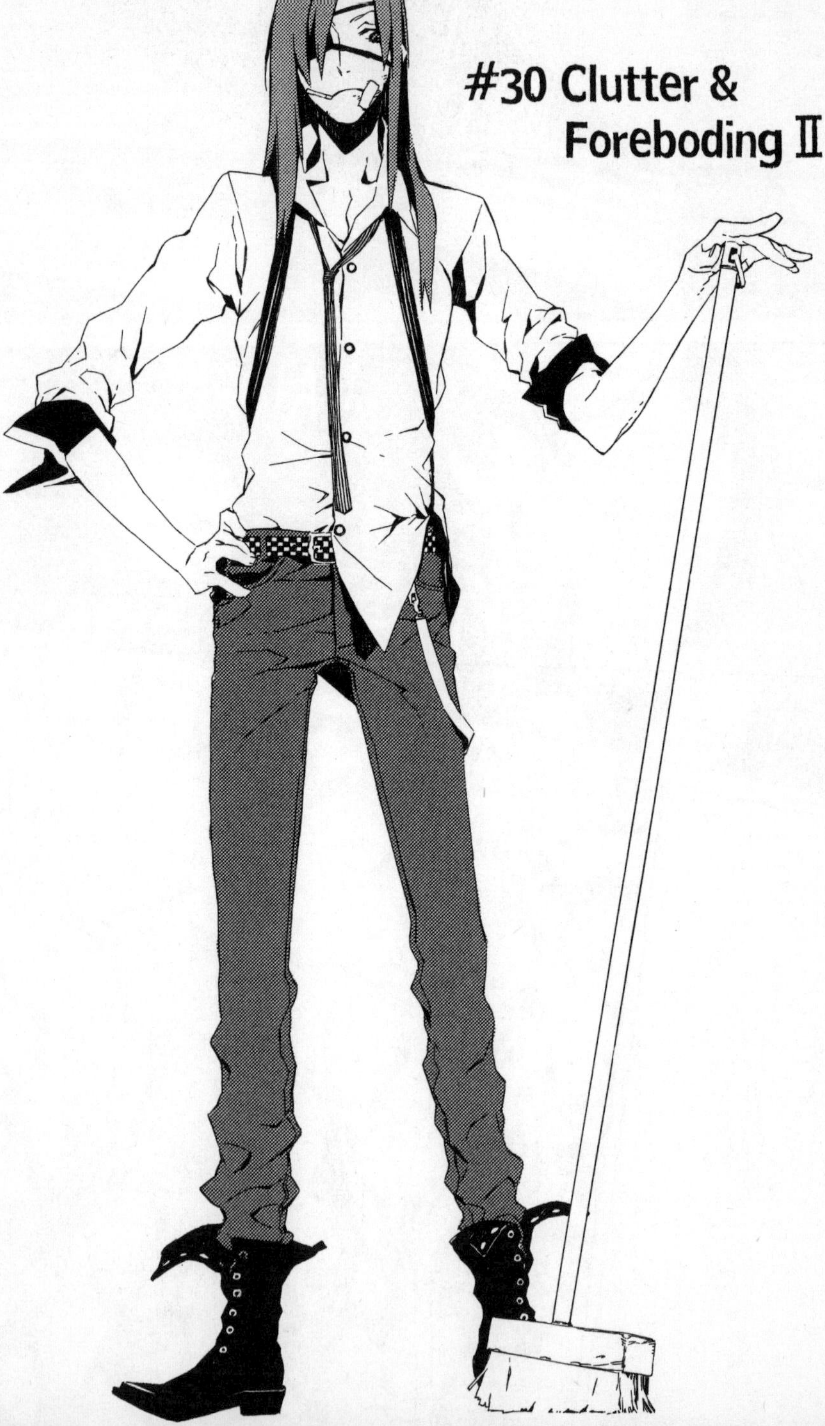

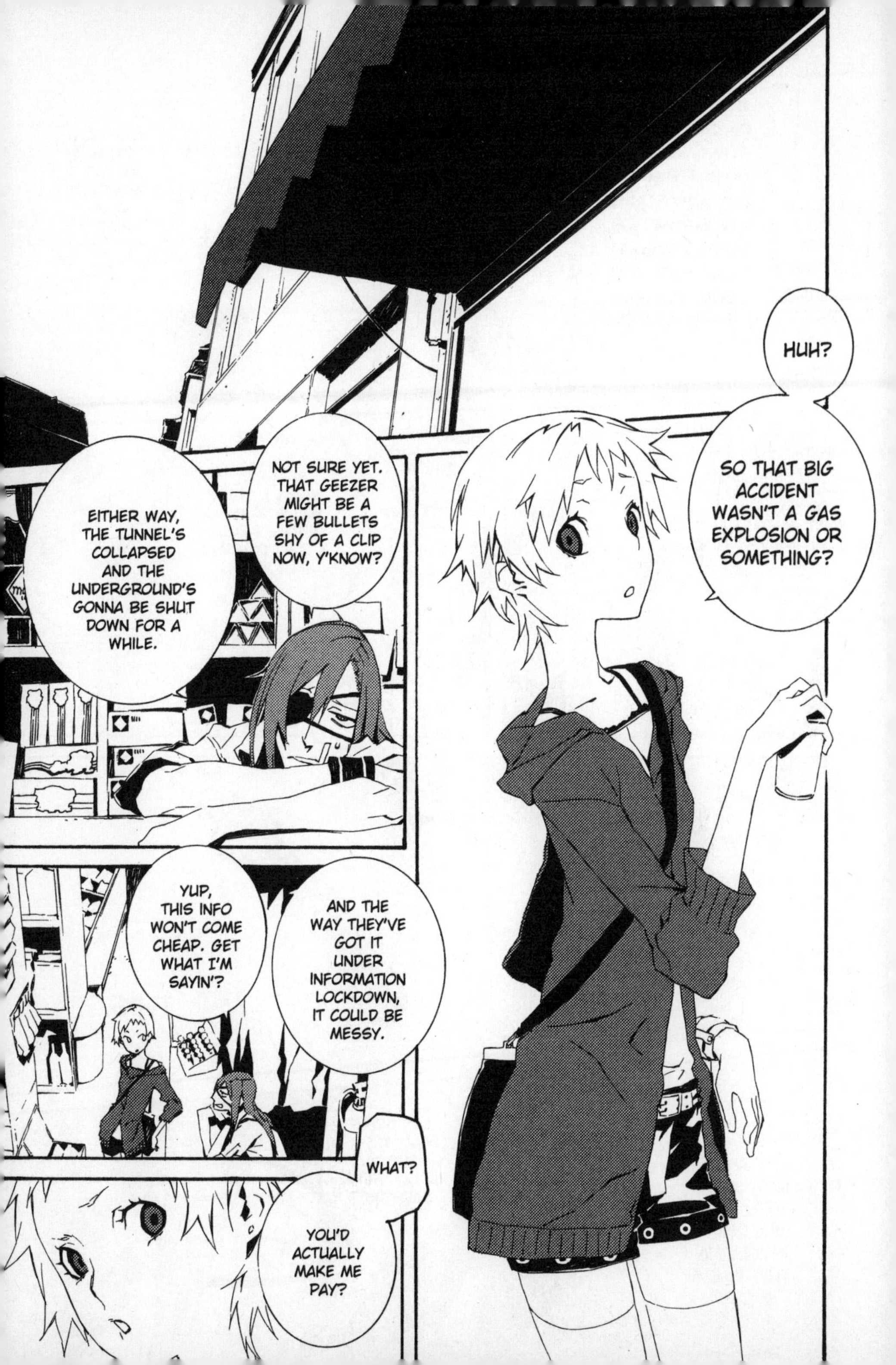
HUH?
SO THAT BIG ACCIDENT WASN'T A GAS EXPLOSION OR SOMETHING?
NOT SURE YET. THAT GEEZER MIGHT BE A FEW BULLETS SHY OF A CLIP NOW, Y'KNOW?
EITHER WAY, THE TUNNEL'S COLLAPSED AND THE UNDERGROUND'S GONNA BE SHUT DOWN FOR A WHILE.
AND THE WAY THEY'VE GOT IT UNDER INFORMATION LOCKDOWN, IT COULD BE MESSY.
YUP, THIS INFO WON'T COME CHEAP. GET WHAT I'M SAYIN'?
WHAT?
YOU'D ACTUALLY MAKE ME PAY?

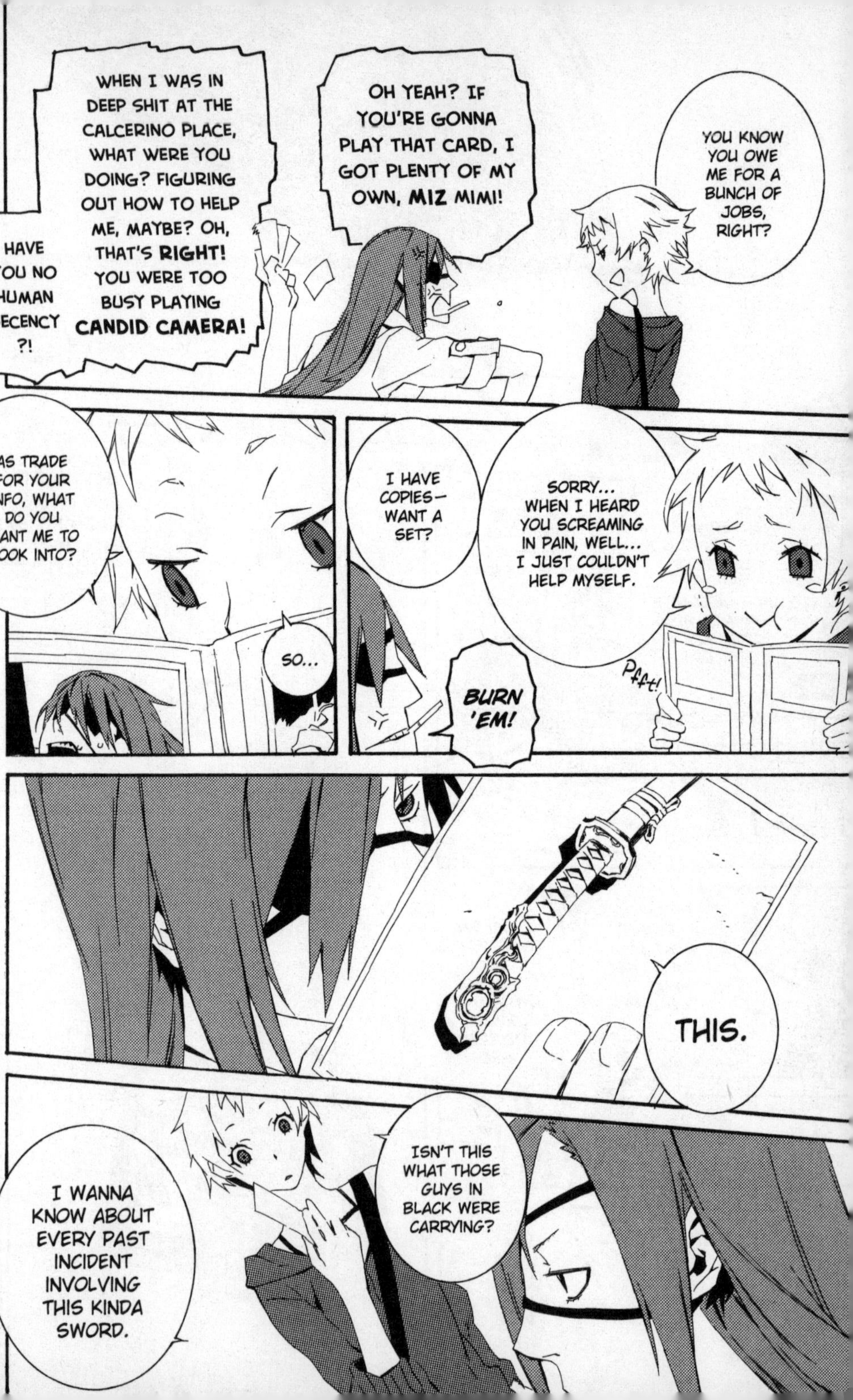
YOU KNOW YOU OWE ME FOR A BUNCH OF JOBS, RIGHT?
OH YEAH? IF YOU'RE GONNA PLAY THAT CARD, I GOT PLENTY OF MY OWN, **MIZ** MIMI!
WHEN I WAS IN DEEP SHIT AT THE CALCERINO PLACE, WHAT WERE YOU DOING? FIGURING OUT HOW TO HELP ME, MAYBE? OH, THAT'S **RIGHT!** YOU WERE TOO BUSY PLAYING **CANDID CAMERA!**
HAVE YOU NO HUMAN DECENCY ?!
SORRY... WHEN I HEARD YOU SCREAMING IN PAIN, WELL... I JUST COULDN'T HELP MYSELF.
Pfft!
I HAVE COPIES— WANT A SET?
BURN 'EM!
AS TRADE FOR YOUR INFO, WHAT DO YOU WANT ME TO LOOK INTO?
SO...
THIS.
ISN'T THIS WHAT THOSE GUYS IN BLACK WERE CARRYING?
I WANNA KNOW ABOUT EVERY PAST INCIDENT INVOLVING THIS KINDA SWORD.

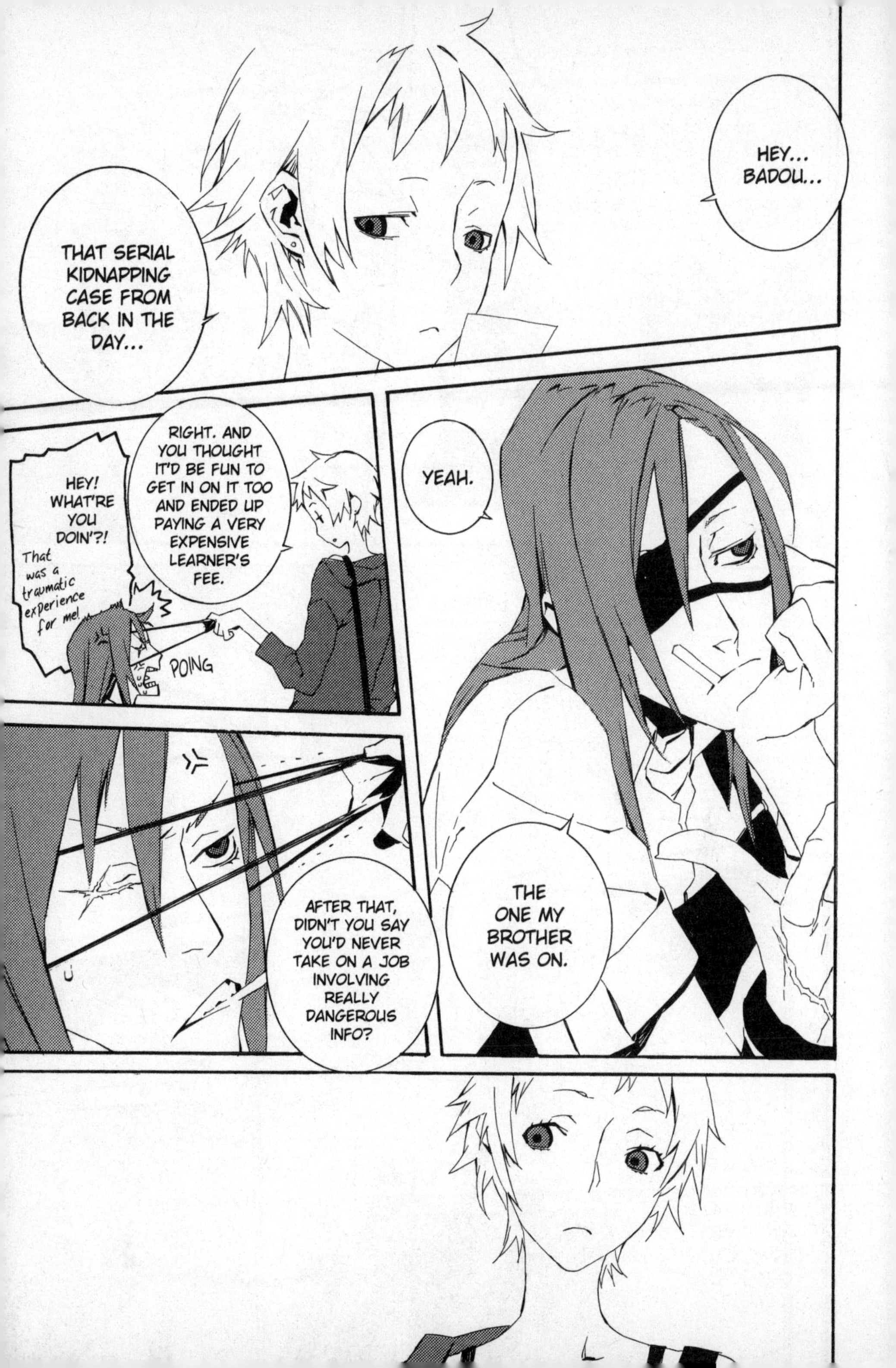
HEY... BADOU...
THAT SERIAL KIDNAPPING CASE FROM BACK IN THE DAY...
YEAH.
THE ONE MY BROTHER WAS ON.
RIGHT. AND YOU THOUGHT IT'D BE FUN TO GET IN ON IT TOO AND ENDED UP PAYING A VERY EXPENSIVE LEARNER'S FEE.
HEY! WHAT'RE YOU DOIN'?!
That was a traumatic experience for me!
POING
AFTER THAT, DIDN'T YOU SAY YOU'D NEVER TAKE ON A JOB INVOLVING REALLY DANGEROUS INFO?

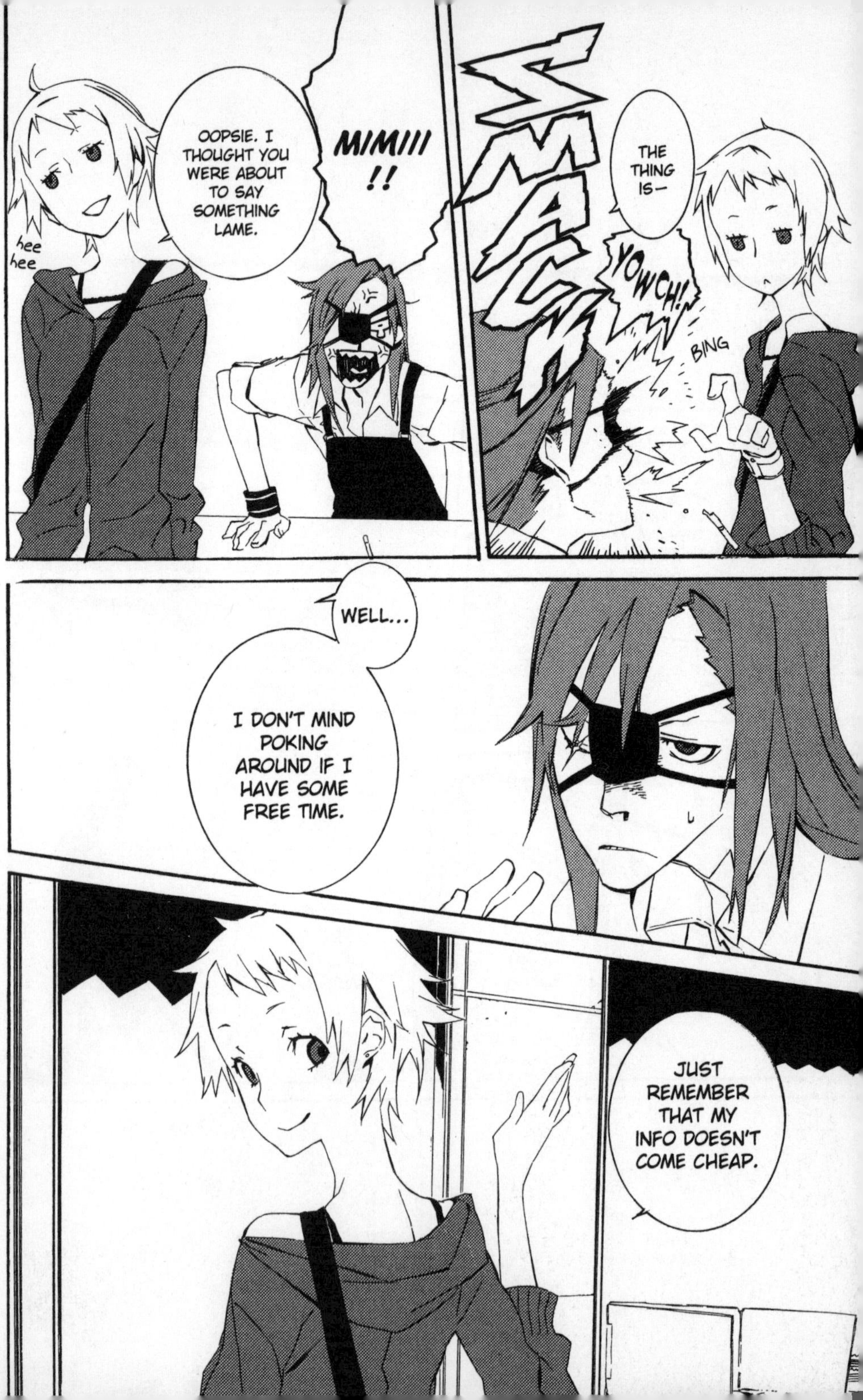
THE THING IS—
SMACK
YOWCH!
BING
MIMI!!! !!
OOPSIE. I THOUGHT YOU WERE ABOUT TO SAY SOMETHING LAME.
hee hee
WELL...
I DON'T MIND POKING AROUND IF I HAVE SOME FREE TIME.
JUST REMEMBER THAT MY INFO DOESN'T COME CHEAP.

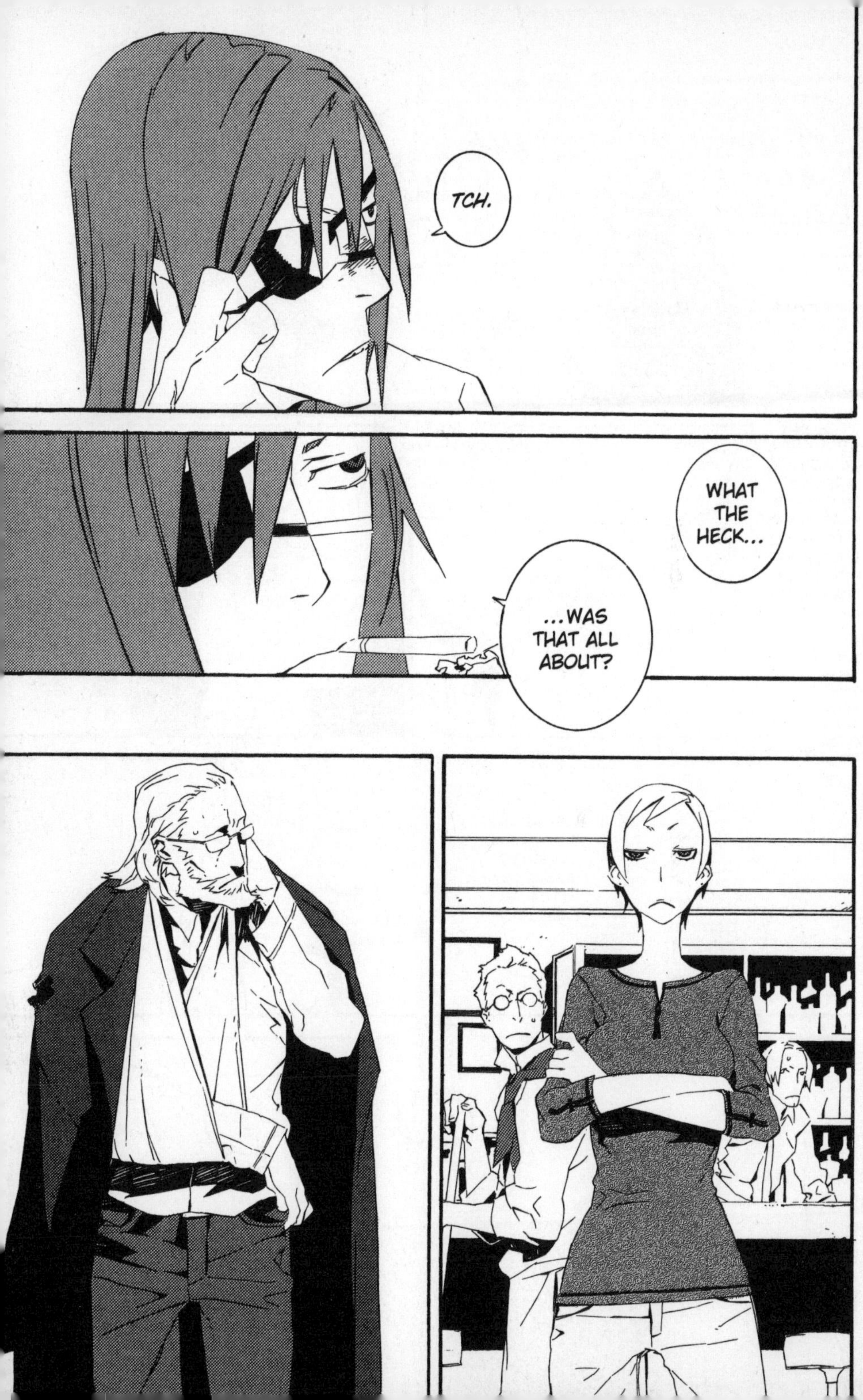
TCH.
WHAT THE HECK...
...WAS THAT ALL ABOUT?

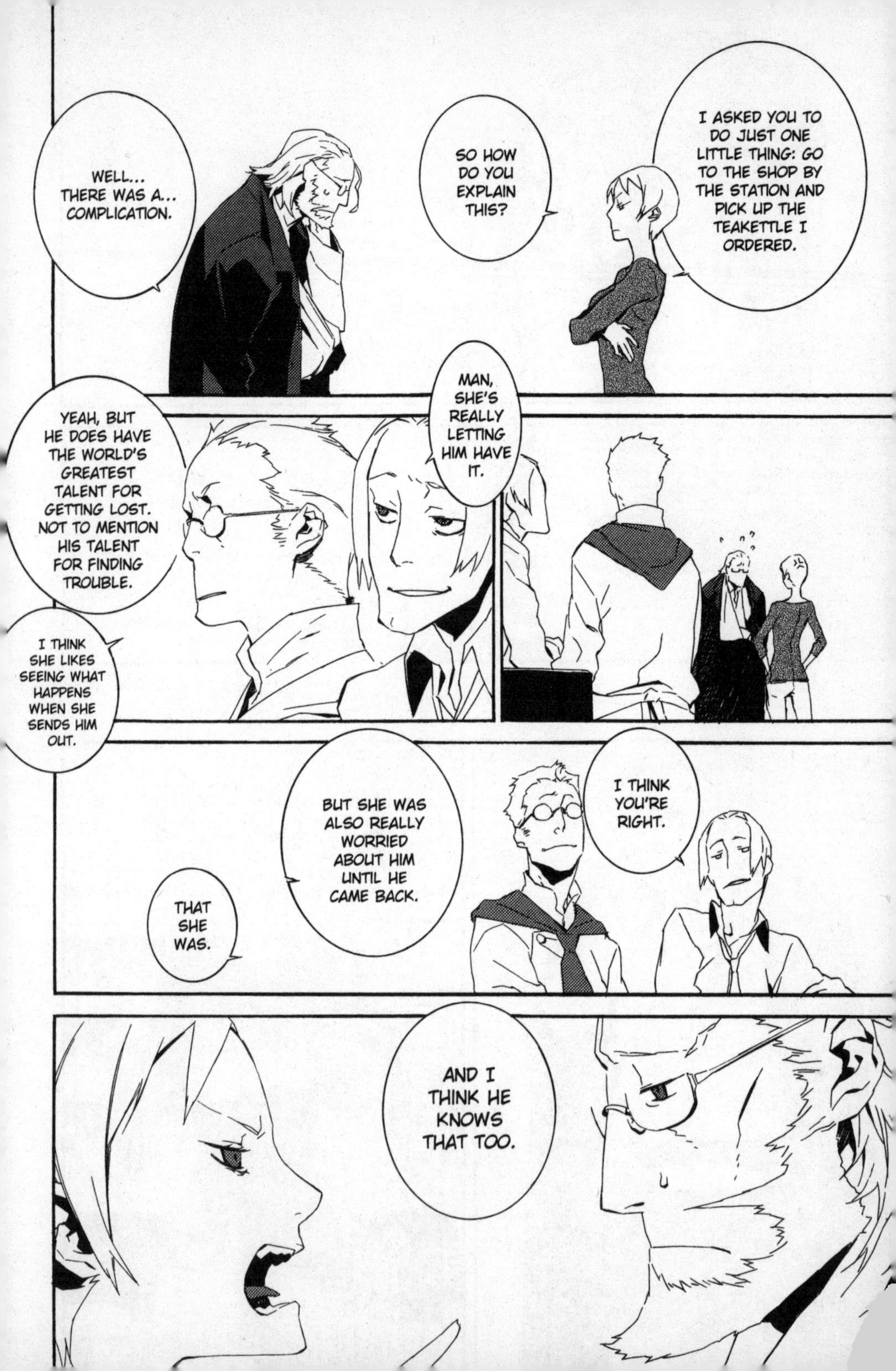
I ASKED YOU TO DO JUST ONE LITTLE THING: GO TO THE SHOP BY THE STATION AND PICK UP THE TEAKETTLE I ORDERED.
SO HOW DO YOU EXPLAIN THIS?
WELL... THERE WAS A... COMPLICATION.
MAN, SHE'S REALLY LETTING HIM HAVE IT.
YEAH, BUT HE DOES HAVE THE WORLD'S GREATEST TALENT FOR GETTING LOST. NOT TO MENTION HIS TALENT FOR FINDING TROUBLE.
I THINK SHE LIKES SEEING WHAT HAPPENS WHEN SHE SENDS HIM OUT.
I THINK YOU'RE RIGHT.
BUT SHE WAS ALSO REALLY WORRIED ABOUT HIM UNTIL HE CAME BACK.
THAT SHE WAS.
AND I THINK HE KNOWS THAT TOO.

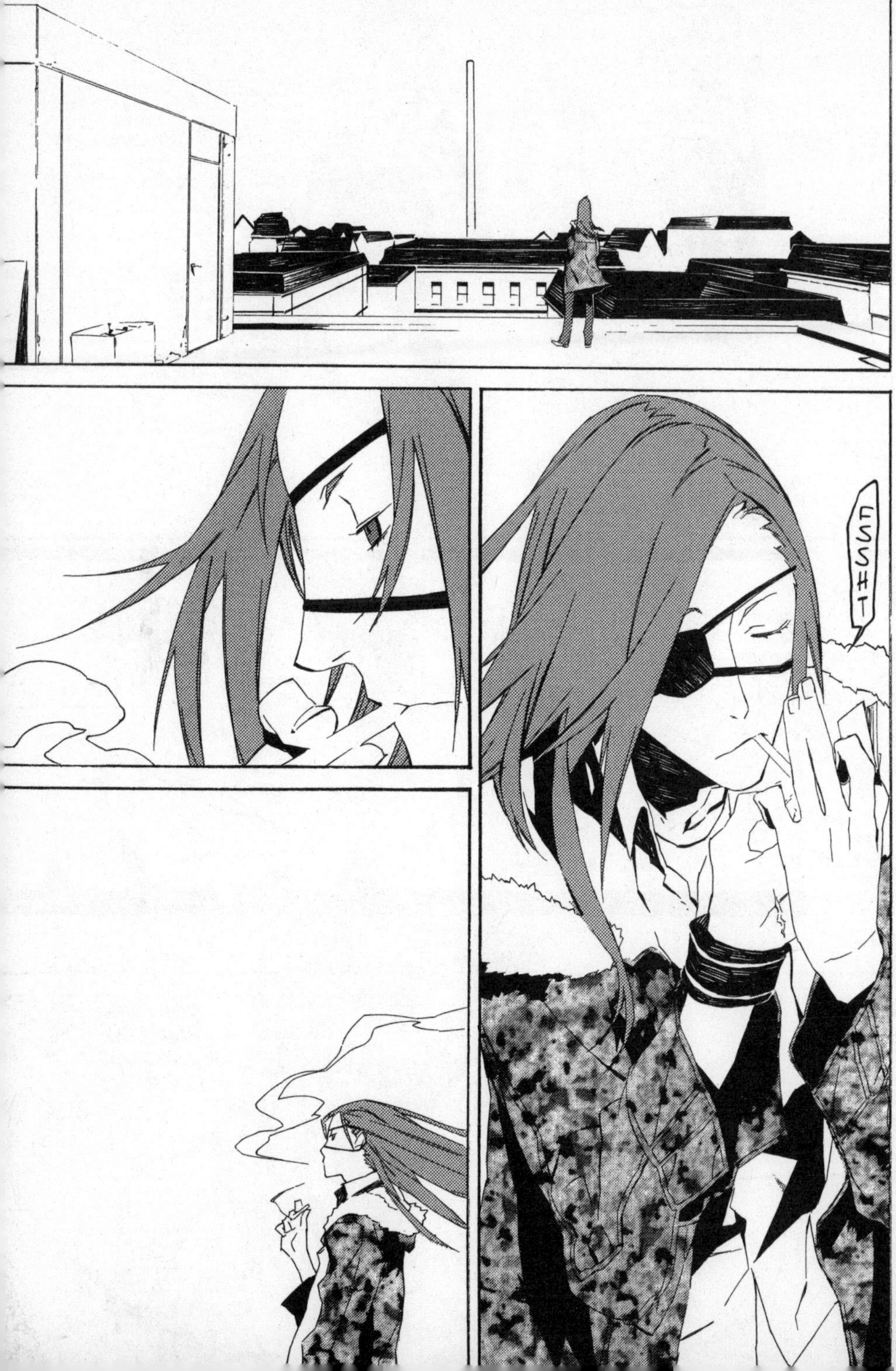
FSSHT

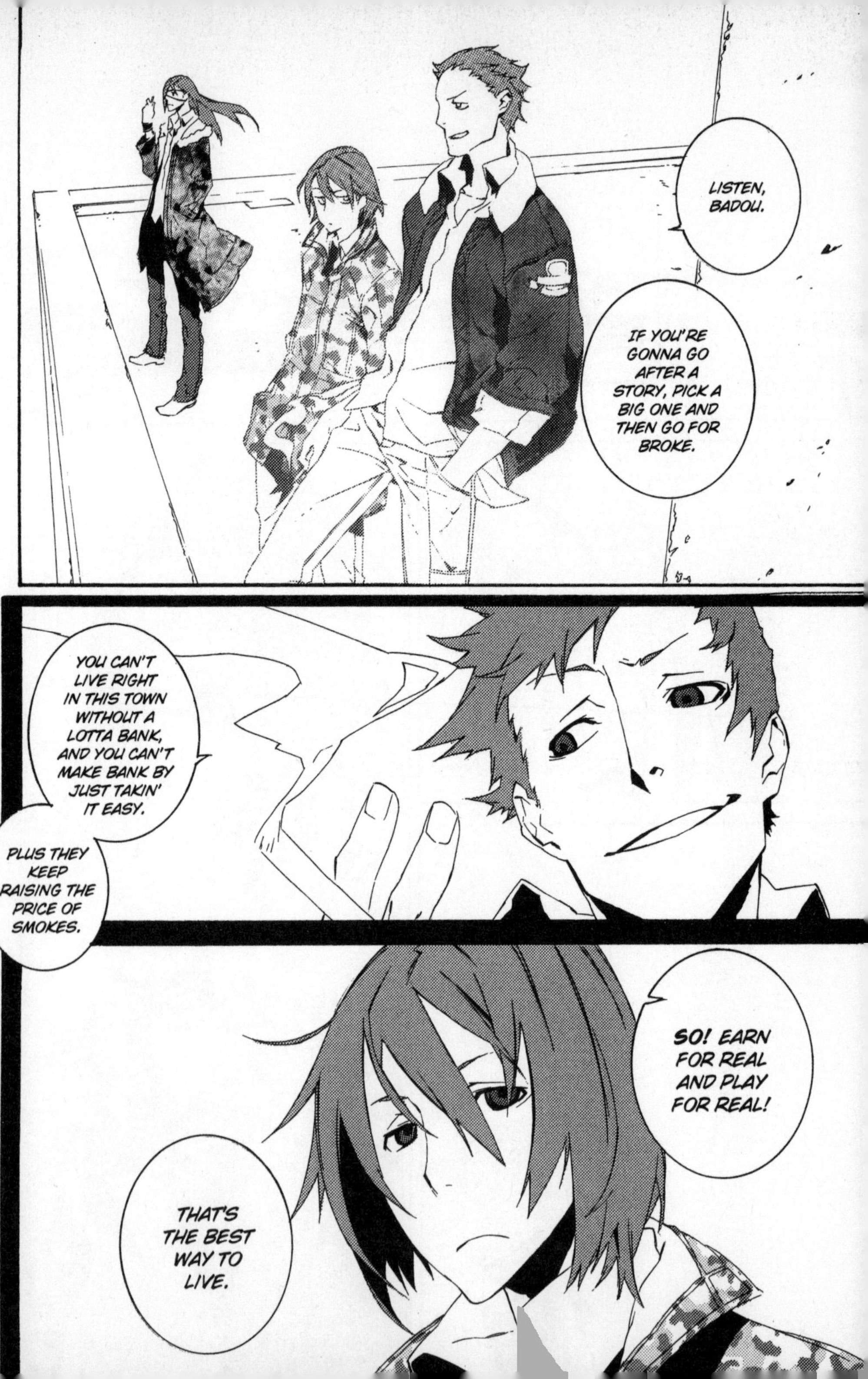
LISTEN, BADOU.
IF YOU'RE GONNA GO AFTER A STORY, PICK A BIG ONE AND THEN GO FOR BROKE.
YOU CAN'T LIVE RIGHT IN THIS TOWN WITHOUT A LOTTA BANK, AND YOU CAN'T MAKE BANK BY JUST TAKIN' IT EASY.
PLUS THEY KEEP RAISING THE PRICE OF SMOKES.
SO! EARN FOR REAL AND PLAY FOR REAL!
THAT'S THE BEST WAY TO LIVE.

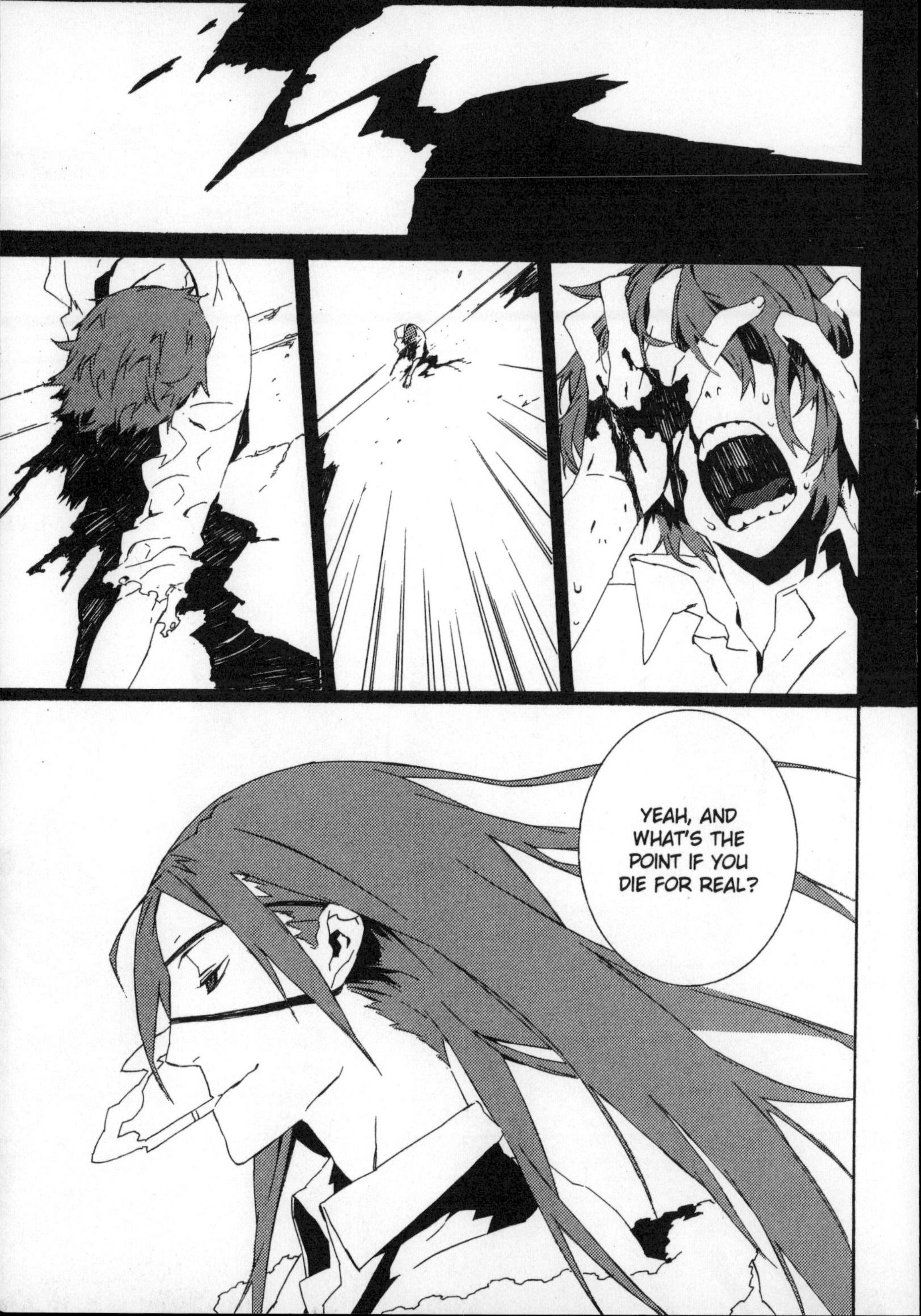
YEAH, AND WHAT'S THE POINT IF YOU DIE FOR REAL?

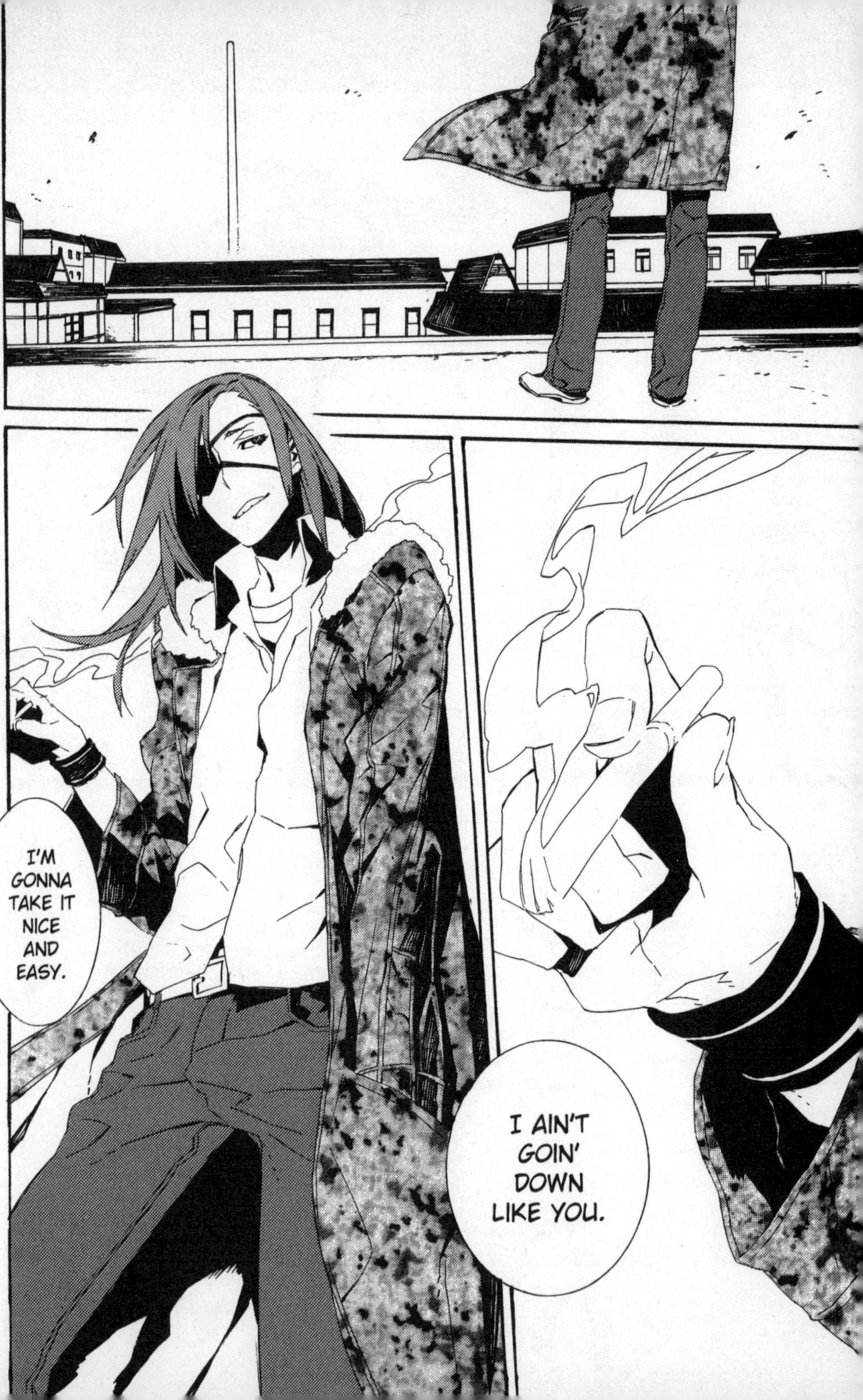
I AIN'T GOIN' DOWN LIKE YOU.
I'M GONNA TAKE IT NICE AND EASY.

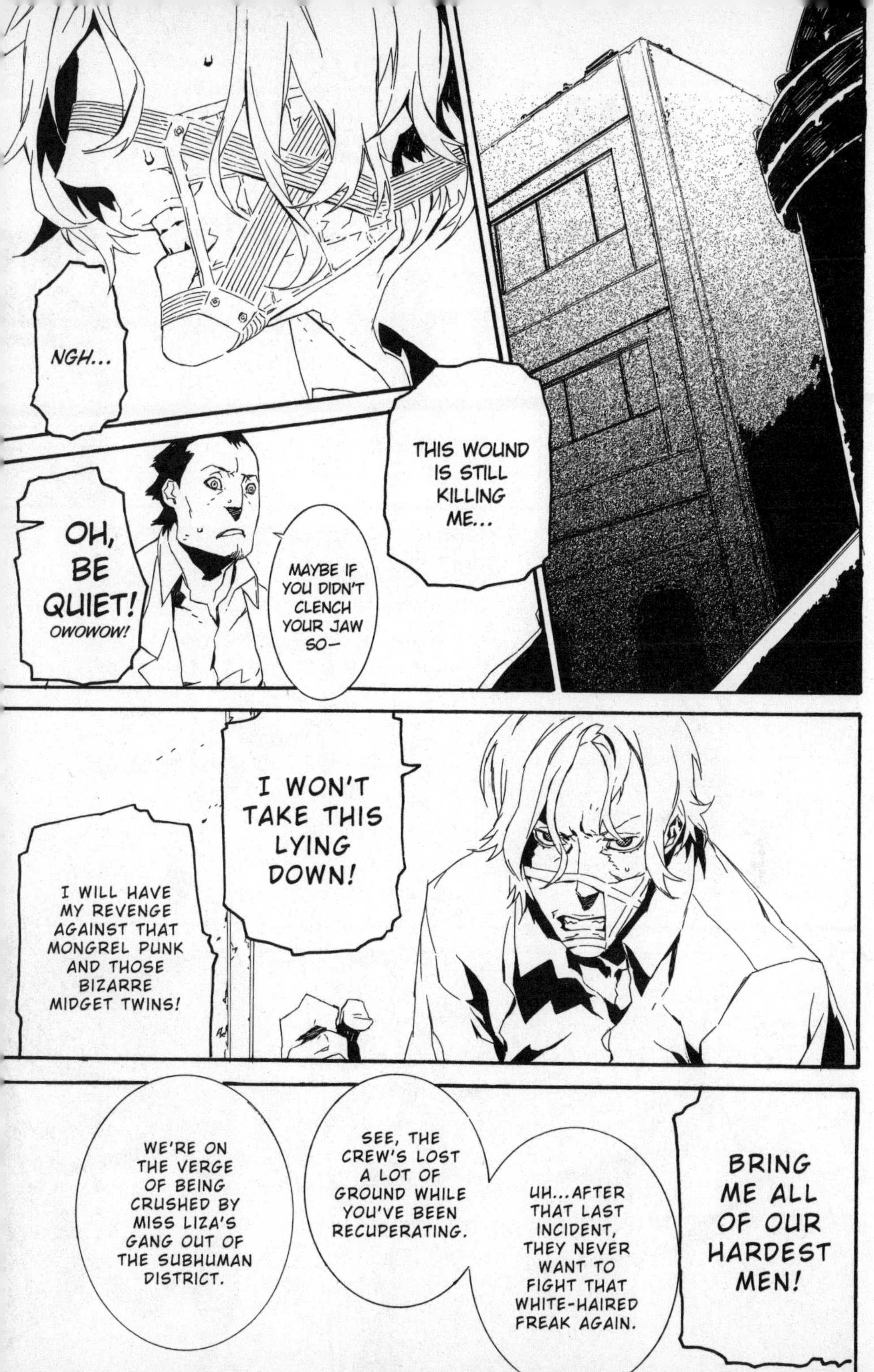
NGH...
THIS WOUND IS STILL KILLING ME...
MAYBE IF YOU DIDN'T CLENCH YOUR JAW SO—
OH, BE QUIET! OWOWOW!
I WON'T TAKE THIS LYING DOWN!
I WILL HAVE MY REVENGE AGAINST THAT MONGREL PUNK AND THOSE BIZARRE MIDGET TWINS!
BRING ME ALL OF OUR HARDEST MEN!
UH...AFTER THAT LAST INCIDENT, THEY NEVER WANT TO FIGHT THAT WHITE-HAIRED FREAK AGAIN.
SEE, THE CREW'S LOST A LOT OF GROUND WHILE YOU'VE BEEN RECUPERATING.
WE'RE ON THE VERGE OF BEING CRUSHED BY MISS LIZA'S GANG OUT OF THE SUBHUMAN DISTRICT.

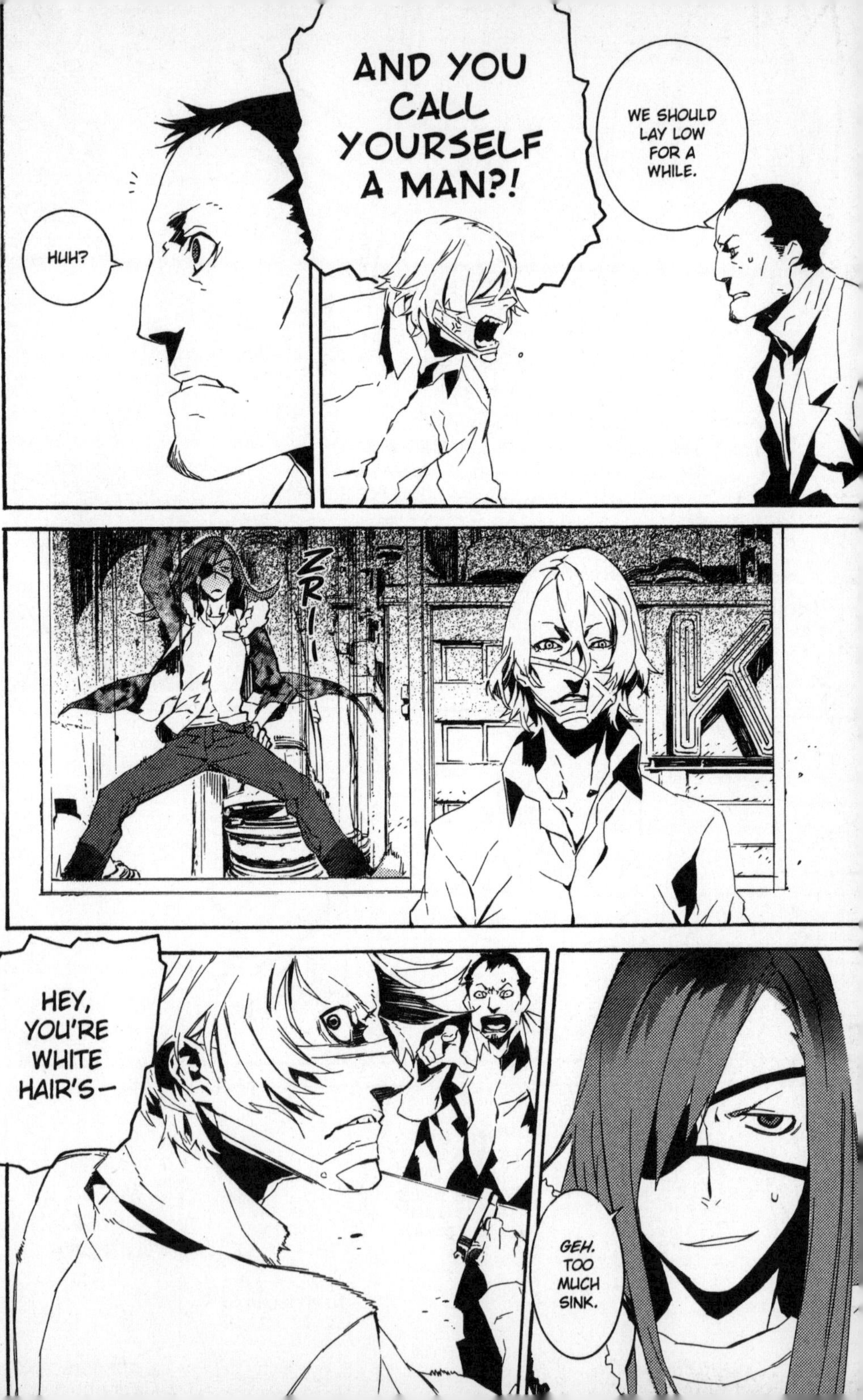
WE SHOULD LAY LOW FOR A WHILE.
AND YOU CALL YOURSELF A MAN?!
HUH?
ZRI-
GEH. TOO MUCH SINK.
HEY, YOU'RE WHITE HAIR'S—

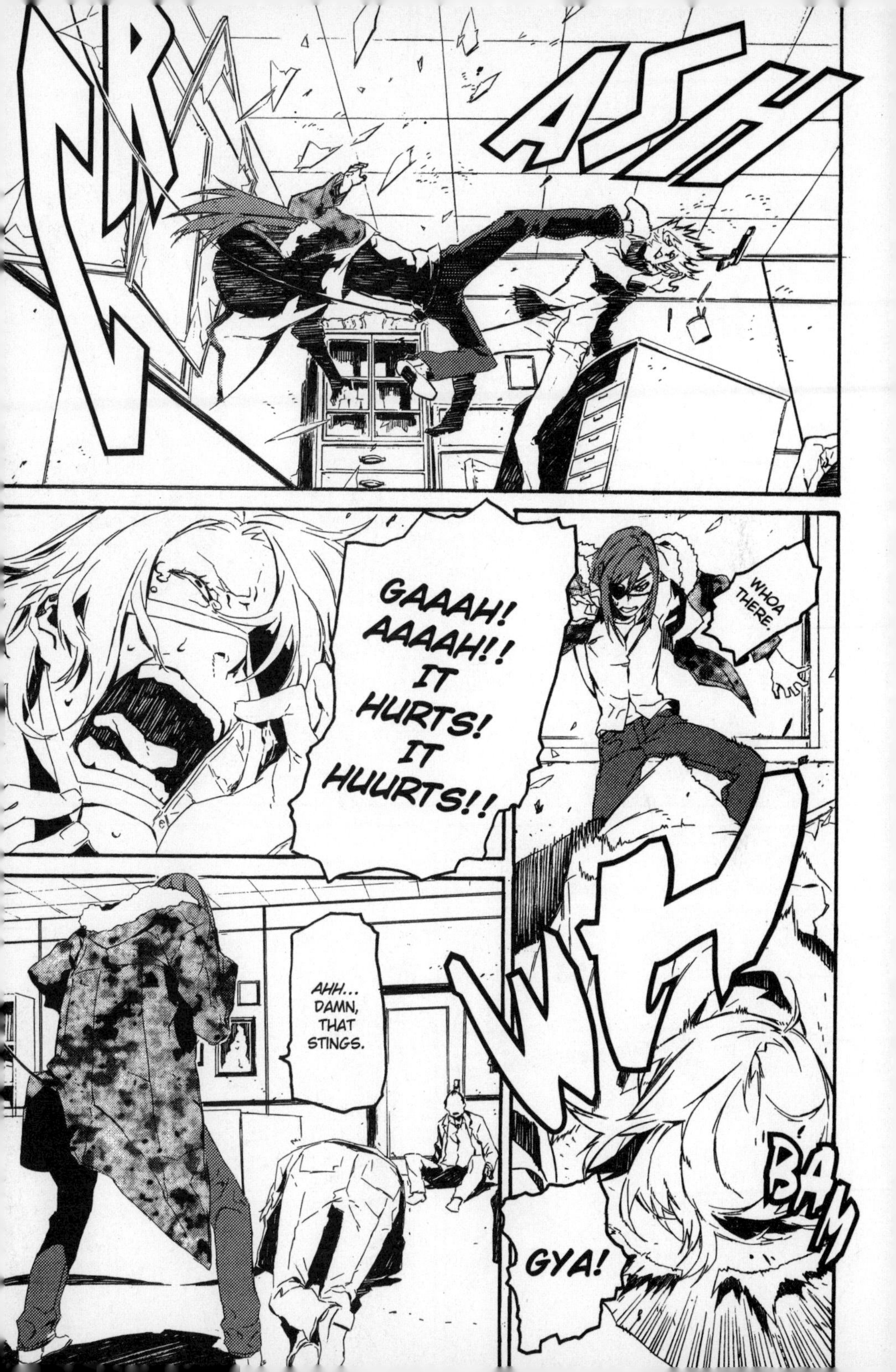
CRASH
WHOA THERE.
GAAAH! AAAAH!! IT HURTS! IT HUURTS!!
BAM
GYA!
AHH... DAMN, THAT STINGS.

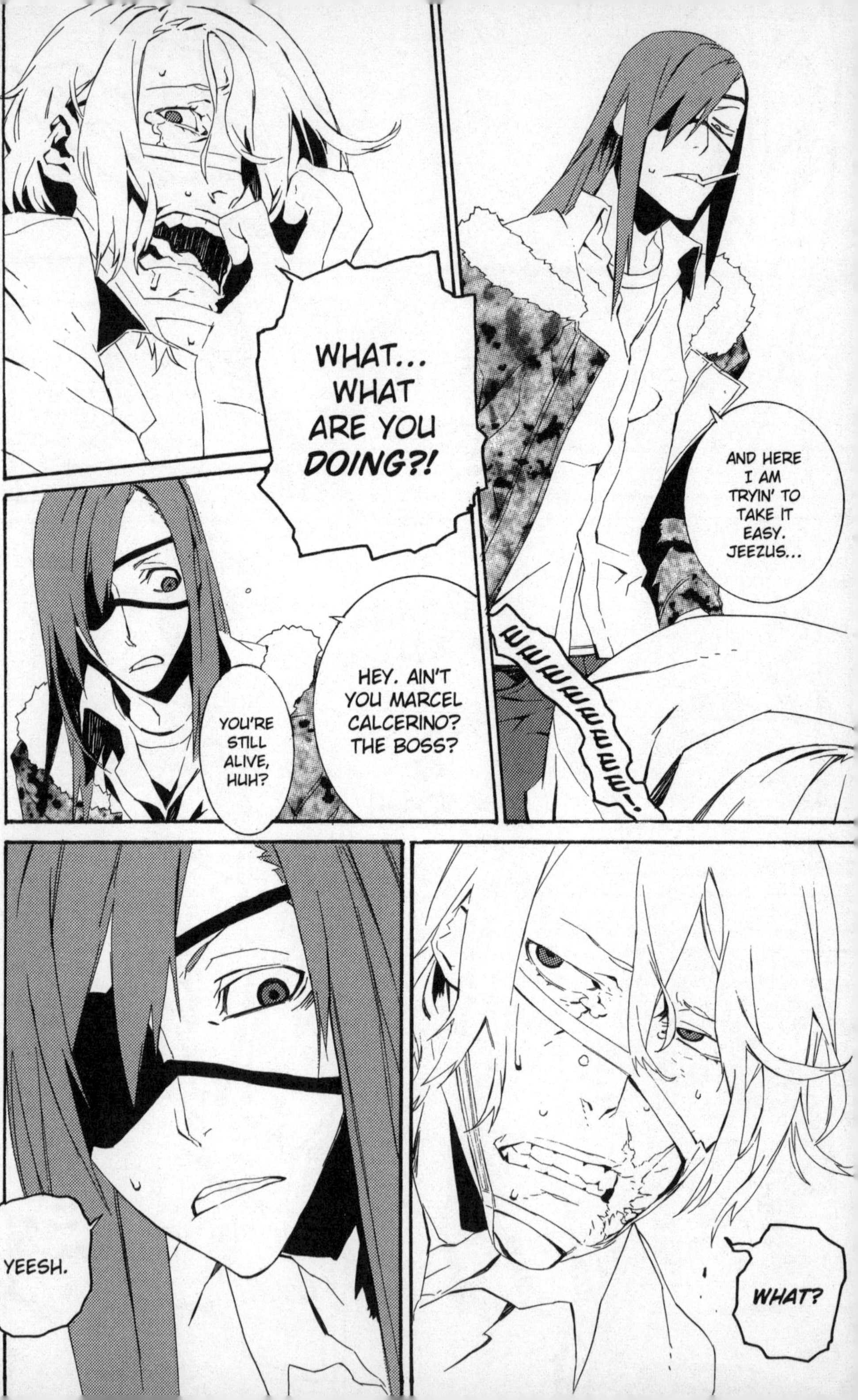
AND HERE I AM TRYIN' TO TAKE IT EASY. JEEZUS...
WWWWWWWWWWW!
WHAT... WHAT ARE YOU *DOING?!*
HEY. AIN'T YOU MARCEL CALCERINO? THE BOSS?
YOU'RE STILL ALIVE, HUH?
WHAT?
YEESH.

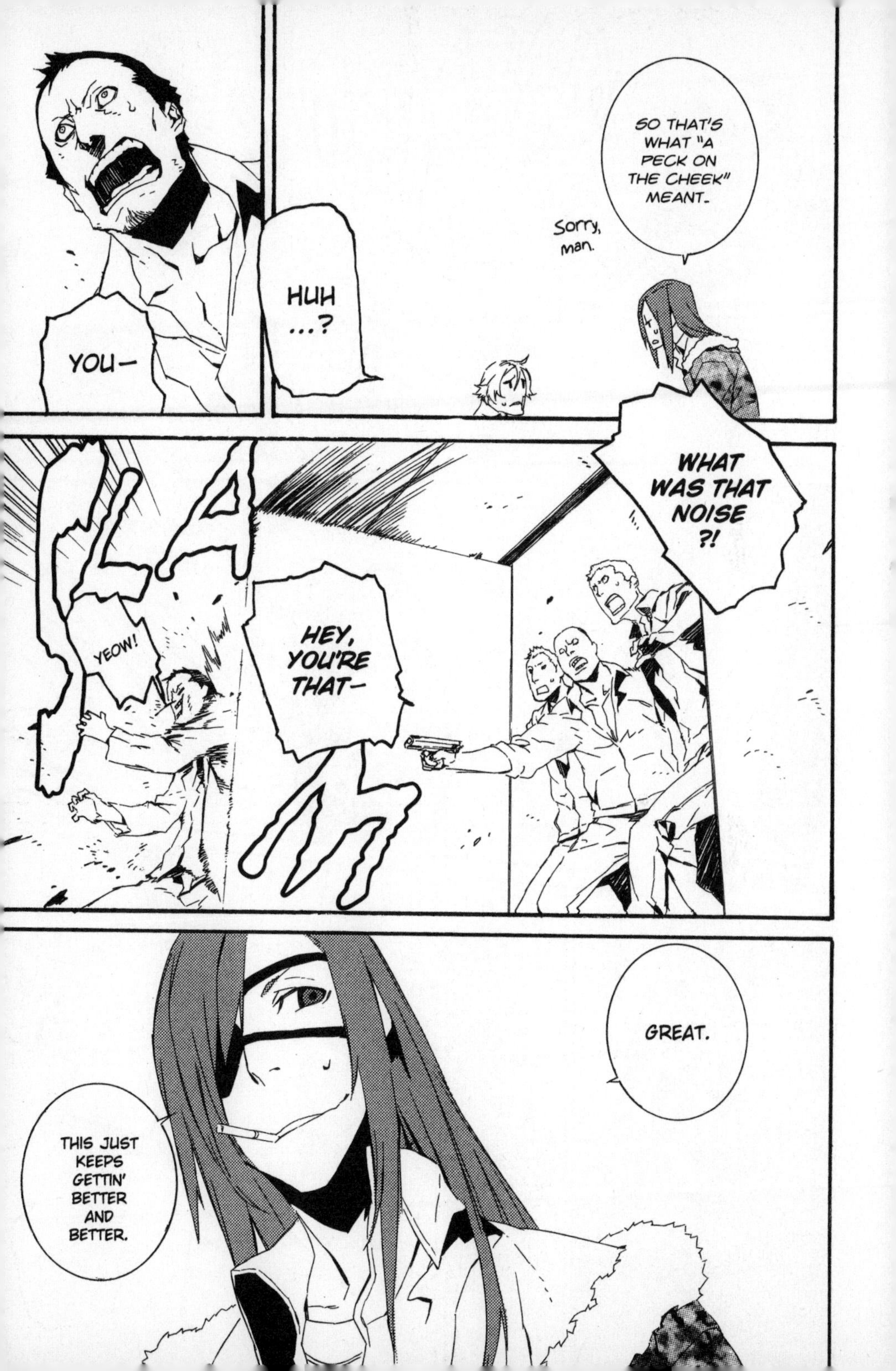
SO THAT'S WHAT "A PECK ON THE CHEEK" MEANT.
Sorry, man.
HUH ...?
YOU—
WHAT WAS THAT NOISE ?!
HEY, YOU'RE THAT—
YEOW!
GREAT.
THIS JUST KEEPS GETTIN' BETTER AND BETTER.

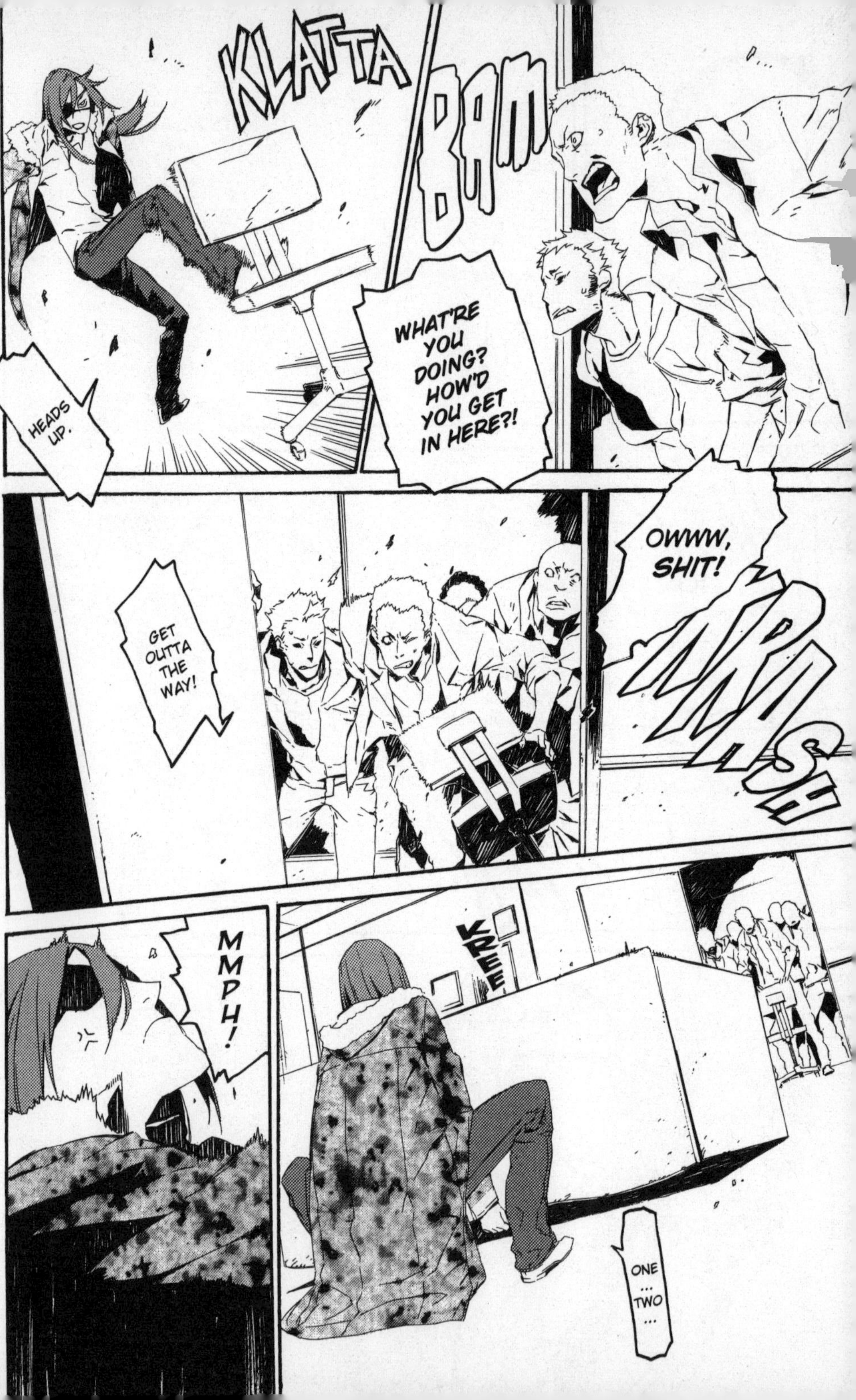
BAM
WHAT'RE YOU DOING? HOW'D YOU GET IN HERE?!
KLATTA
HEADS UP.
OWWW, SHIT!
SMASH
GET OUTTA THE WAY!
KREE
ONE ... TWO ...
MMPH!

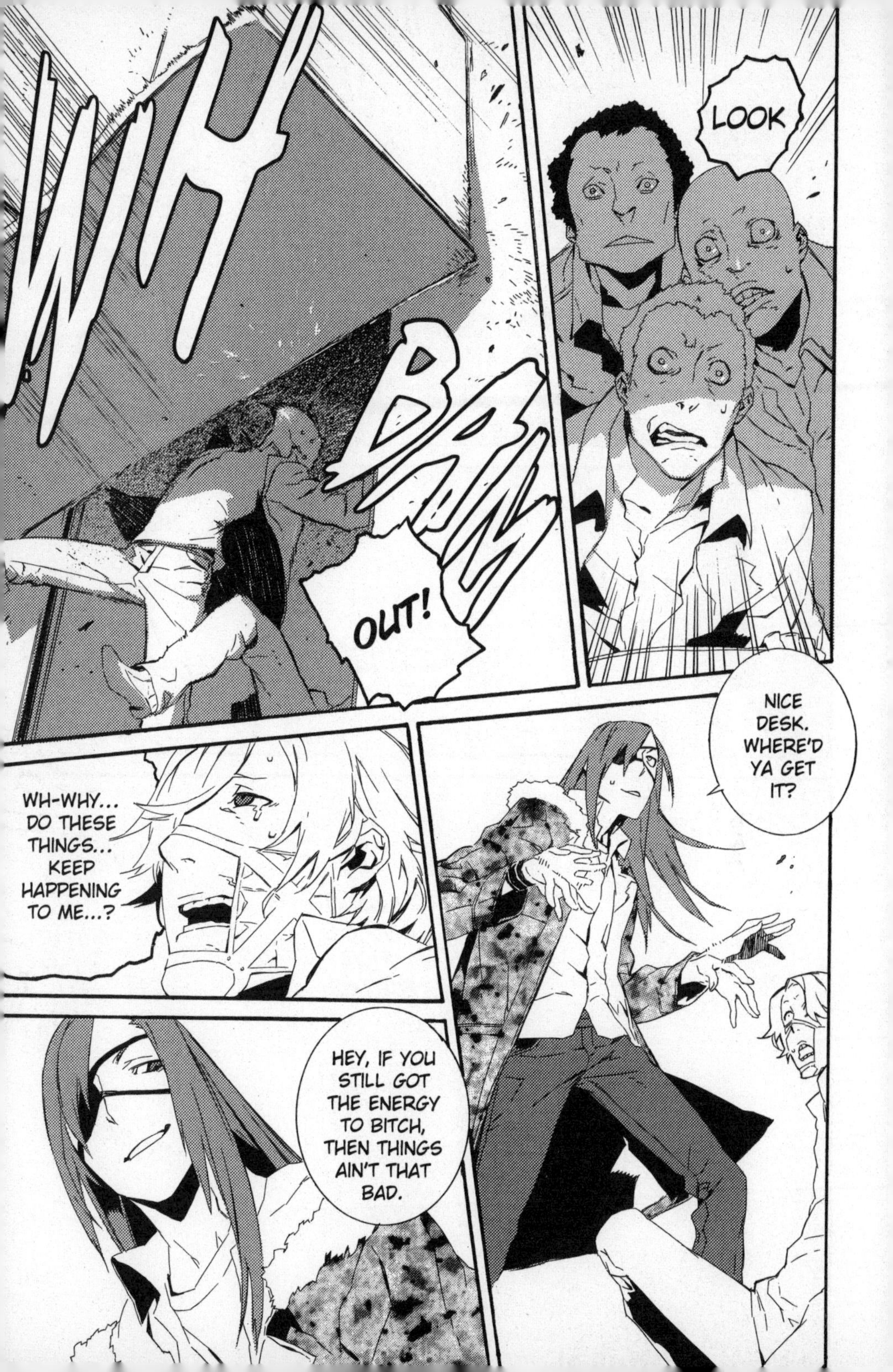
LOOK
WHY
BAM
OUT!
NICE DESK. WHERE'D YA GET IT?
WH-WHY... DO THESE THINGS... KEEP HAPPENING TO ME...?
HEY, IF YOU STILL GOT THE ENERGY TO BITCH, THEN THINGS AIN'T THAT BAD.

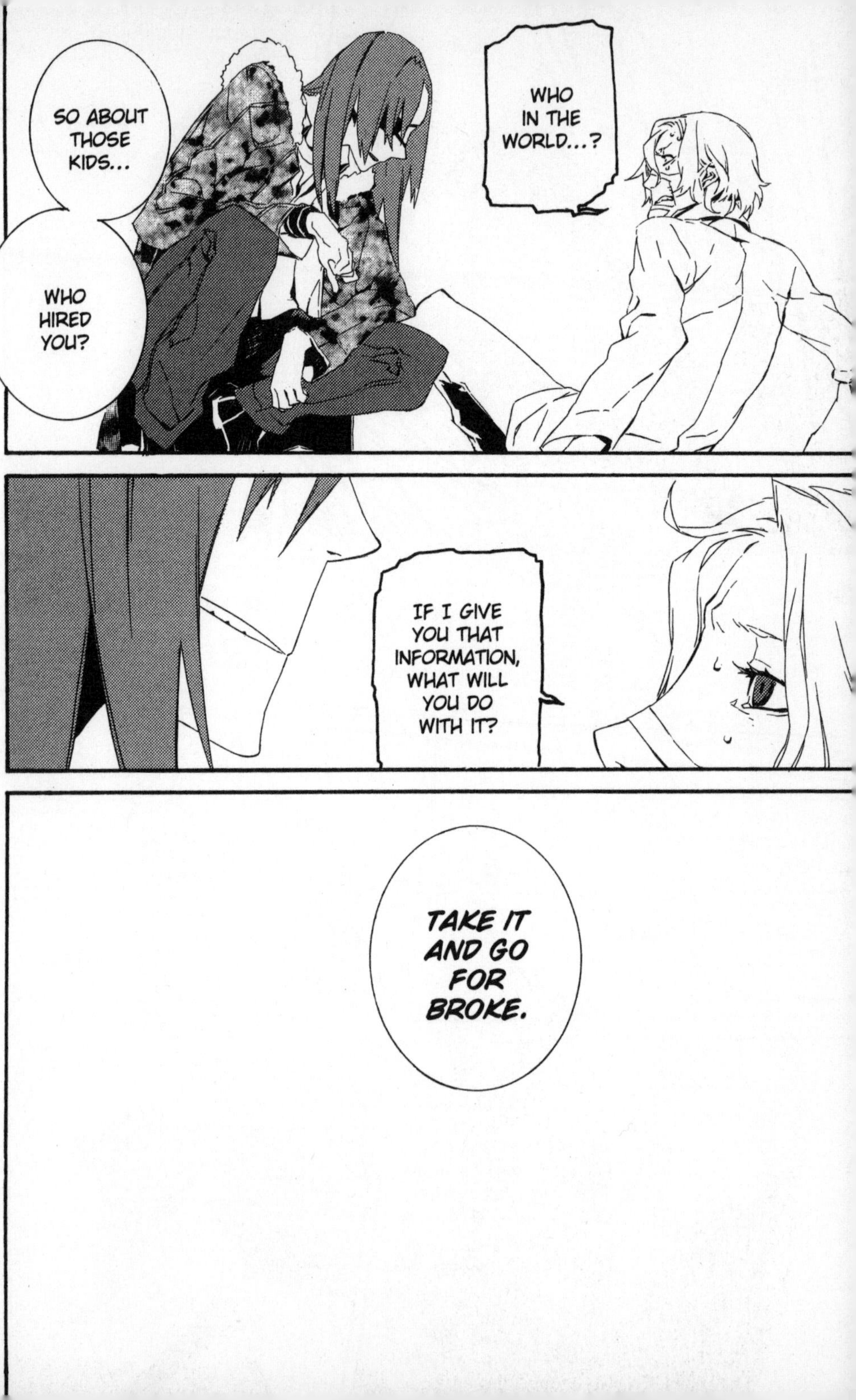
WHO IN THE WORLD...?
SO ABOUT THOSE KIDS...
WHO HIRED YOU?
IF I GIVE YOU THAT INFORMATION, WHAT WILL YOU DO WITH IT?
TAKE IT AND GO FOR BROKE.

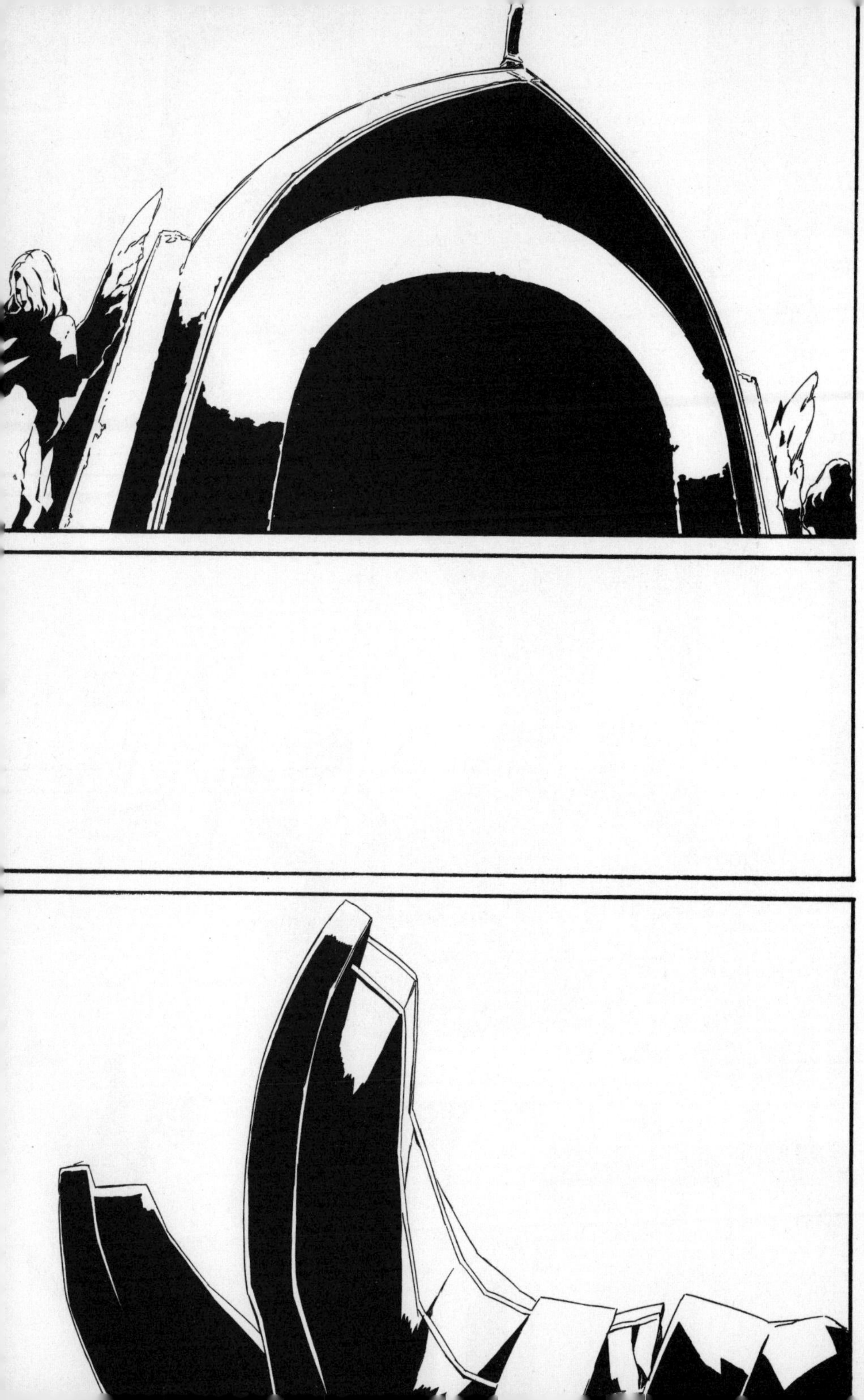

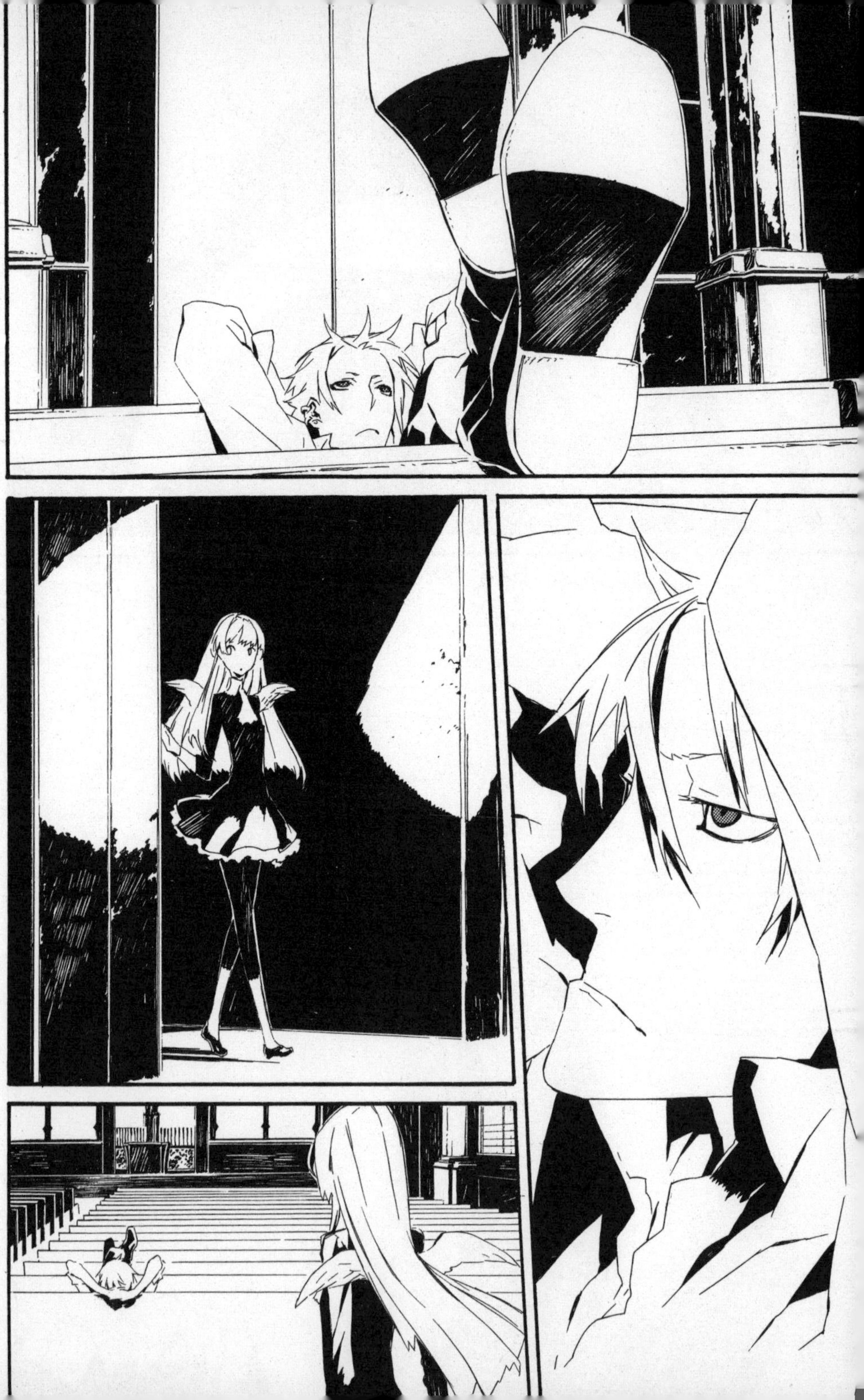

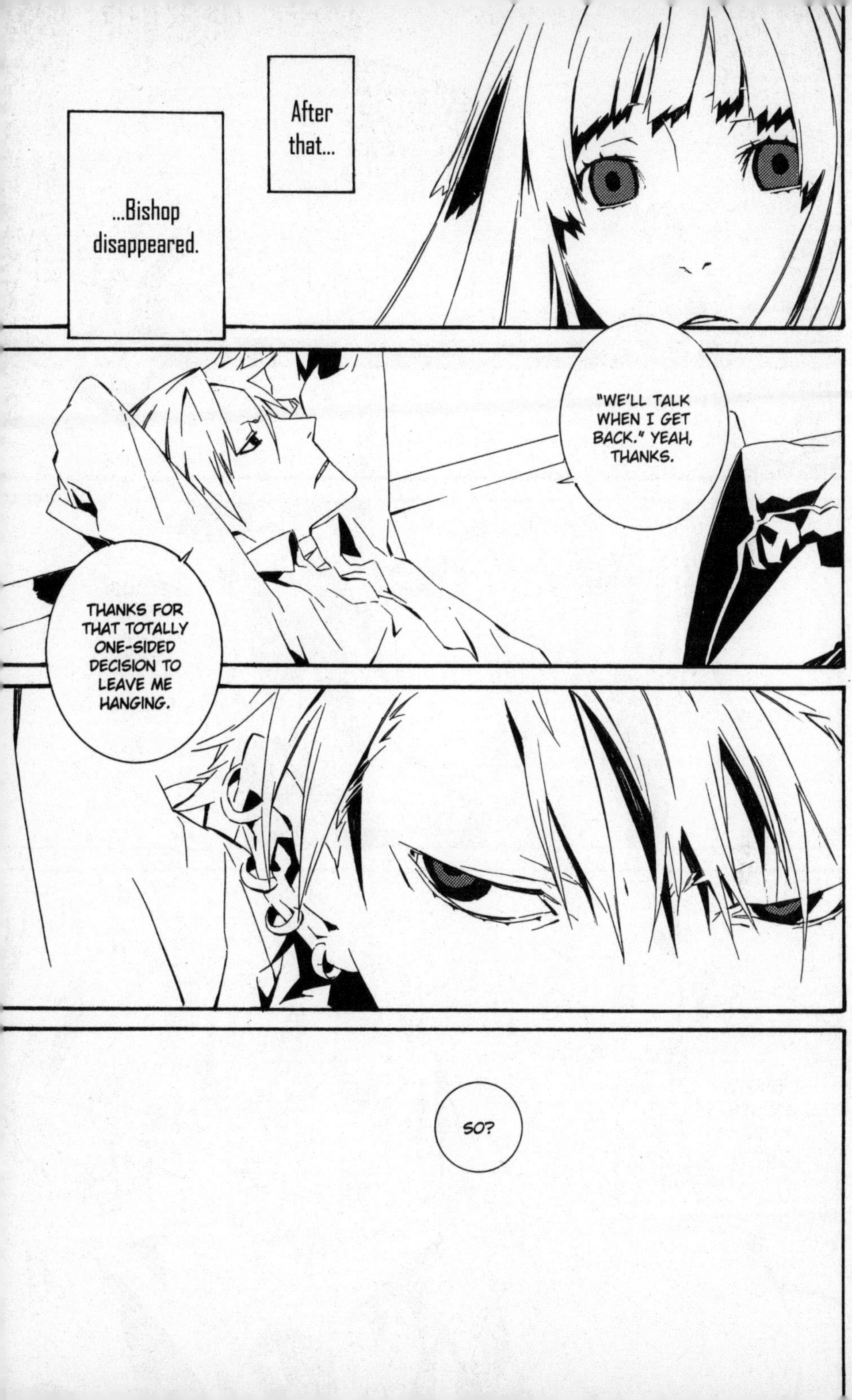
After that...
...Bishop disappeared.
"WE'LL TALK WHEN I GET BACK." YEAH, THANKS.
THANKS FOR THAT TOTALLY ONE-SIDED DECISION TO LEAVE ME HANGING.
SO?

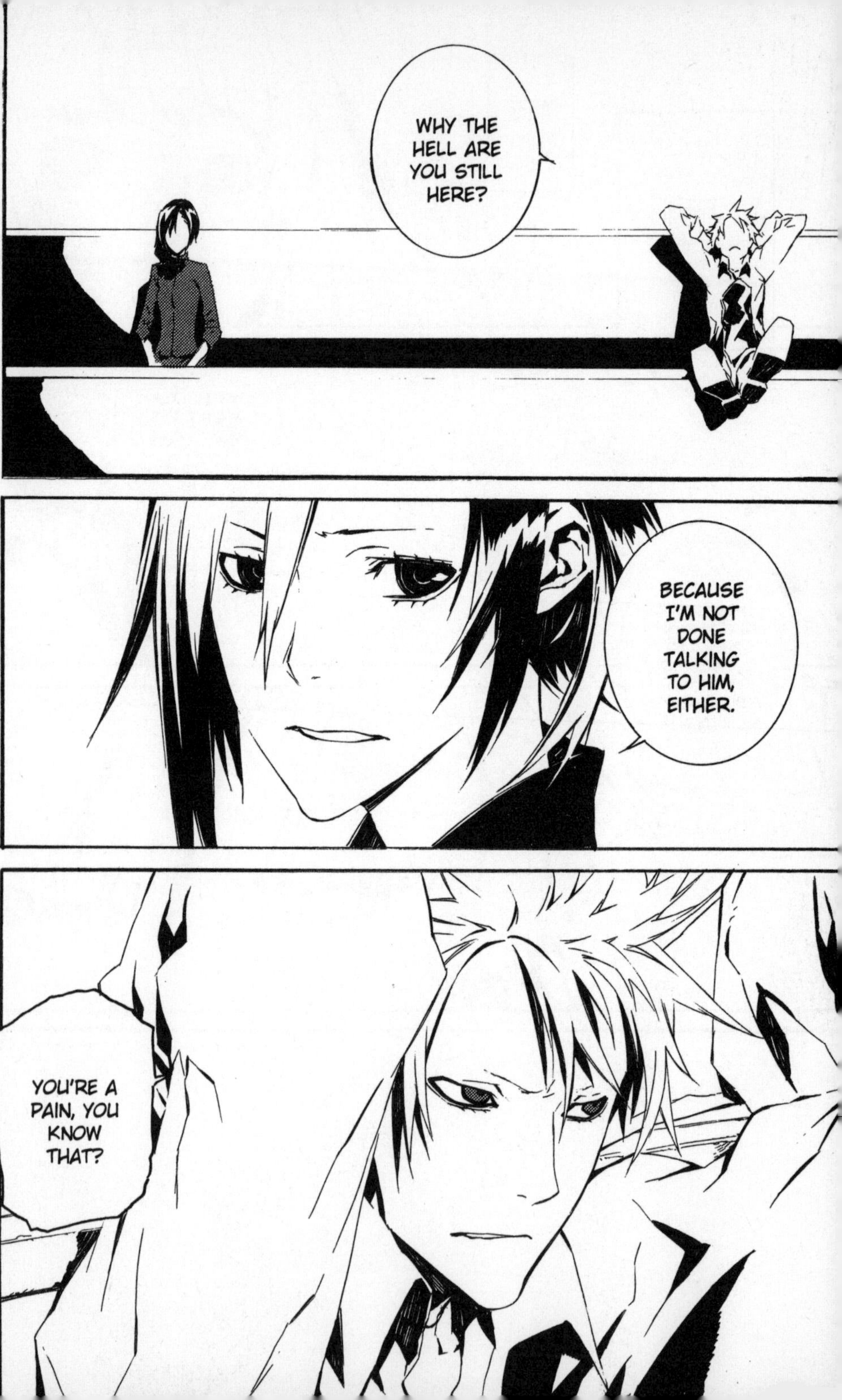
WHY THE HELL ARE YOU STILL HERE?
BECAUSE I'M NOT DONE TALKING TO HIM, EITHER.
YOU'RE A PAIN, YOU KNOW THAT?

#31 Clutter & Foreboding Ⅲ

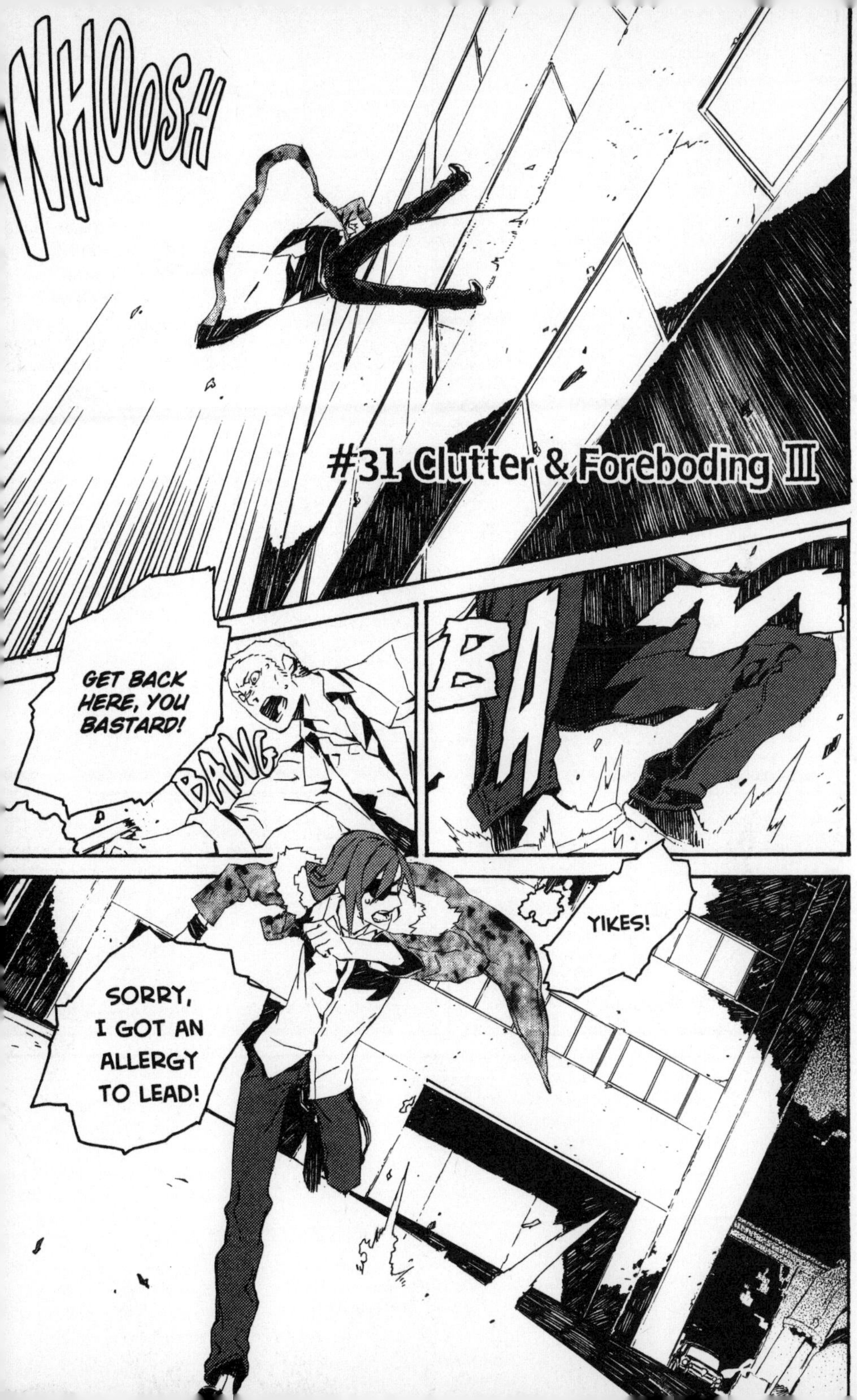
WHOOSH
BAM
GET BACK HERE, YOU BASTARD!
BANG
YIKES!
SORRY, I GOT AN ALLERGY TO LEAD!

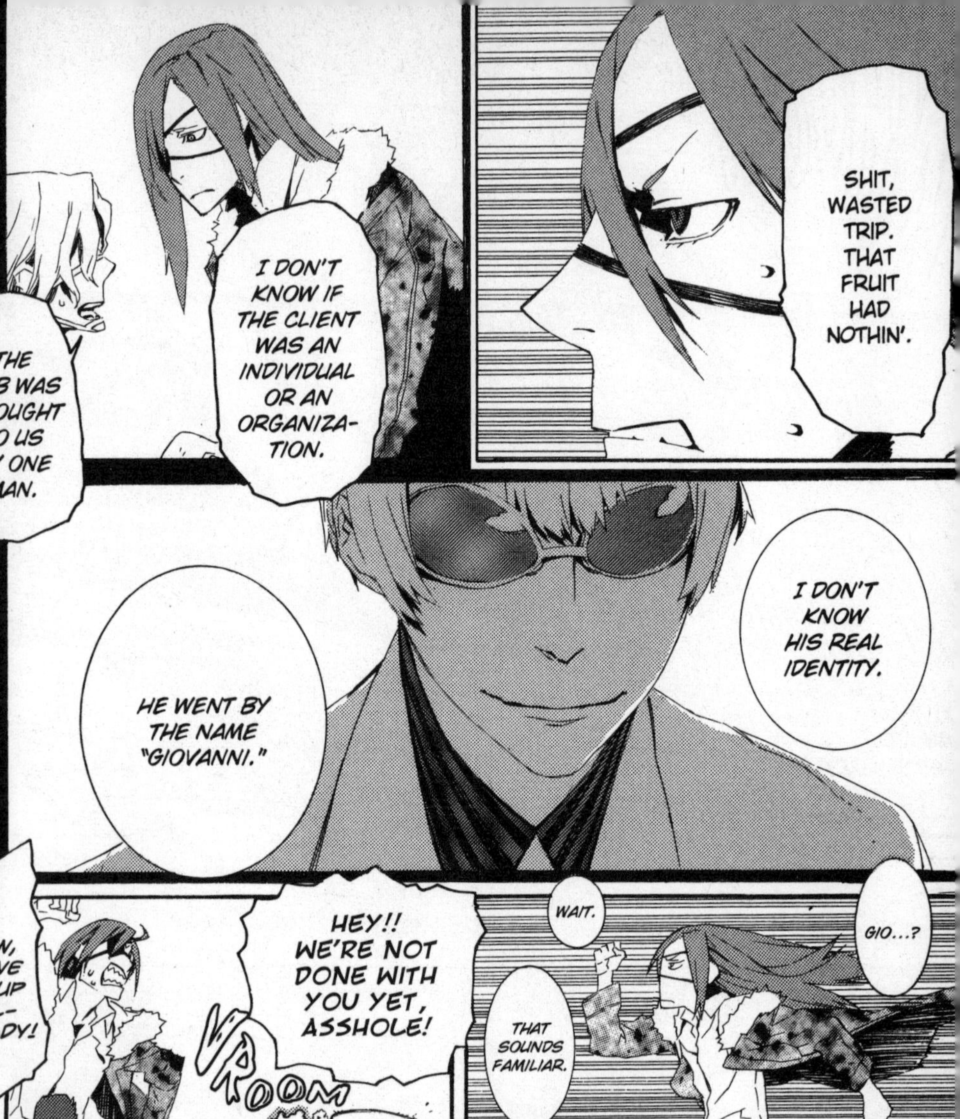
SHIT, WASTED TRIP. THAT FRUIT HAD NOTHIN'.
I DON'T KNOW IF THE CLIENT WAS AN INDIVIDUAL OR AN ORGANIZA- TION.
THE JOB WAS BROUGHT TO US BY ONE MAN.
I DON'T KNOW HIS REAL IDENTITY.
HE WENT BY THE NAME "GIOVANNI."
GIO...?
WAIT.
THAT SOUNDS FAMILIAR.
HEY!! WE'RE NOT DONE WITH YOU YET, ASSHOLE!
AW, GIVE IT UP AL- READY!
VROOOM
BANG BANG

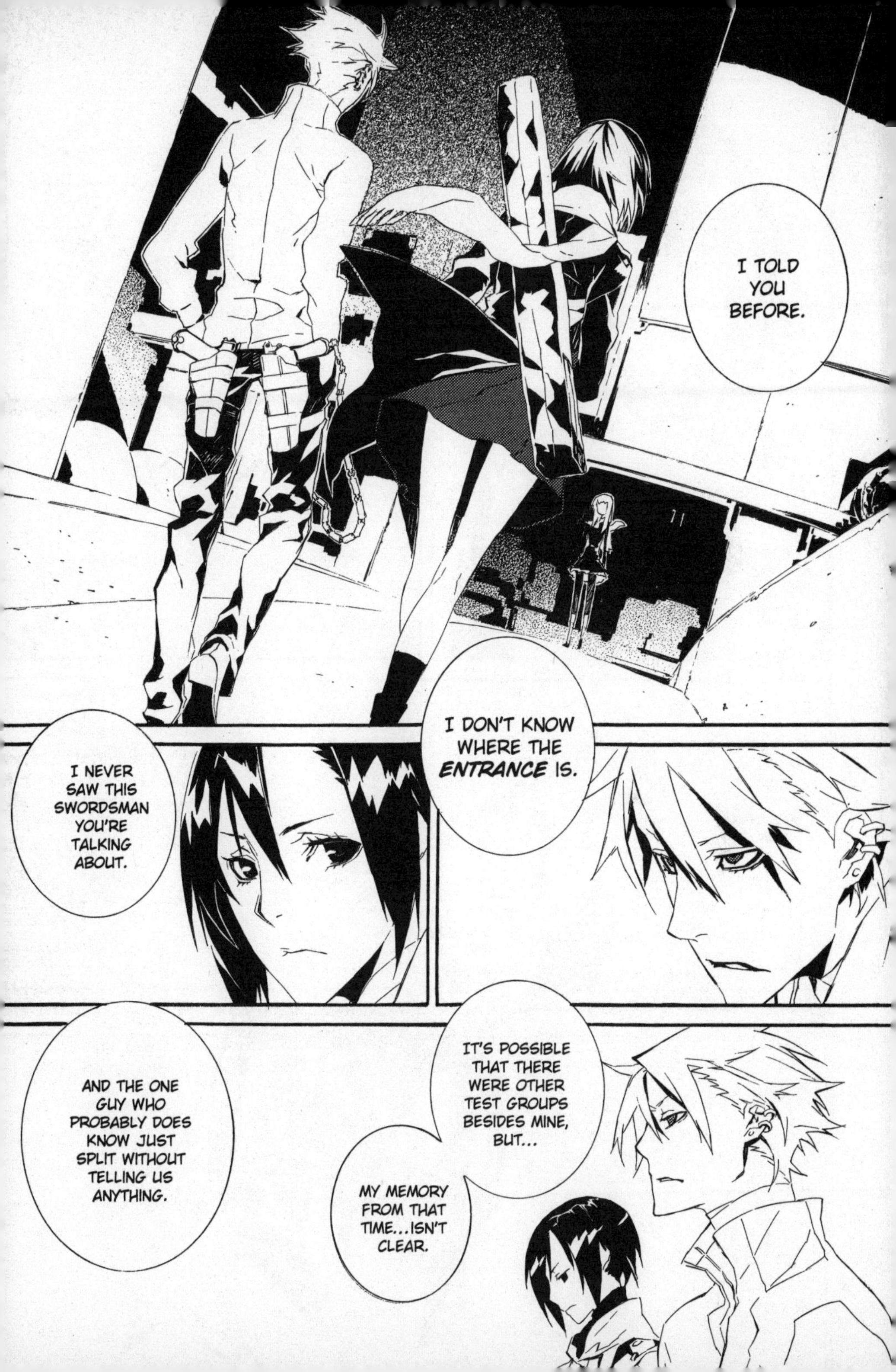
I TOLD YOU BEFORE.
I DON'T KNOW WHERE THE *ENTRANCE* IS.
I NEVER SAW THIS SWORDSMAN YOU'RE TALKING ABOUT.
IT'S POSSIBLE THAT THERE WERE OTHER TEST GROUPS BESIDES MINE, BUT...
MY MEMORY FROM THAT TIME...ISN'T CLEAR.
AND THE ONE GUY WHO PROBABLY DOES KNOW JUST SPLIT WITHOUT TELLING US ANYTHING.

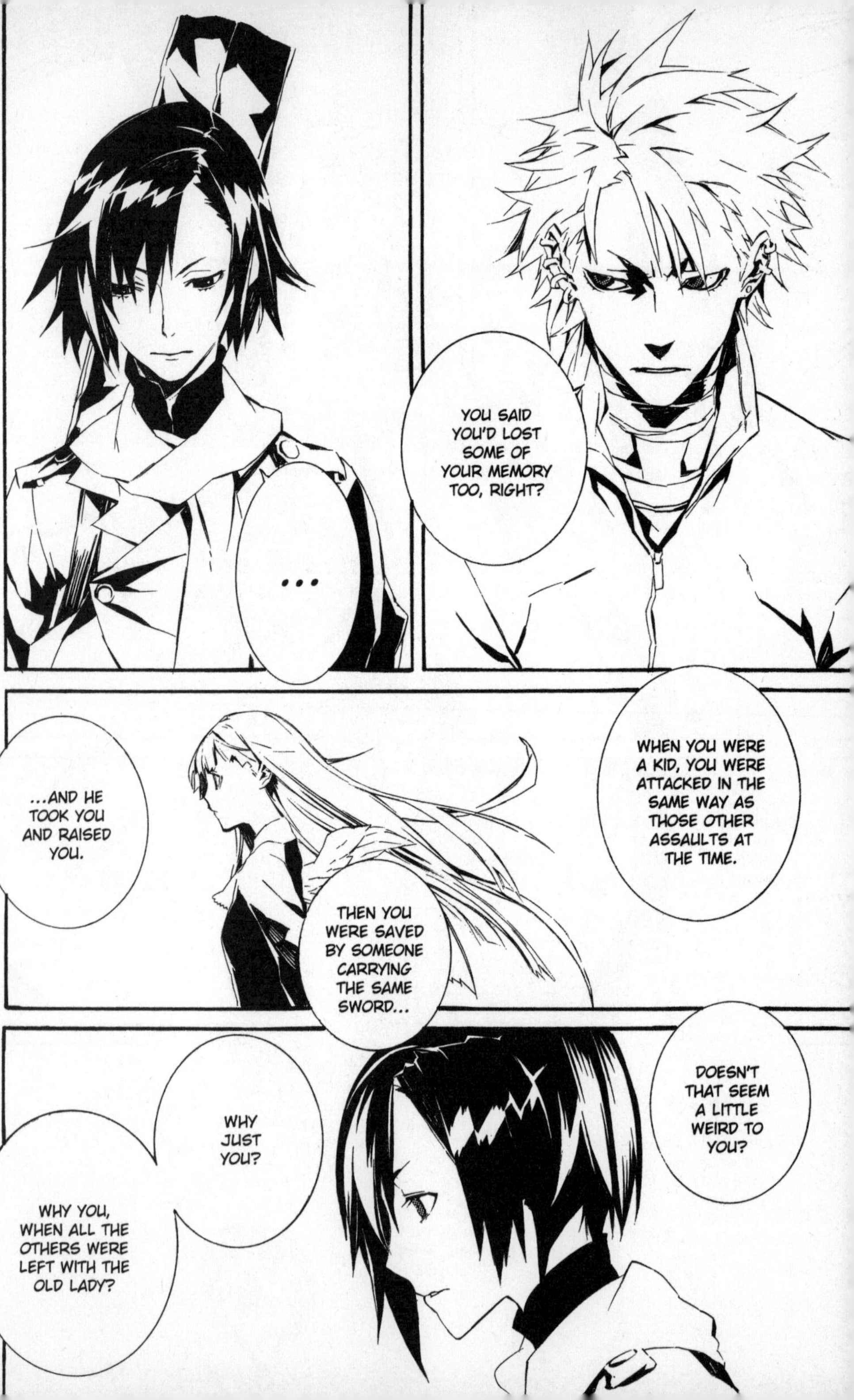
YOU SAID YOU'D LOST SOME OF YOUR MEMORY TOO, RIGHT?
...
WHEN YOU WERE A KID, YOU WERE ATTACKED IN THE SAME WAY AS THOSE OTHER ASSAULTS AT THE TIME.
THEN YOU WERE SAVED BY SOMEONE CARRYING THE SAME SWORD...
...AND HE TOOK YOU AND RAISED YOU.
DOESN'T THAT SEEM A LITTLE WEIRD TO YOU?
WHY JUST YOU?
WHY YOU, WHEN ALL THE OTHERS WERE LEFT WITH THE OLD LADY?

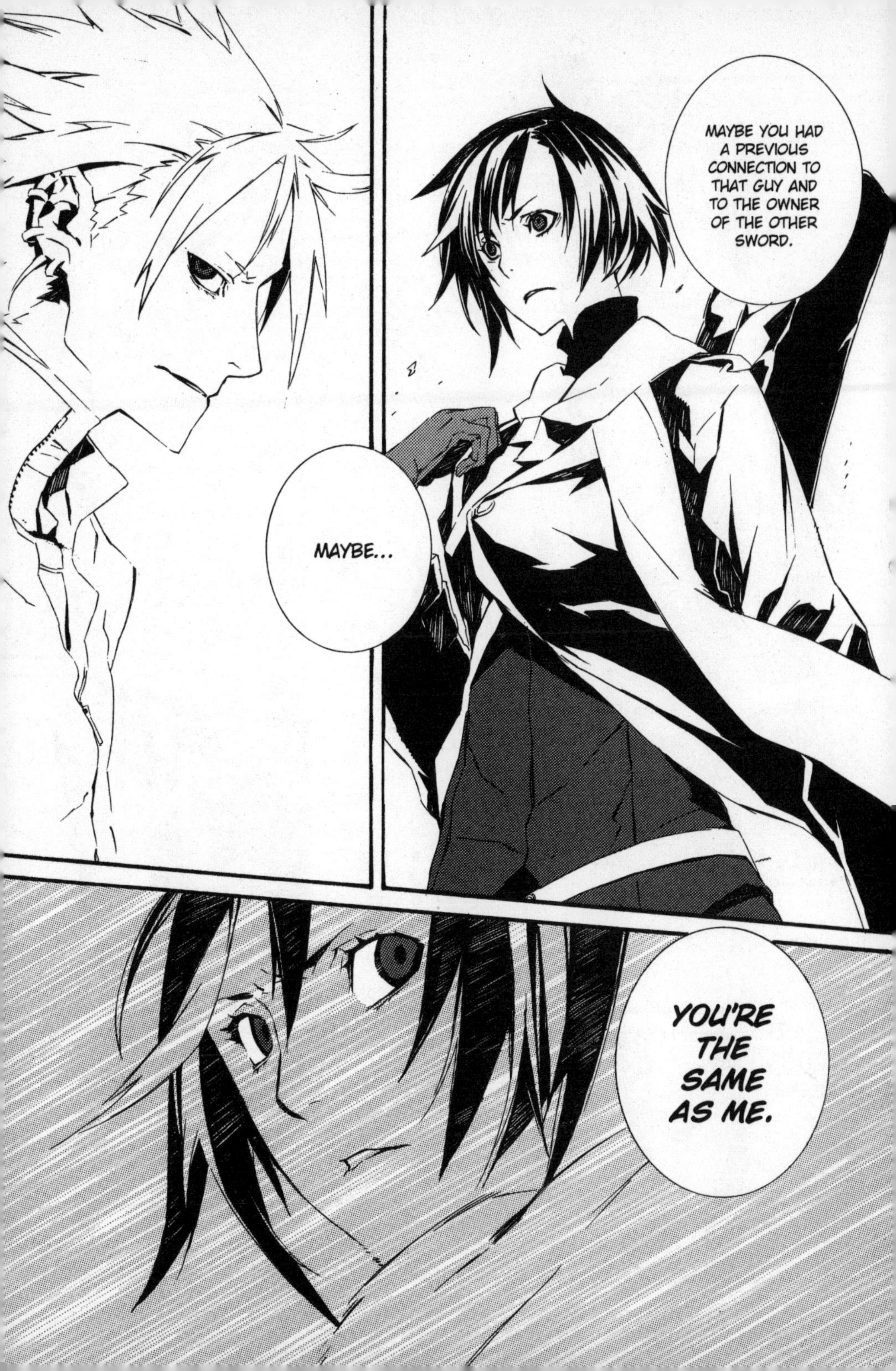
MAYBE YOU HAD A PREVIOUS CONNECTION TO THAT GUY AND TO THE OWNER OF THE OTHER SWORD.
MAYBE...
YOU'RE THE SAME AS ME.

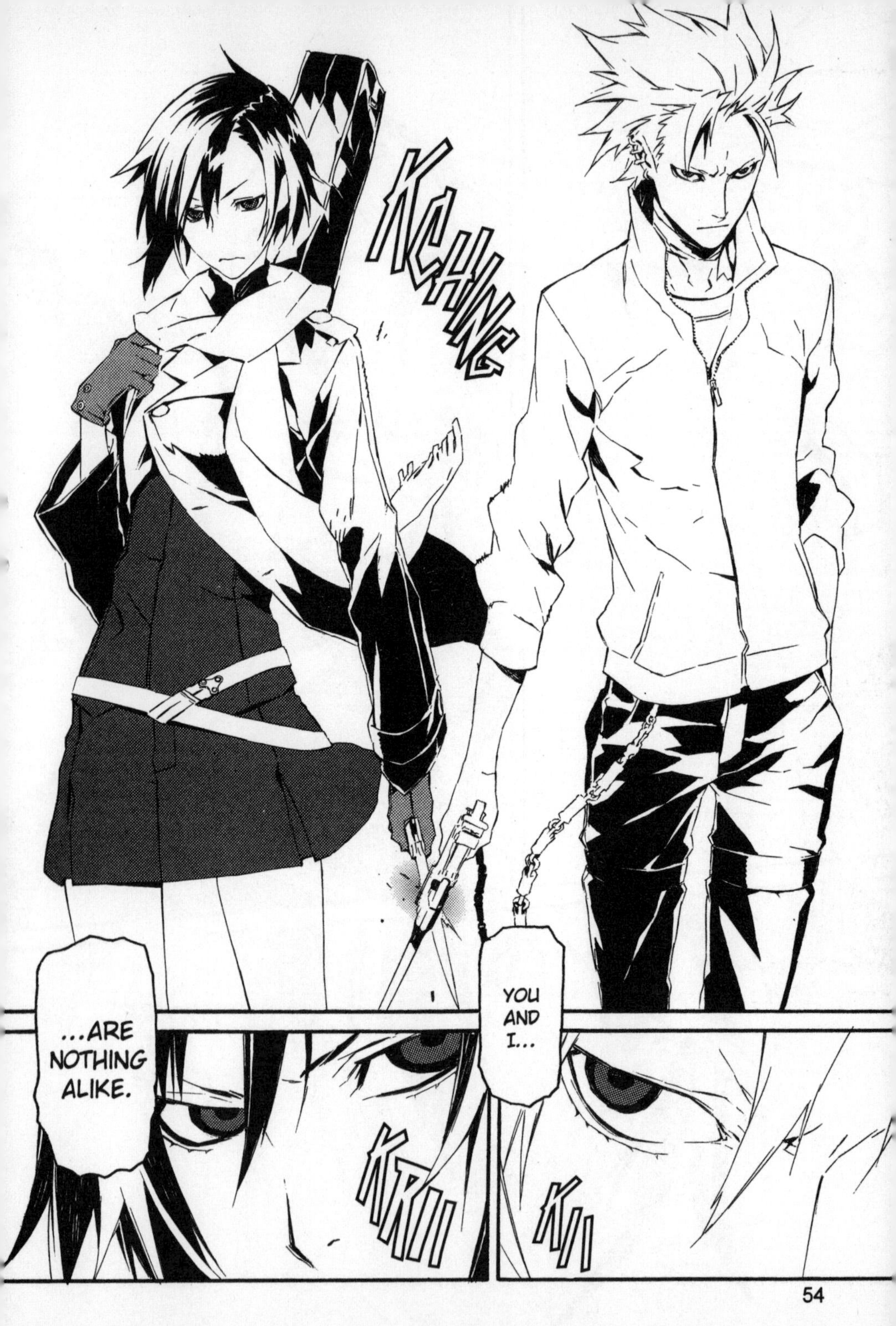
KCHING
YOU AND I...
KII
...ARE NOTHING ALIKE.
KRII

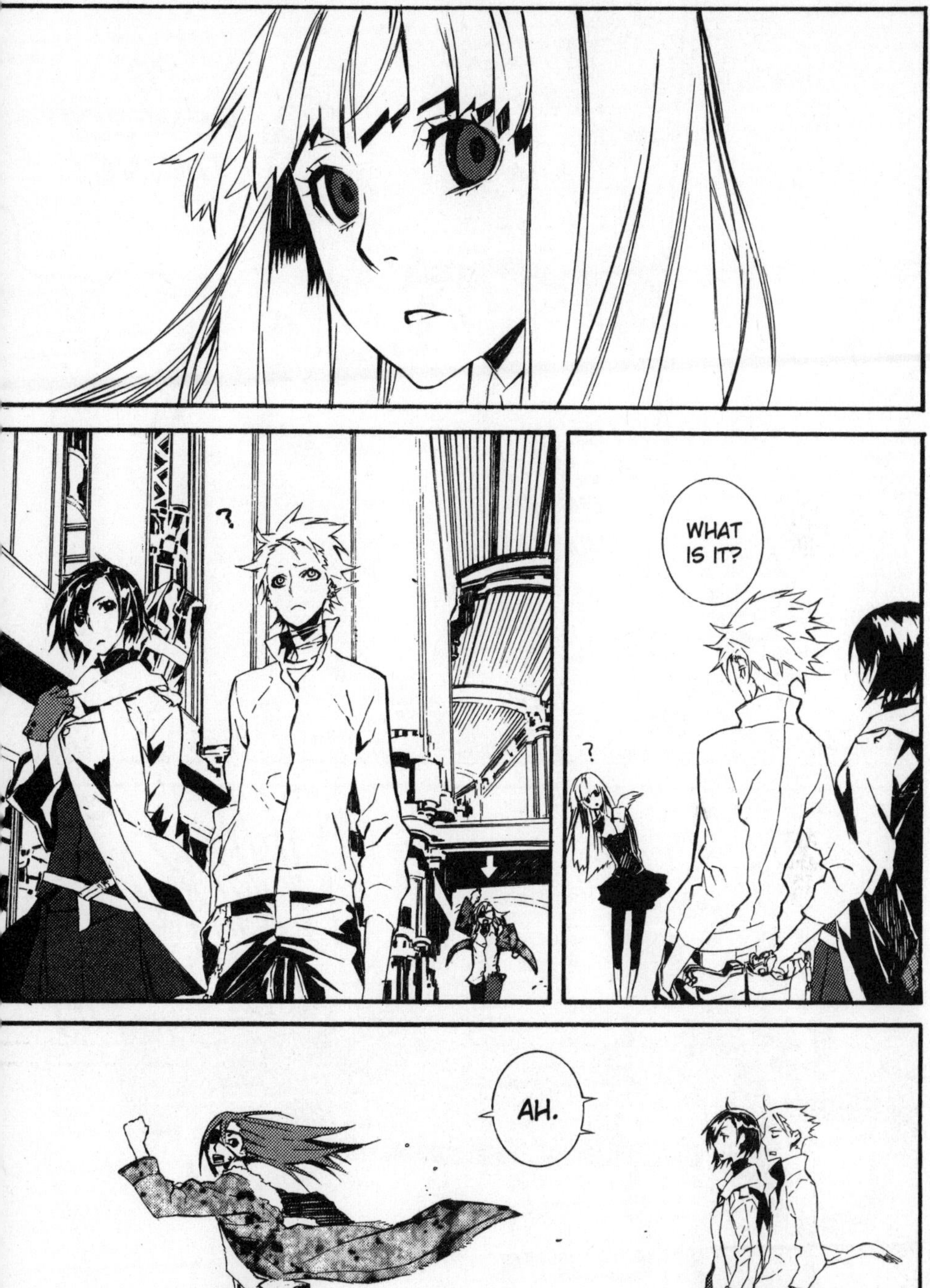
WHAT IS IT?
?
?
AH.

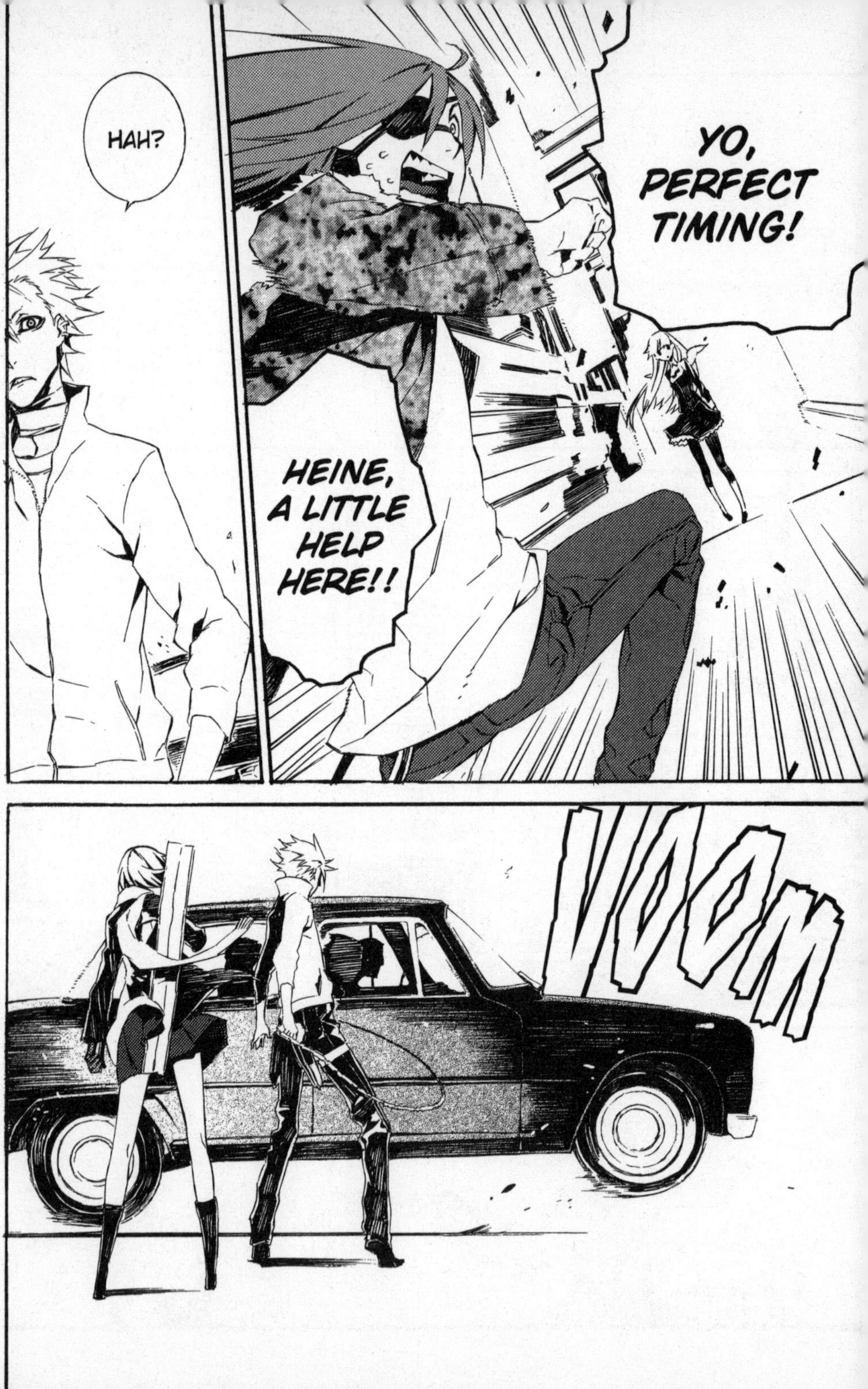
YO, PERFECT TIMING!
HEINE, A LITTLE HELP HERE!!
HAH?
VOOM

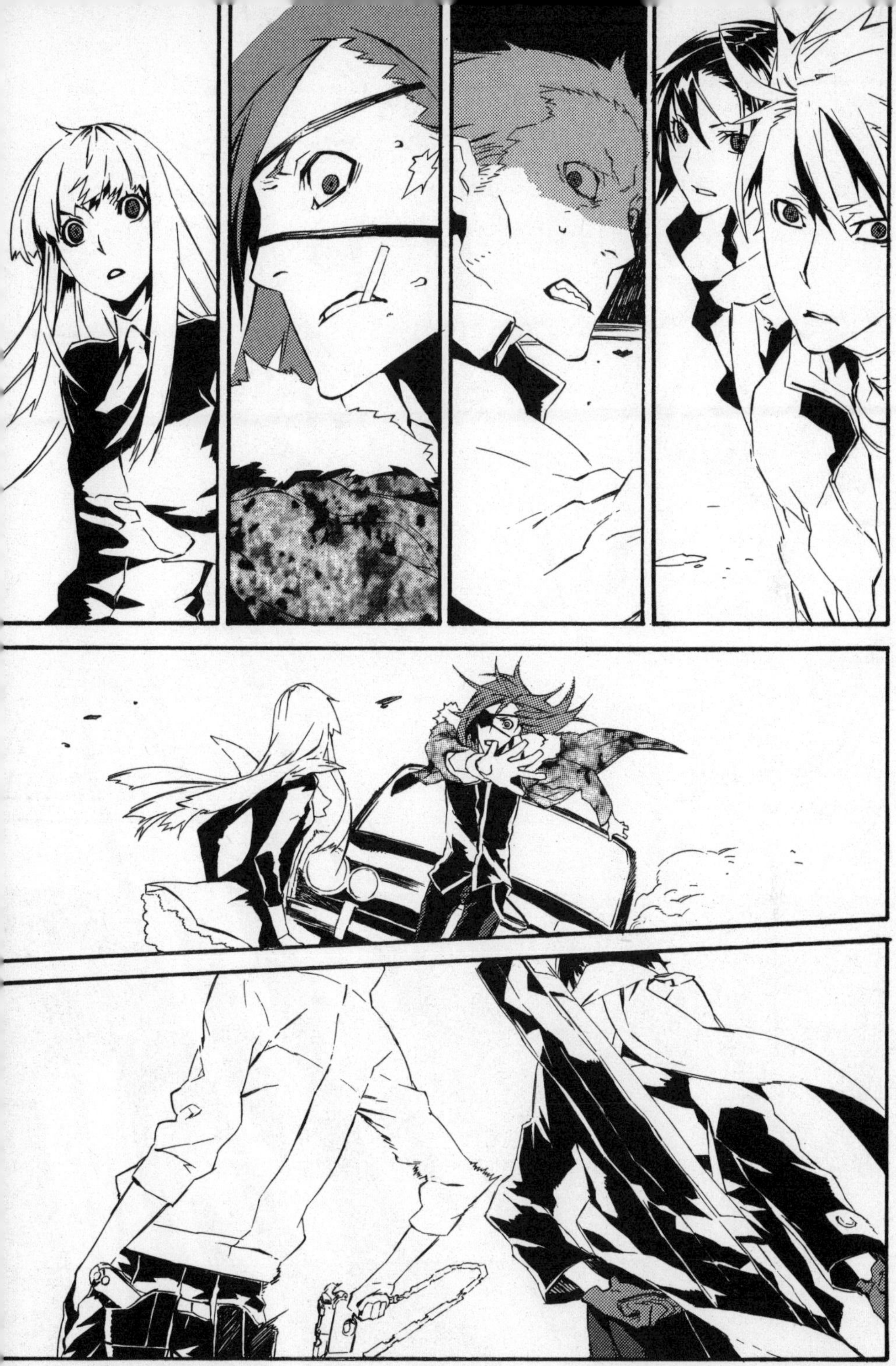

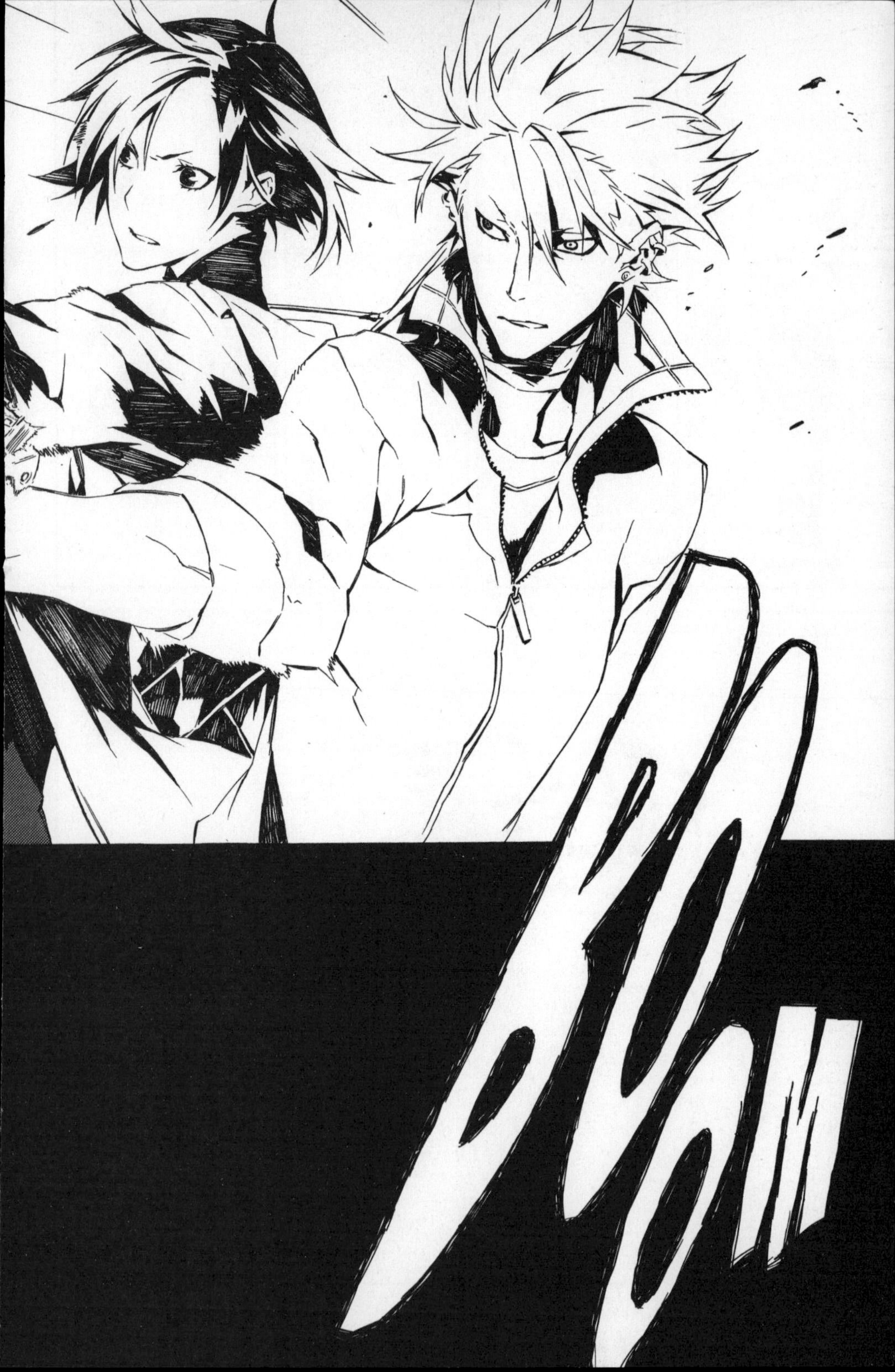

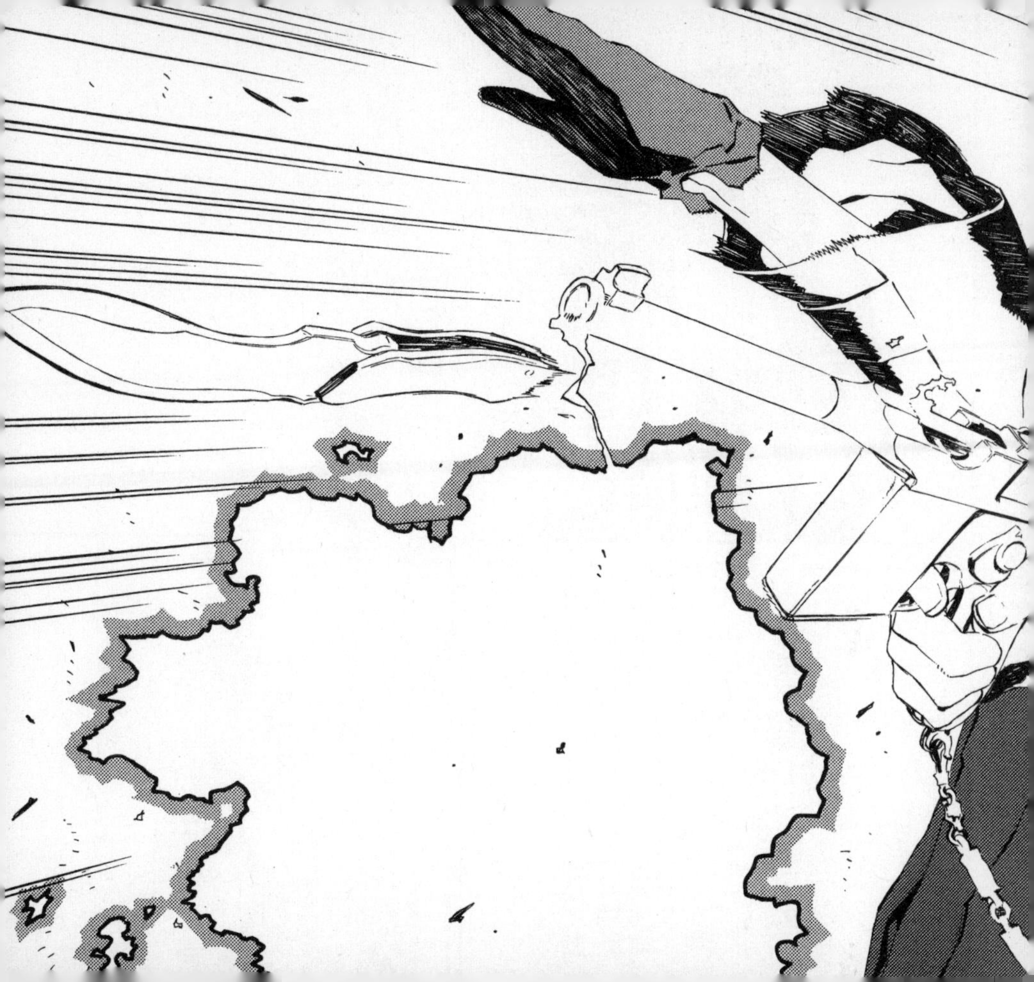

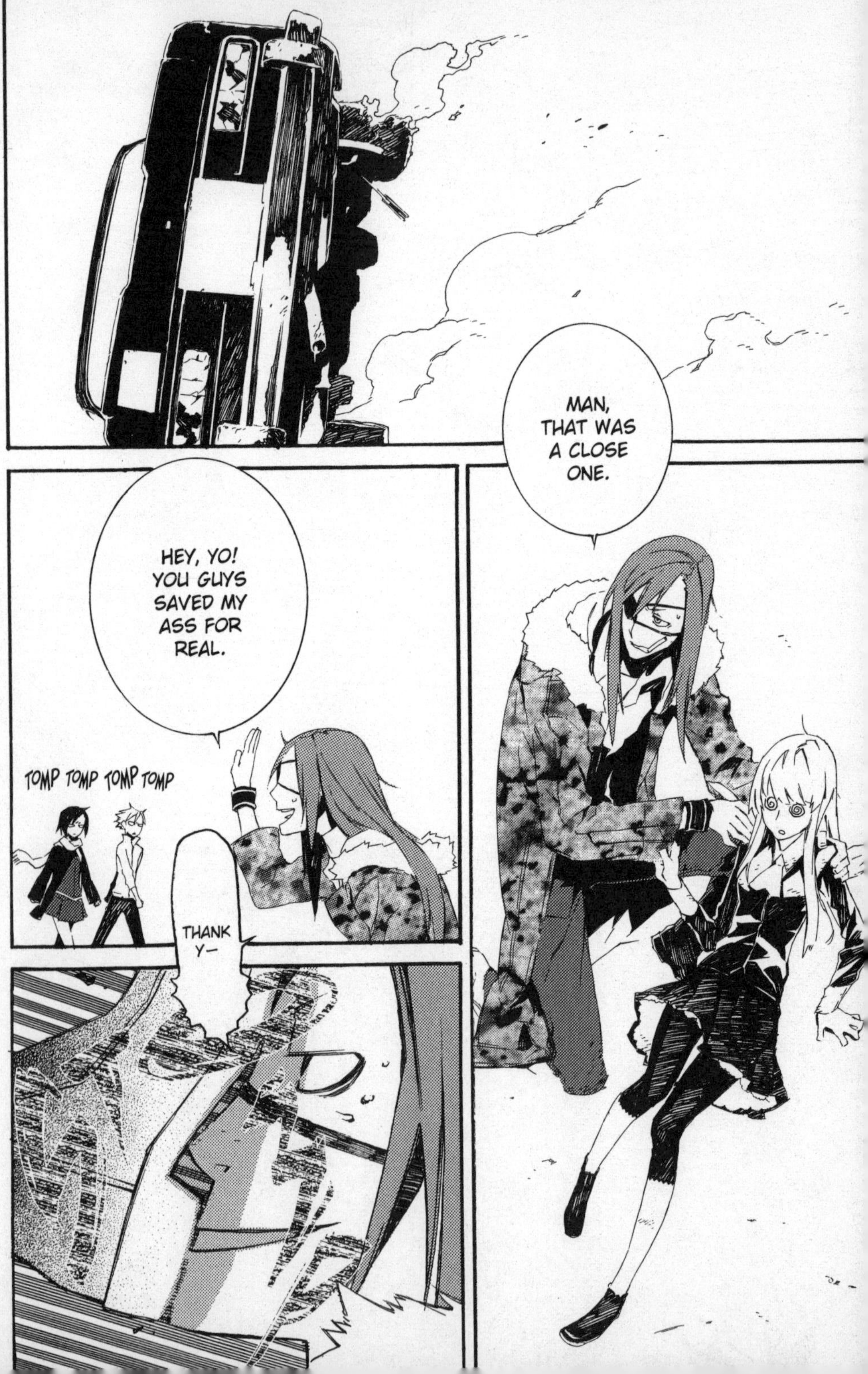
MAN, THAT WAS A CLOSE ONE.
HEY, YO! YOU GUYS SAVED MY ASS FOR REAL.
TOMP TOMP TOMP TOMP
THANK Y—

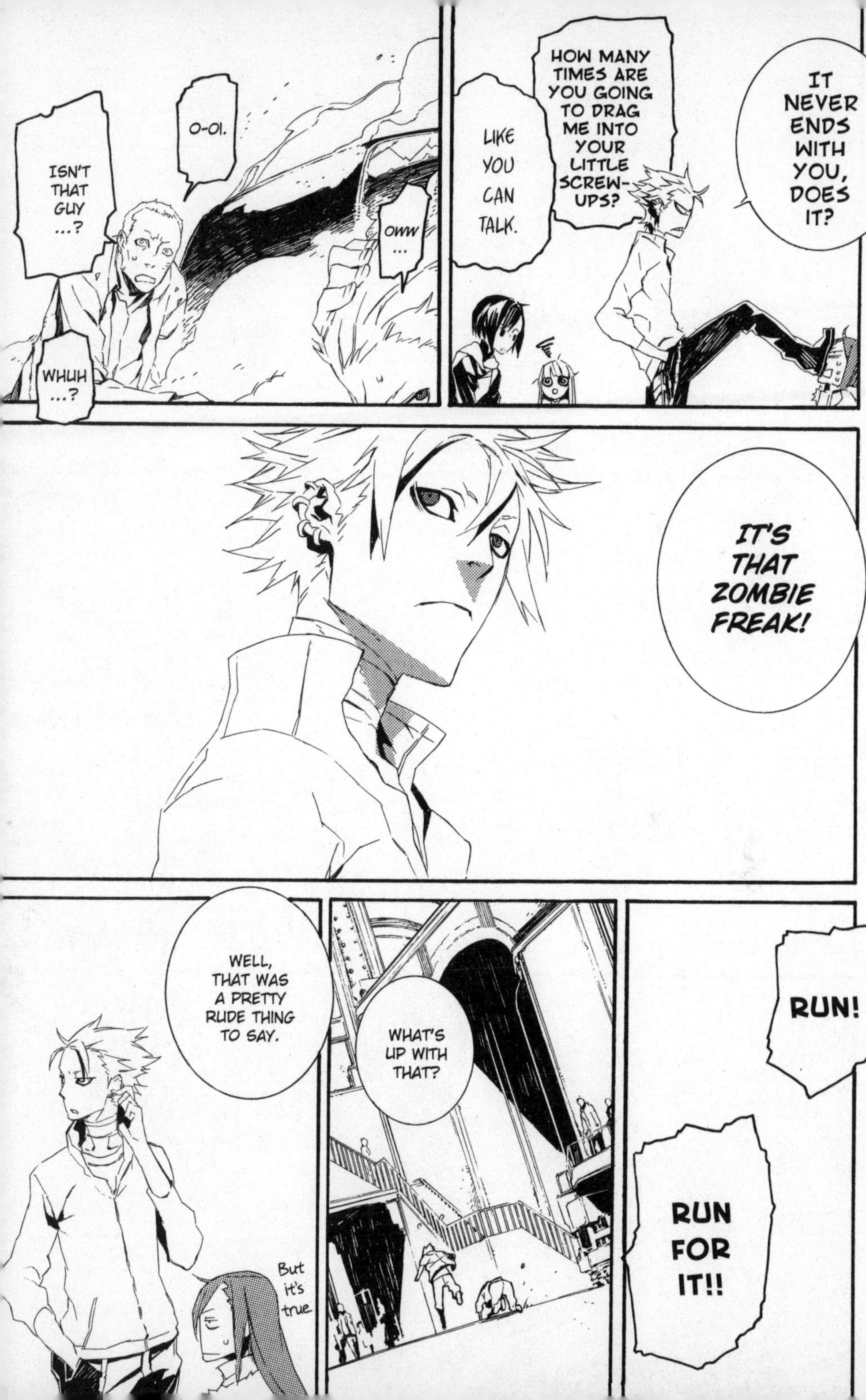
IT NEVER ENDS WITH YOU, DOES IT?
HOW MANY TIMES ARE YOU GOING TO DRAG ME INTO YOUR LITTLE SCREW-UPS?
LIKE YOU CAN TALK.
OWW ...
O-OI.
ISN'T THAT GUY ...?
WHUH ...?
IT'S THAT ZOMBIE FREAK!
RUN!
RUN FOR IT!!
WHAT'S UP WITH THAT?
WELL, THAT WAS A PRETTY RUDE THING TO SAY.
But it's true.

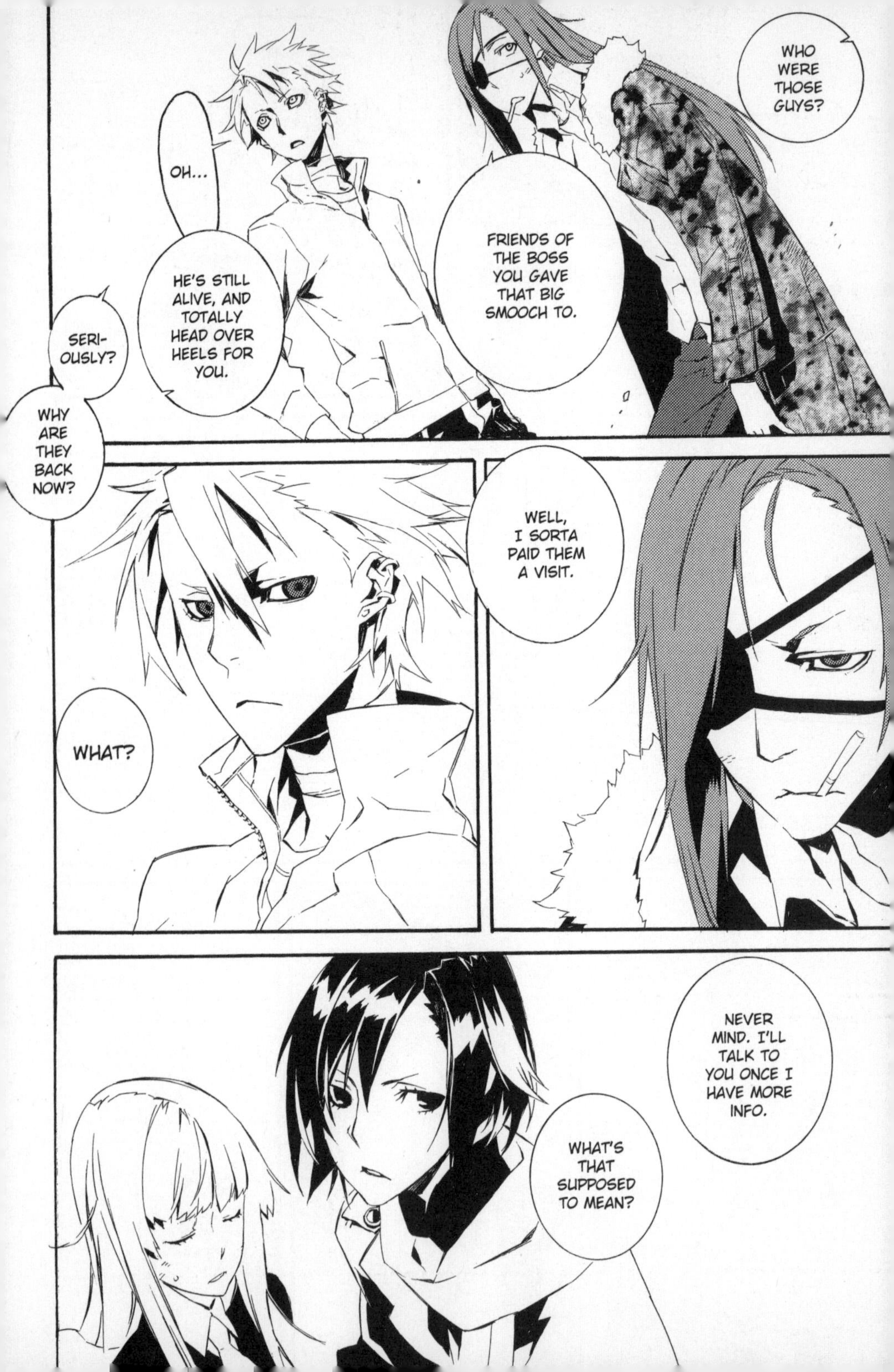
WHO WERE THOSE GUYS?
FRIENDS OF THE BOSS YOU GAVE THAT BIG SMOOCH TO.
OH...
HE'S STILL ALIVE, AND TOTALLY HEAD OVER HEELS FOR YOU.
SERI-OUSLY?
WHY ARE THEY BACK NOW?
WELL, I SORTA PAID THEM A VISIT.
WHAT?
NEVER MIND. I'LL TALK TO YOU ONCE I HAVE MORE INFO.
WHAT'S THAT SUPPOSED TO MEAN?

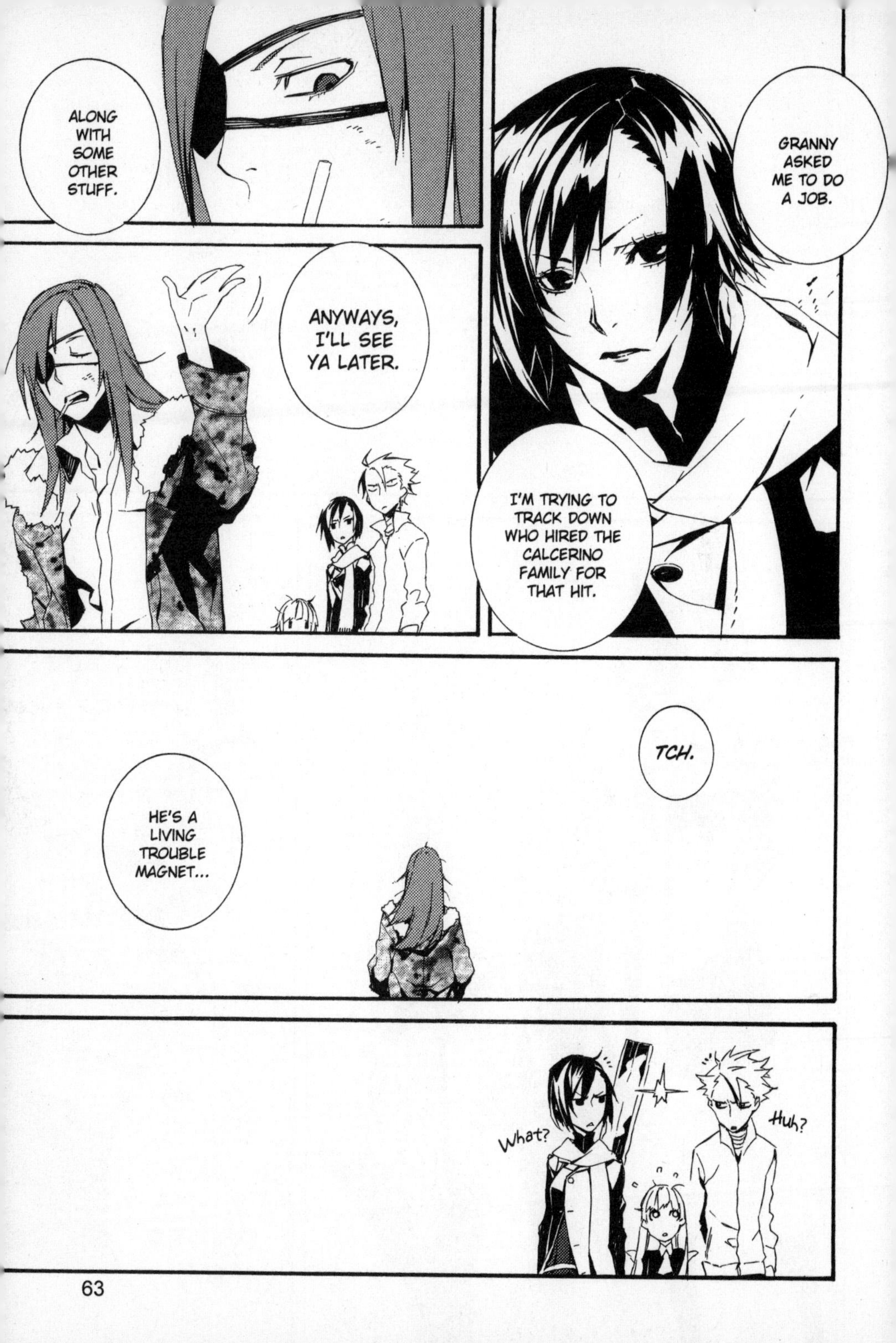
GRANNY ASKED ME TO DO A JOB.
I'M TRYING TO TRACK DOWN WHO HIRED THE CALCERINO FAMILY FOR THAT HIT.
ALONG WITH SOME OTHER STUFF.
ANYWAYS, I'LL SEE YA LATER.
TCH.
HE'S A LIVING TROUBLE MAGNET...
Huh?
What?

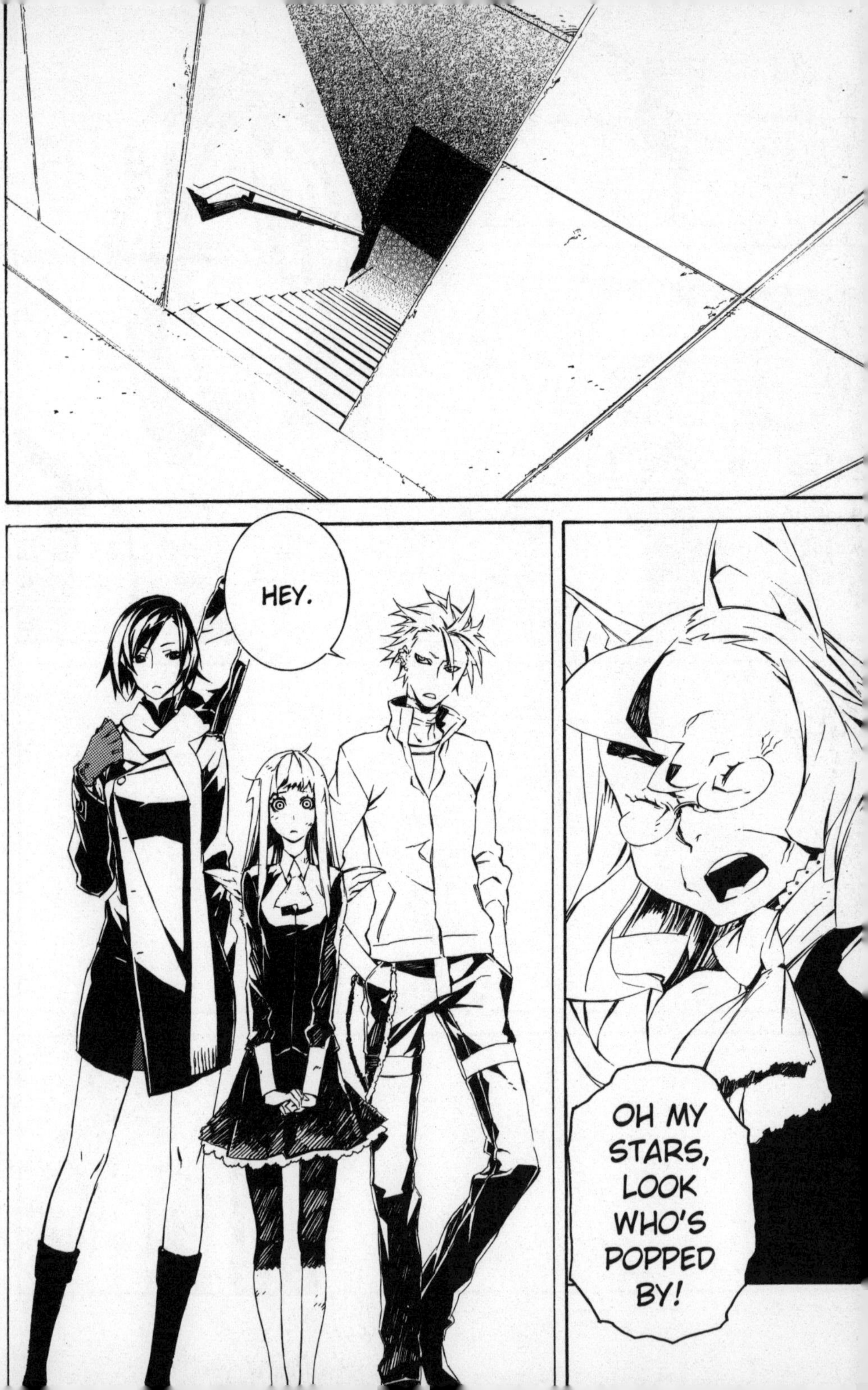
OH MY STARS, LOOK WHO'S POPPED BY!
HEY.

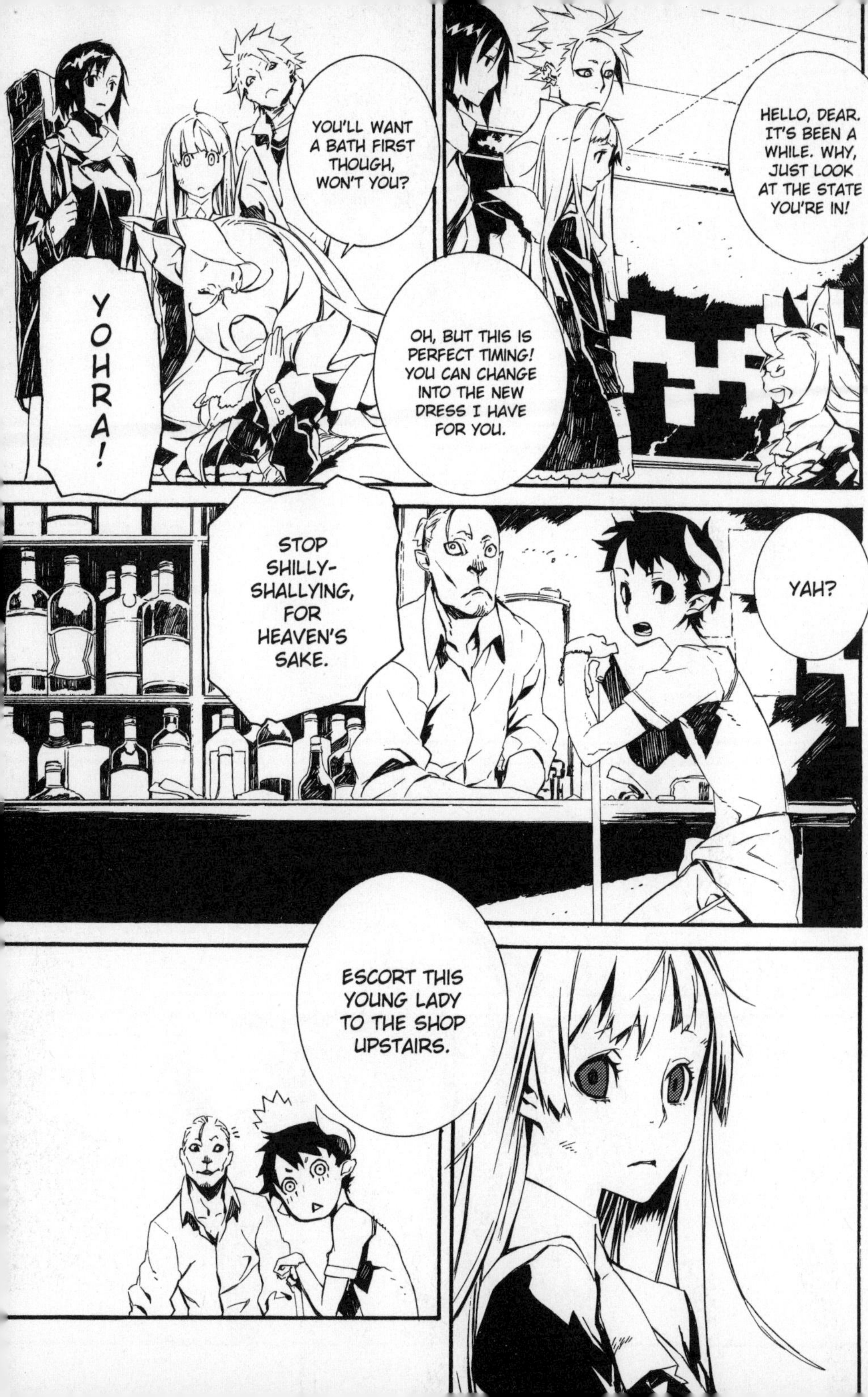
HELLO, DEAR. IT'S BEEN A WHILE. WHY, JUST LOOK AT THE STATE YOU'RE IN!
OH, BUT THIS IS PERFECT TIMING! YOU CAN CHANGE INTO THE NEW DRESS I HAVE FOR YOU.
YOU'LL WANT A BATH FIRST THOUGH, WON'T YOU?
YOHRA!
STOP SHILLY-SHALLYING, FOR HEAVEN'S SAKE.
YAH?
ESCORT THIS YOUNG LADY TO THE SHOP UPSTAIRS.

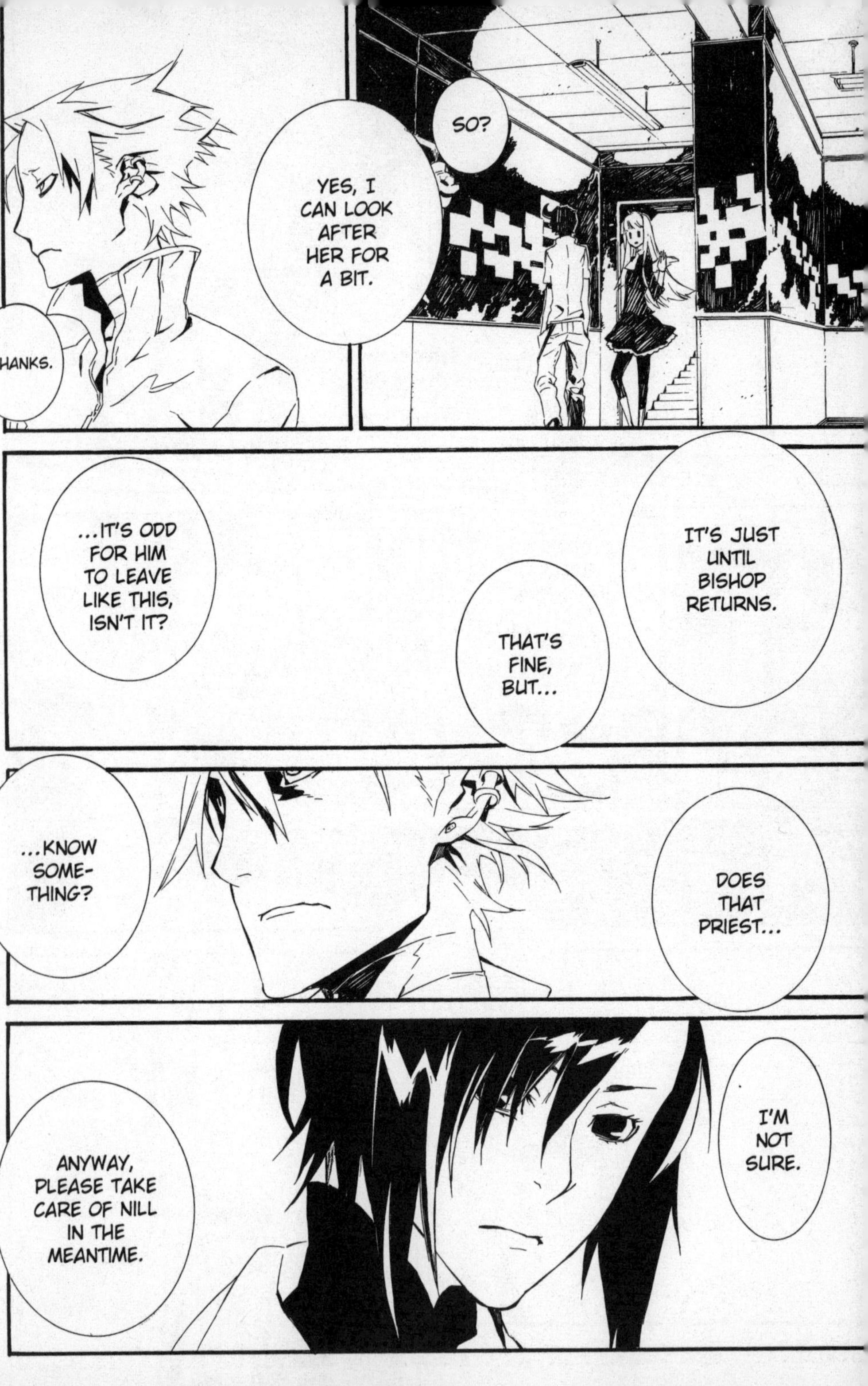
SO?
YES, I CAN LOOK AFTER HER FOR A BIT.
THANKS.
IT'S JUST UNTIL BISHOP RETURNS.
THAT'S FINE, BUT...
...IT'S ODD FOR HIM TO LEAVE LIKE THIS, ISN'T IT?
DOES THAT PRIEST...
...KNOW SOME-THING?
I'M NOT SURE.
ANYWAY, PLEASE TAKE CARE OF NILL IN THE MEANTIME.

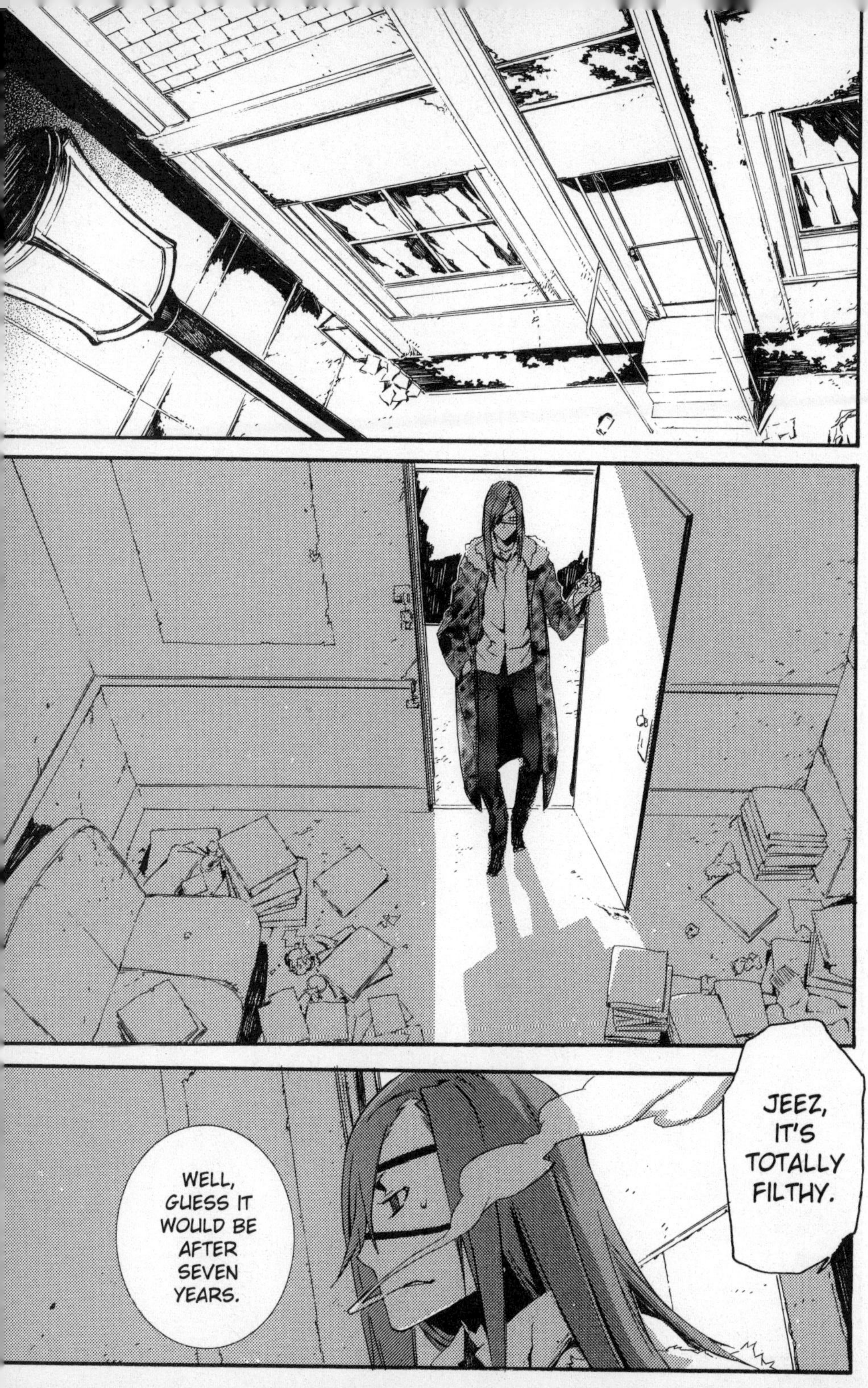
JEEZ, IT'S TOTALLY FILTHY.
WELL, GUESS IT WOULD BE AFTER SEVEN YEARS.

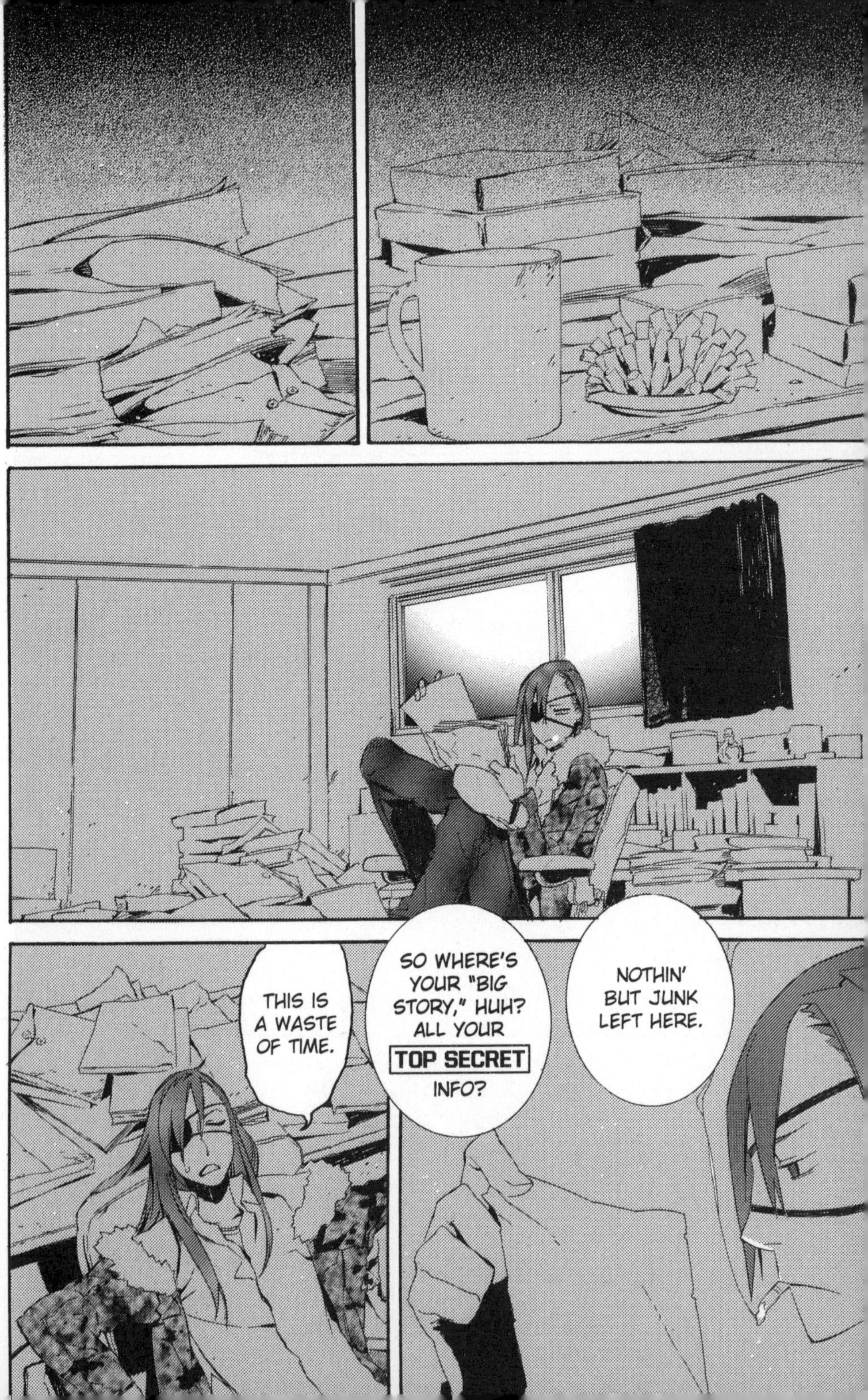
NOTHIN' BUT JUNK LEFT HERE.
SO WHERE'S YOUR "BIG STORY," HUH? ALL YOUR TOP SECRET INFO?
THIS IS A WASTE OF TIME.

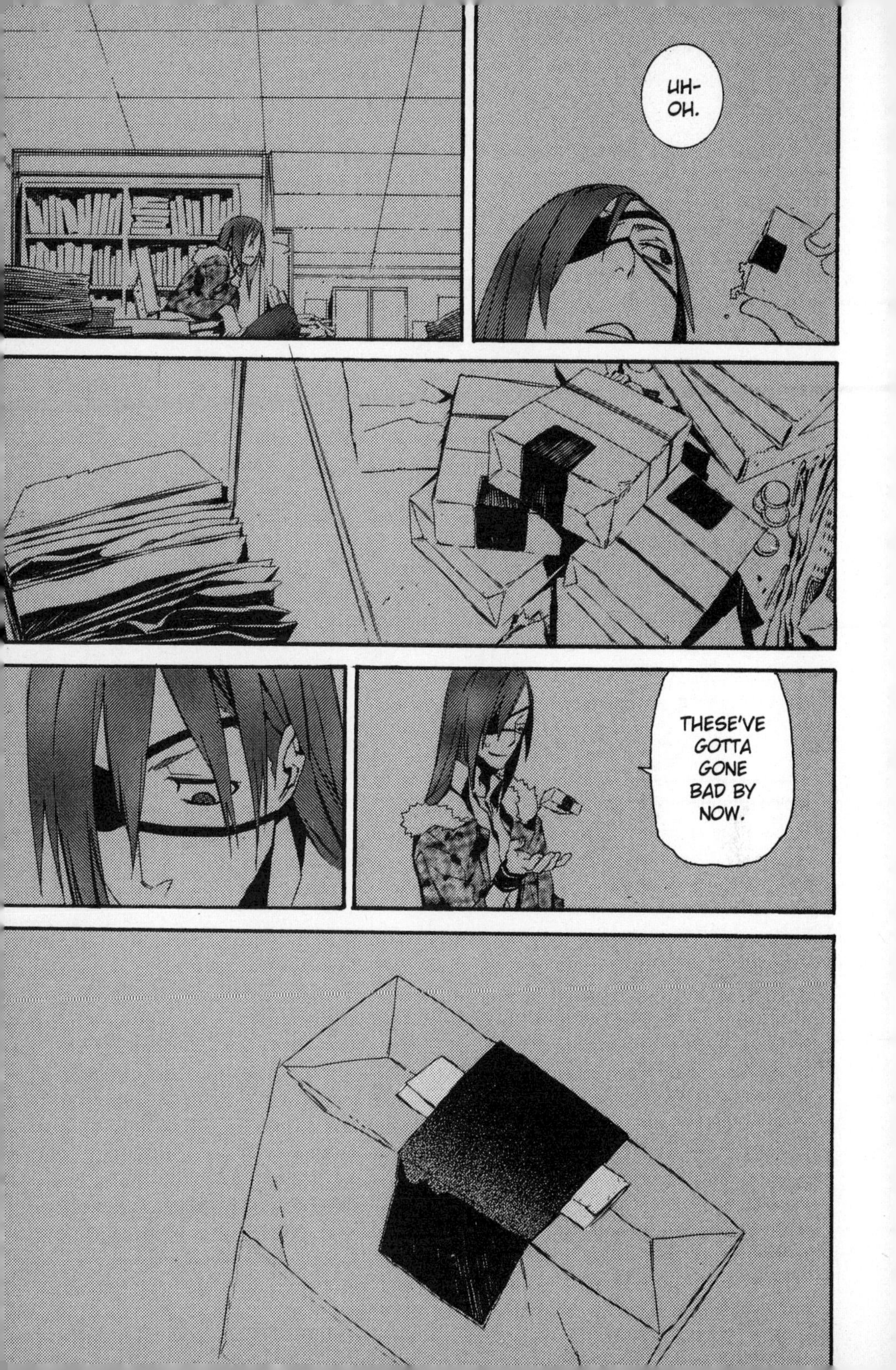
UH-OH.
THESE'VE GOTTA GONE BAD BY NOW.

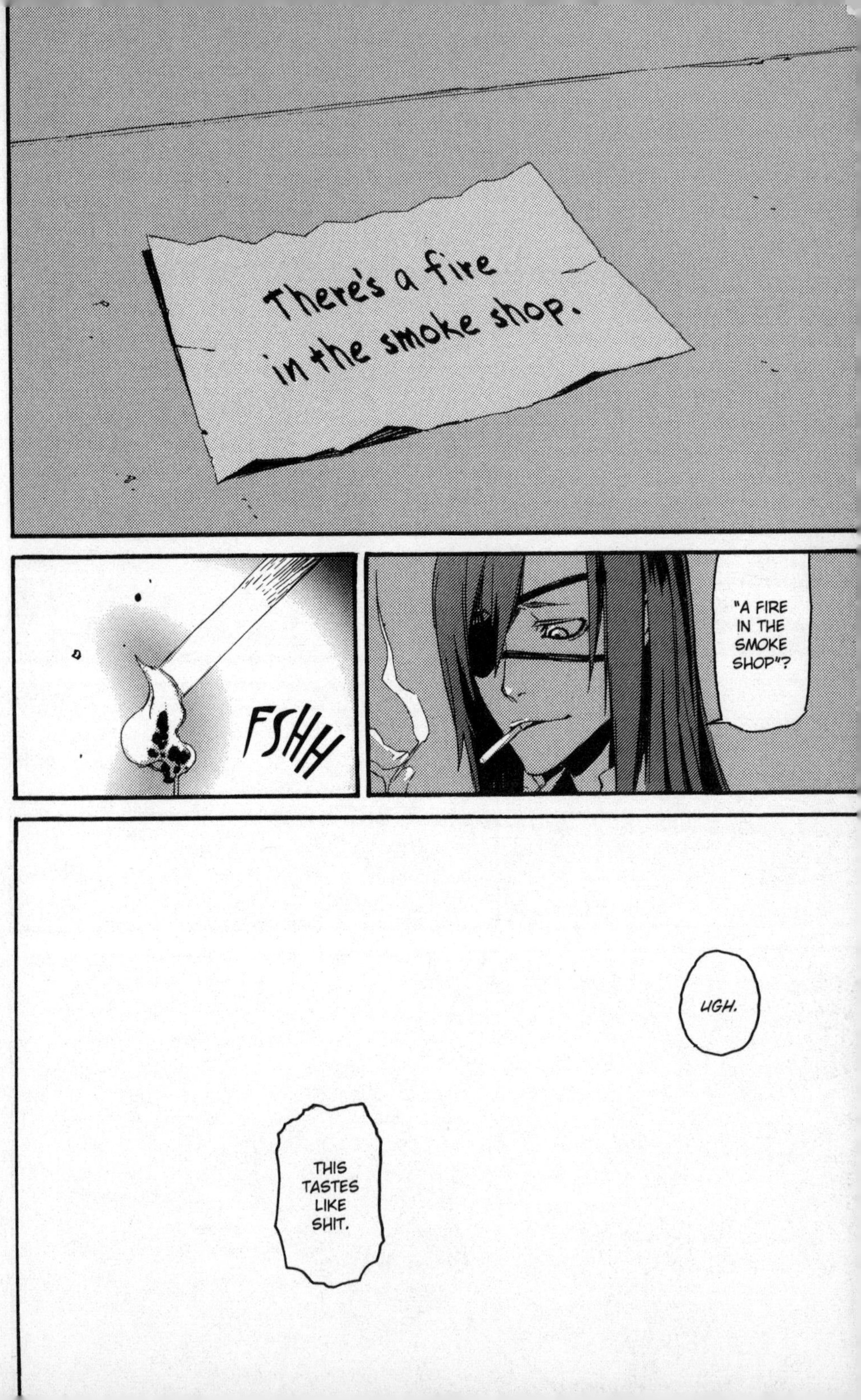
There's a fire
in the smoke shop.
"A FIRE IN THE SMOKE SHOP"?
FSHH
UGH.
THIS TASTES LIKE SHIT.

#32 Cigarette & Bad Boy

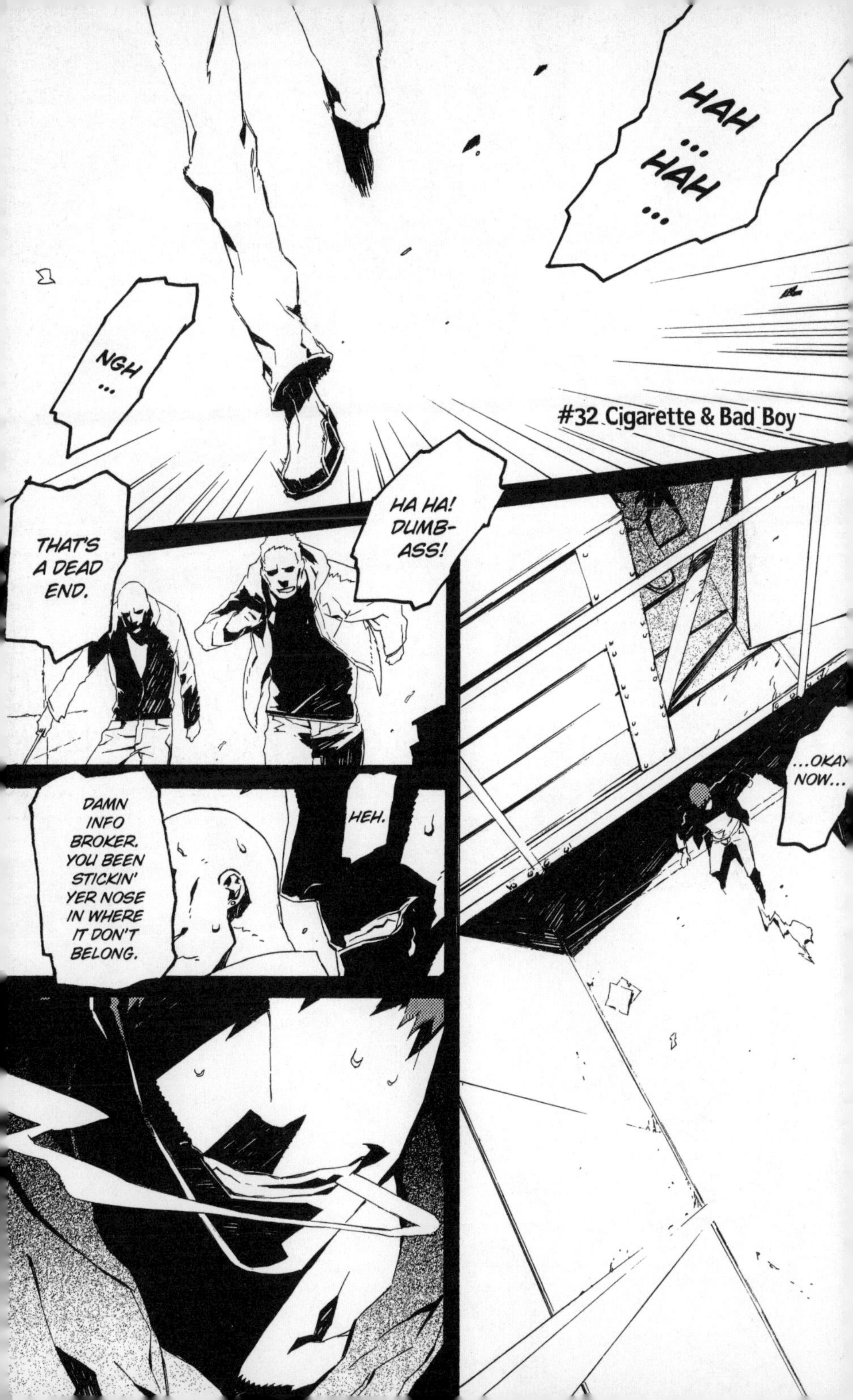
HAH ... HAH ...
NGH ...
...OKAY NOW...
HA HA! DUMB-ASS!
THAT'S A DEAD END.
HEH.
DAMN INFO BROKER. YOU BEEN STICKIN' YER NOSE IN WHERE IT DON'T BELONG.

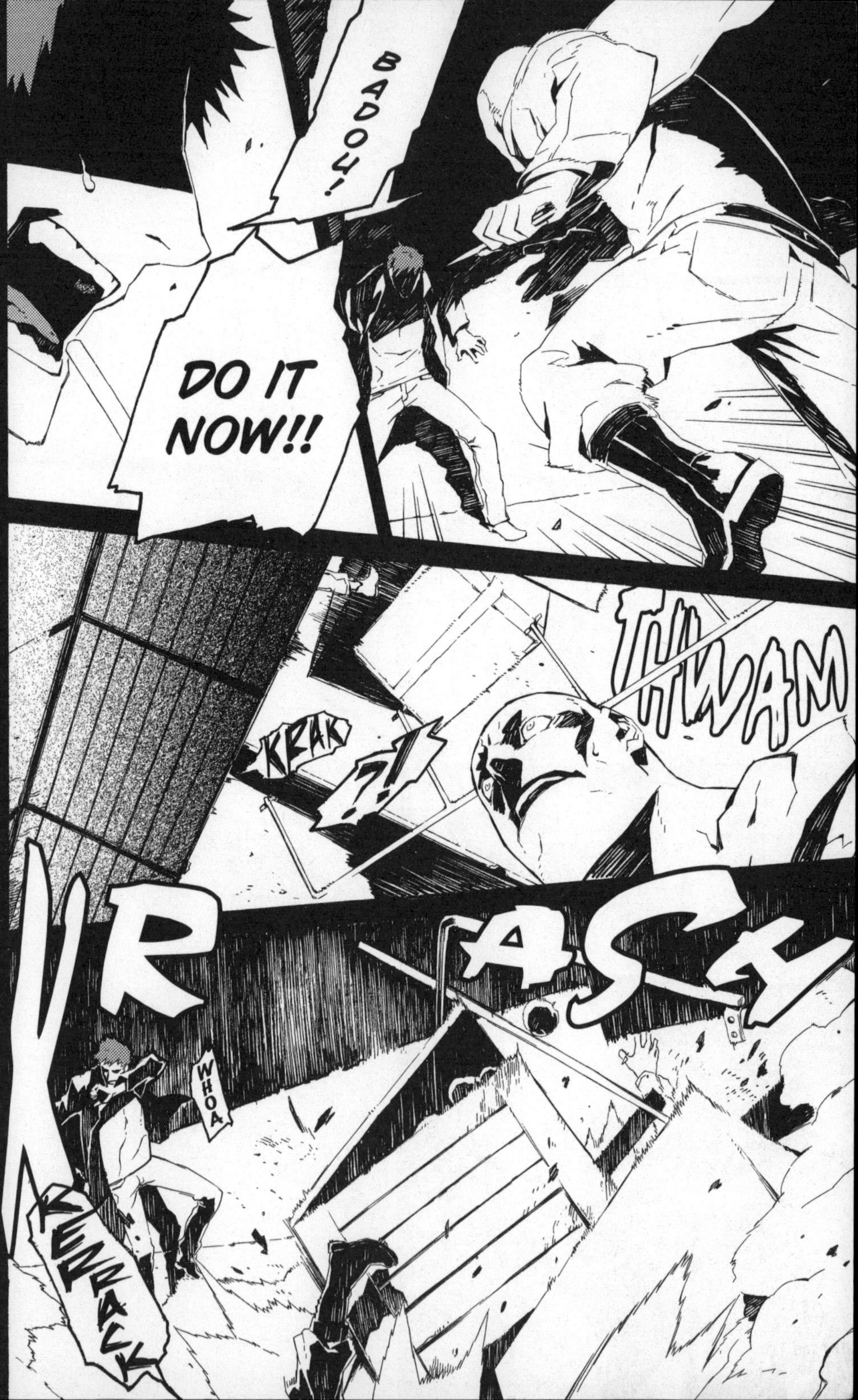
BADOOM!
DO IT NOW!!
THWAM
?!
KRAK
CRASH
WHOA
KERRACK

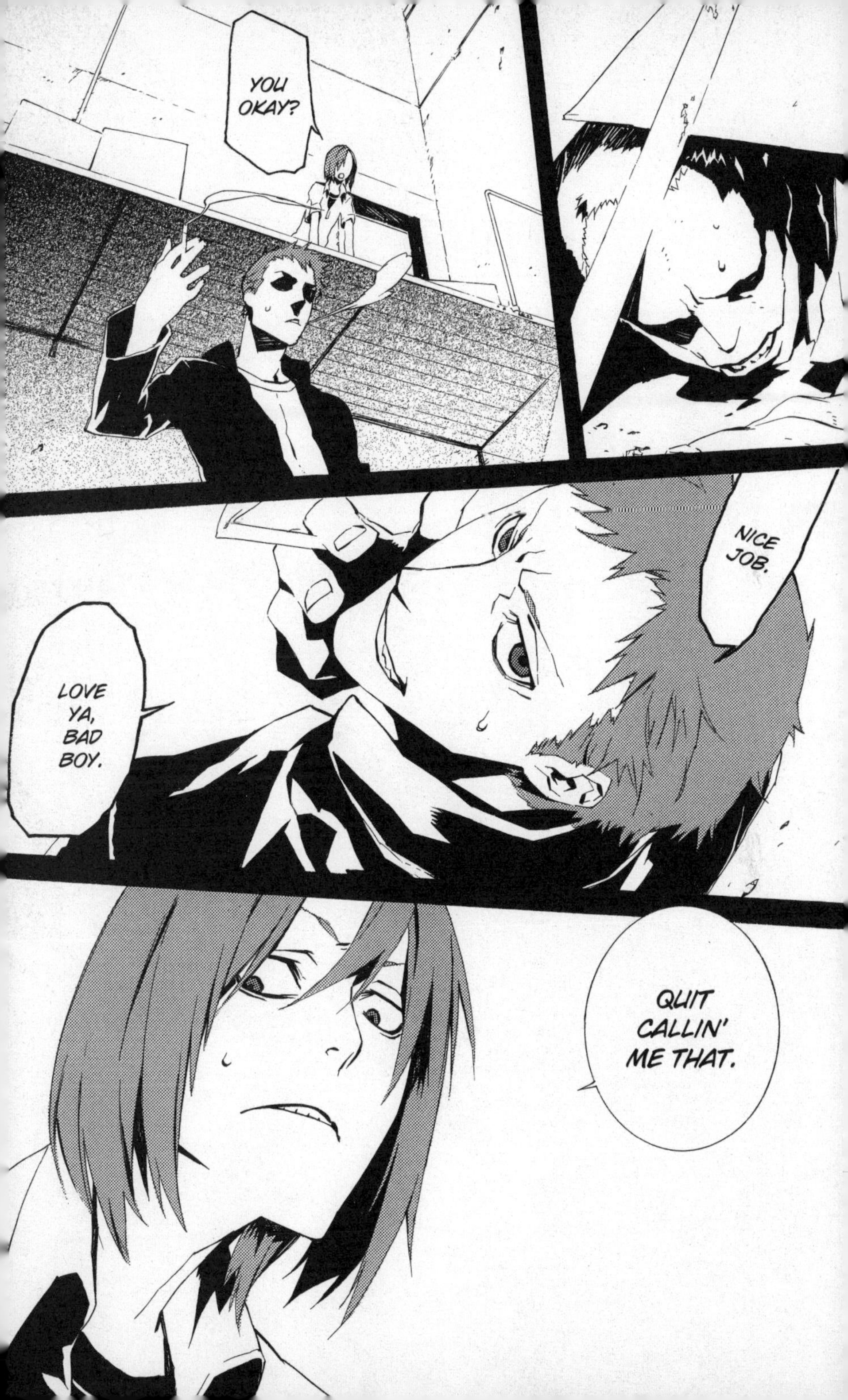
YOU OKAY?
NICE JOB.
LOVE YA, BAD BOY.
QUIT CALLIN' ME THAT.

#32 Cigarette & Bad Boy

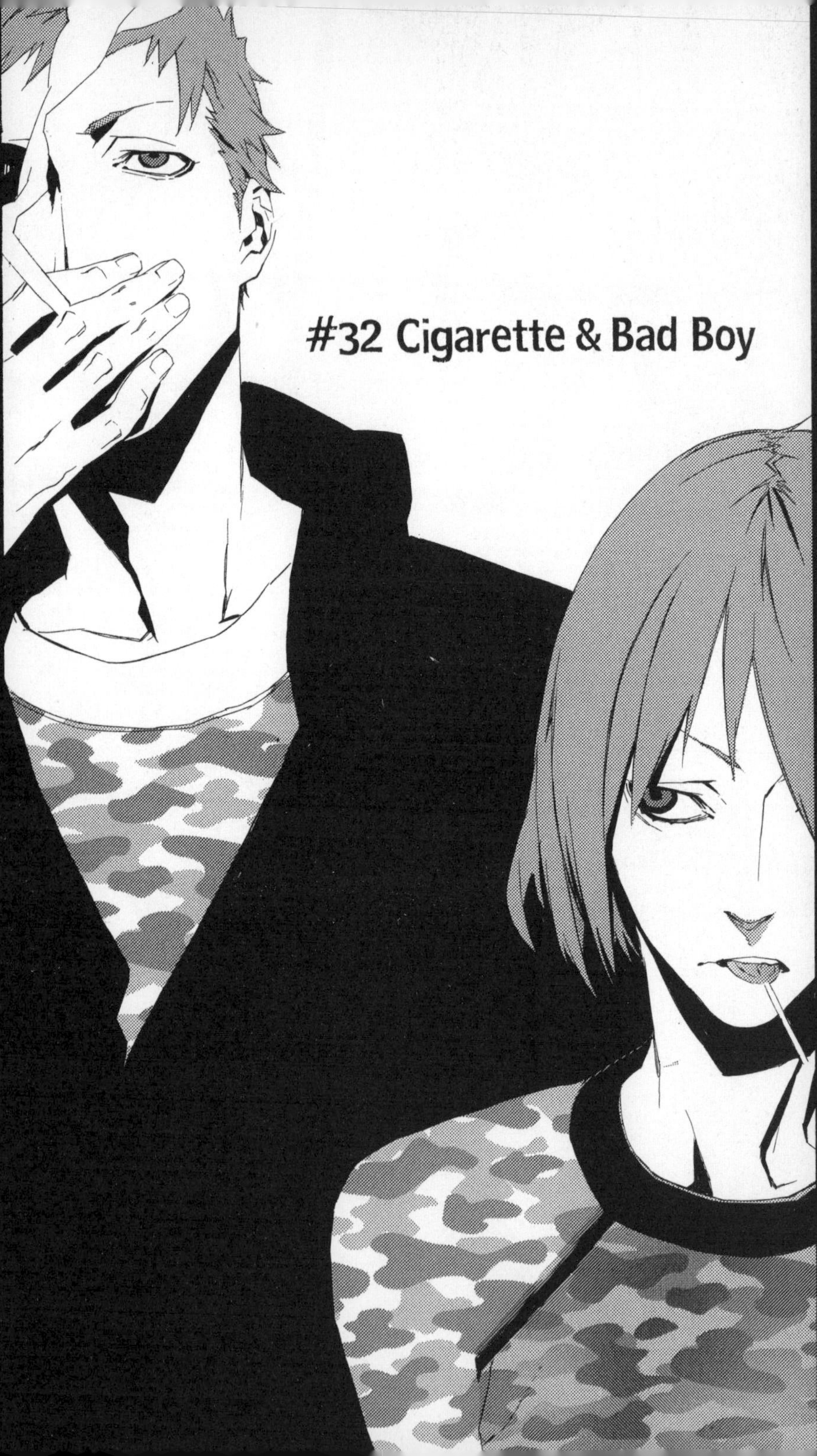

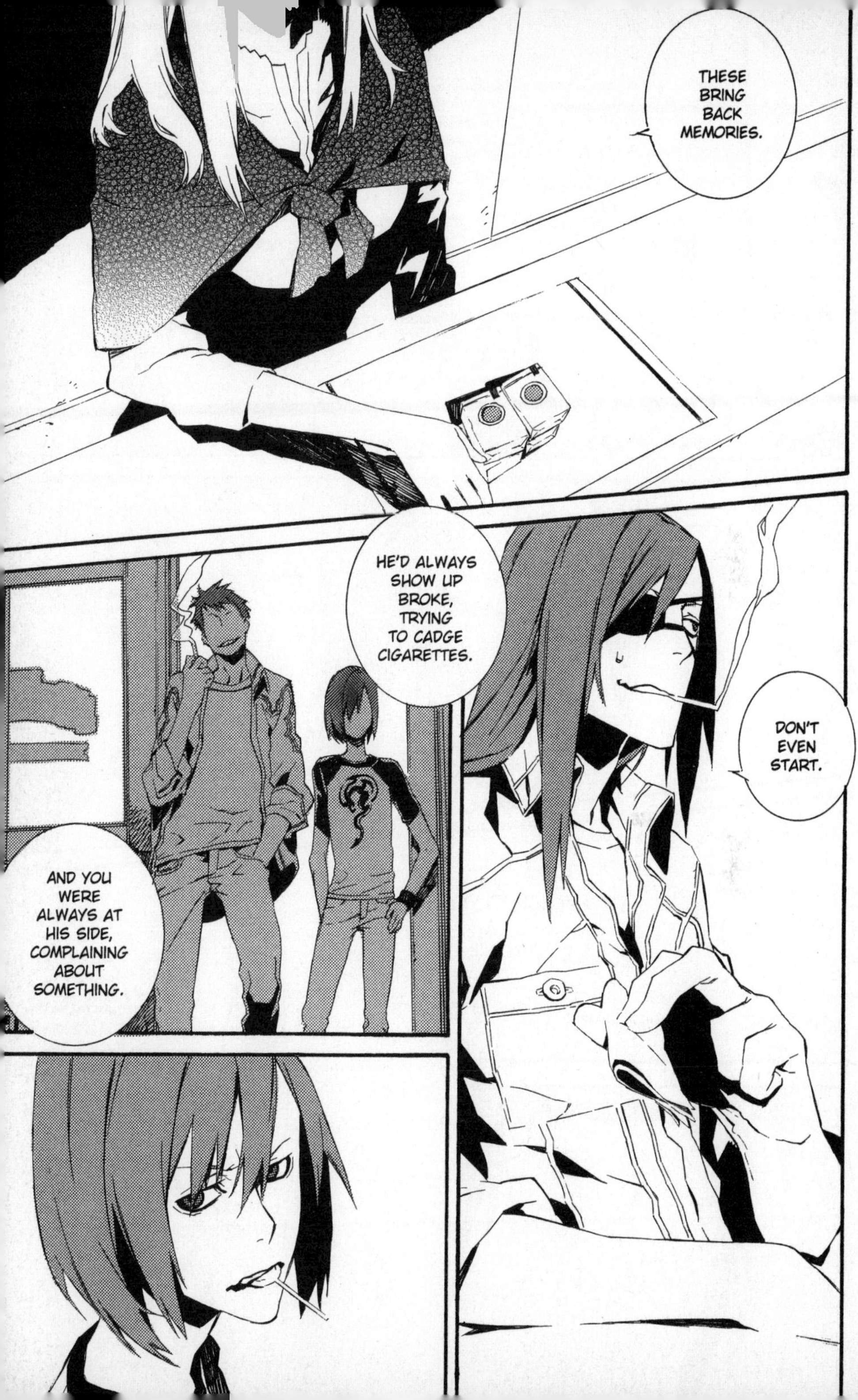
THESE BRING BACK MEMORIES.
HE'D ALWAYS SHOW UP BROKE, TRYING TO CADGE CIGARETTES.
AND YOU WERE ALWAYS AT HIS SIDE, COMPLAINING ABOUT SOMETHING.
DON'T EVEN START.

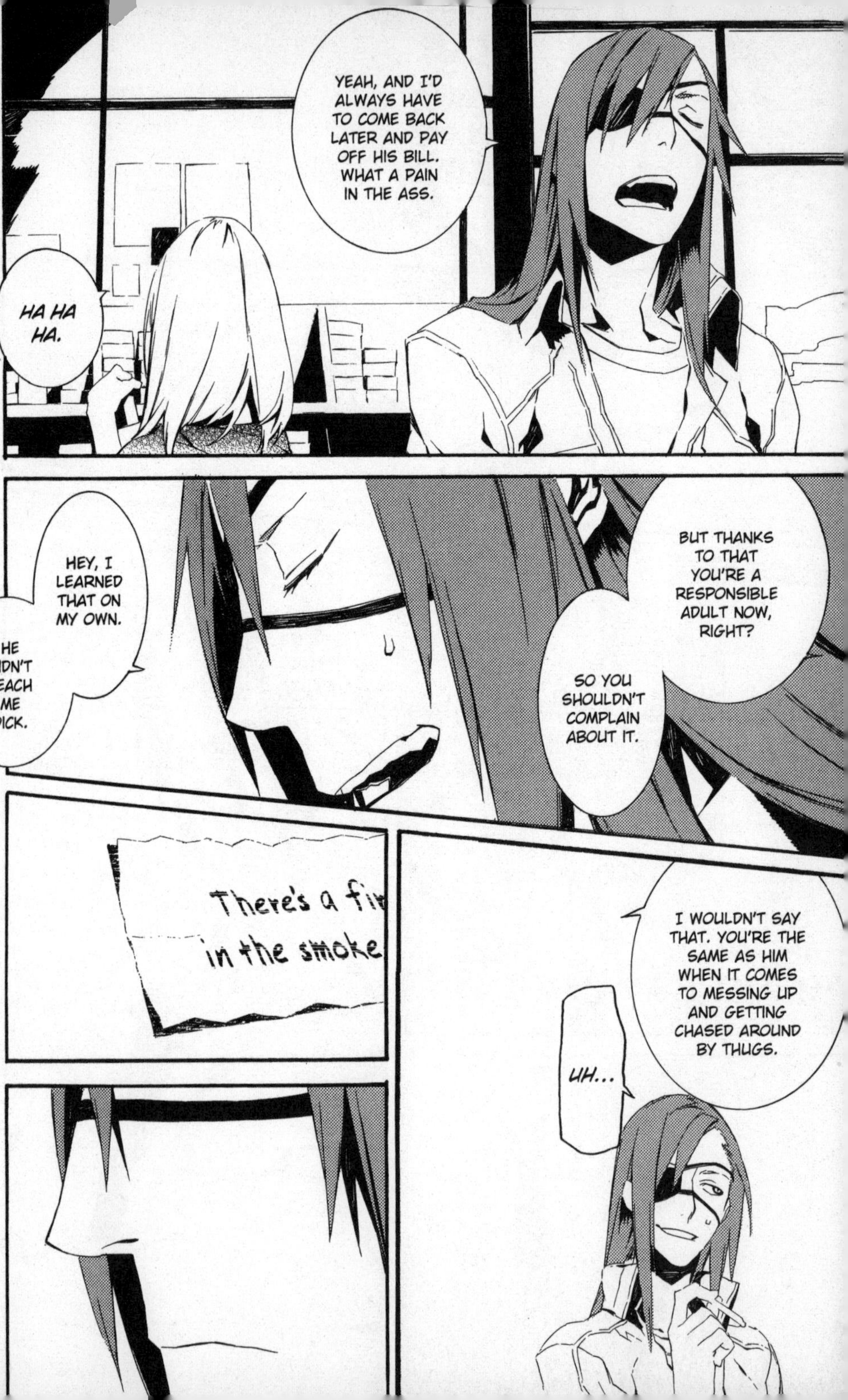
YEAH, AND I'D ALWAYS HAVE TO COME BACK LATER AND PAY OFF HIS BILL. WHAT A PAIN IN THE ASS.
HA HA HA.
BUT THANKS TO THAT YOU'RE A RESPONSIBLE ADULT NOW, RIGHT?
SO YOU SHOULDN'T COMPLAIN ABOUT IT.
HEY, I LEARNED THAT ON MY OWN.
HE DIDN'T TEACH ME DICK.
I WOULDN'T SAY THAT. YOU'RE THE SAME AS HIM WHEN IT COMES TO MESSING UP AND GETTING CHASED AROUND BY THUGS.
UH...
There's a fir
in the smoke

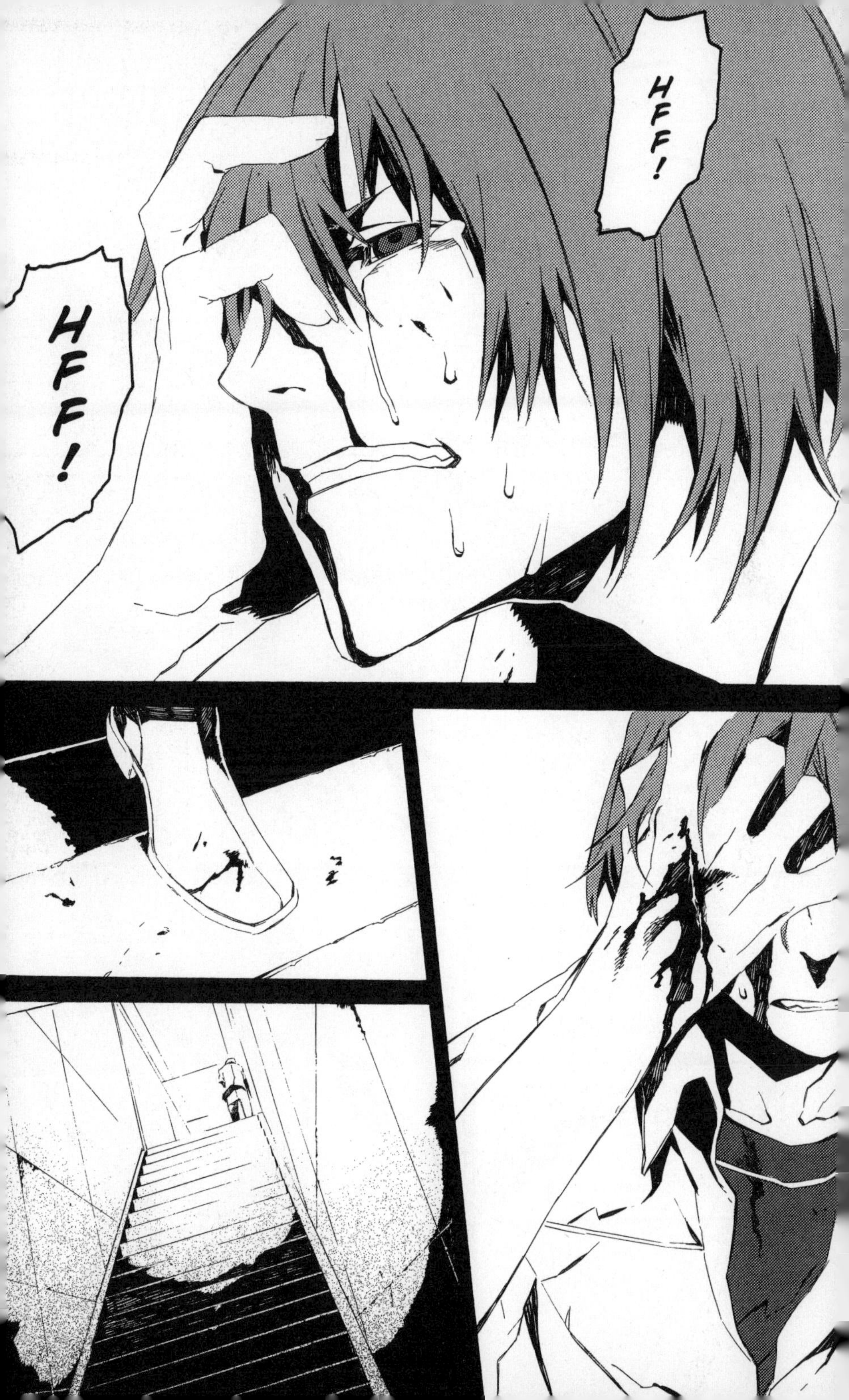
HFF!
HFF!

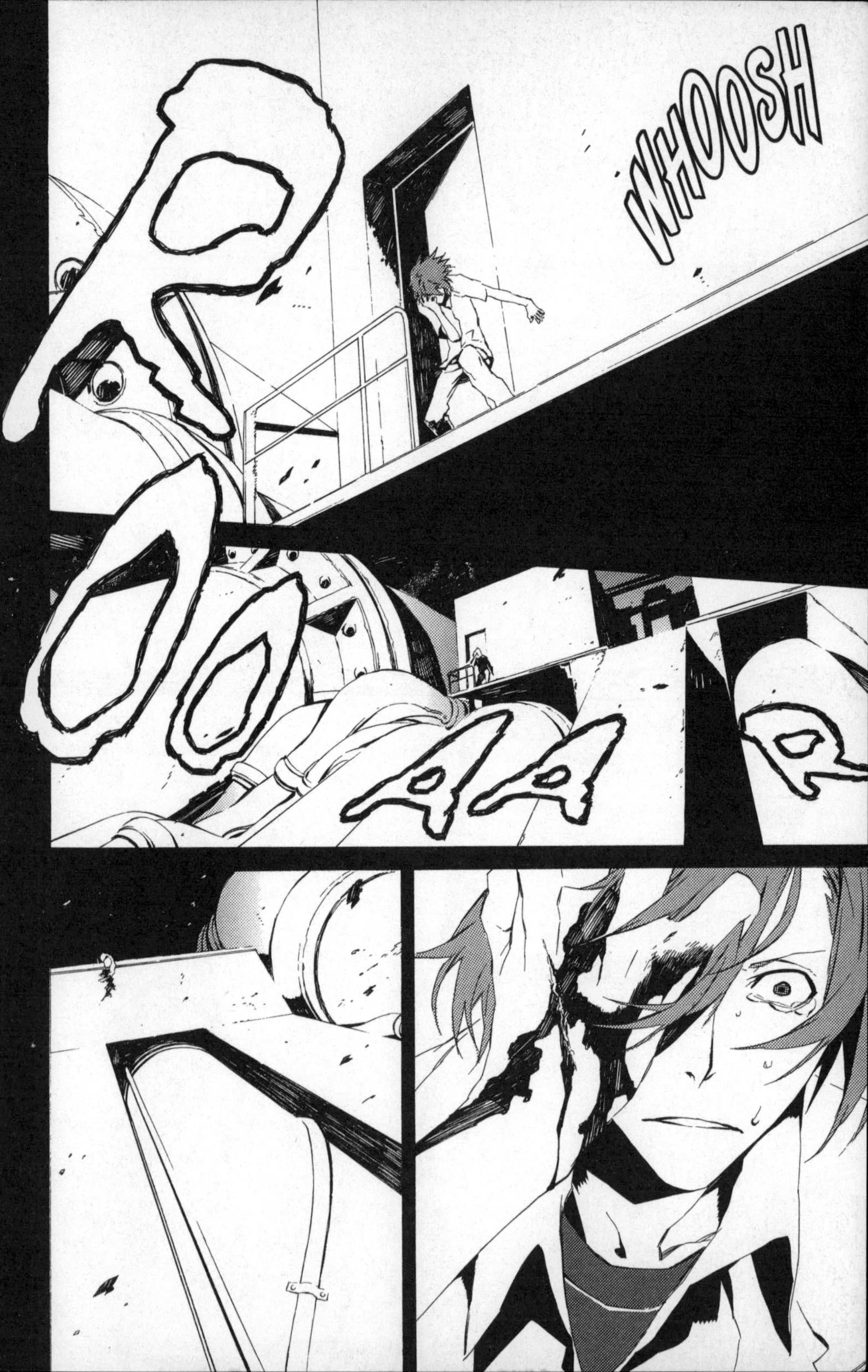
WHOOSH
ROOAAR

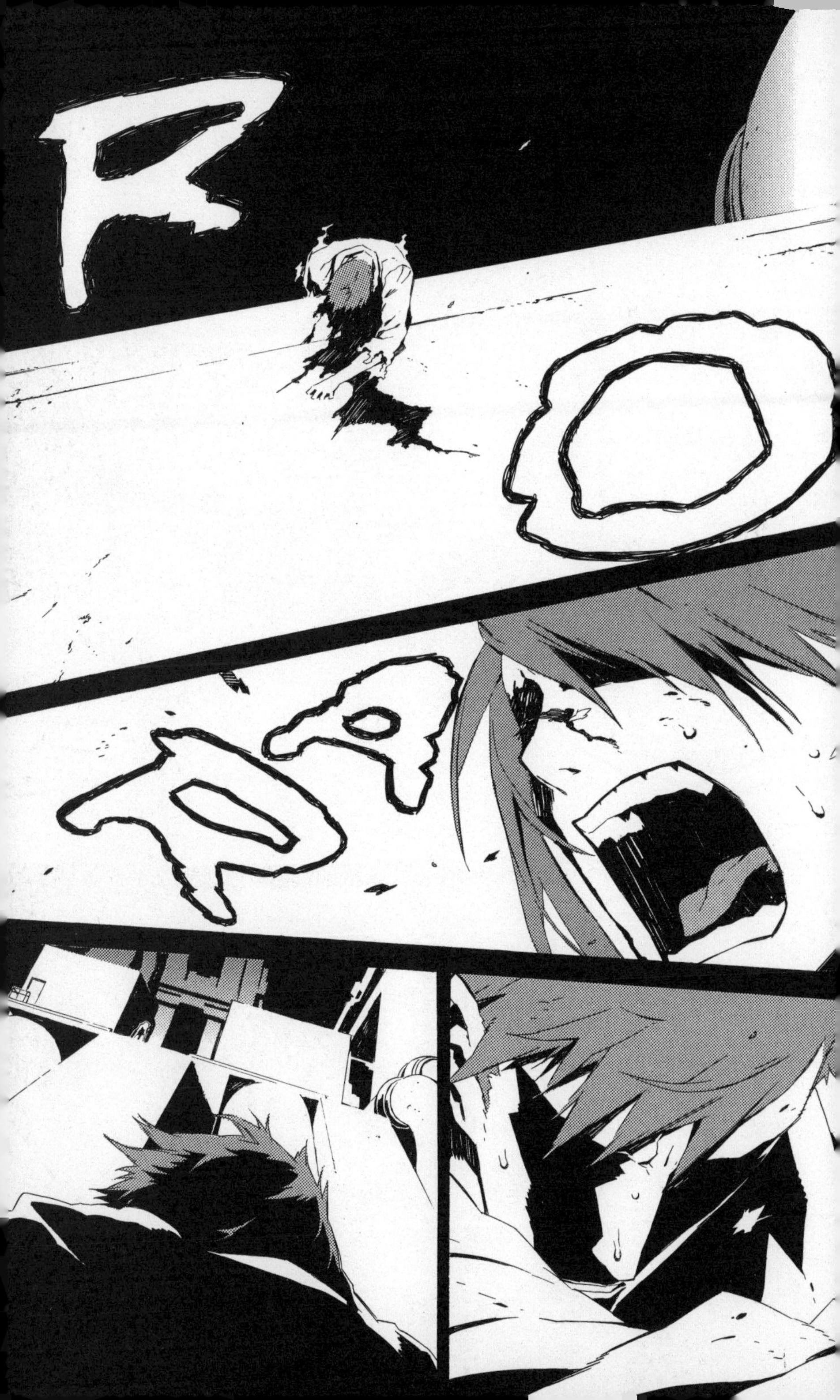
R
O

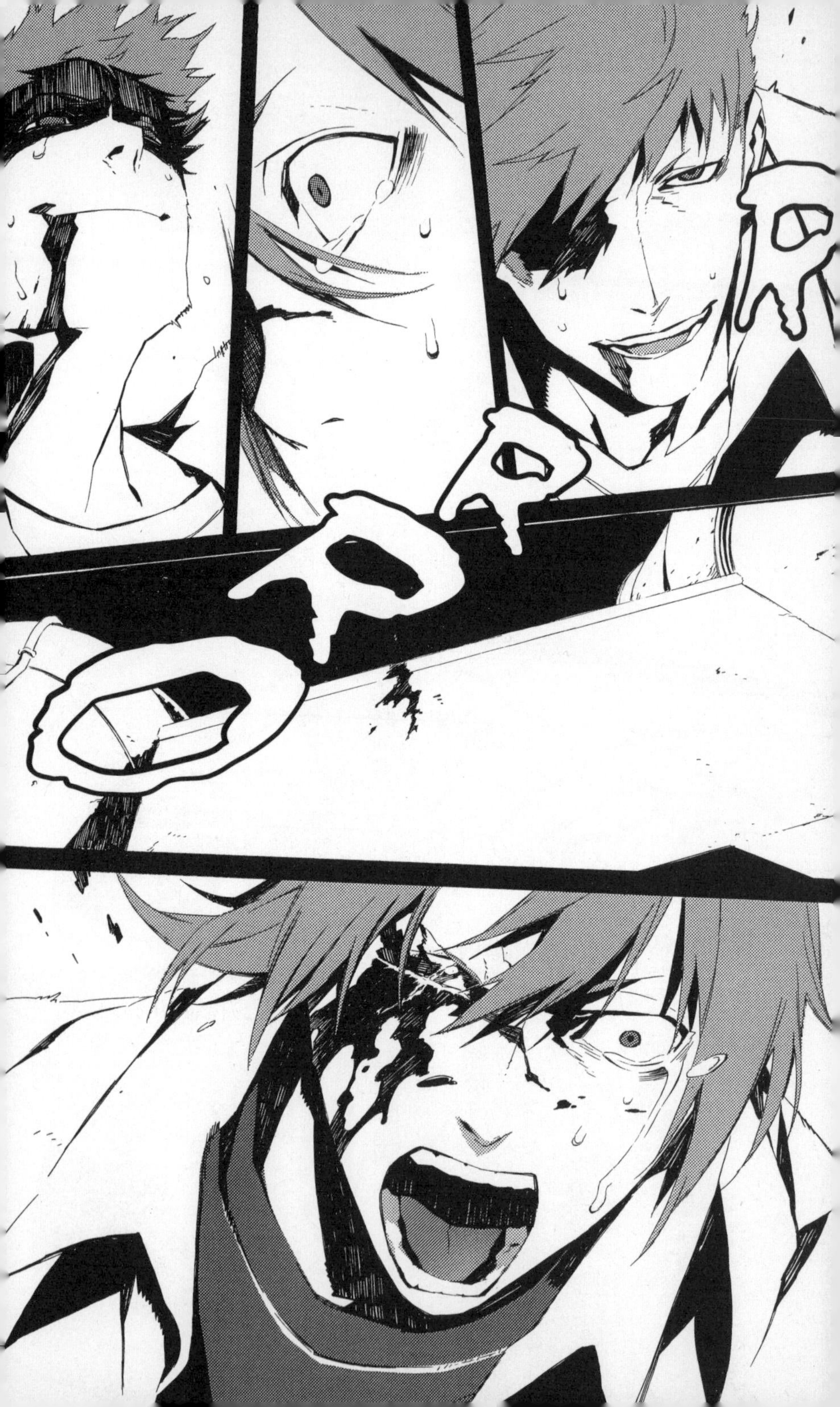

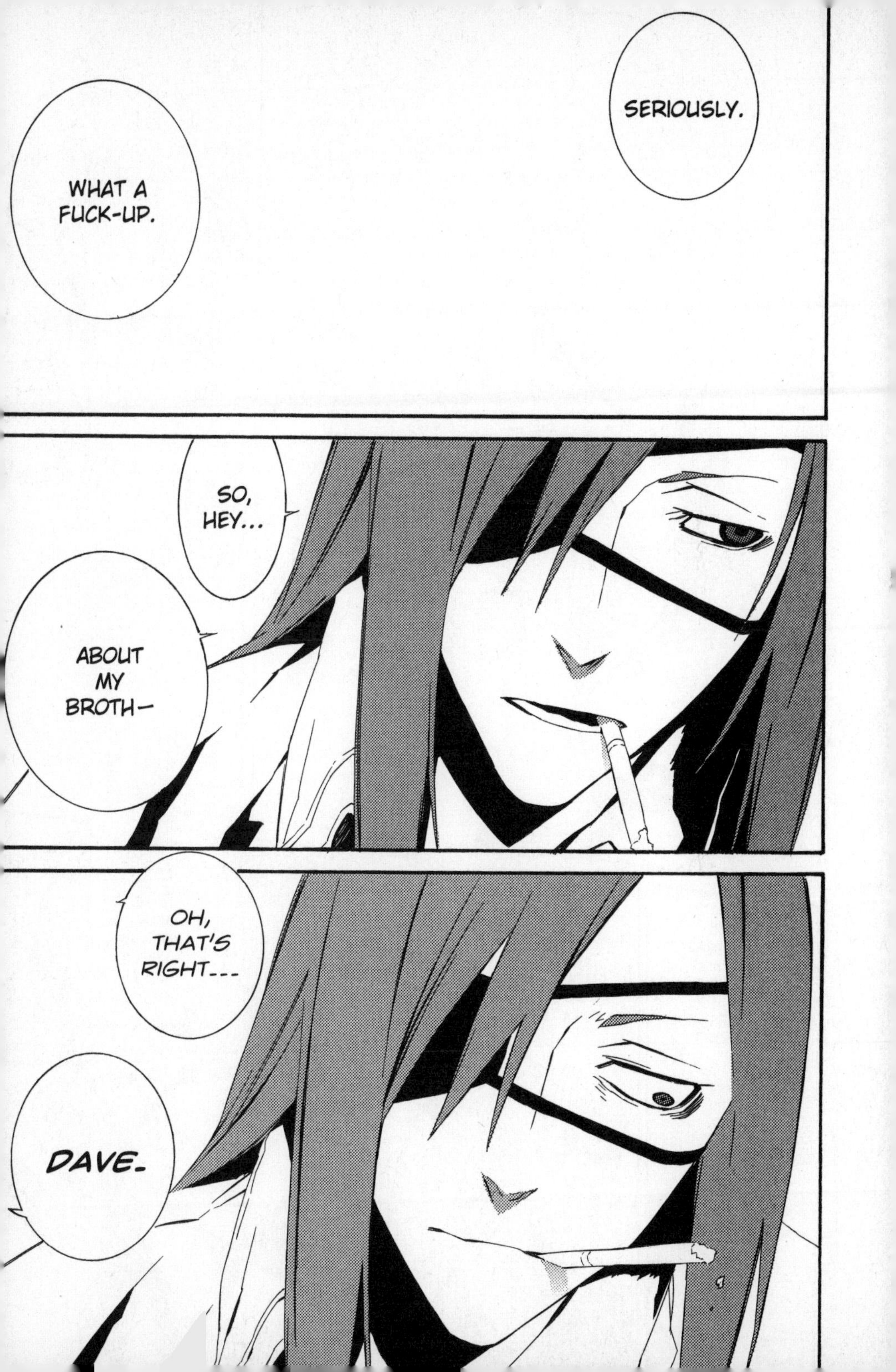
SERIOUSLY.
WHAT A FUCK-UP.
SO, HEY...
ABOUT MY BROTH—
OH, THAT'S RIGHT...
DAVE.

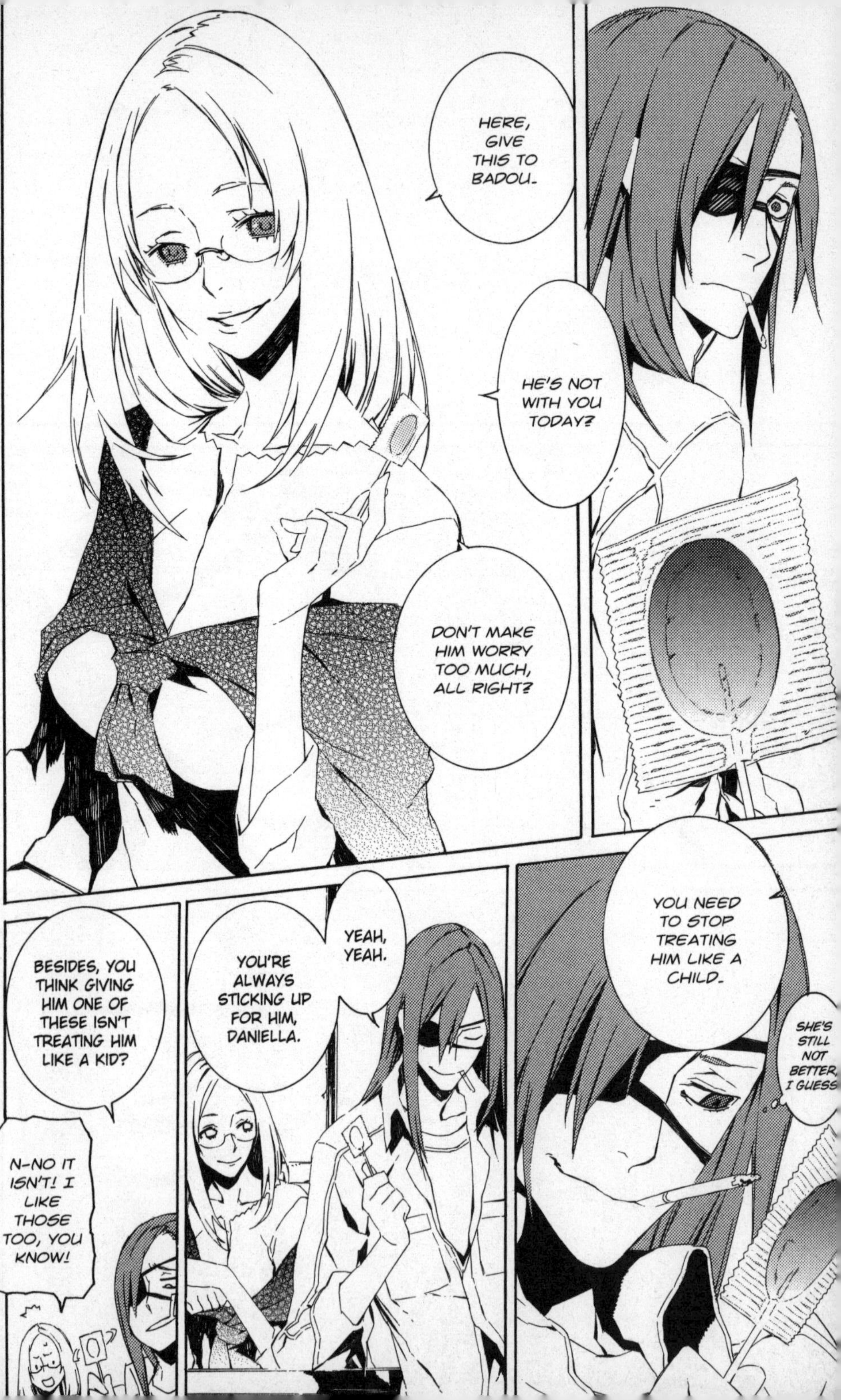
HERE, GIVE THIS TO BADOU.
HE'S NOT WITH YOU TODAY?
DON'T MAKE HIM WORRY TOO MUCH, ALL RIGHT?
YOU NEED TO STOP TREATING HIM LIKE A CHILD.
SHE'S STILL NOT BETTER, I GUESS.
YEAH, YEAH.
YOU'RE ALWAYS STICKING UP FOR HIM, DANIELLA.
BESIDES, YOU THINK GIVING HIM ONE OF THESE ISN'T TREATING HIM LIKE A KID?
N-NO IT ISN'T! I LIKE THOSE TOO, YOU KNOW!

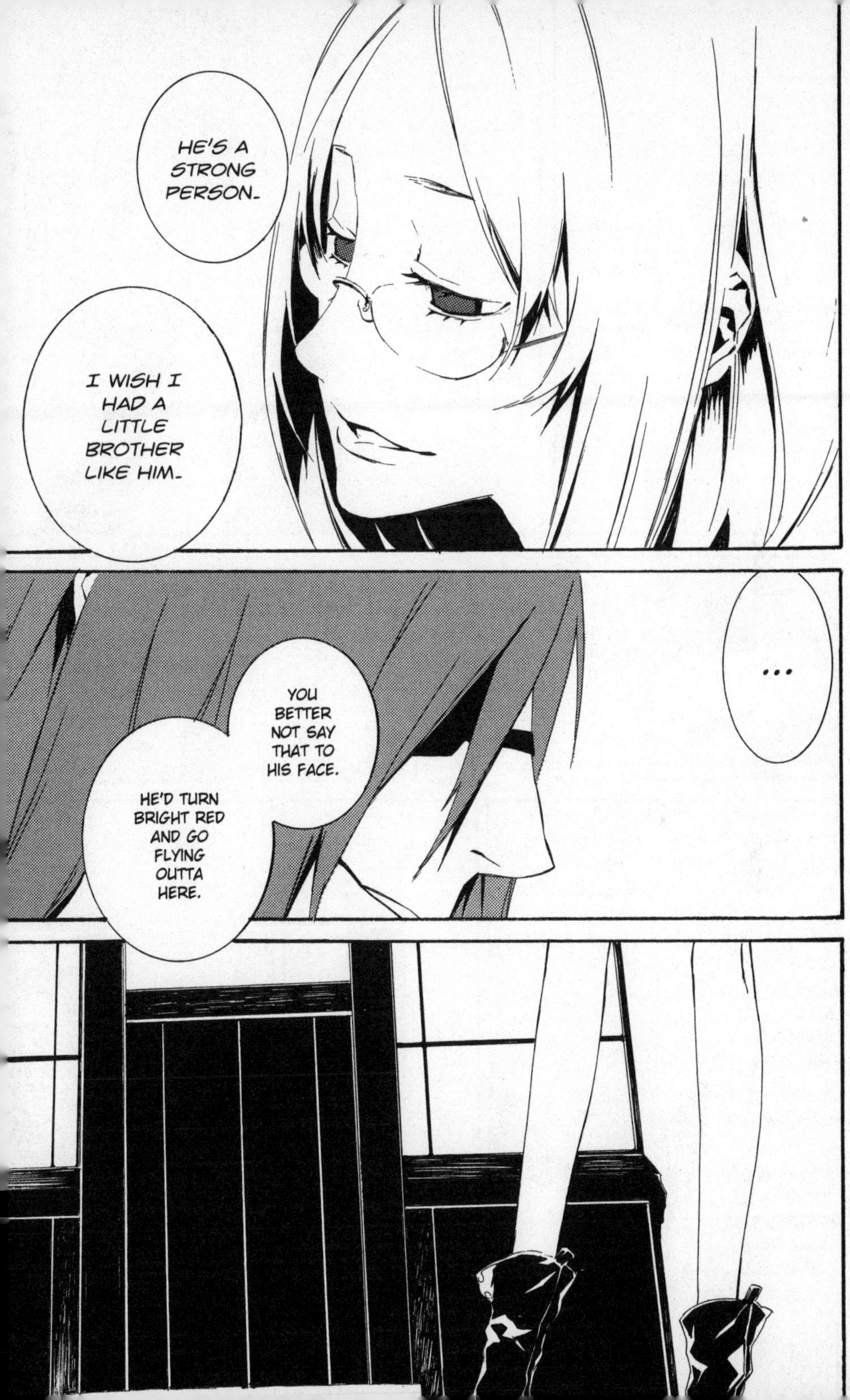
HE'S A STRONG PERSON...
I WISH I HAD A LITTLE BROTHER LIKE HIM...
...
YOU BETTER NOT SAY THAT TO HIS FACE.
HE'D TURN BRIGHT RED AND GO FLYING OUTTA HERE.

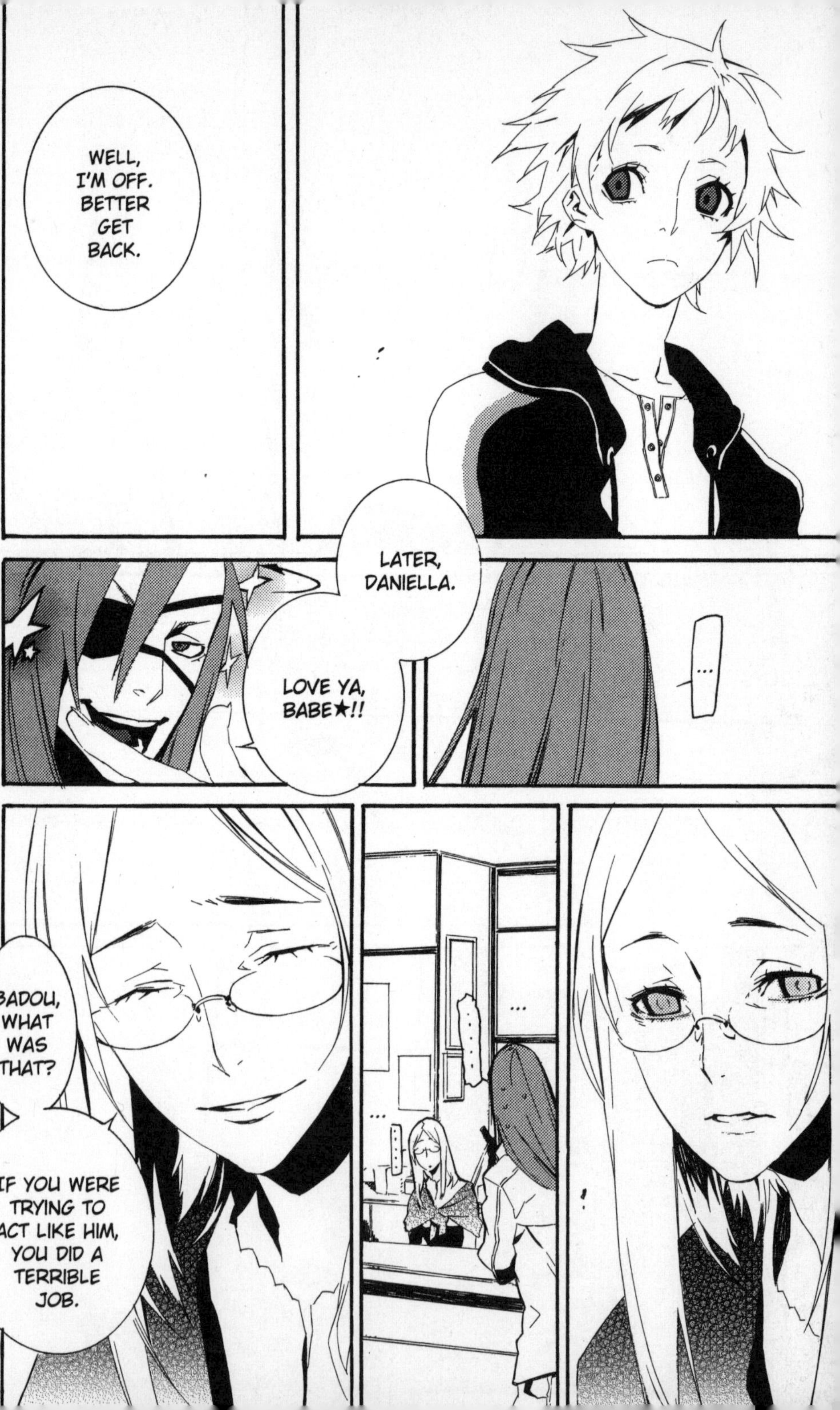
WELL, I'M OFF. BETTER GET BACK.
...
LATER, DANIELLA.
LOVE YA, BABE★!!
...
...
BADOU, WHAT WAS THAT?
IF YOU WERE TRYING TO ACT LIKE HIM, YOU DID A TERRIBLE JOB.

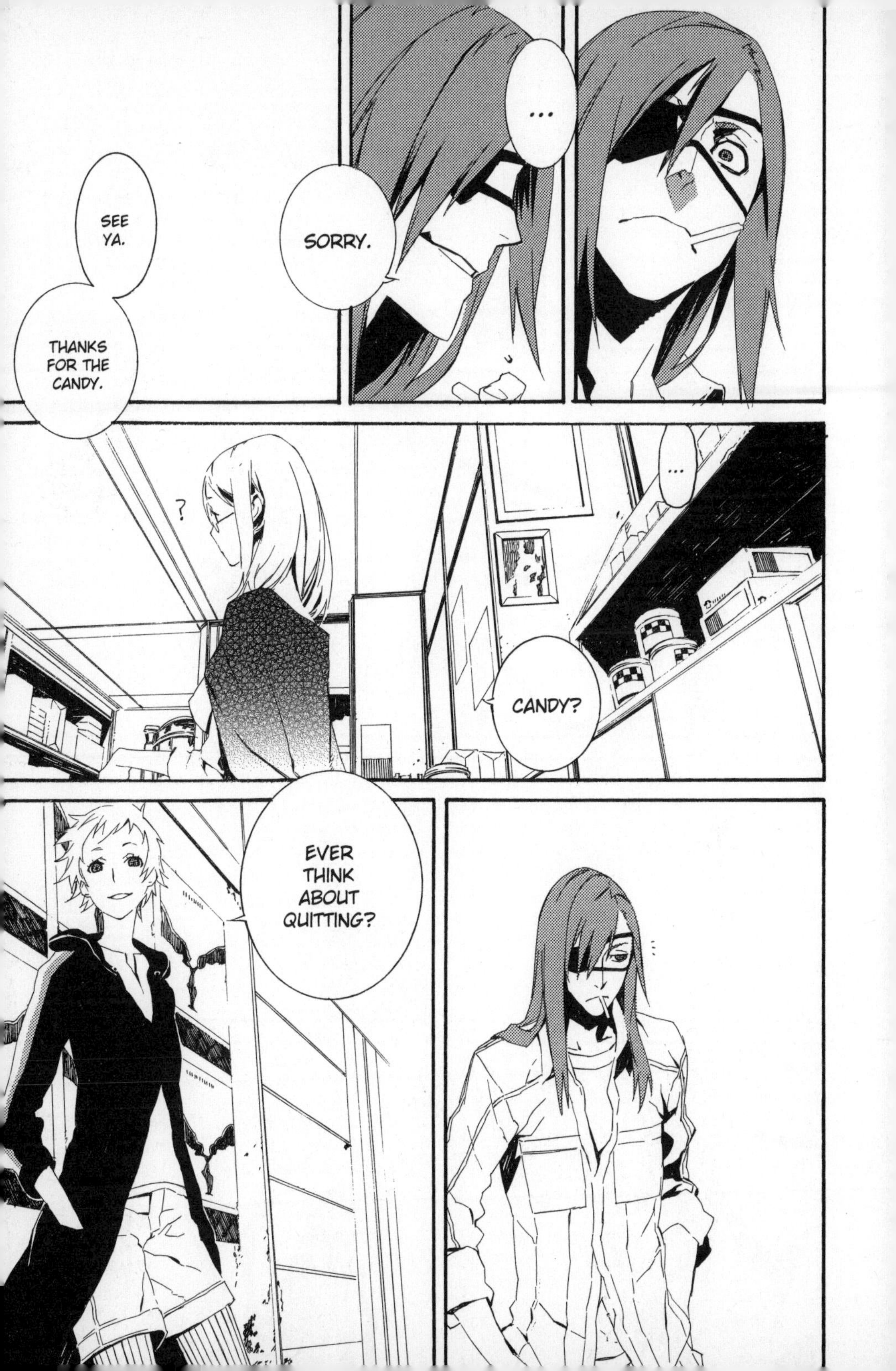
...
SORRY.
SEE YA.
THANKS FOR THE CANDY.
...
CANDY?
?
EVER THINK ABOUT QUITTING?

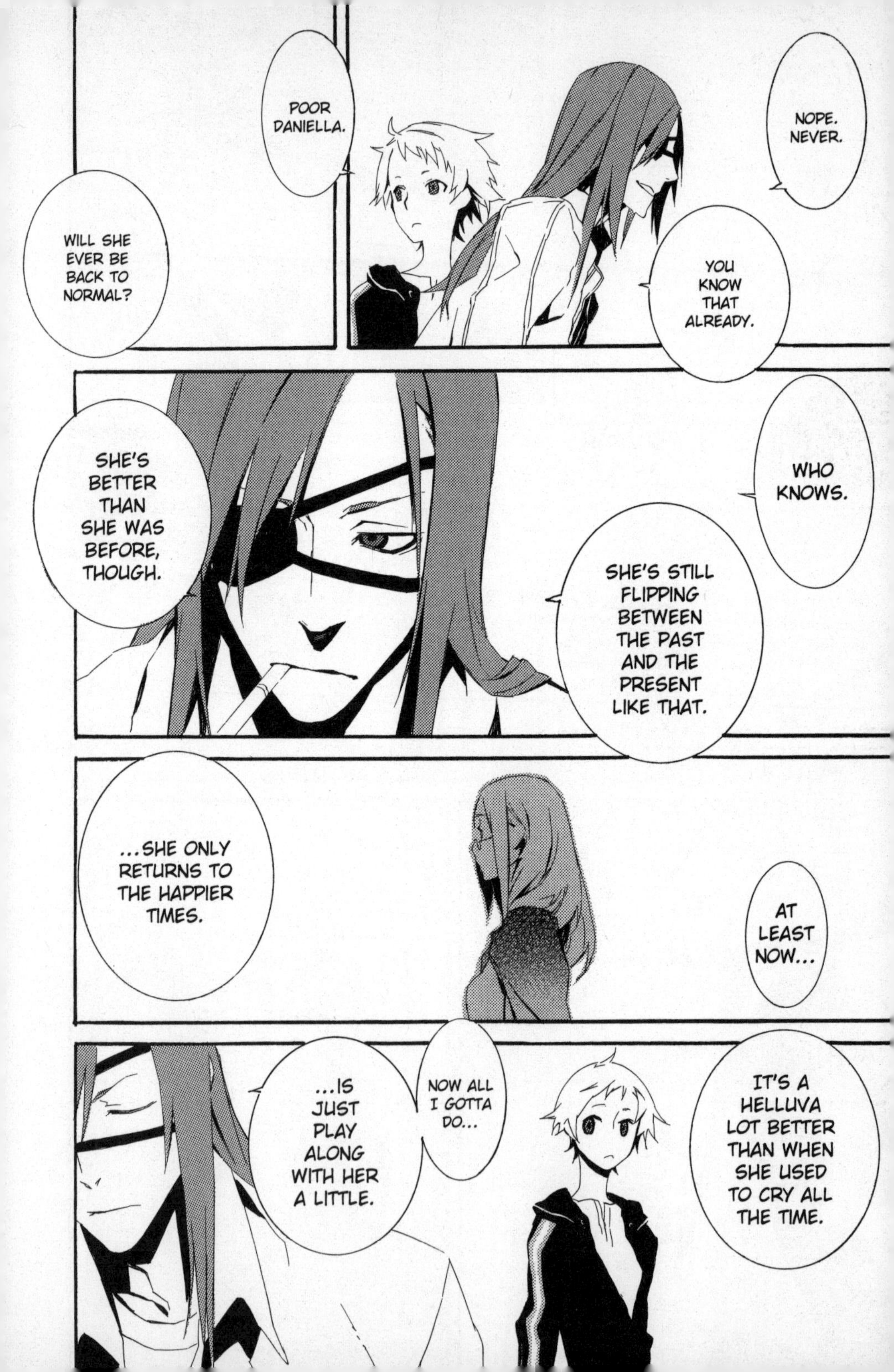
NOPE. NEVER.
YOU KNOW THAT ALREADY.
POOR DANIELLA.
WILL SHE EVER BE BACK TO NORMAL?
WHO KNOWS.
SHE'S STILL FLIPPING BETWEEN THE PAST AND THE PRESENT LIKE THAT.
SHE'S BETTER THAN SHE WAS BEFORE, THOUGH.
AT LEAST NOW...
...SHE ONLY RETURNS TO THE HAPPIER TIMES.
IT'S A HELLUVA LOT BETTER THAN WHEN SHE USED TO CRY ALL THE TIME.
NOW ALL I GOTTA DO...
...IS JUST PLAY ALONG WITH HER A LITTLE.

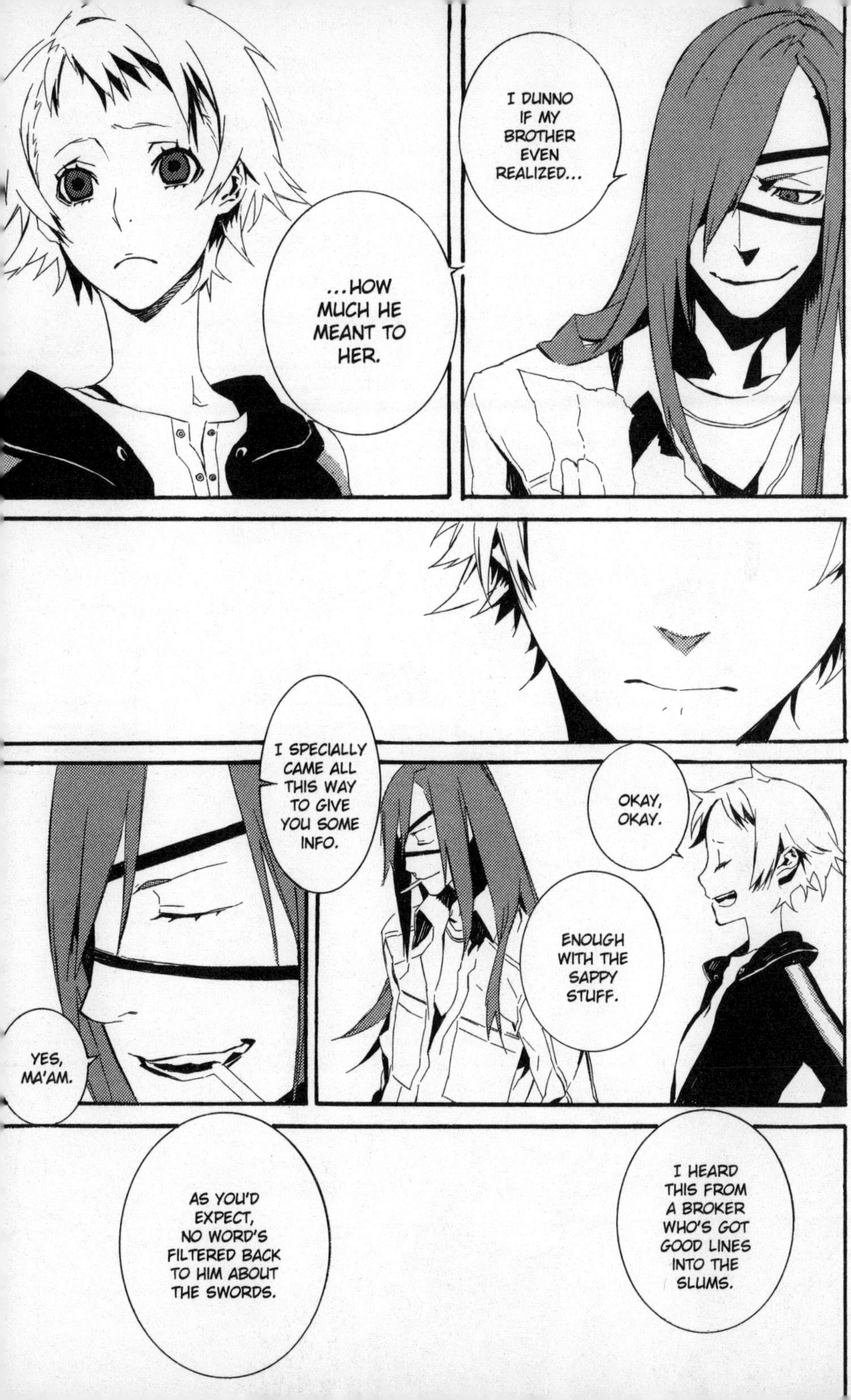
I DUNNO IF MY BROTHER EVEN REALIZED...
...HOW MUCH HE MEANT TO HER.
OKAY, OKAY.
ENOUGH WITH THE SAPPY STUFF.
I SPECIALLY CAME ALL THIS WAY TO GIVE YOU SOME INFO.
YES, MA'AM.
I HEARD THIS FROM A BROKER WHO'S GOT GOOD LINES INTO THE SLUMS.
AS YOU'D EXPECT, NO WORD'S FILTERED BACK TO HIM ABOUT THE SWORDS.

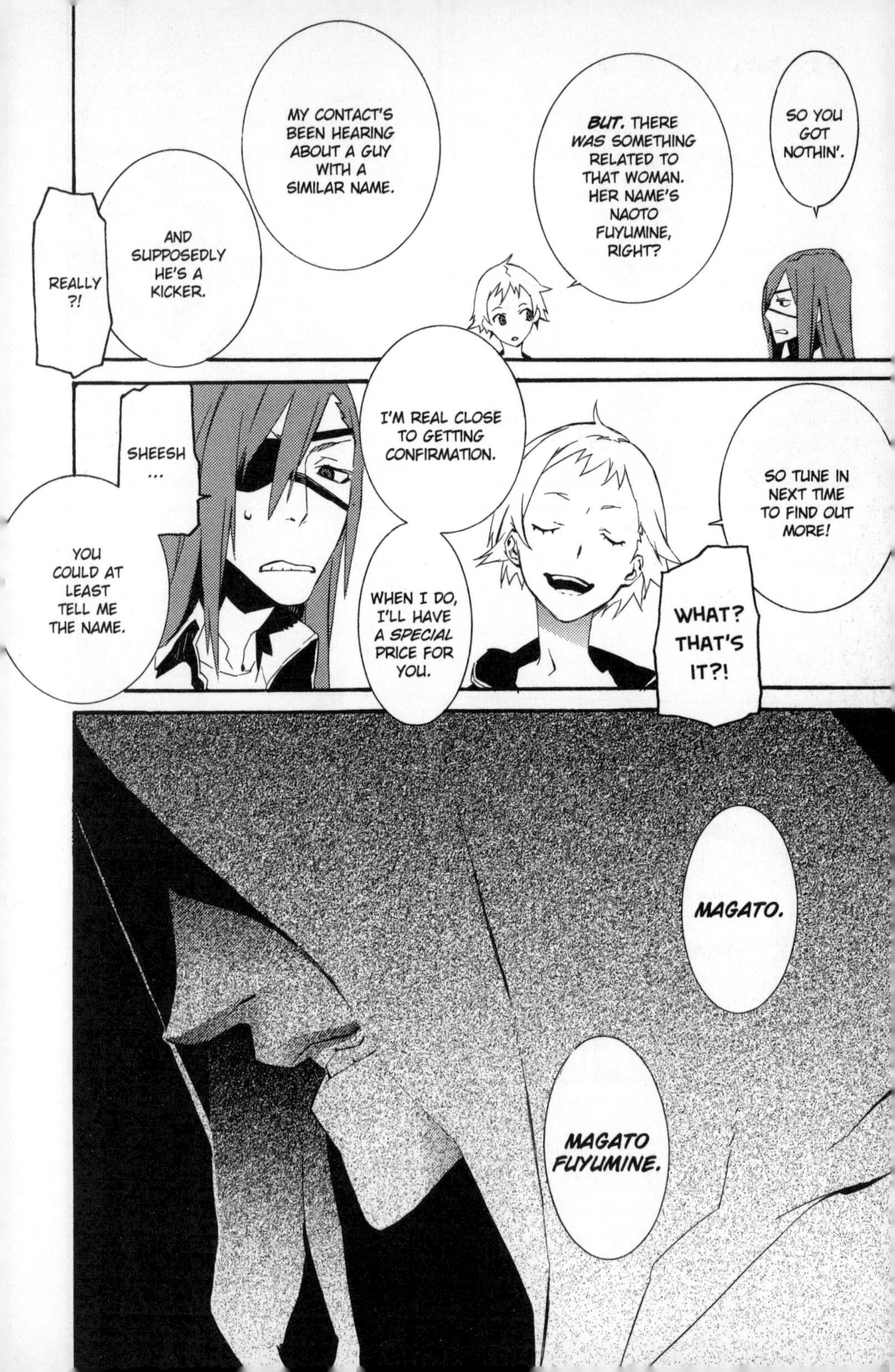
SO YOU GOT NOTHIN'.
BUT. THERE WAS SOMETHING RELATED TO THAT WOMAN. HER NAME'S NAOTO FUYUMINE, RIGHT?
MY CONTACT'S BEEN HEARING ABOUT A GUY WITH A SIMILAR NAME.
AND SUPPOSEDLY HE'S A KICKER.
REALLY?!
I'M REAL CLOSE TO GETTING CONFIRMATION.
WHEN I DO, I'LL HAVE A SPECIAL PRICE FOR YOU.
SO TUNE IN NEXT TIME TO FIND OUT MORE!
WHAT? THAT'S IT?!
SHEESH...
YOU COULD AT LEAST TELL ME THE NAME.
MAGATO.
MAGATO FUYUMINE.

#33 Good Day & Good Die

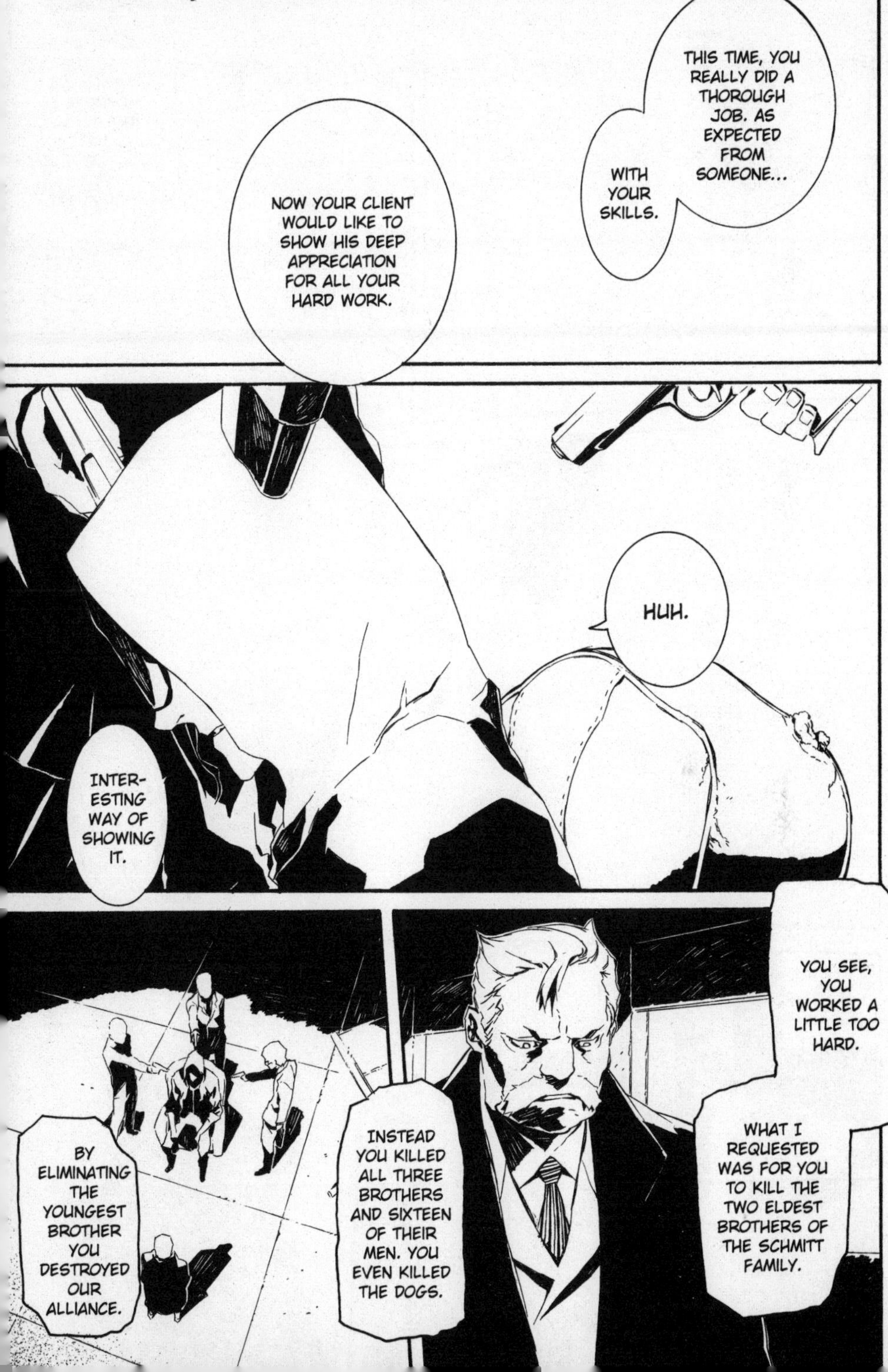

THIS TIME, YOU REALLY DID A THOROUGH JOB. AS EXPECTED FROM SOMEONE...
WITH YOUR SKILLS.
NOW YOUR CLIENT WOULD LIKE TO SHOW HIS DEEP APPRECIATION FOR ALL YOUR HARD WORK.
HUH.
INTER-ESTING WAY OF SHOWING IT.
YOU SEE, YOU WORKED A LITTLE TOO HARD.
WHAT I REQUESTED WAS FOR YOU TO KILL THE TWO ELDEST BROTHERS OF THE SCHMITT FAMILY.
INSTEAD YOU KILLED ALL THREE BROTHERS AND SIXTEEN OF THEIR MEN. YOU EVEN KILLED THE DOGS.
BY ELIMINATING THE YOUNGEST BROTHER YOU DESTROYED OUR ALLIANCE.

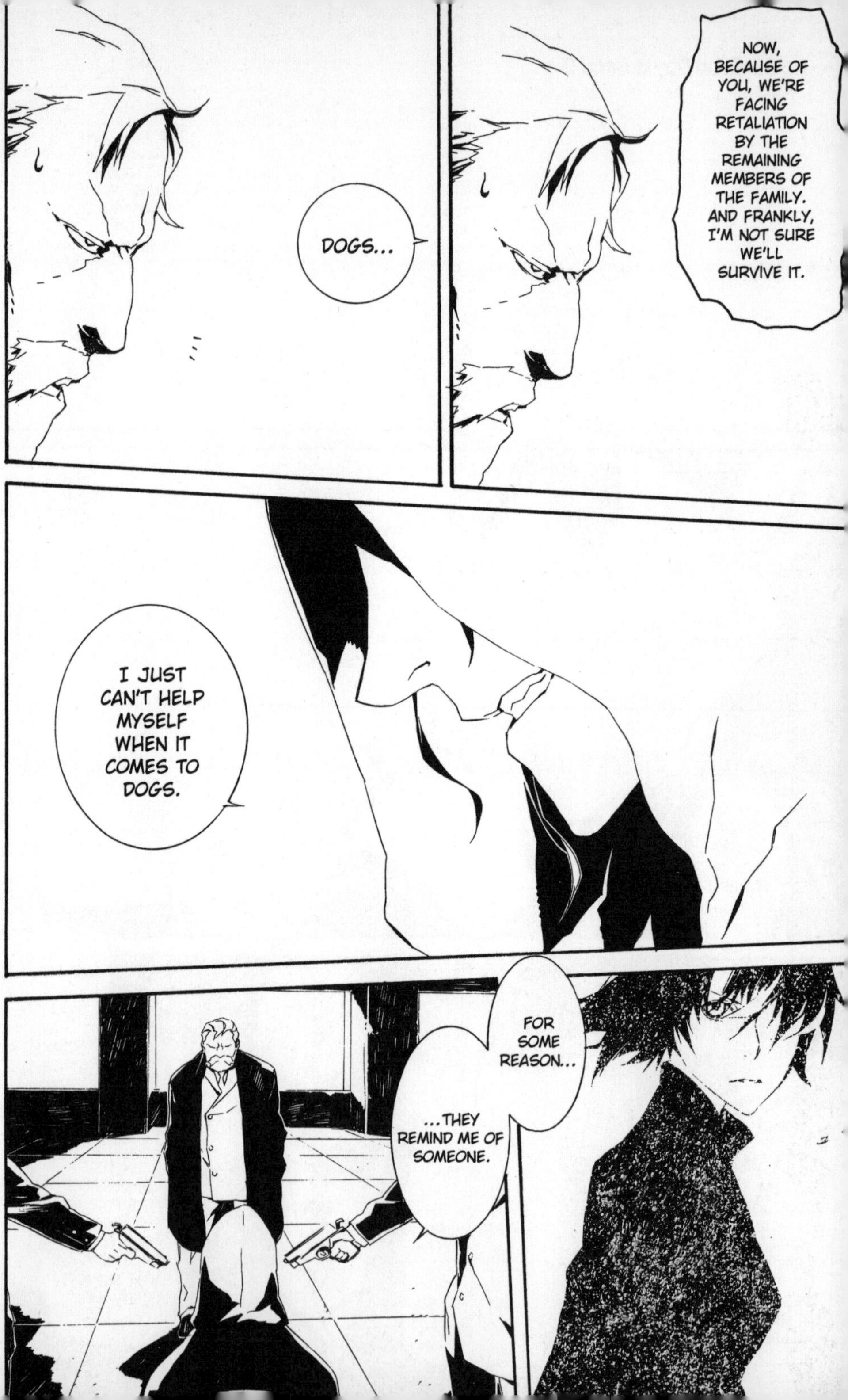
NOW, BECAUSE OF YOU, WE'RE FACING RETALIATION BY THE REMAINING MEMBERS OF THE FAMILY. AND FRANKLY, I'M NOT SURE WE'LL SURVIVE IT.
DOGS...
I JUST CAN'T HELP MYSELF WHEN IT COMES TO DOGS.
FOR SOME REASON...
...THEY REMIND ME OF SOMEONE.

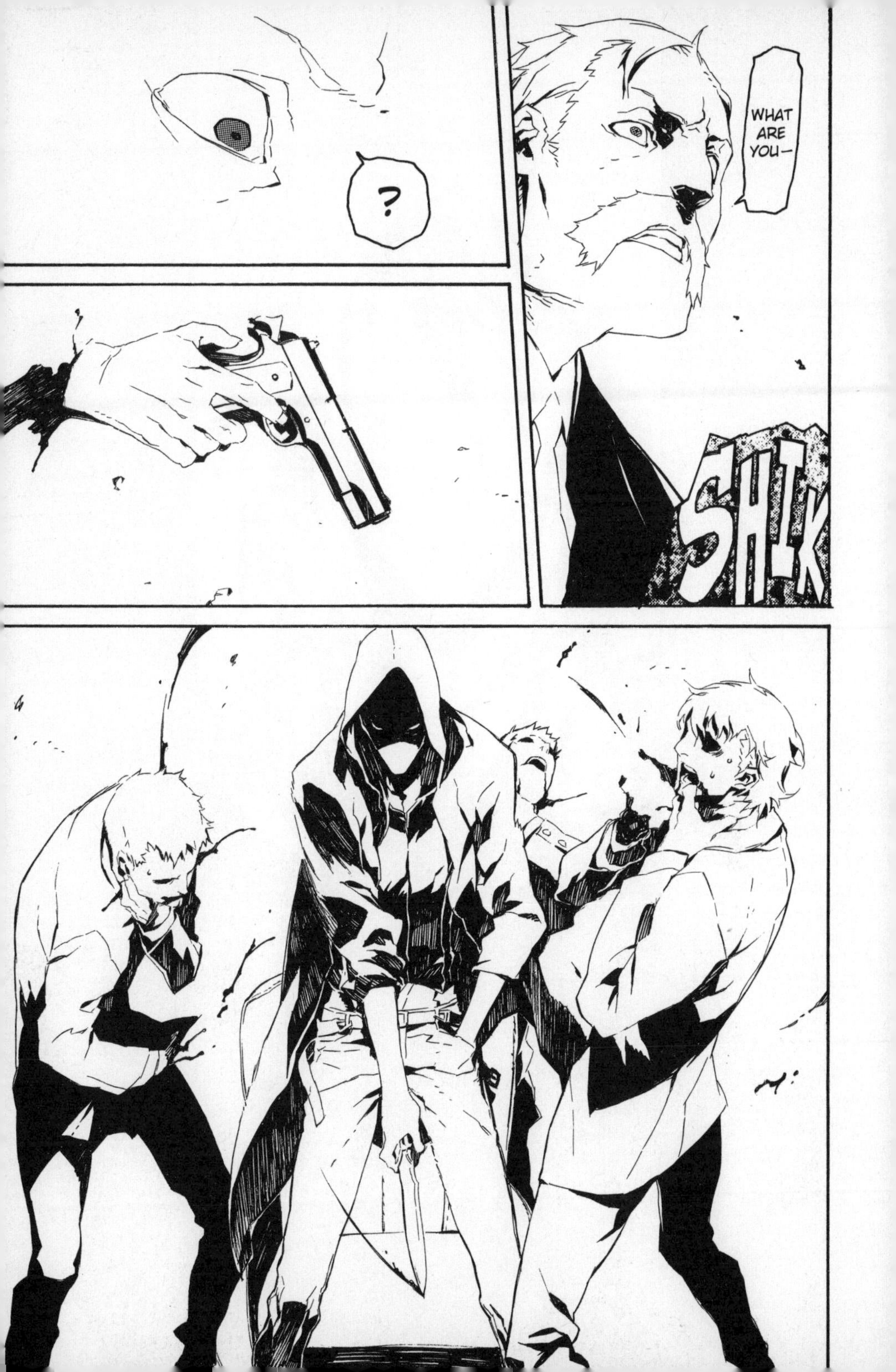
WHAT ARE YOU—
SHIK
?

#33 Good Day & Good Die

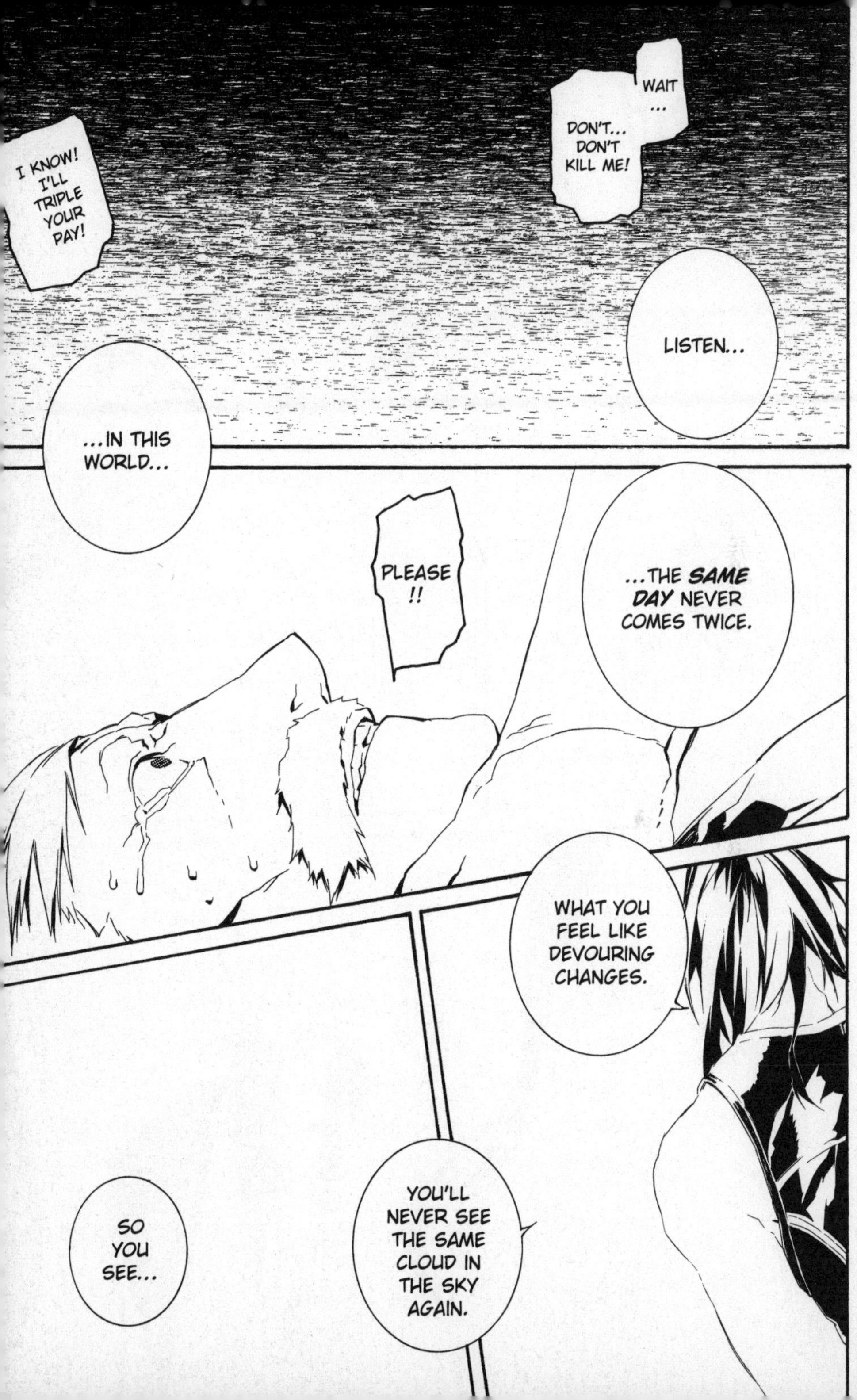
WAIT ...
DON'T... DON'T KILL ME!
I KNOW! I'LL TRIPLE YOUR PAY!
LISTEN...
...IN THIS WORLD...
...THE ***SAME DAY*** NEVER COMES TWICE.
PLEASE !!
WHAT YOU FEEL LIKE DEVOURING CHANGES.
YOU'LL NEVER SEE THE SAME CLOUD IN THE SKY AGAIN.
SO YOU SEE...

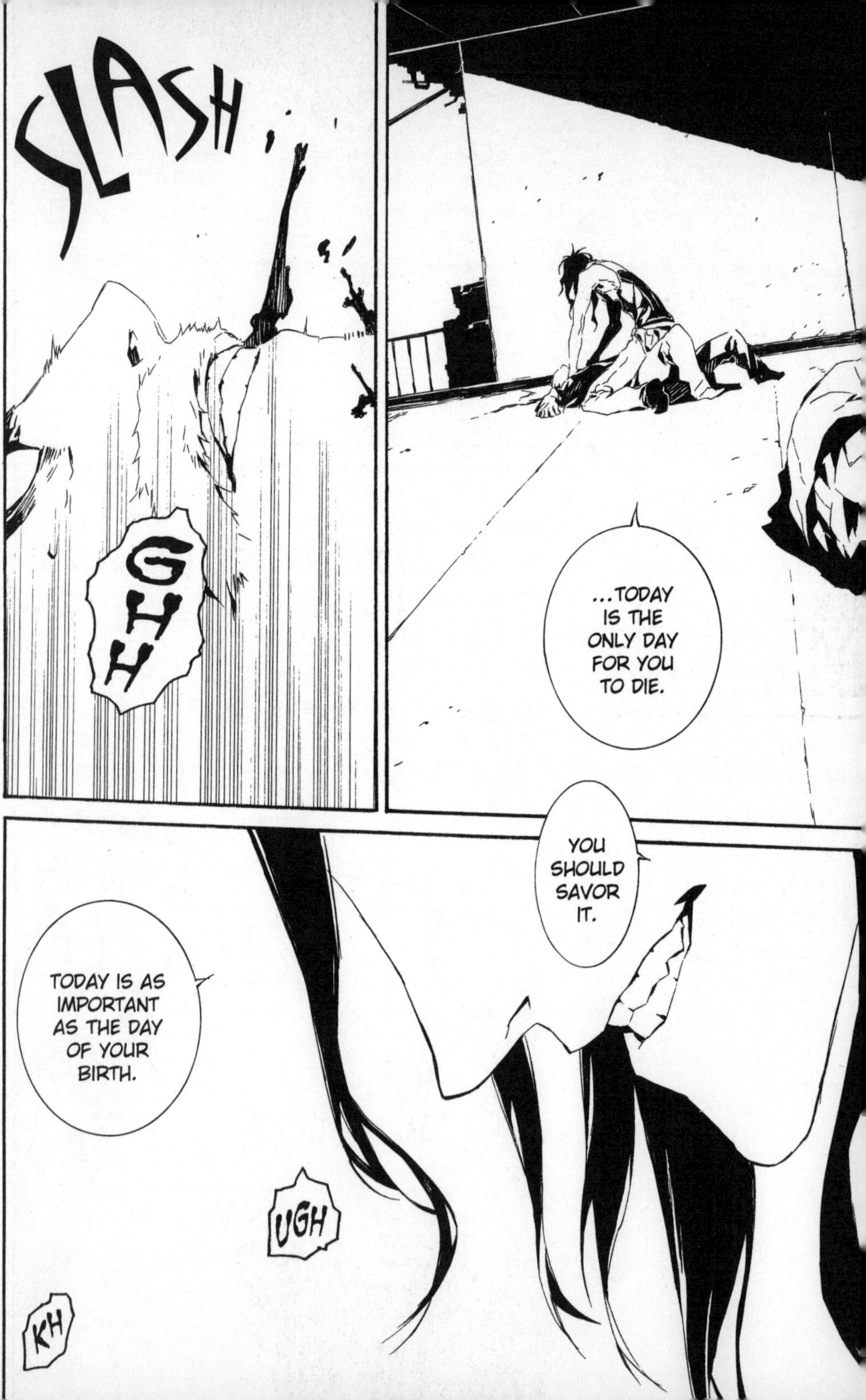
...TODAY IS THE ONLY DAY FOR YOU TO DIE.
SLASH
GHH
YOU SHOULD SAVOR IT.
TODAY IS AS IMPORTANT AS THE DAY OF YOUR BIRTH.
UGH
KH

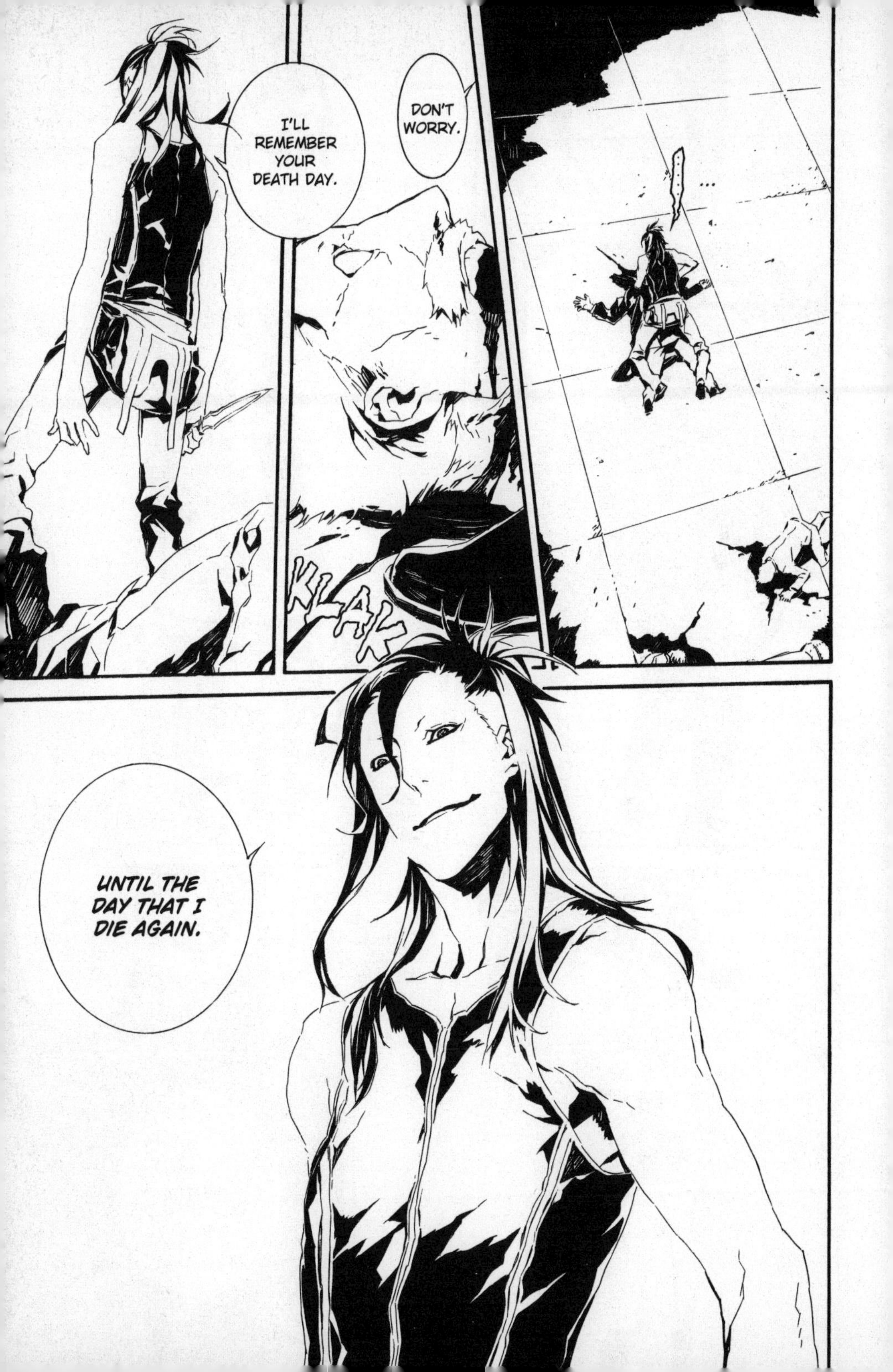
!
...
DON'T WORRY.
KLAK
I'LL REMEMBER YOUR DEATH DAY.
UNTIL THE DAY THAT I DIE AGAIN.

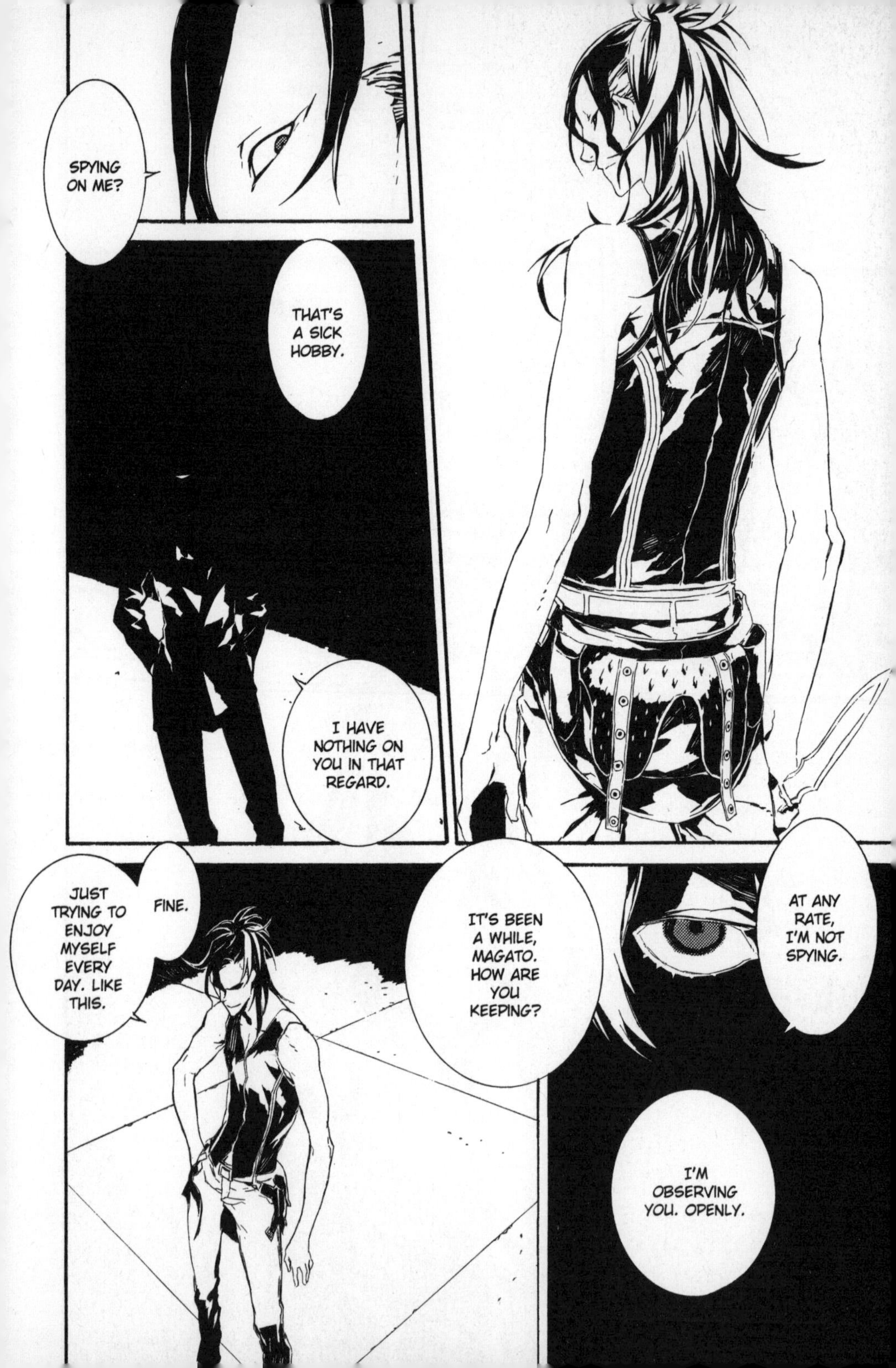
SPYING ON ME?
THAT'S A SICK HOBBY.
I HAVE NOTHING ON YOU IN THAT REGARD.
AT ANY RATE, I'M NOT SPYING.
I'M OBSERVING YOU. OPENLY.
IT'S BEEN A WHILE, MAGATO. HOW ARE YOU KEEPING?
FINE.
JUST TRYING TO ENJOY MYSELF EVERY DAY. LIKE THIS.

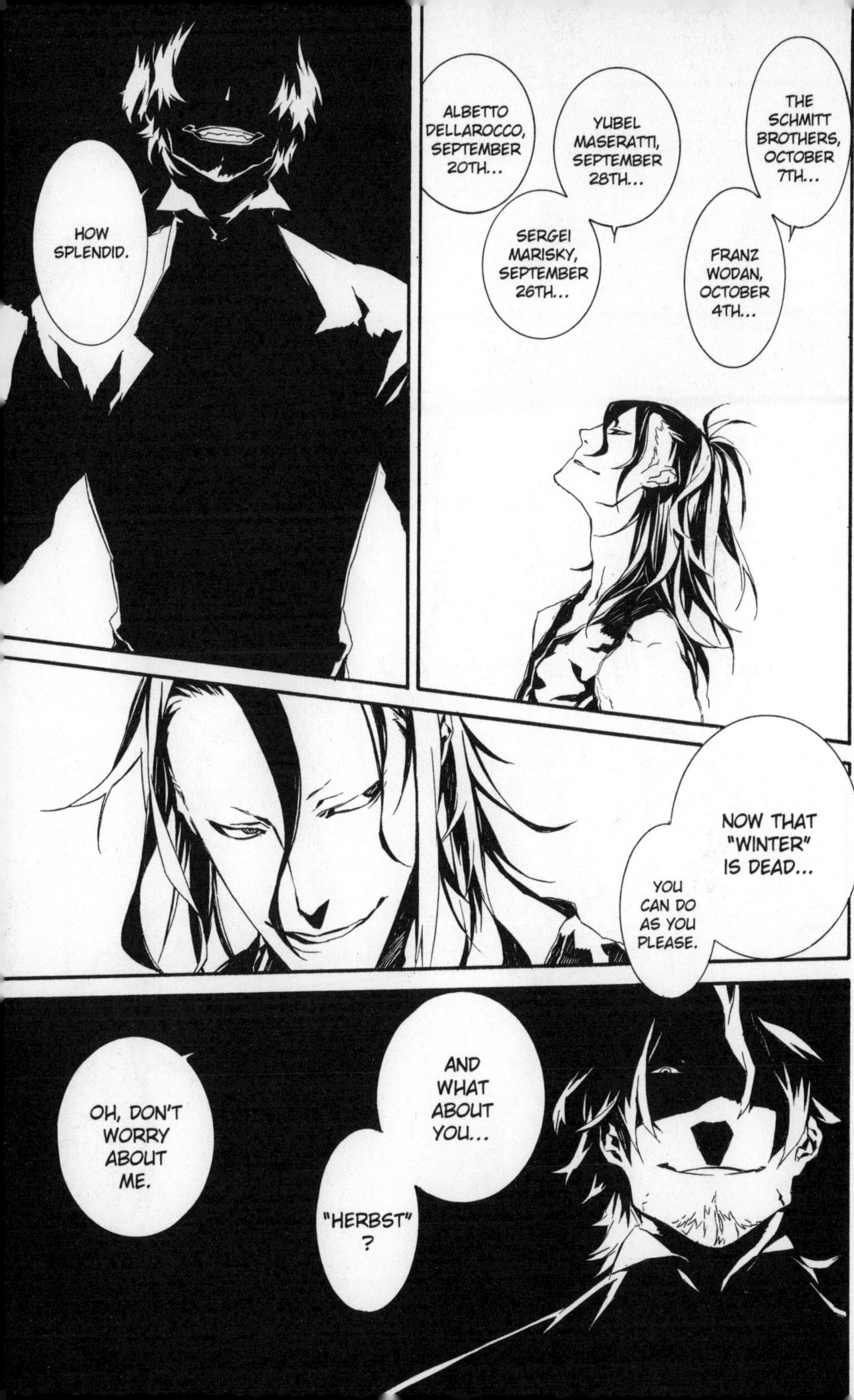
THE SCHMITT BROTHERS, OCTOBER 7TH...
FRANZ WODAN, OCTOBER 4TH...
YUBEL MASERATTI, SEPTEMBER 28TH...
SERGEI MARISKY, SEPTEMBER 26TH...
ALBETTO DELLAROCCO, SEPTEMBER 20TH...
HOW SPLENDID.
NOW THAT "WINTER" IS DEAD...
YOU CAN DO AS YOU PLEASE.
AND WHAT ABOUT YOU...
"HERBST"?
OH, DON'T WORRY ABOUT ME.

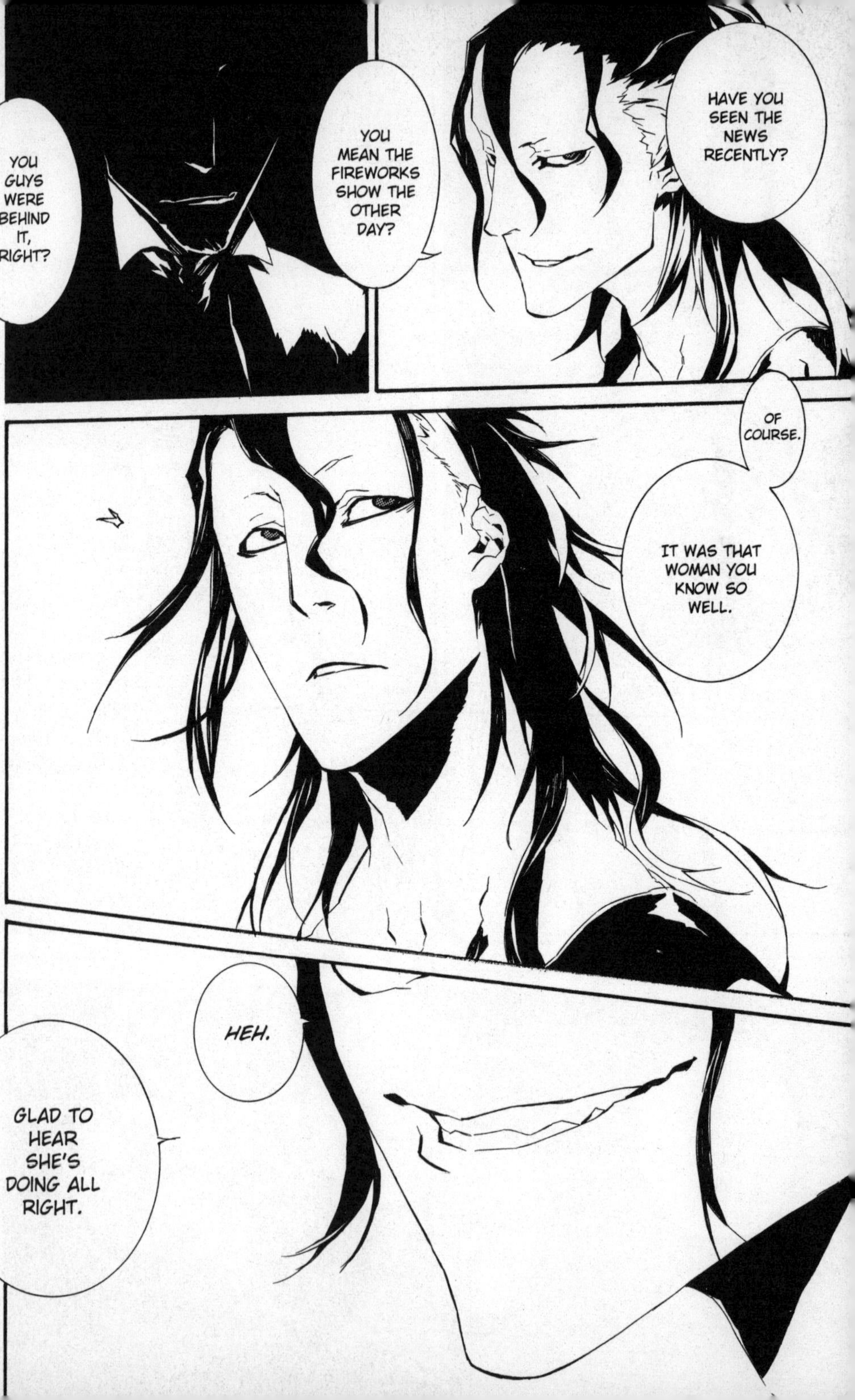
HAVE YOU SEEN THE NEWS RECENTLY?
YOU MEAN THE FIREWORKS SHOW THE OTHER DAY?
YOU GUYS WERE BEHIND IT, RIGHT?
OF COURSE.
IT WAS THAT WOMAN YOU KNOW SO WELL.
HEH.
GLAD TO HEAR SHE'S DOING ALL RIGHT.

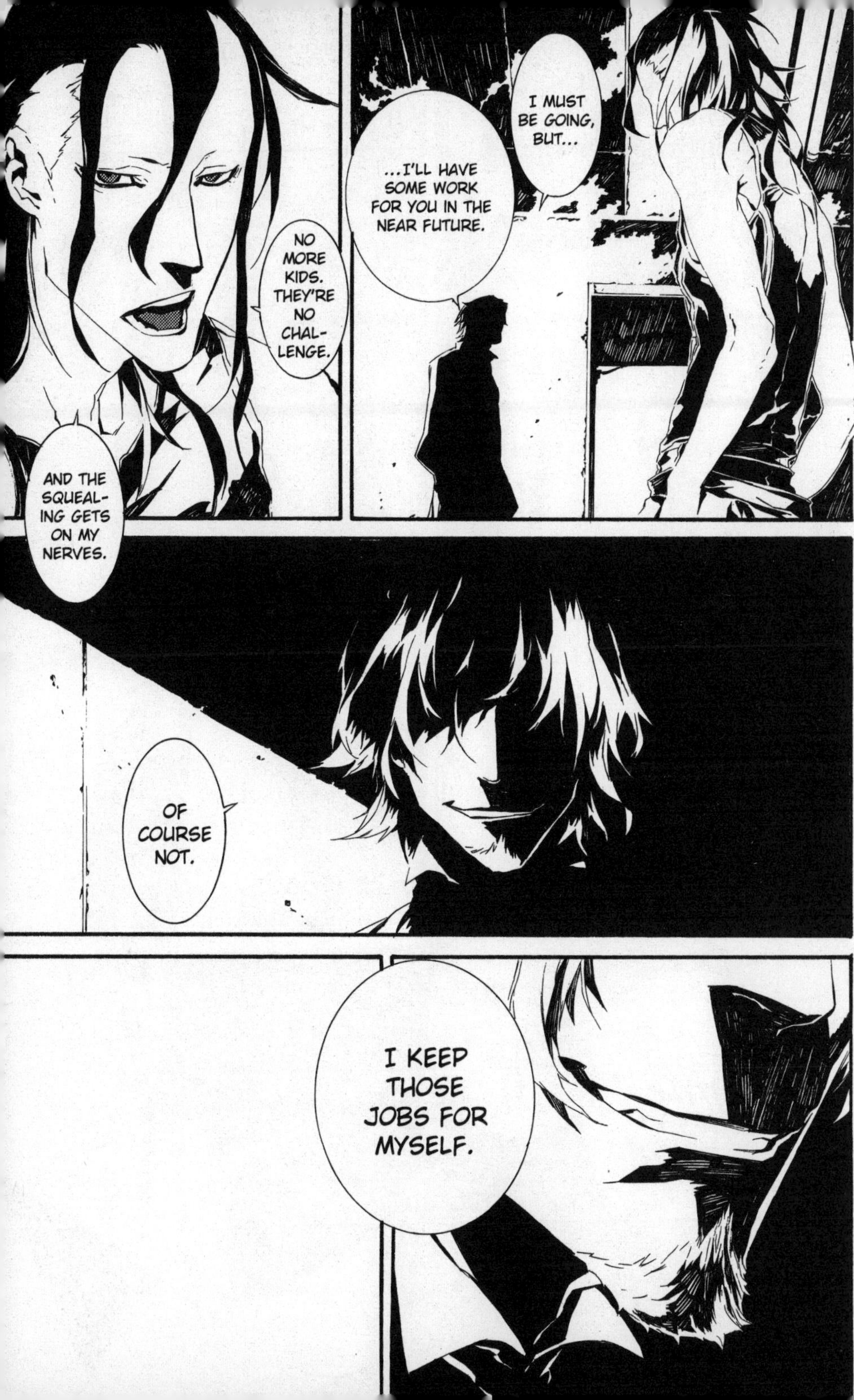
I MUST BE GOING, BUT...
...I'LL HAVE SOME WORK FOR YOU IN THE NEAR FUTURE.
NO MORE KIDS. THEY'RE NO CHAL-LENGE.
AND THE SQUEAL-ING GETS ON MY NERVES.
OF COURSE NOT.
I KEEP THOSE JOBS FOR MYSELF.

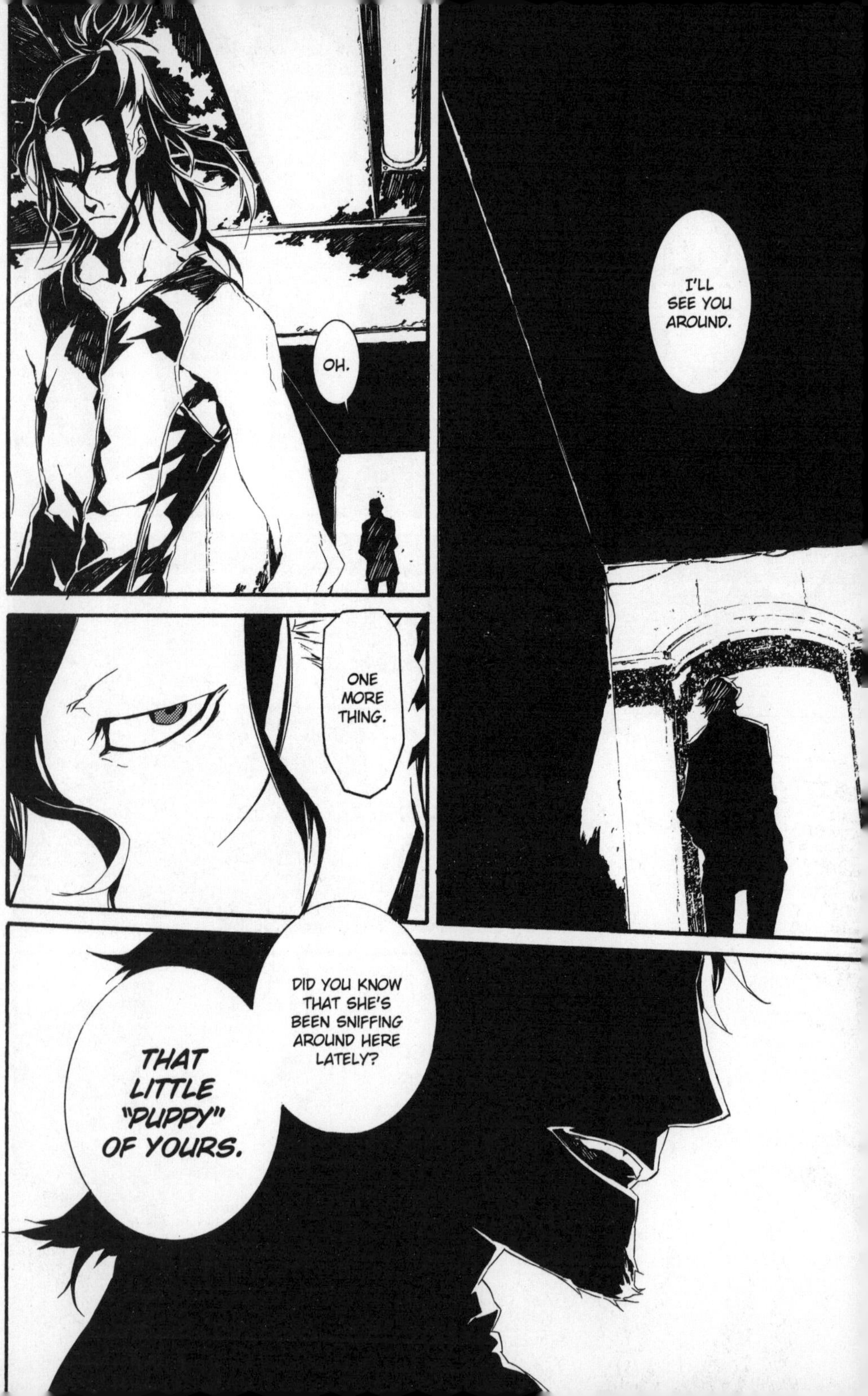
I'LL SEE YOU AROUND.
OH.
ONE MORE THING.
DID YOU KNOW THAT SHE'S BEEN SNIFFING AROUND HERE LATELY?
THAT LITTLE "PUPPY" OF YOURS.

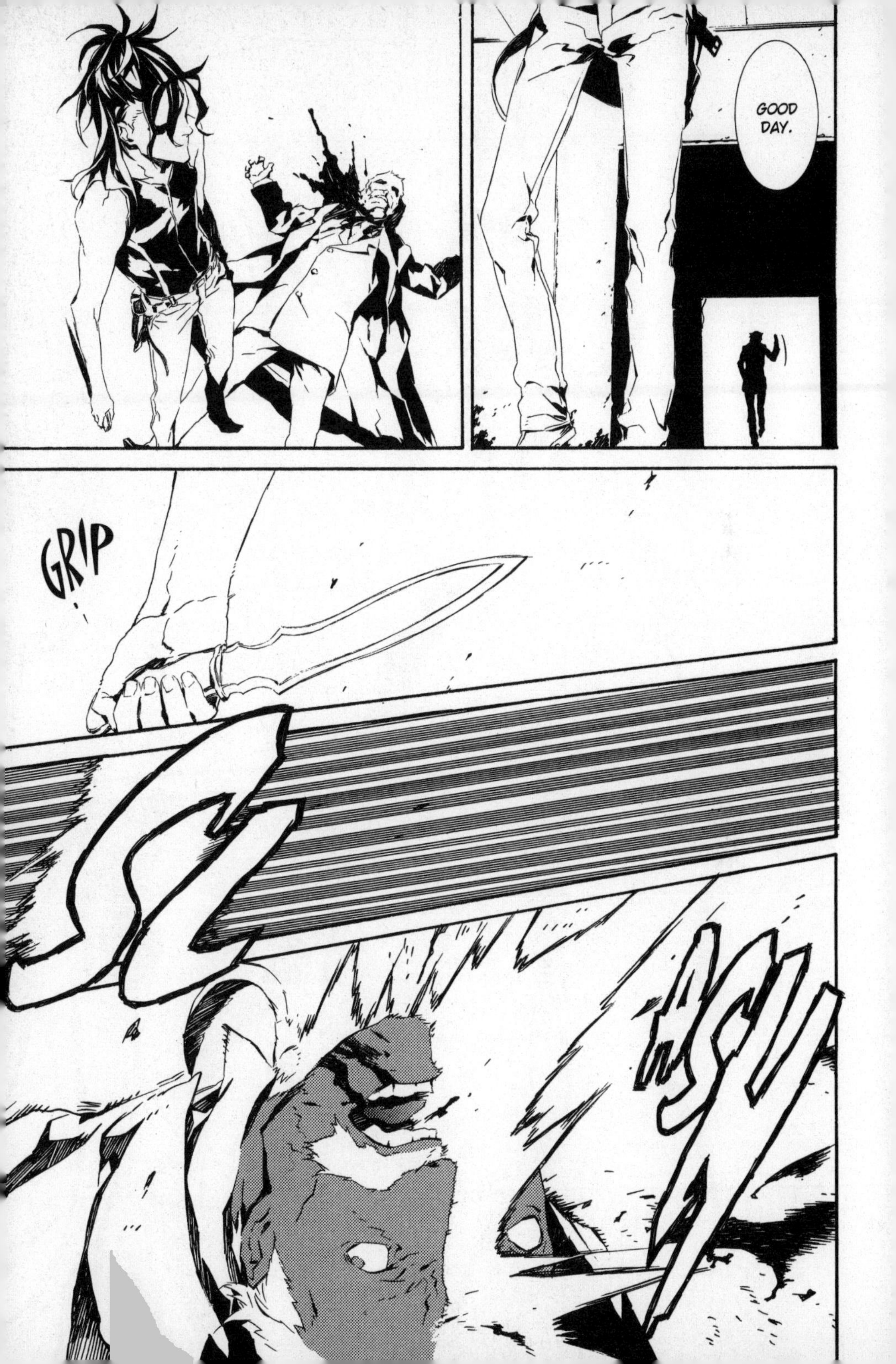
GOOD DAY.
GRIP

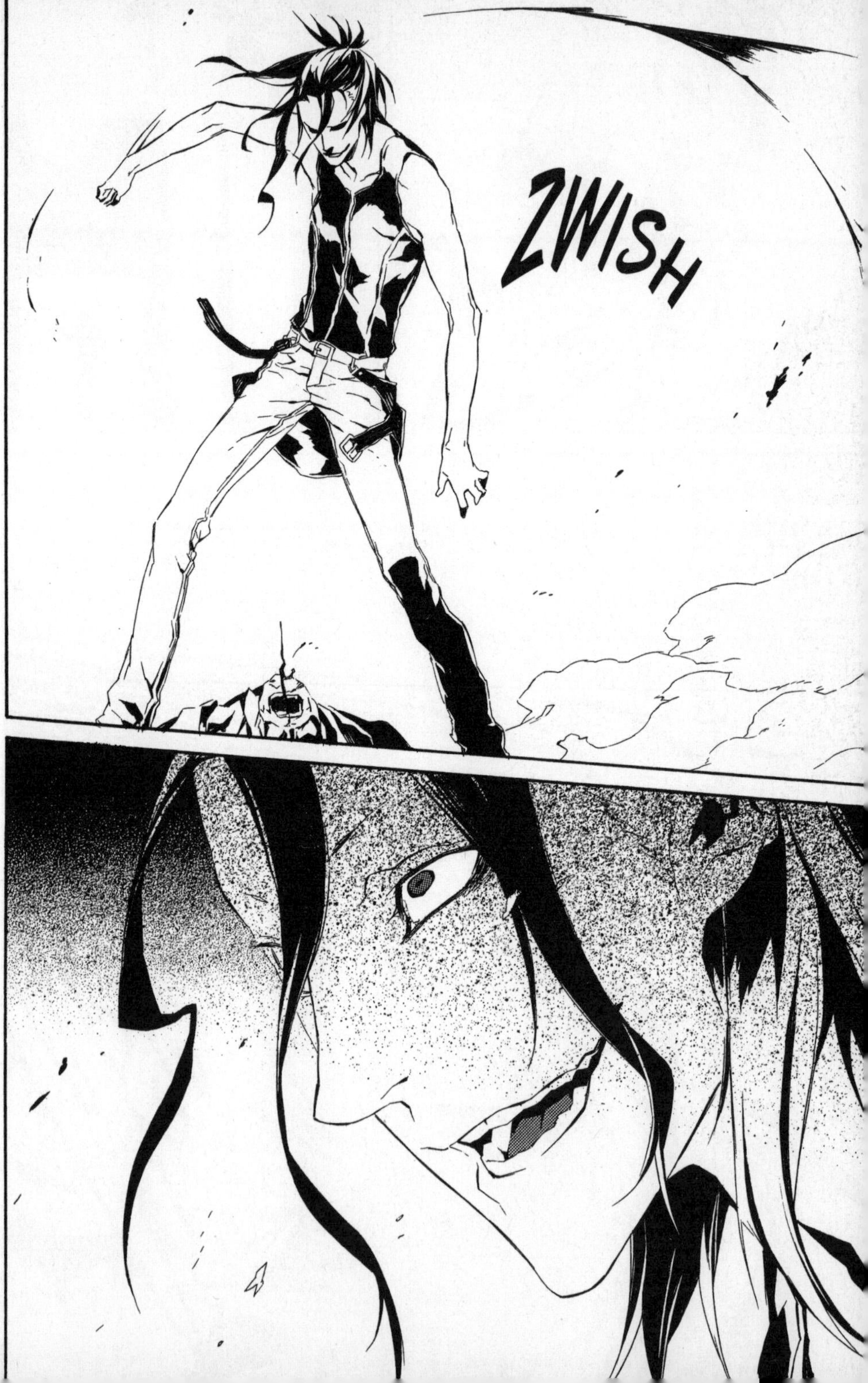
ZWISH

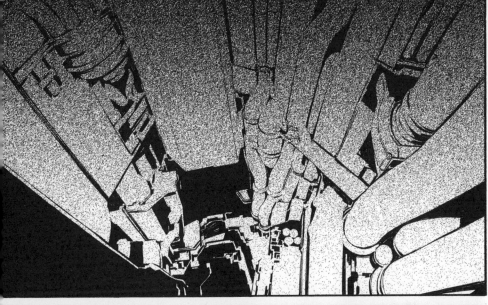

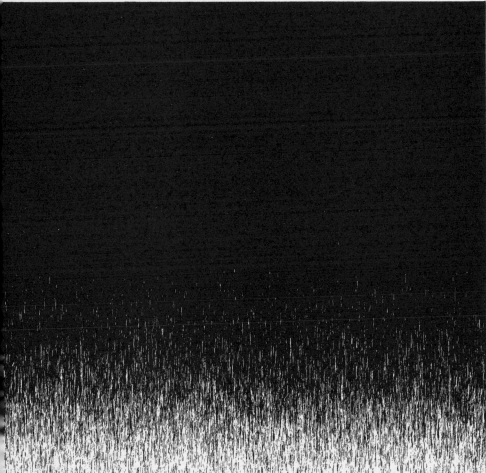

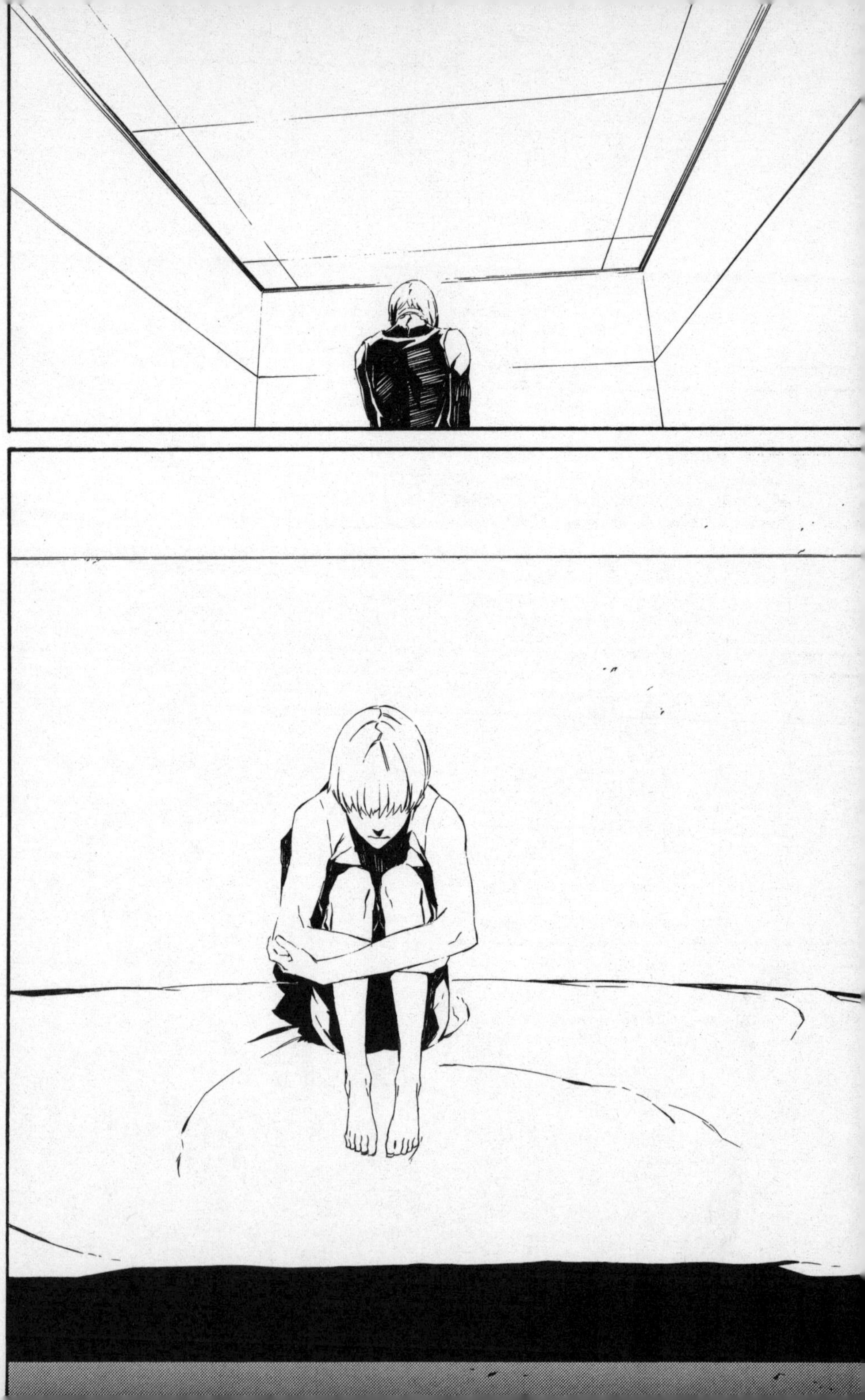

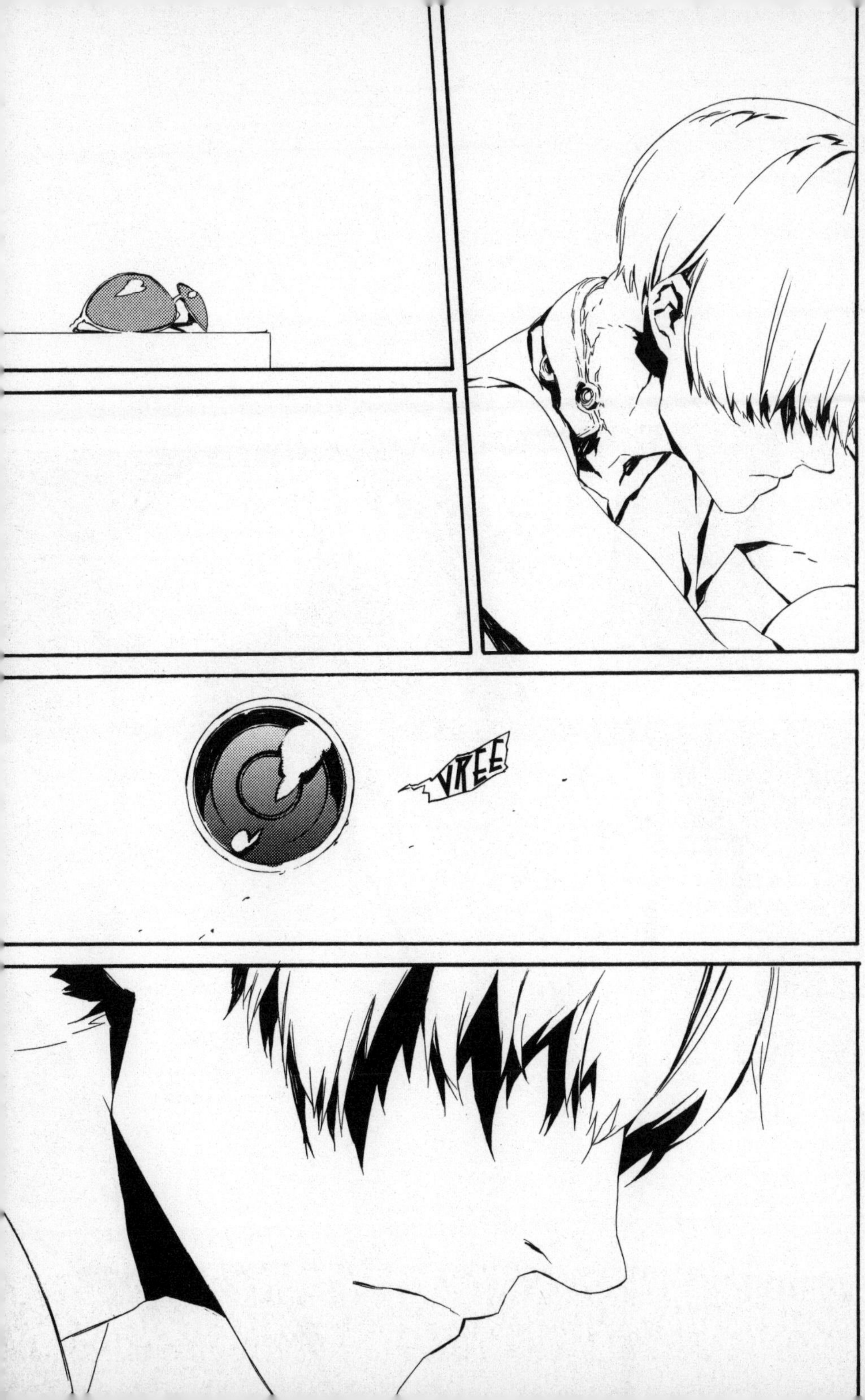
VREE

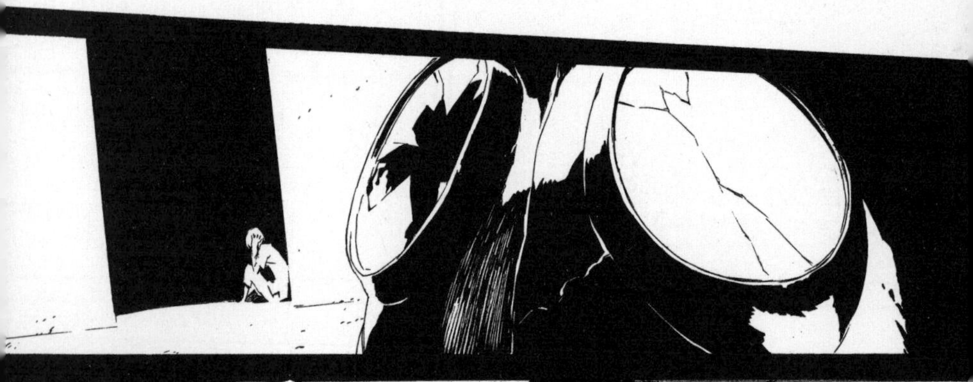

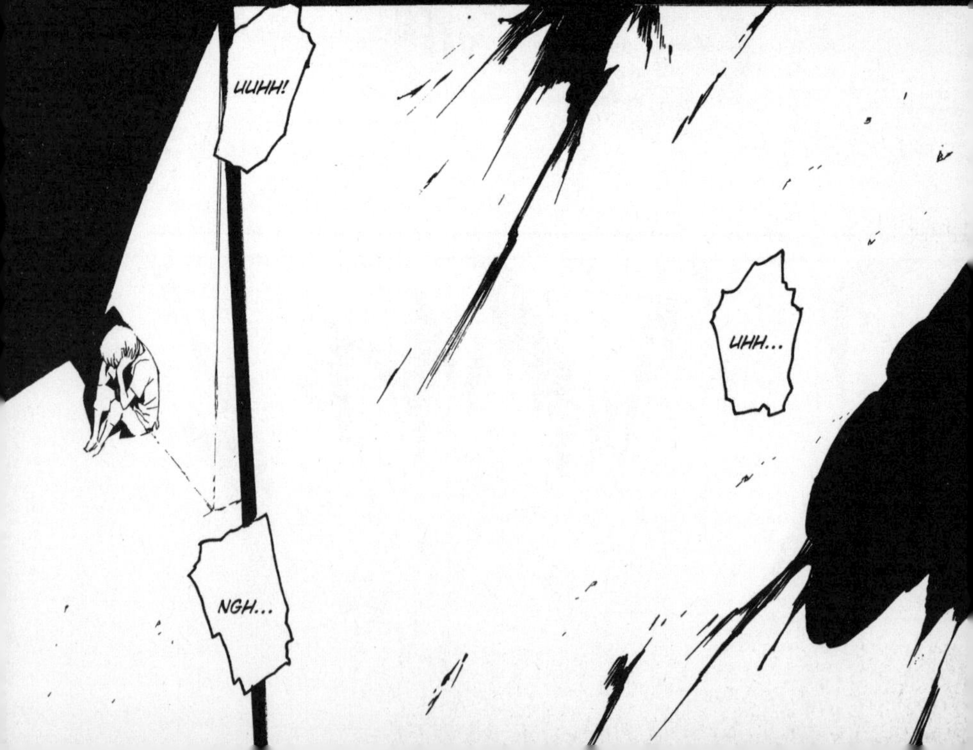
UUHH!
UHH...
NGH...

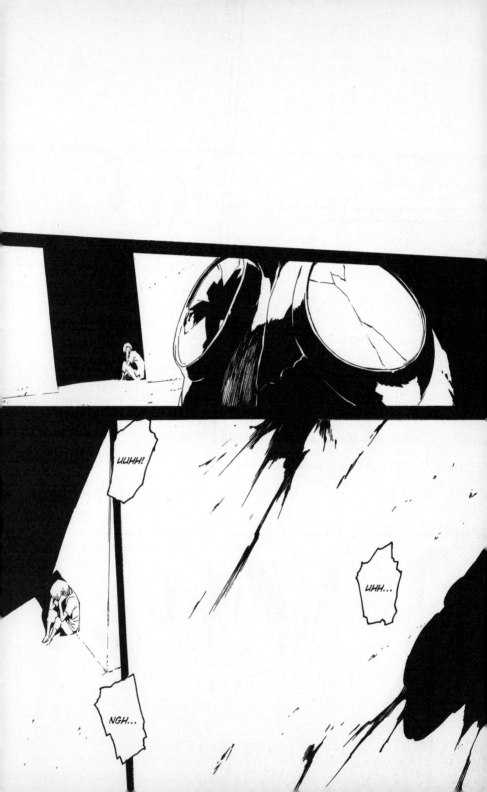

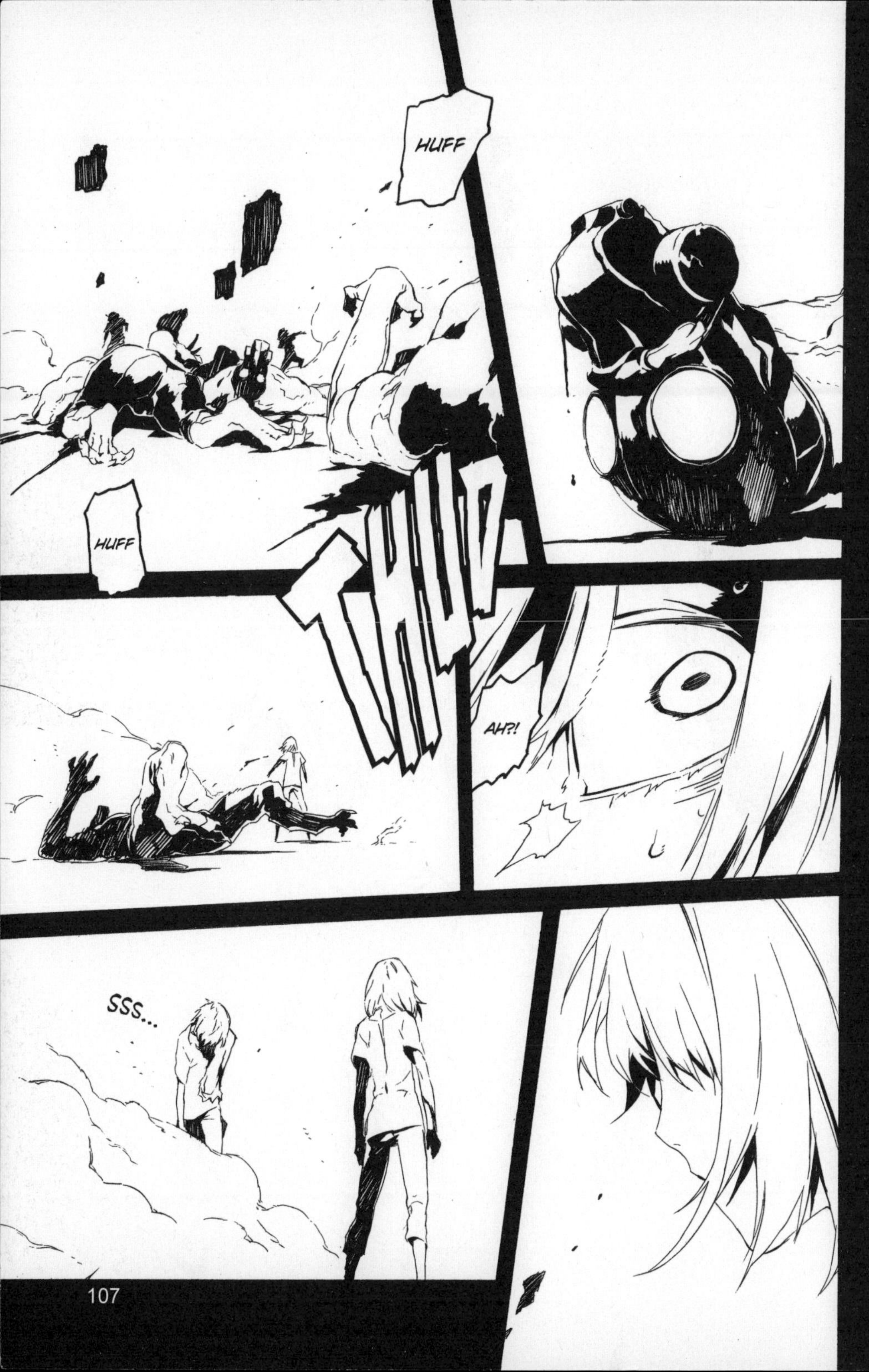
HUFF
HUFF
THUD
AH?!
SSS...

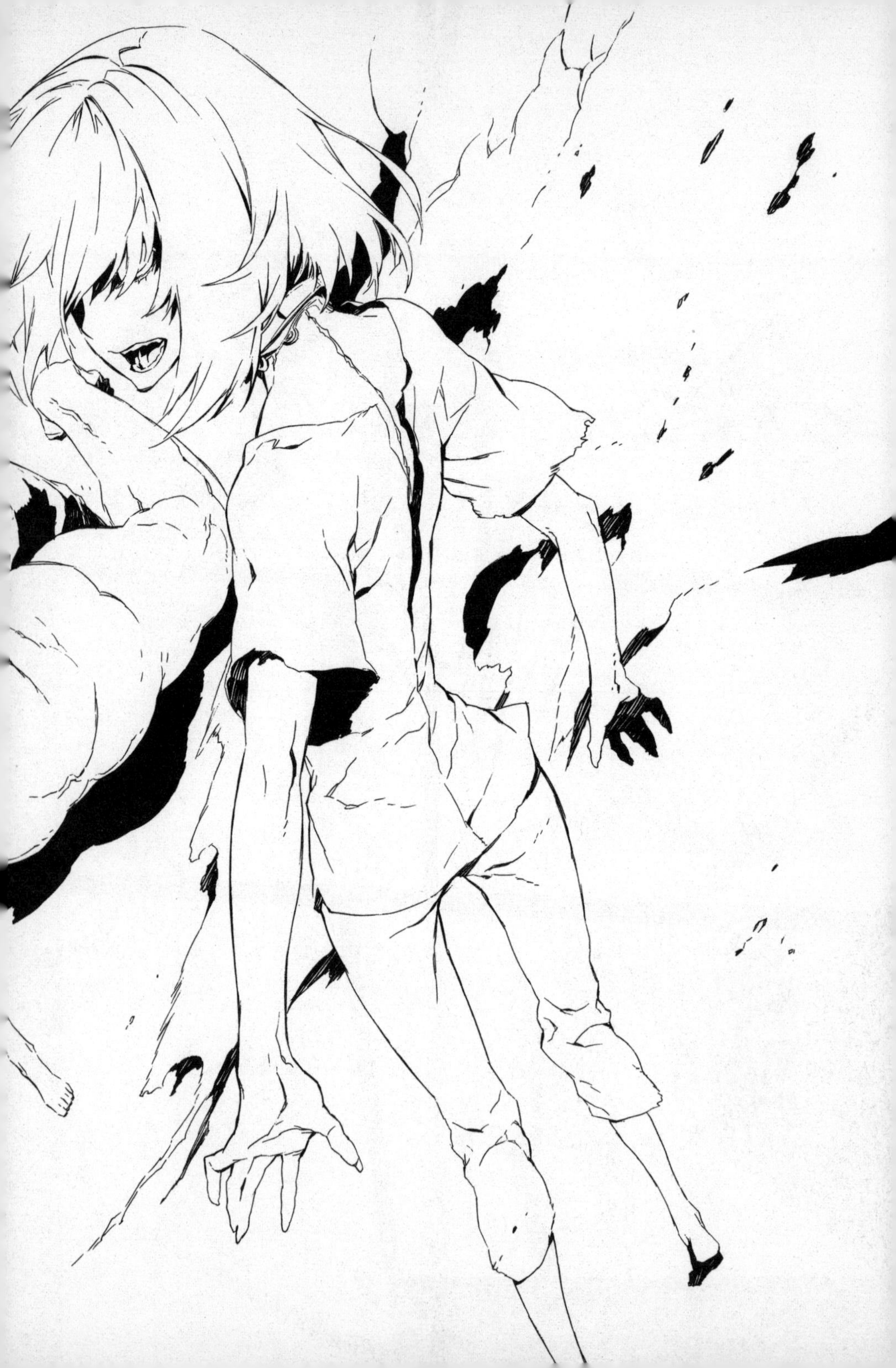

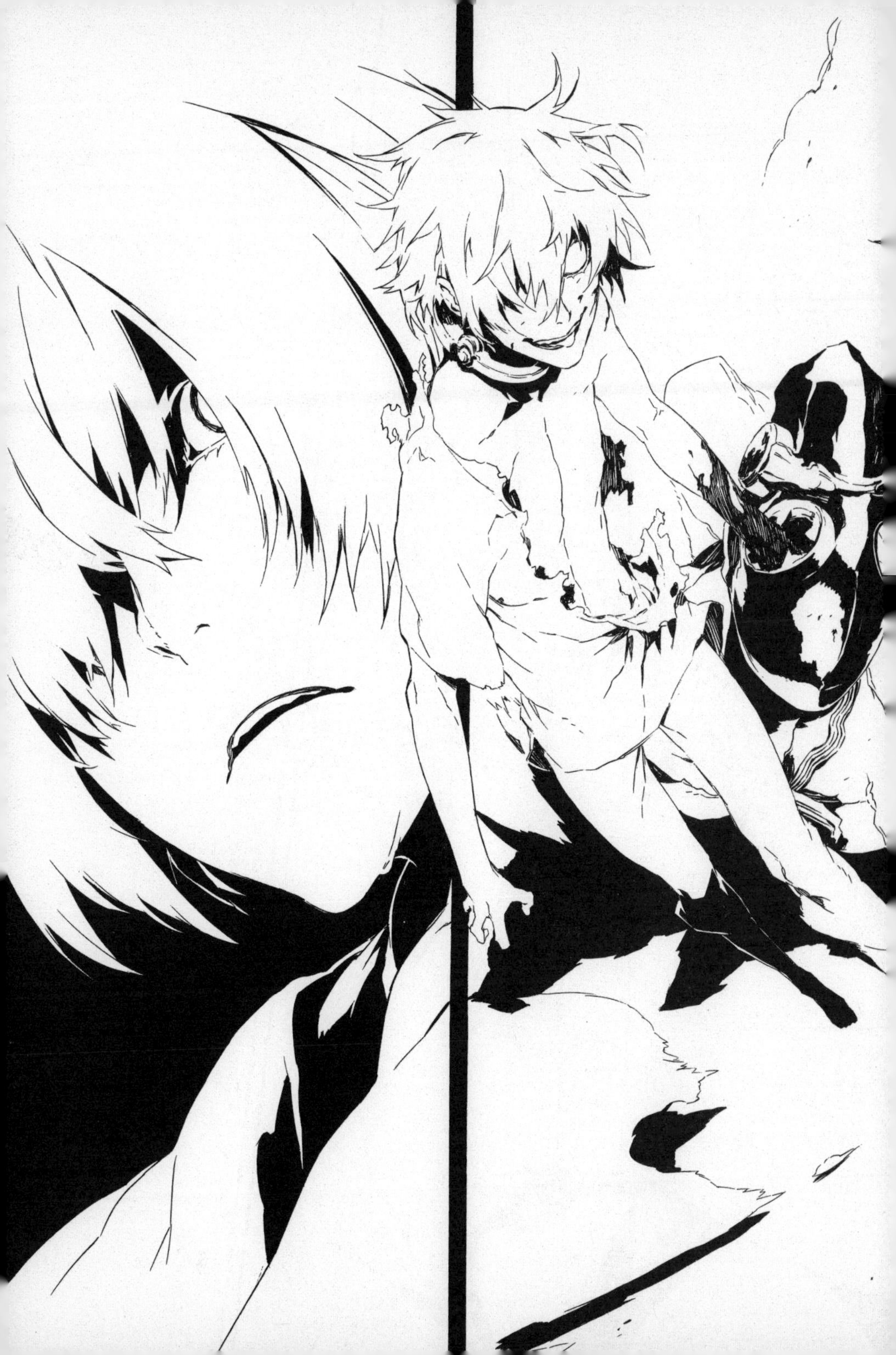

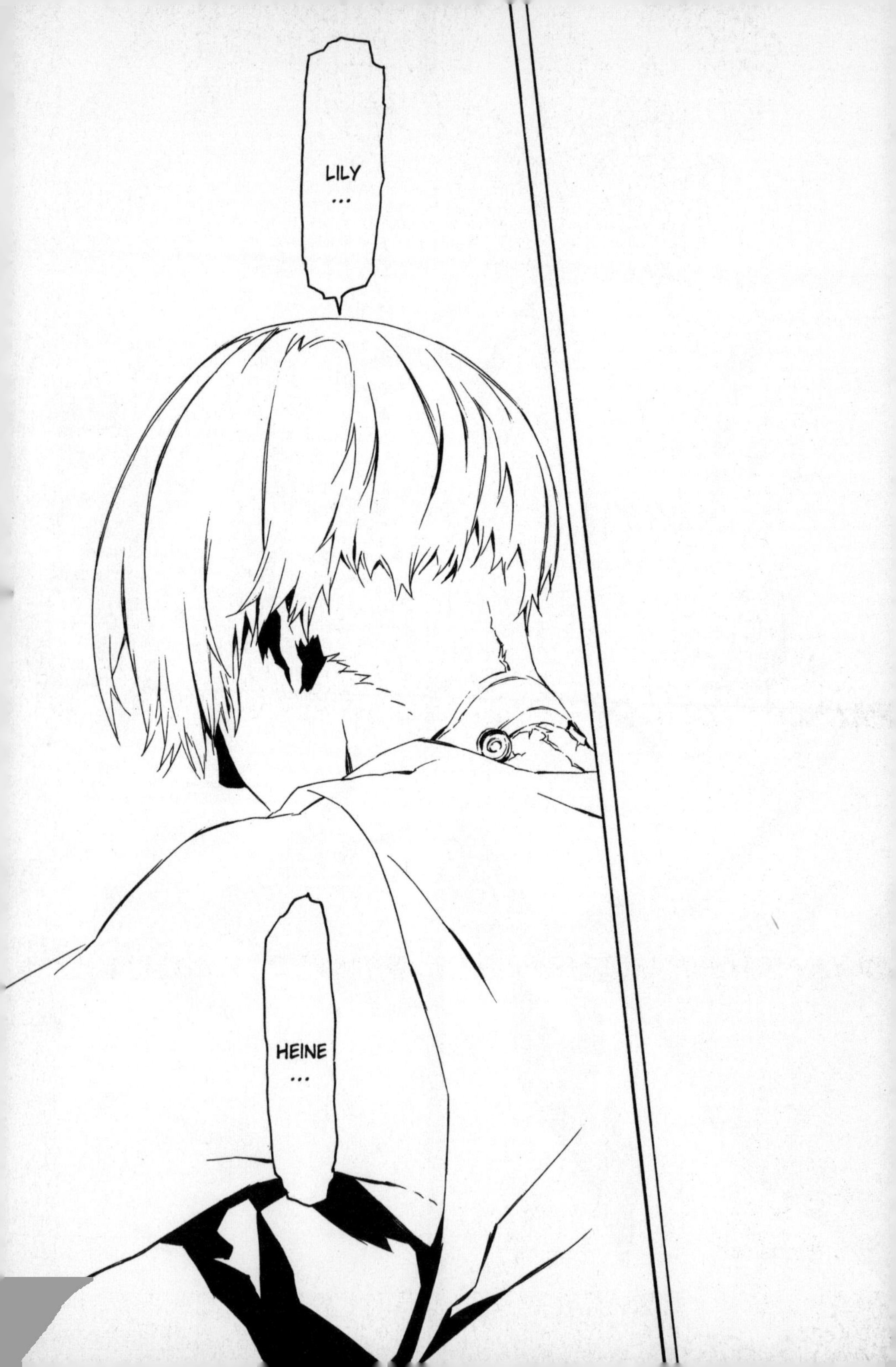
LILY
...
HEINE
...

#34 Envy & Curse

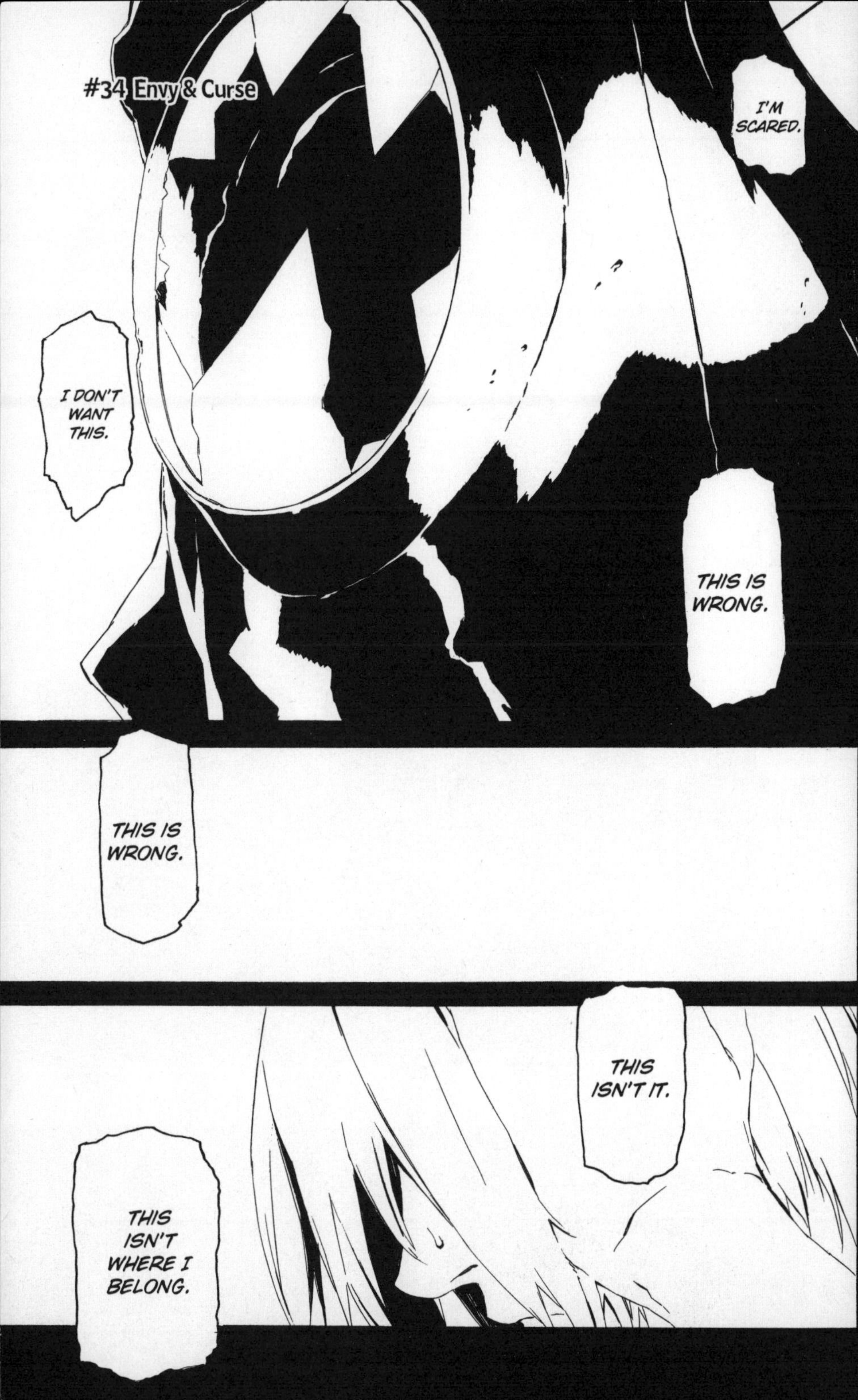
I'M SCARED.
THIS IS WRONG.
I DON'T WANT THIS.
THIS IS WRONG.
THIS ISN'T IT.
THIS ISN'T WHERE I BELONG.

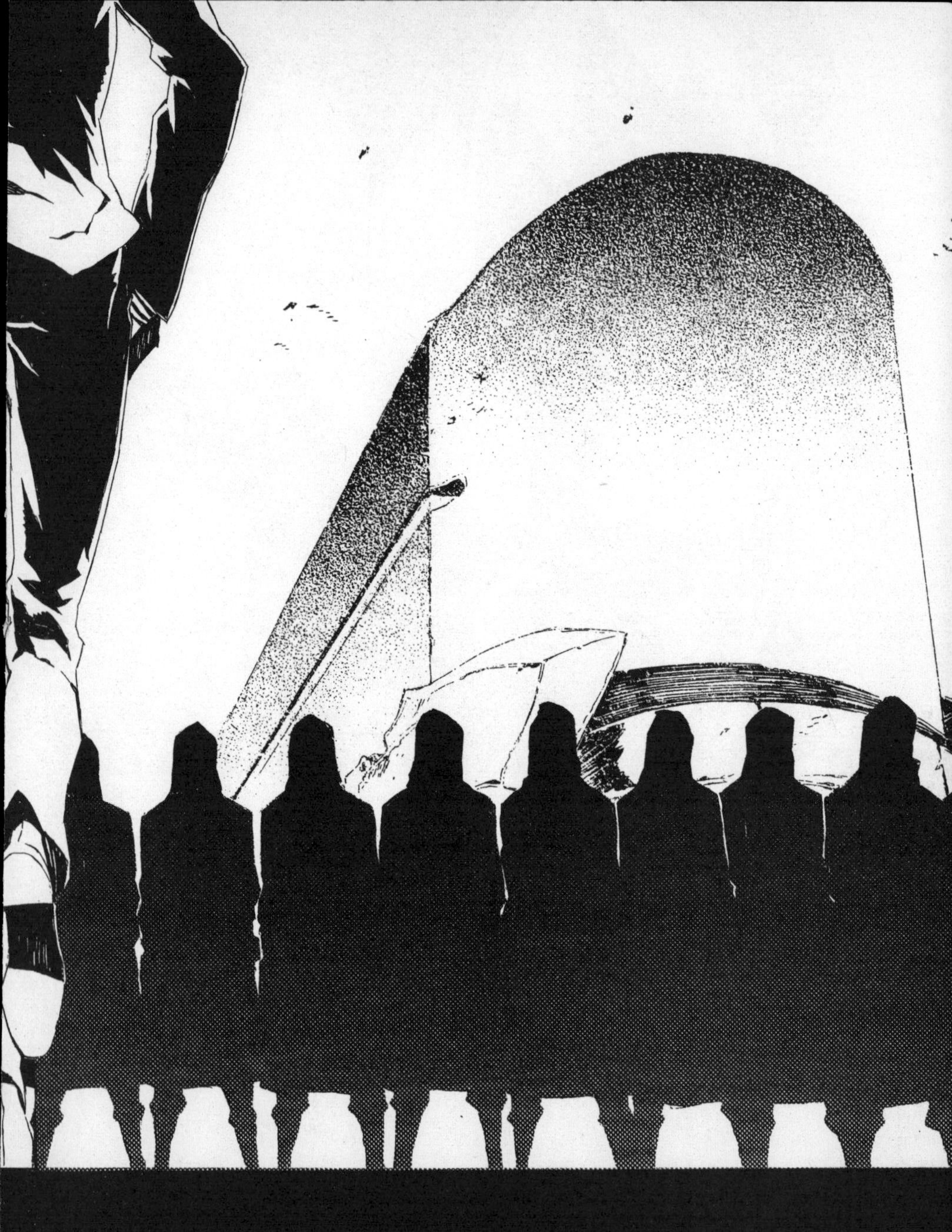

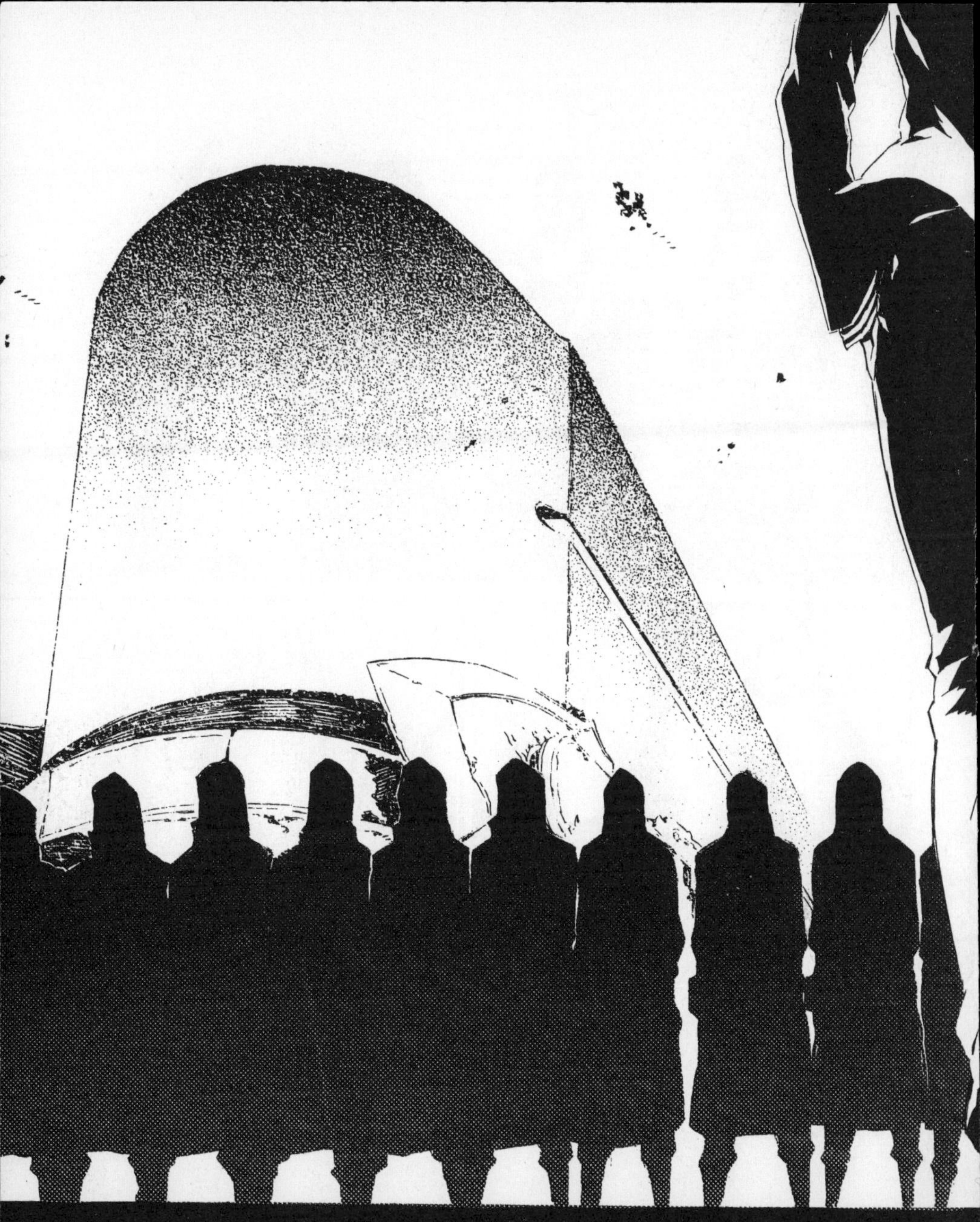

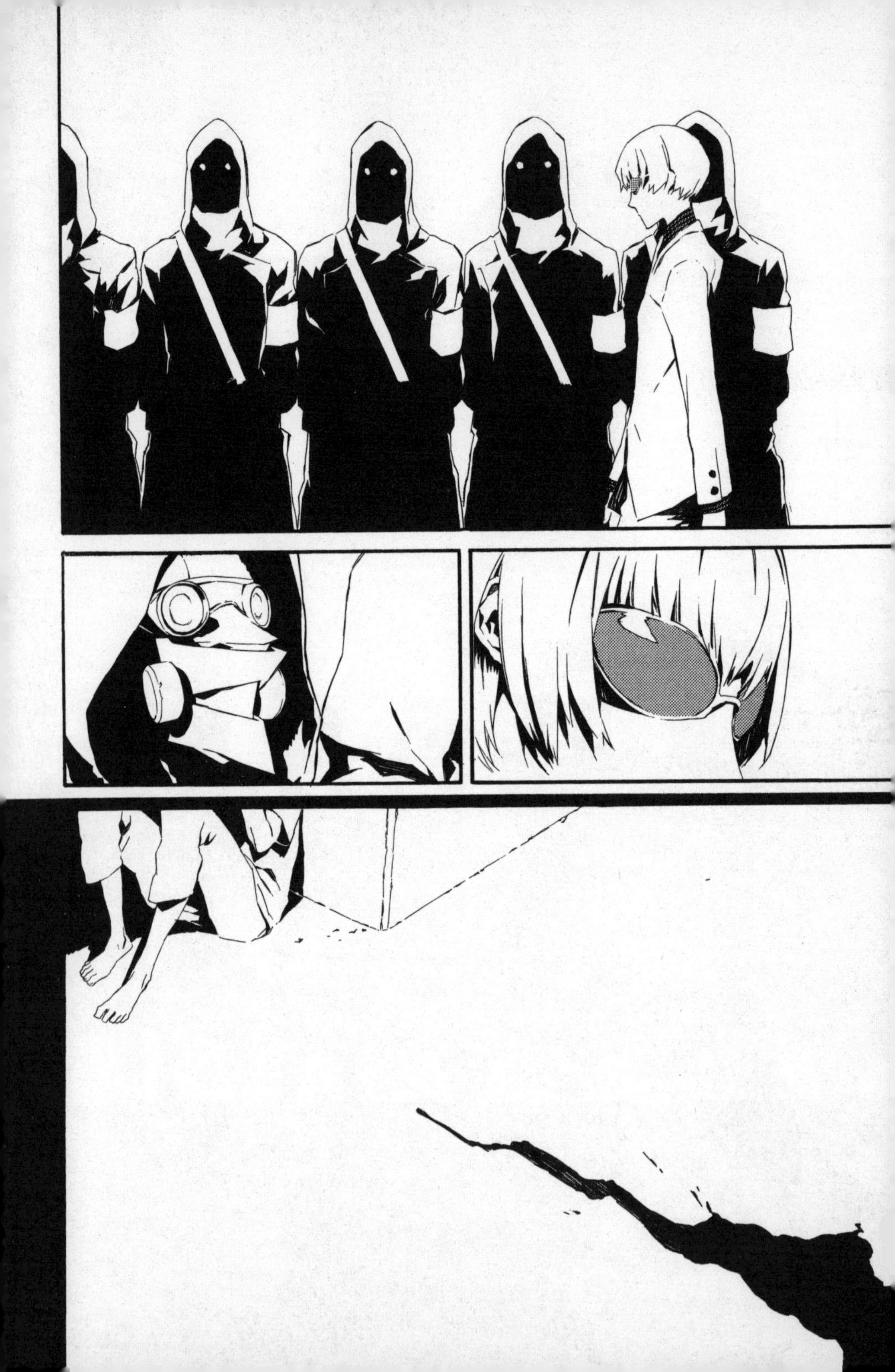

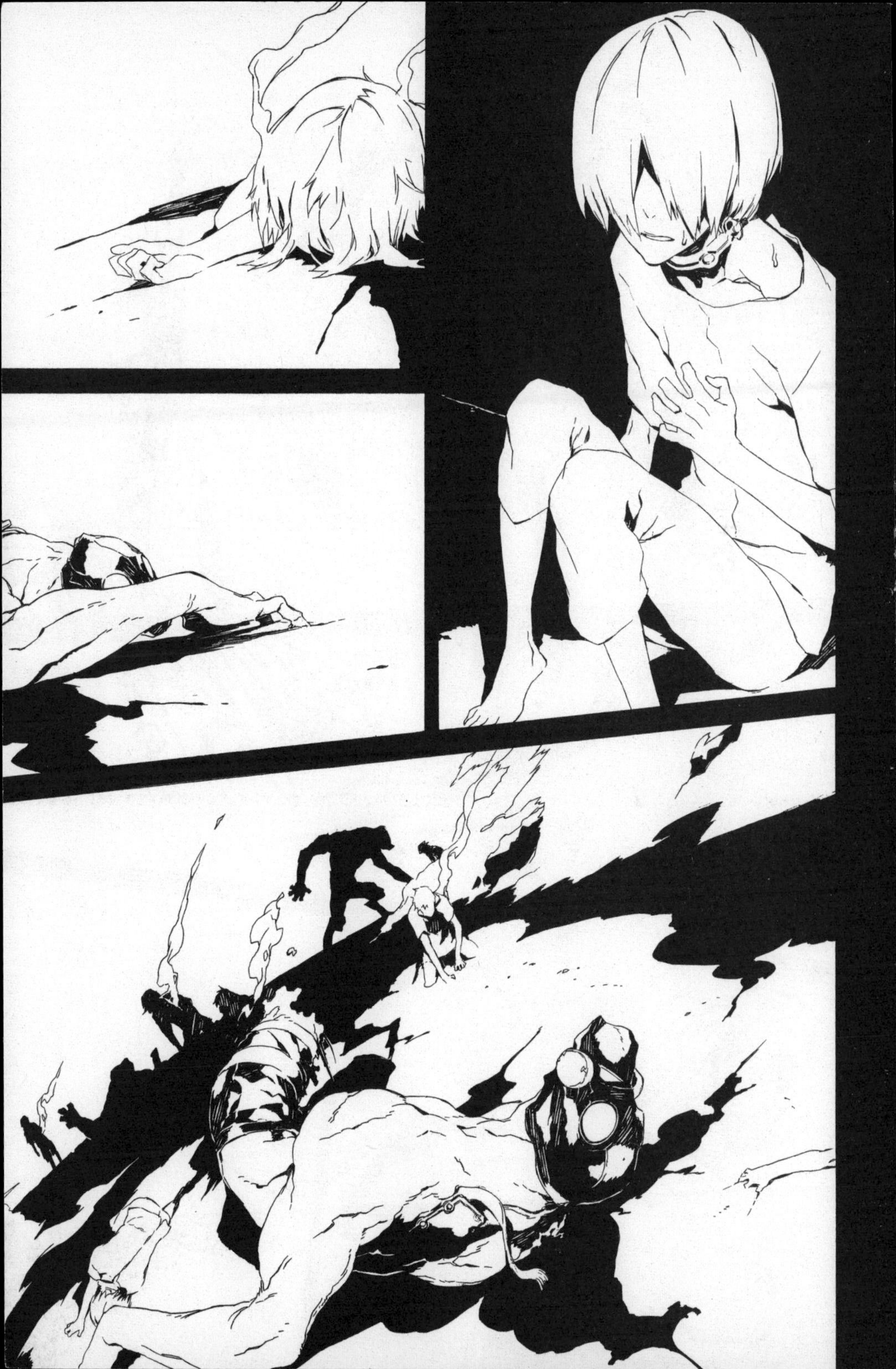

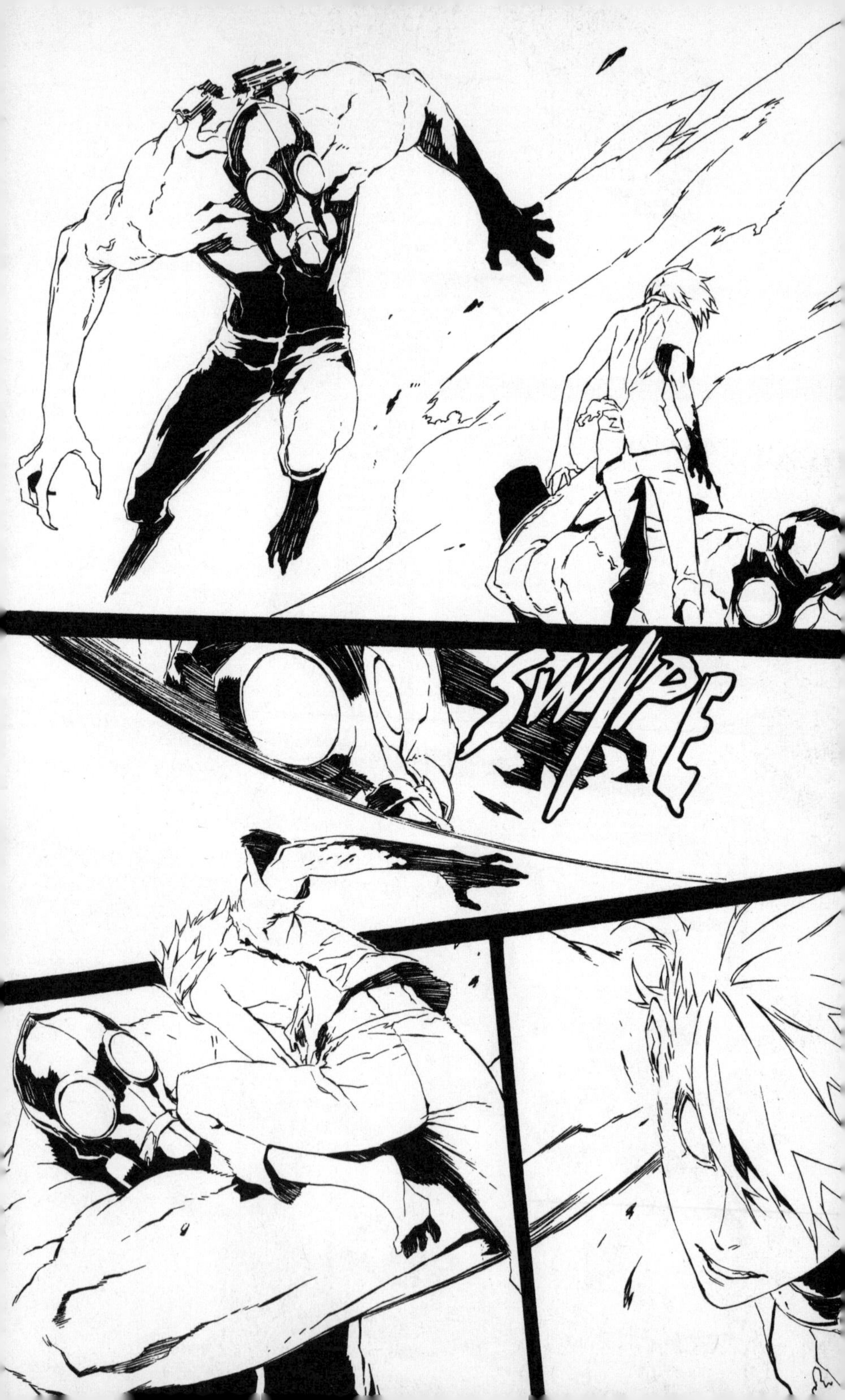
SWIPE

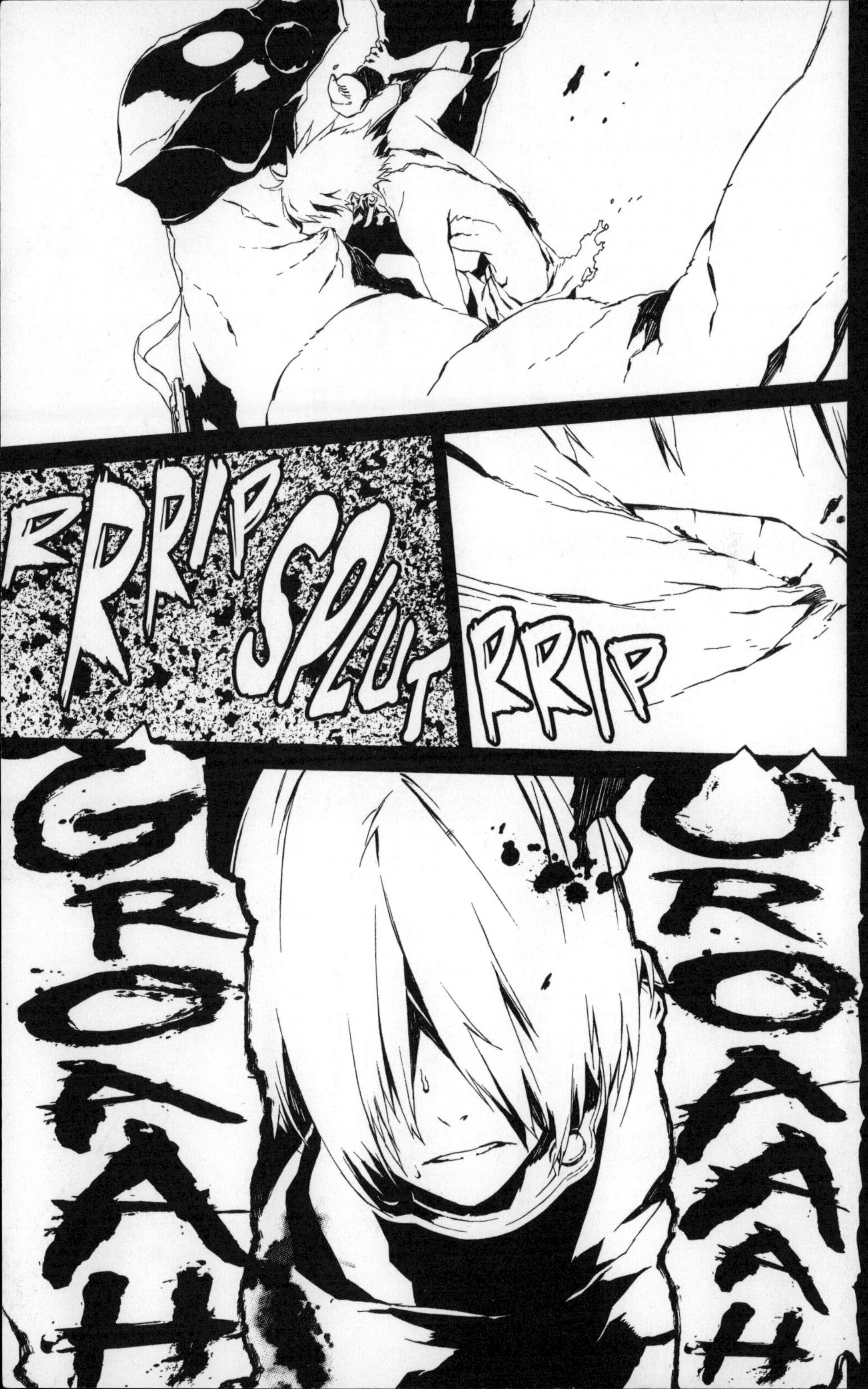
RRIP
RRIP
SPLUT
UROAAAH
GROAAH

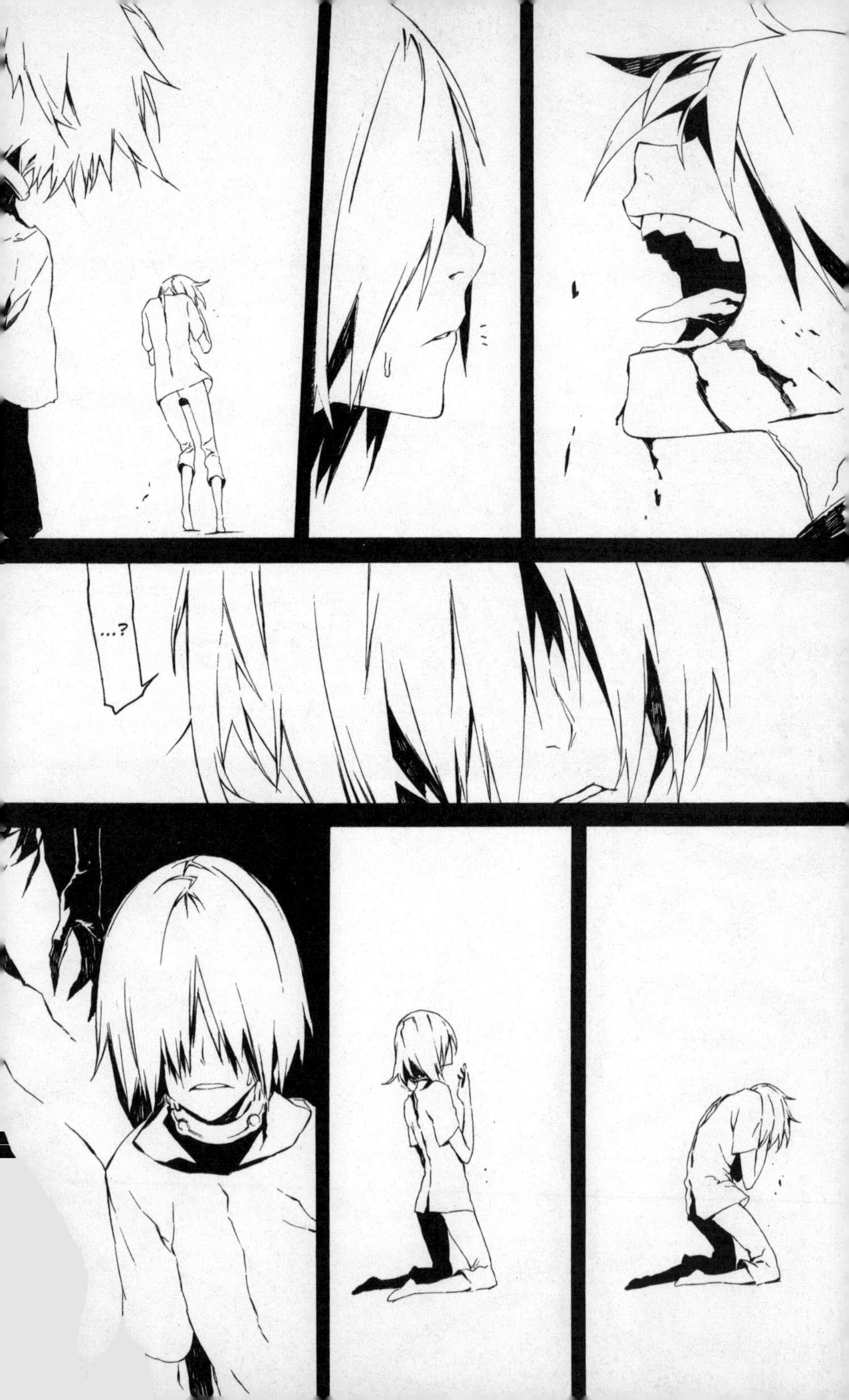
...?

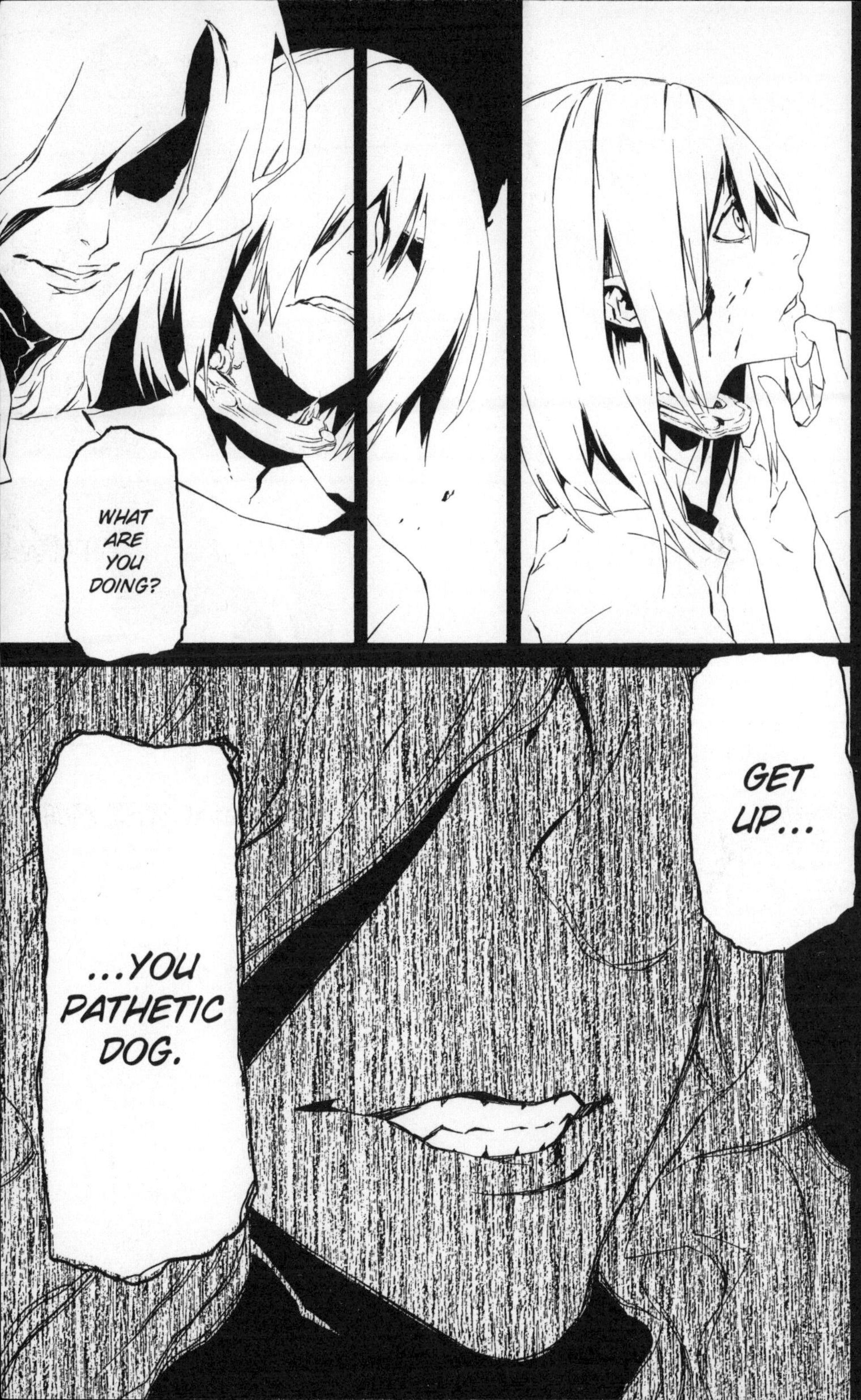
WHAT ARE YOU DOING?
GET UP...
...YOU PATHETIC DOG.

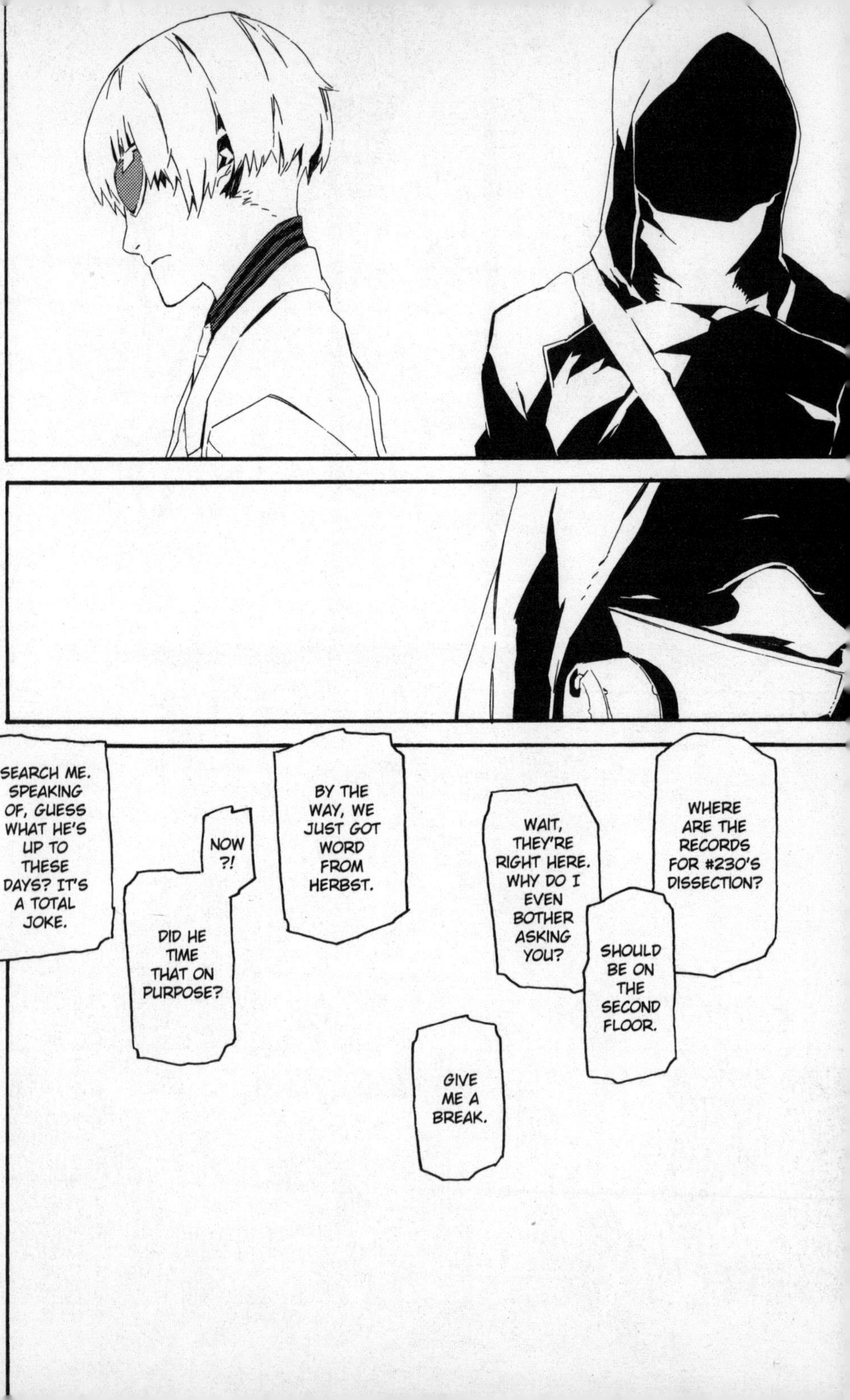
WHERE ARE THE RECORDS FOR #230'S DISSECTION?
SHOULD BE ON THE SECOND FLOOR.
WAIT, THEY'RE RIGHT HERE. WHY DO I EVEN BOTHER ASKING YOU?
GIVE ME A BREAK.
BY THE WAY, WE JUST GOT WORD FROM HERBST.
NOW?!
DID HE TIME THAT ON PURPOSE?
SEARCH ME. SPEAKING OF, GUESS WHAT HE'S UP TO THESE DAYS? IT'S A TOTAL JOKE.

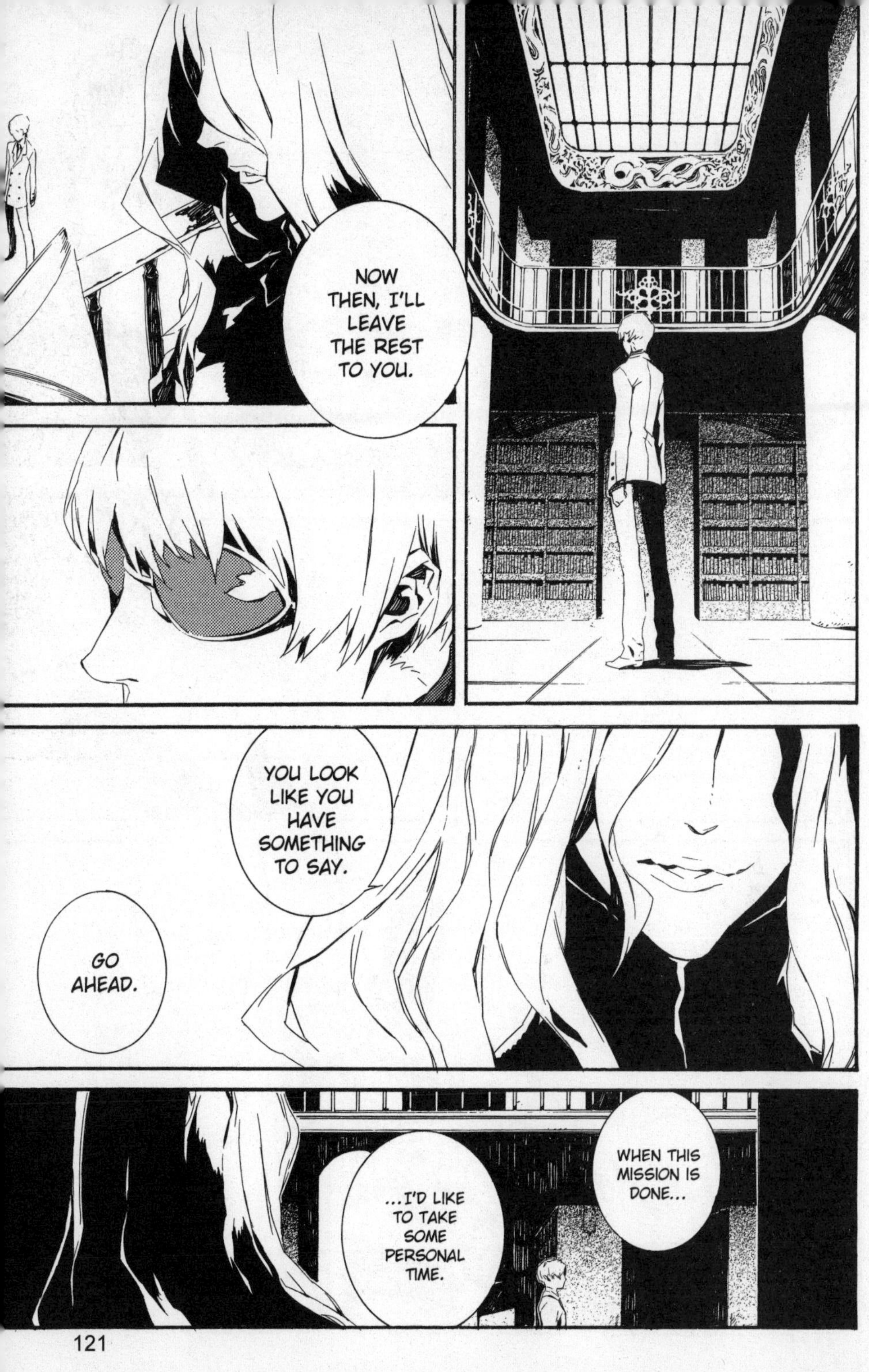
NOW THEN, I'LL LEAVE THE REST TO YOU.
YOU LOOK LIKE YOU HAVE SOMETHING TO SAY.
GO AHEAD.
WHEN THIS MISSION IS DONE...
...I'D LIKE TO TAKE SOME PERSONAL TIME.

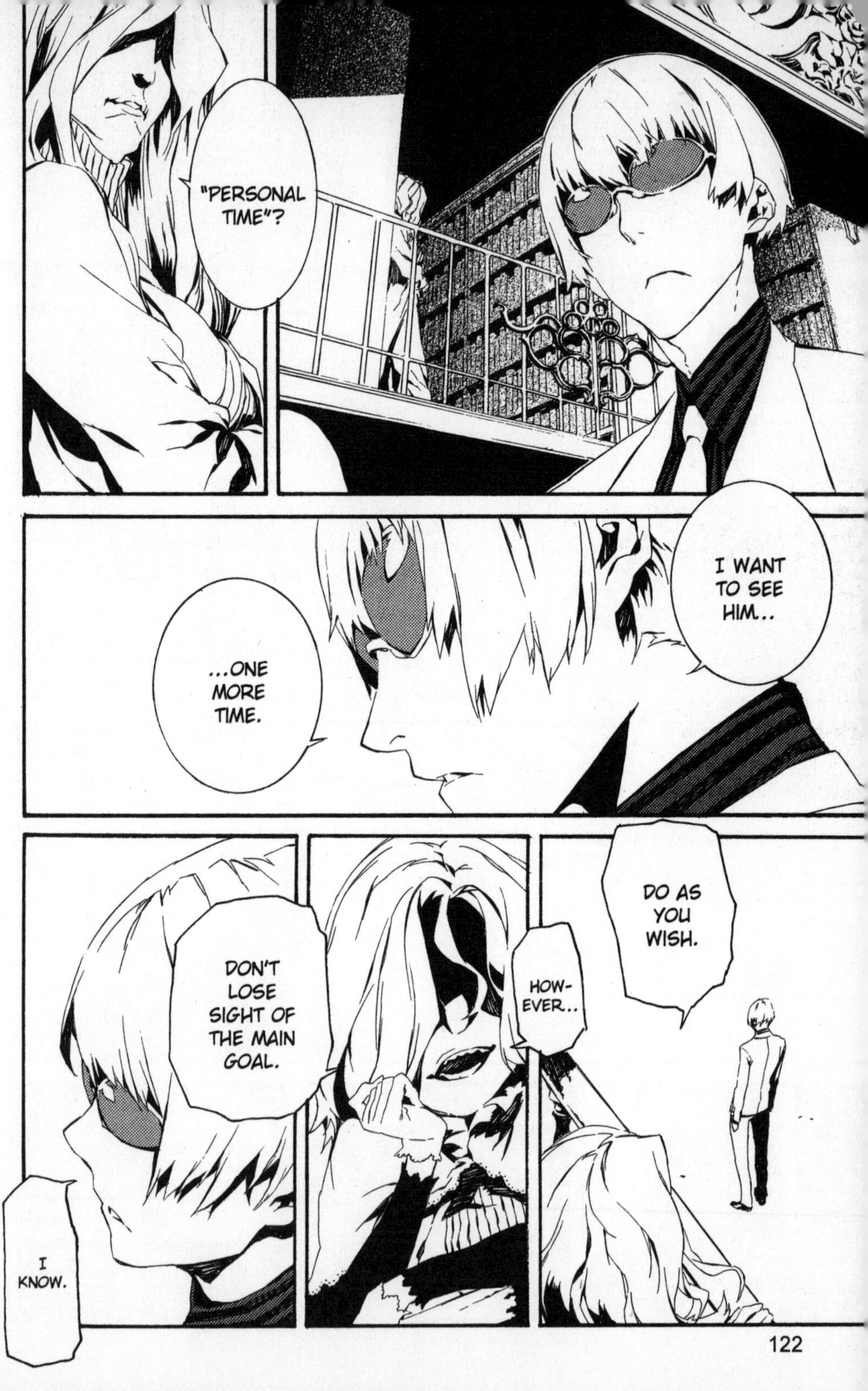
"PERSONAL TIME"?
I WANT TO SEE HIM...
...ONE MORE TIME.
DO AS YOU WISH.
HOW-EVER...
DON'T LOSE SIGHT OF THE MAIN GOAL.
I KNOW.

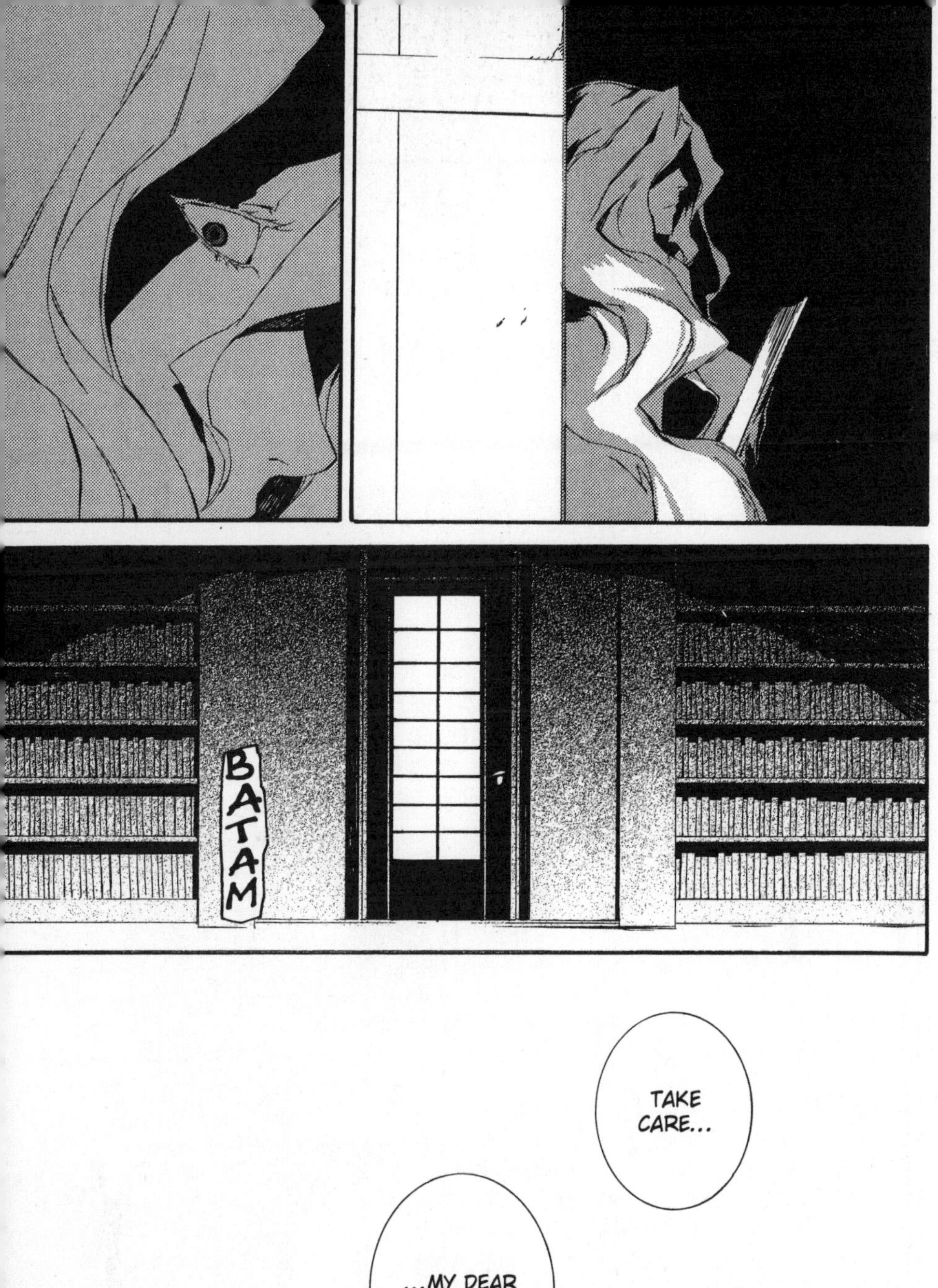
BATAM
TAKE CARE...
...MY DEAR GIOVANNI.

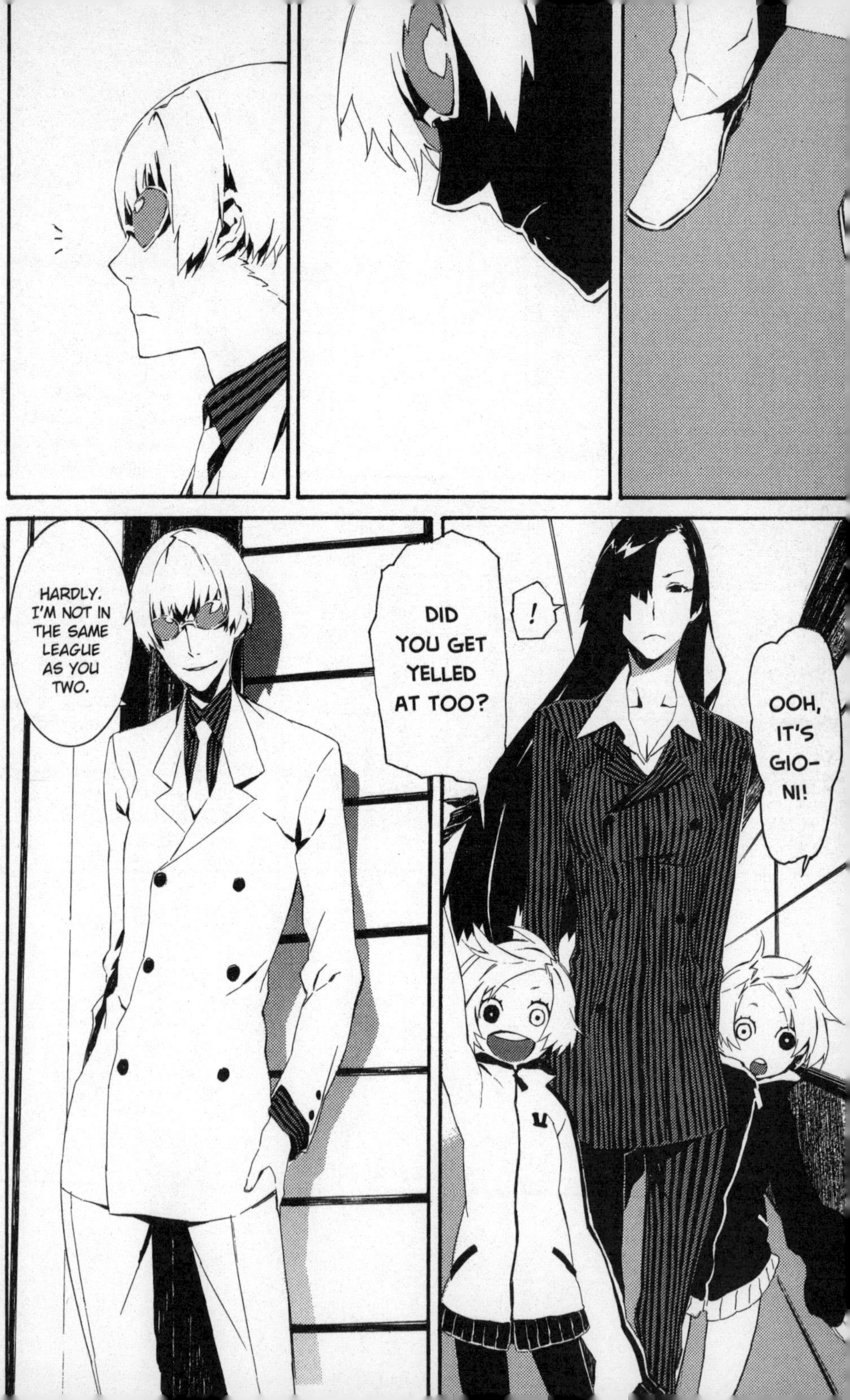
OOH, IT'S GIO-NI!
!
DID YOU GET YELLED AT TOO?
HARDLY. I'M NOT IN THE SAME LEAGUE AS YOU TWO.

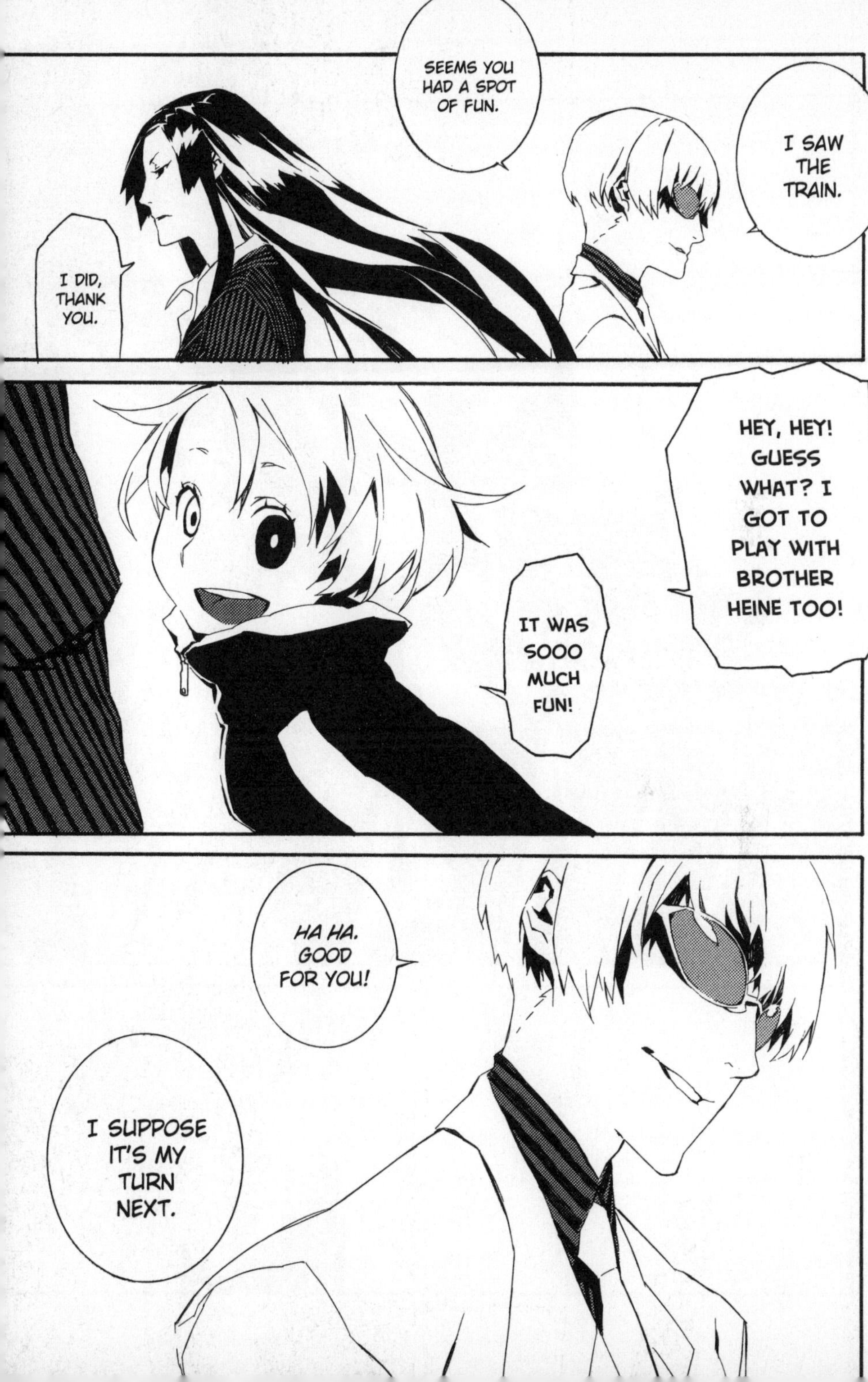
I SAW THE TRAIN.
SEEMS YOU HAD A SPOT OF FUN.
I DID, THANK YOU.
HEY, HEY! GUESS WHAT? I GOT TO PLAY WITH BROTHER HEINE TOO!
IT WAS SOOO MUCH FUN!
HA HA. GOOD FOR YOU!
I SUPPOSE IT'S MY TURN NEXT.

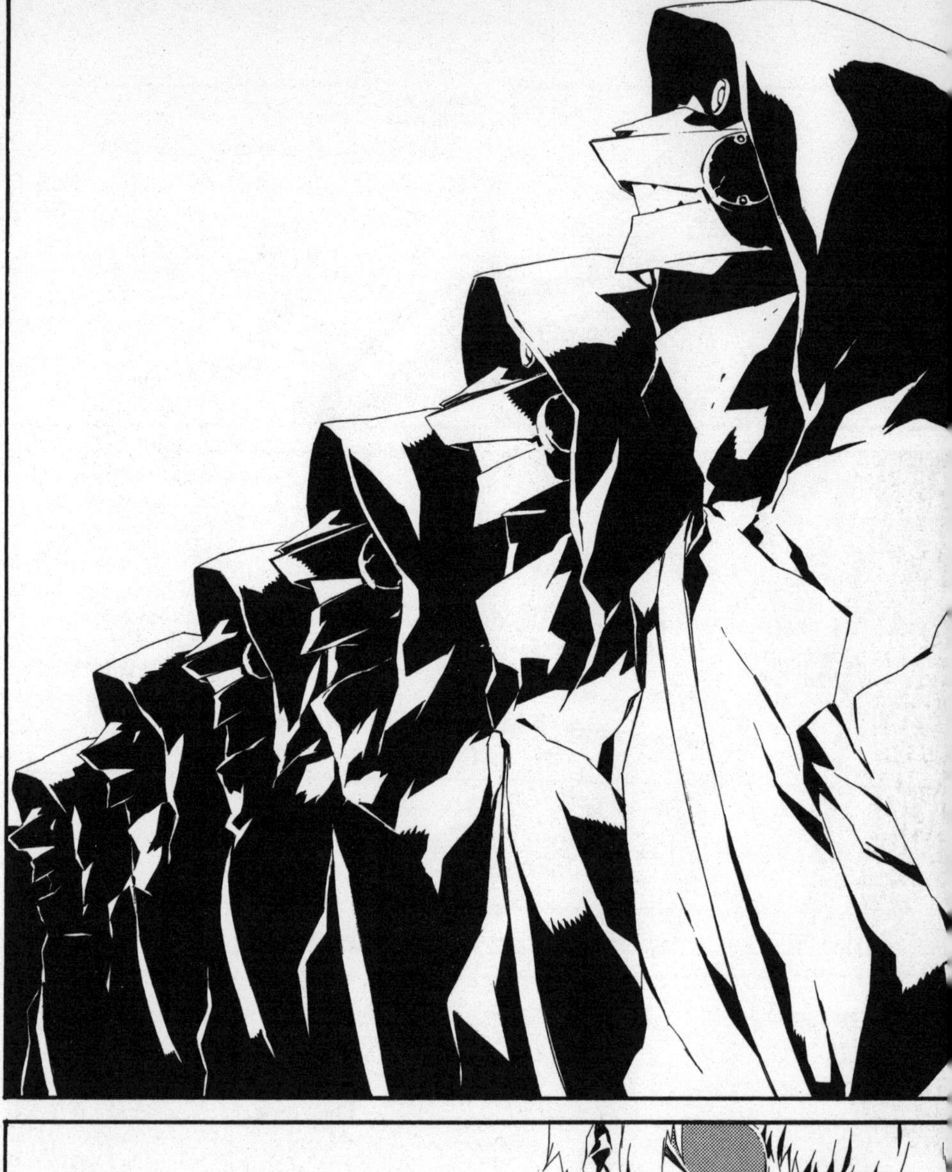
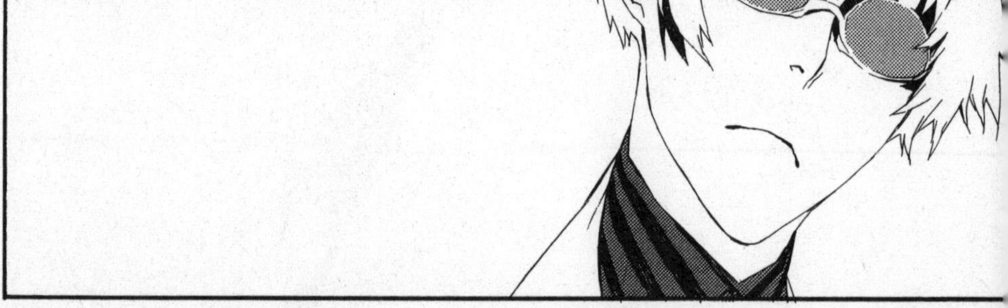

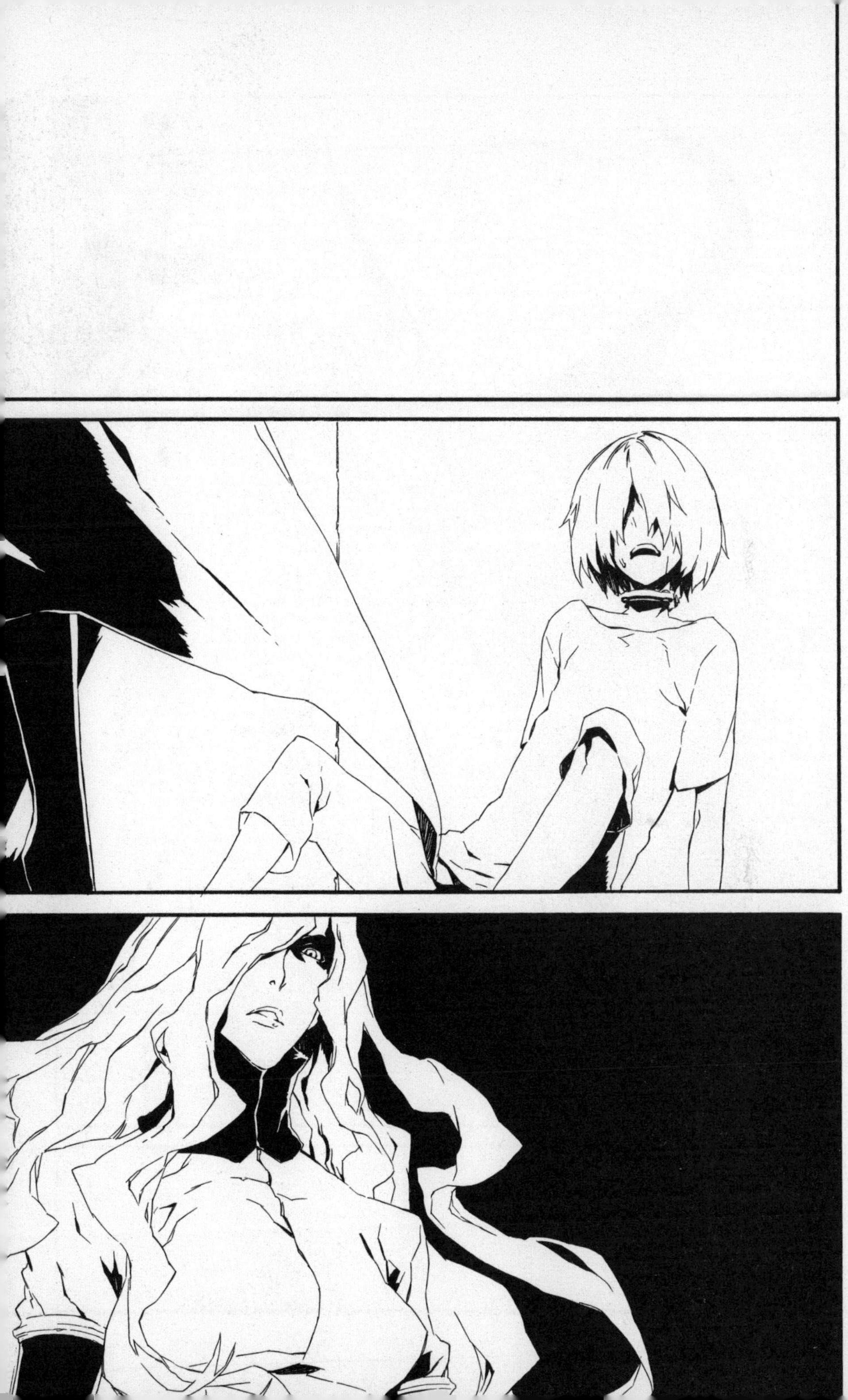

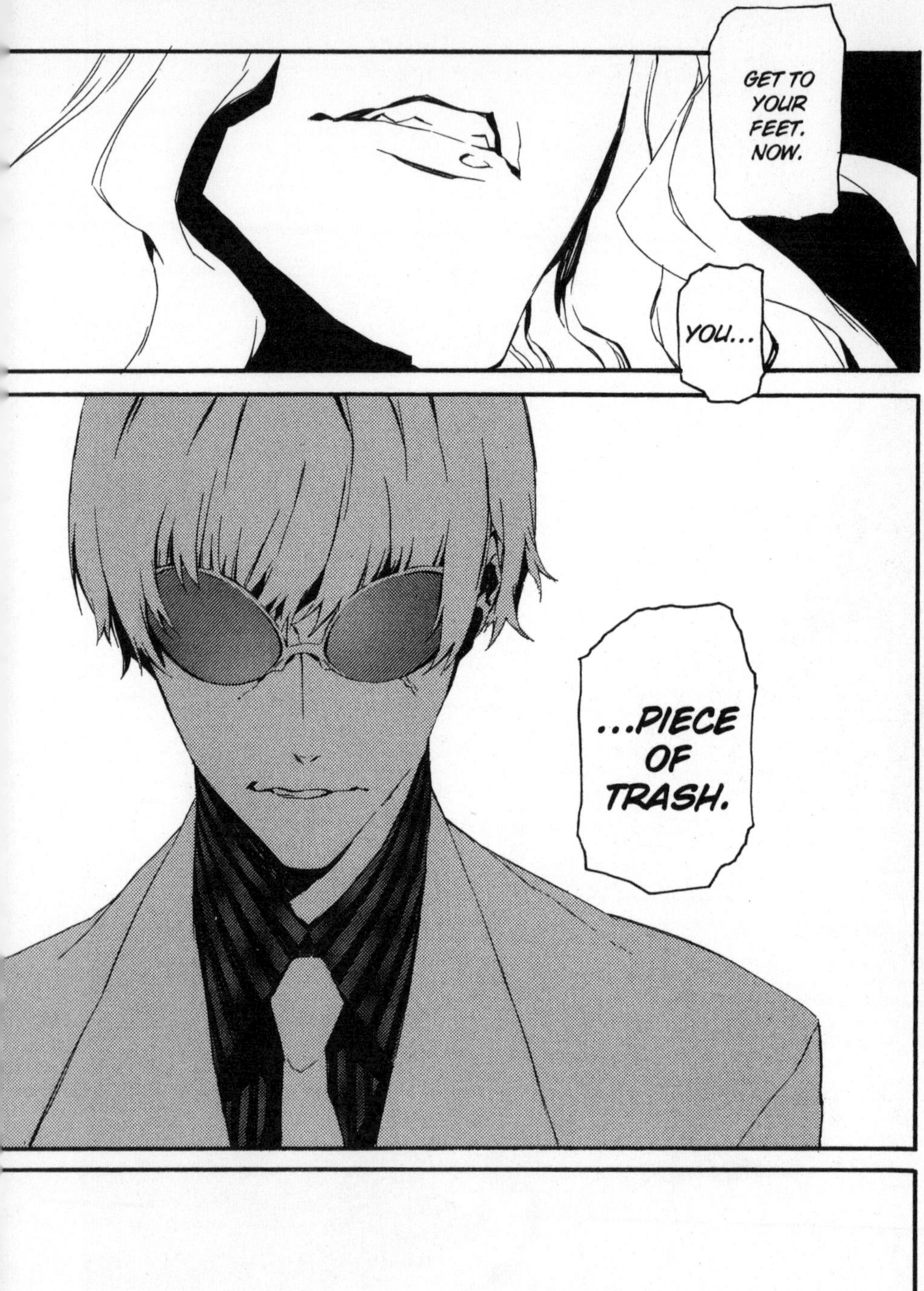
GET TO YOUR FEET. NOW.
YOU...
...PIECE OF TRASH.

#35 Armored Train
& Conductor I

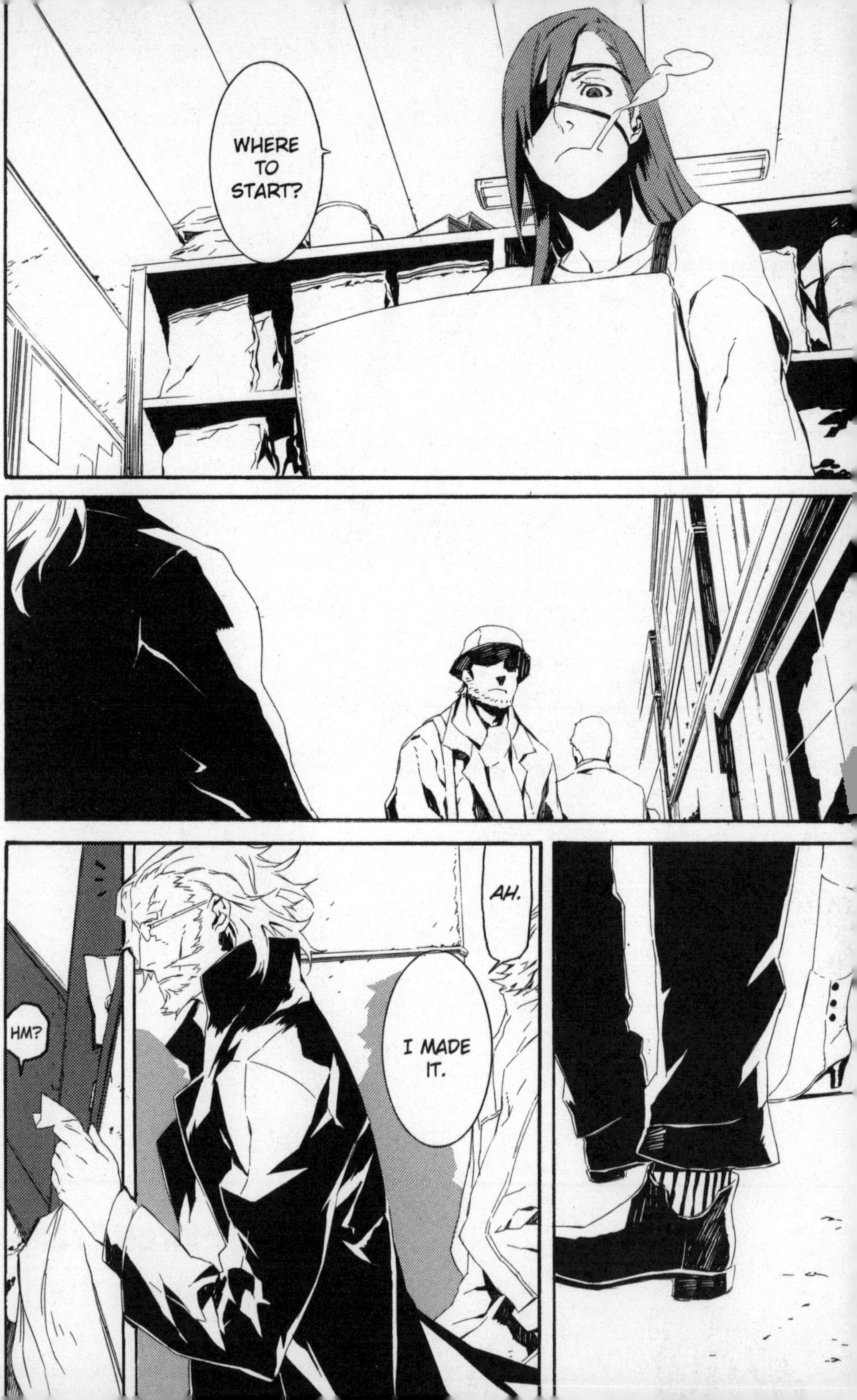
WHERE TO START?
AH.
I MADE IT.
HM?

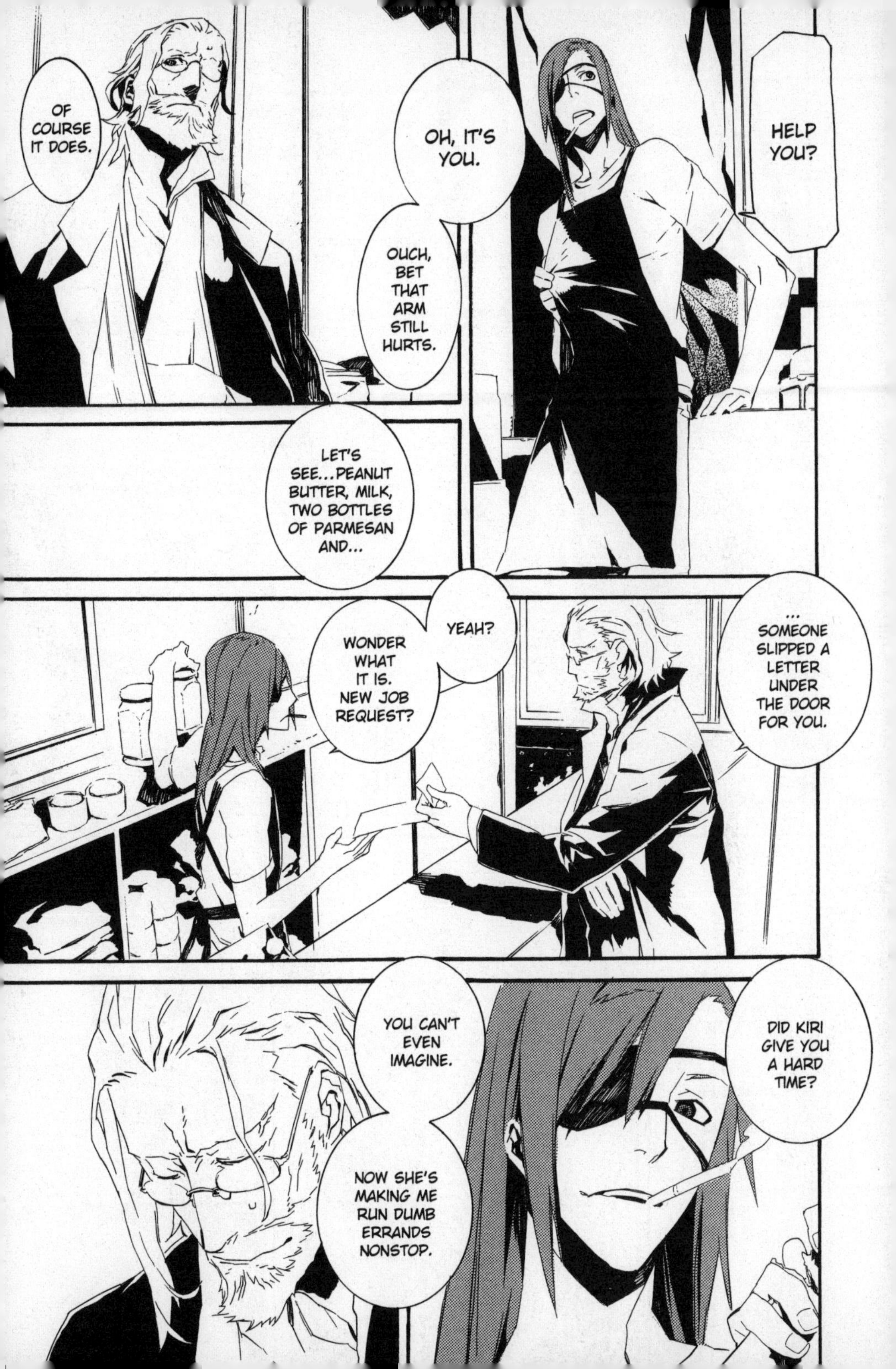
HELP YOU?
OH, IT'S YOU.
OUCH, BET THAT ARM STILL HURTS.
OF COURSE IT DOES.
LET'S SEE...PEANUT BUTTER, MILK, TWO BOTTLES OF PARMESAN AND...
...SOMEONE SLIPPED A LETTER UNDER THE DOOR FOR YOU.
YEAH?
WONDER WHAT IT IS. NEW JOB REQUEST?
DID KIRI GIVE YOU A HARD TIME?
YOU CAN'T EVEN IMAGINE.
NOW SHE'S MAKING ME RUN DUMB ERRANDS NONSTOP.

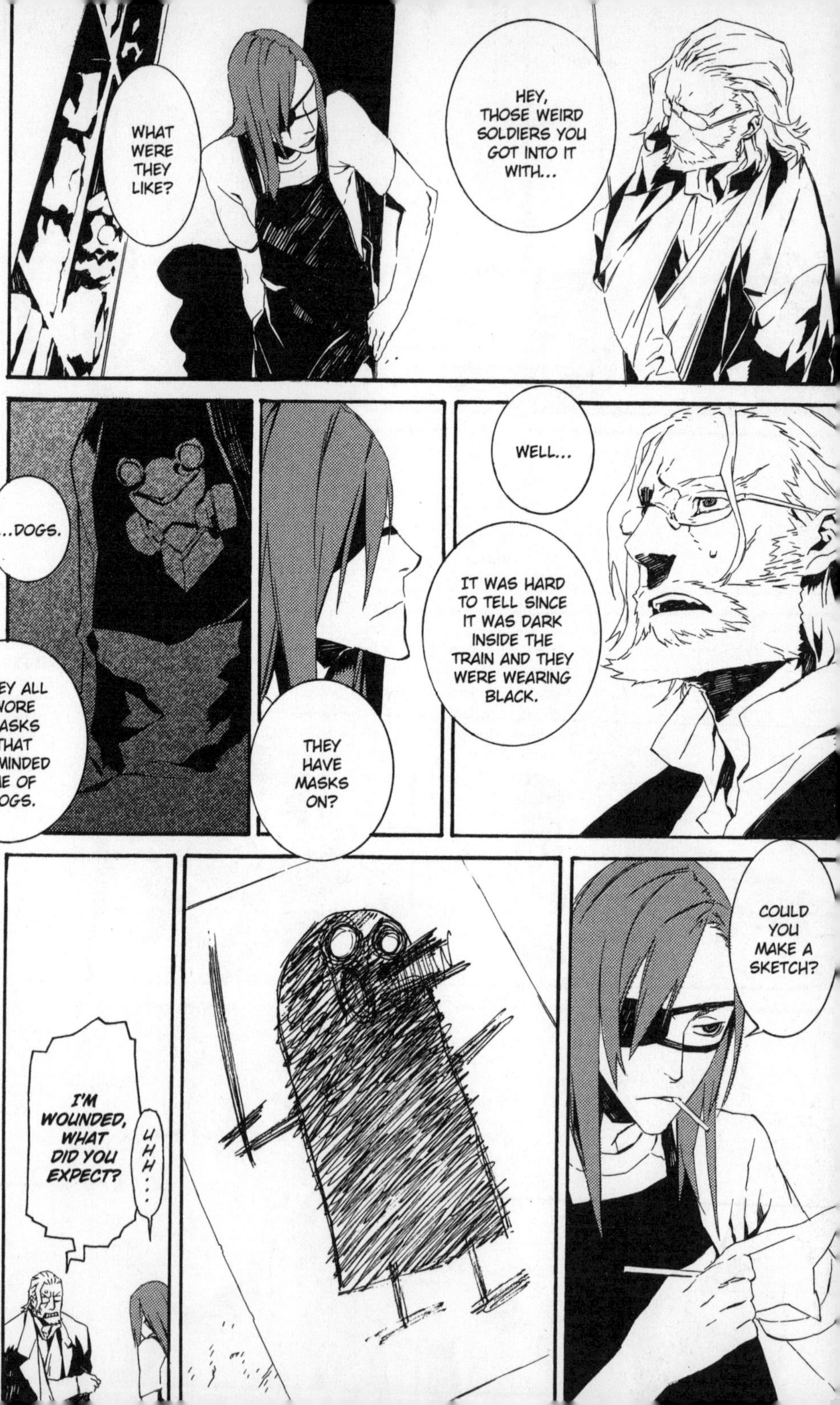
HEY, THOSE WEIRD SOLDIERS YOU GOT INTO IT WITH...
WHAT WERE THEY LIKE?
WELL...
IT WAS HARD TO TELL SINCE IT WAS DARK INSIDE THE TRAIN AND THEY WERE WEARING BLACK.
THEY HAVE MASKS ON?
...DOGS.
THEY ALL WORE MASKS THAT REMINDED ME OF DOGS.
COULD YOU MAKE A SKETCH?
UHH...
I'M WOUNDED, WHAT DID YOU EXPECT?

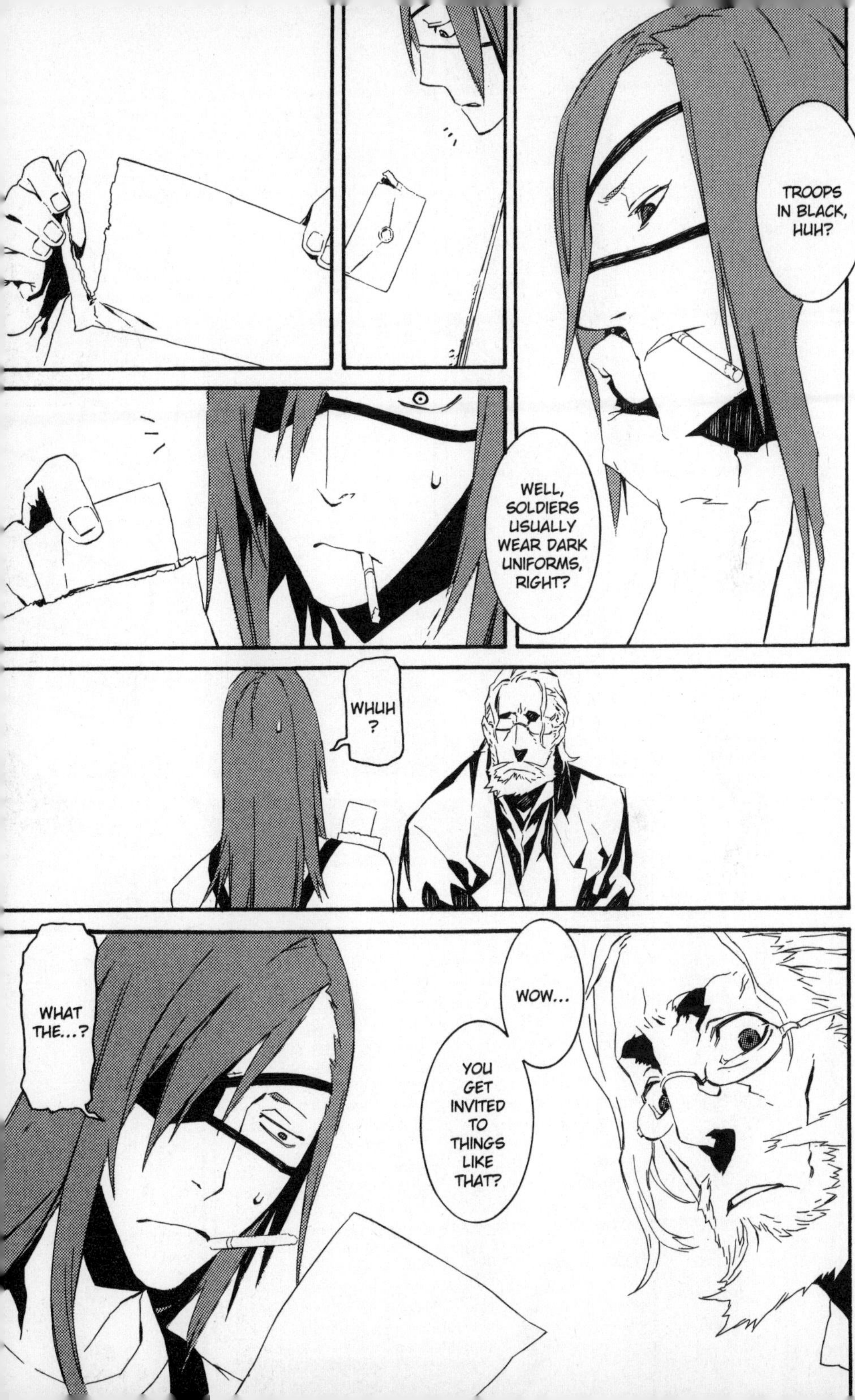
TROOPS IN BLACK, HUH?
WELL, SOLDIERS USUALLY WEAR DARK UNIFORMS, RIGHT?
WHUH?
WOW...
YOU GET INVITED TO THINGS LIKE THAT?
WHAT THE...?

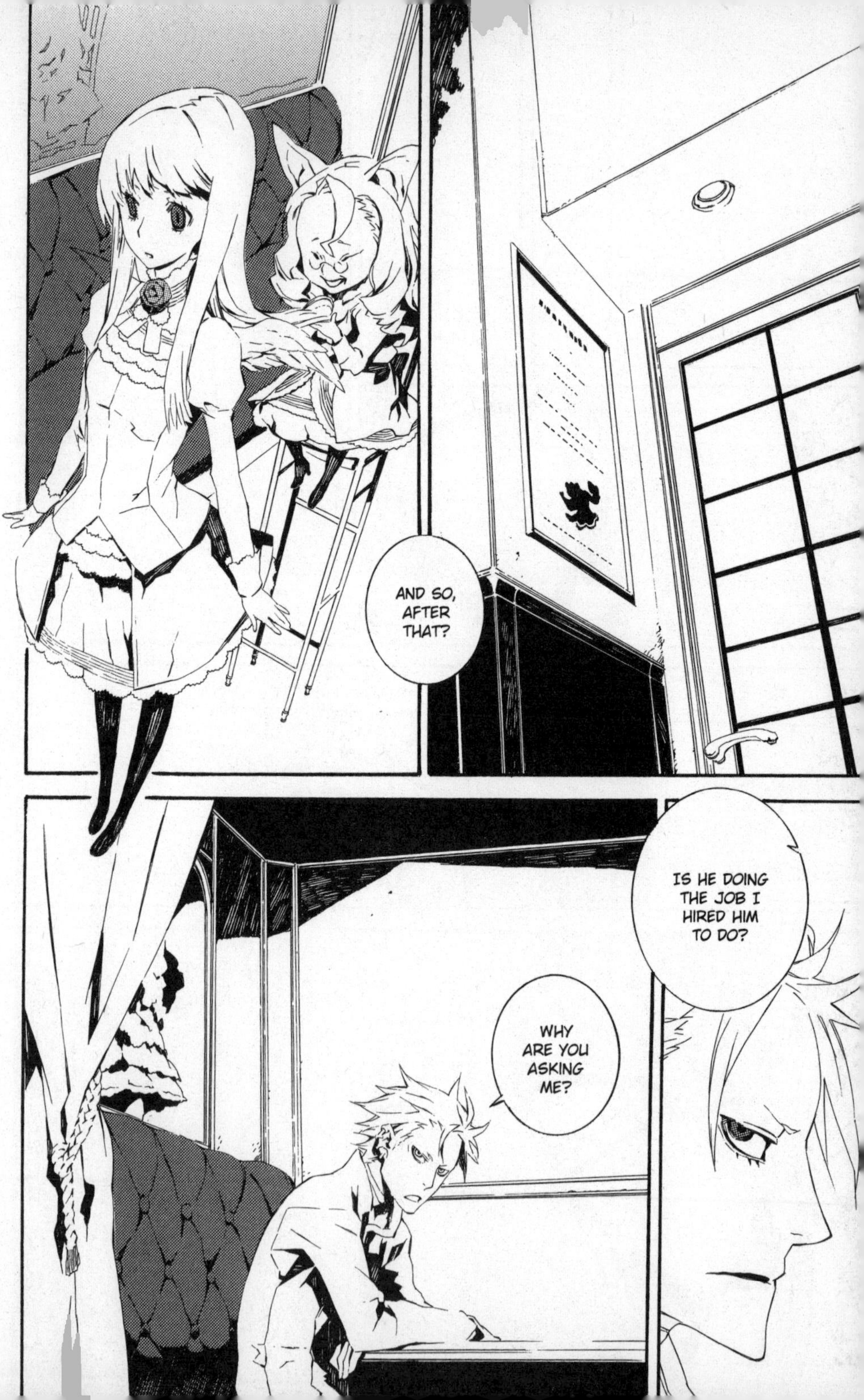
AND SO, AFTER THAT?
IS HE DOING THE JOB I HIRED HIM TO DO?
WHY ARE YOU ASKING ME?

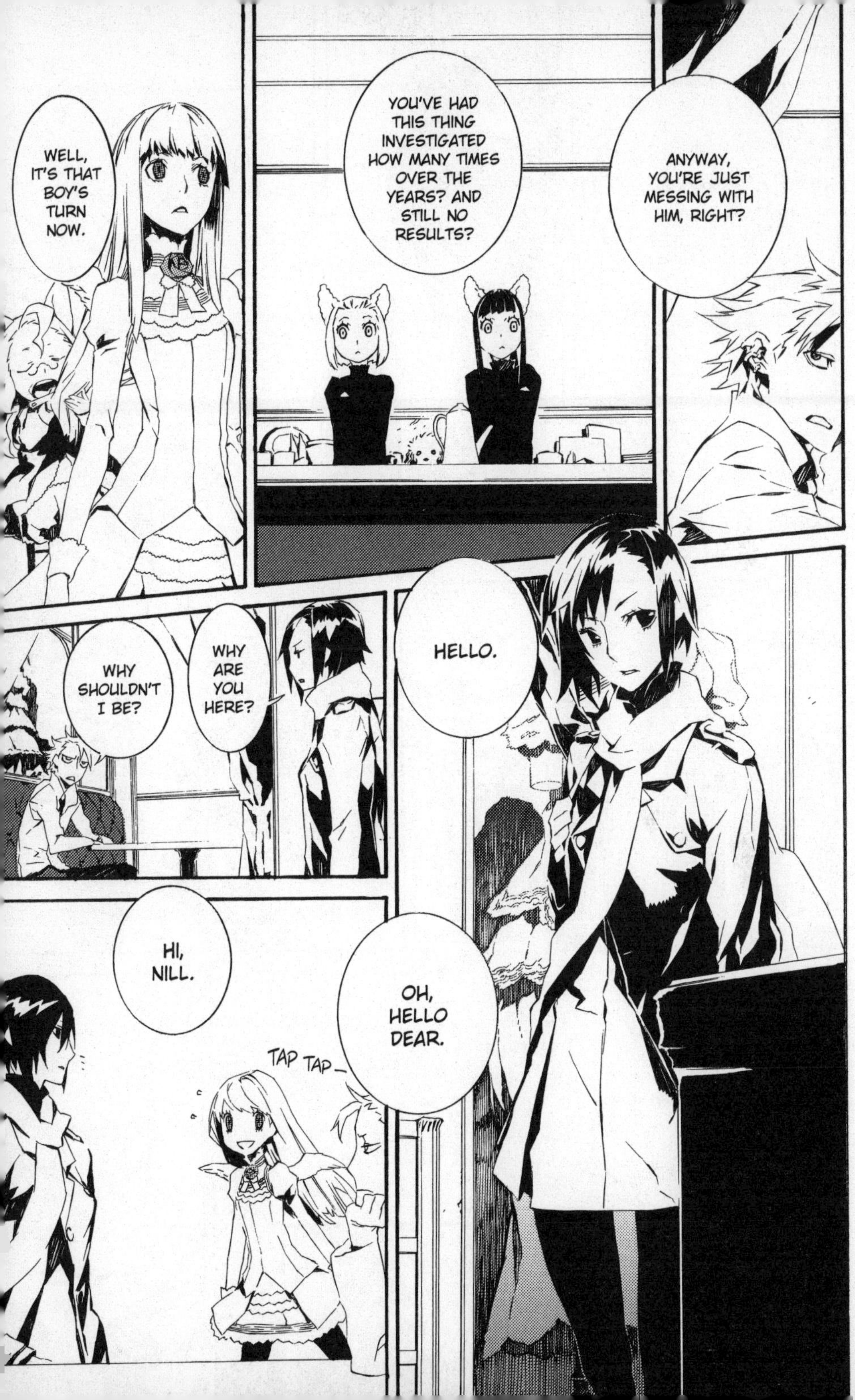
ANYWAY, YOU'RE JUST MESSING WITH HIM, RIGHT?
YOU'VE HAD THIS THING INVESTIGATED HOW MANY TIMES OVER THE YEARS? AND STILL NO RESULTS?
WELL, IT'S THAT BOY'S TURN NOW.
HELLO.
OH, HELLO DEAR.
WHY ARE YOU HERE?
WHY SHOULDN'T I BE?
HI, NILL.
TAP TAP

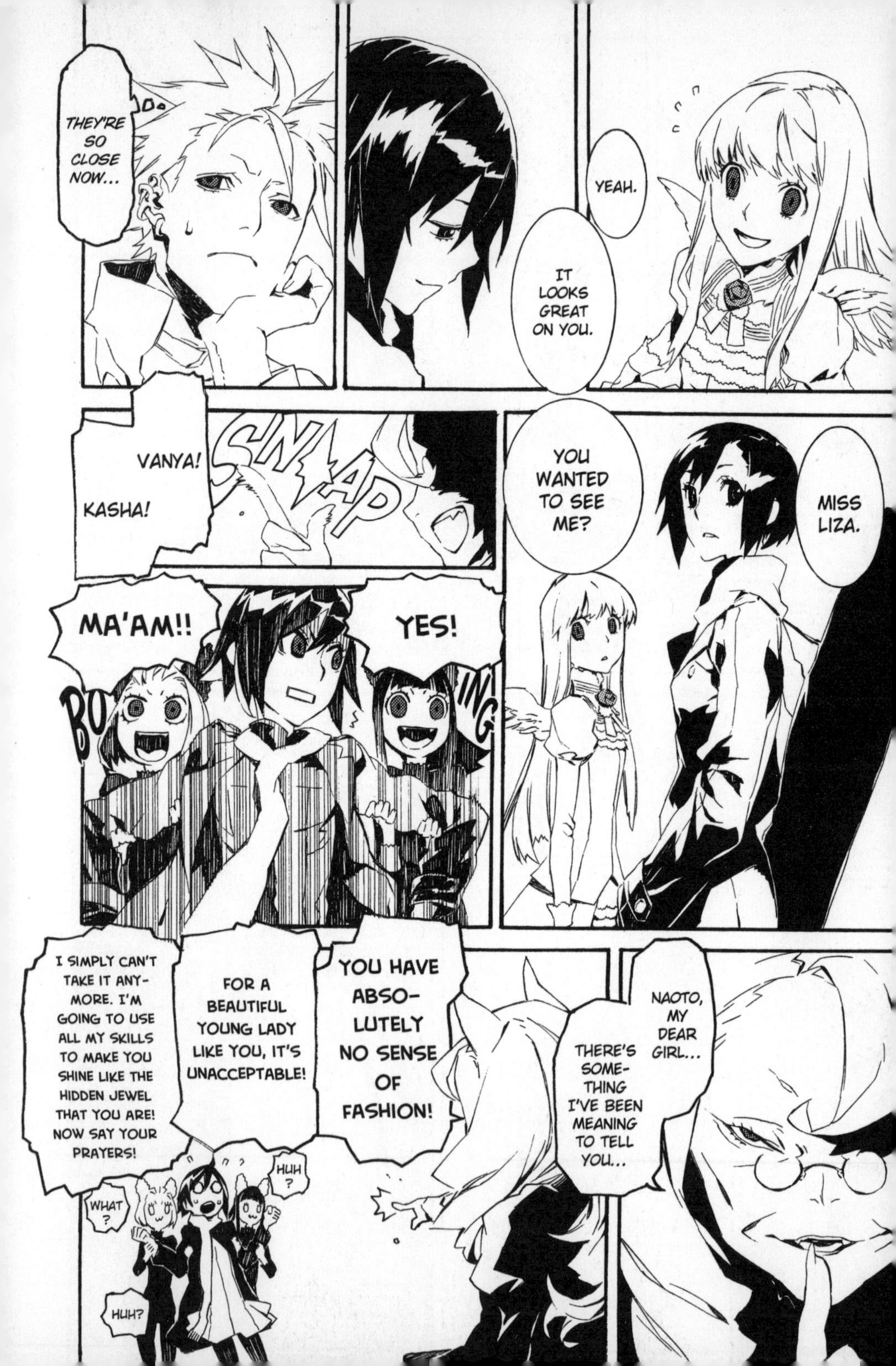
YEAH.
IT LOOKS GREAT ON YOU.
THEY'RE SO CLOSE NOW...
MISS LIZA.
YOU WANTED TO SEE ME?
VANYA!
KASHA!
SNAP
YES!
MA'AM!!
NAOTO, MY DEAR GIRL...
THERE'S SOME-THING I'VE BEEN MEANING TO TELL YOU...
YOU HAVE ABSO-LUTELY NO SENSE OF FASHION!
FOR A BEAUTIFUL YOUNG LADY LIKE YOU, IT'S UNACCEPTABLE!
I SIMPLY CAN'T TAKE IT ANY-MORE. I'M GOING TO USE ALL MY SKILLS TO MAKE YOU SHINE LIKE THE HIDDEN JEWEL THAT YOU ARE! NOW SAY YOUR PRAYERS!
HUH?
WHAT?
HUH?

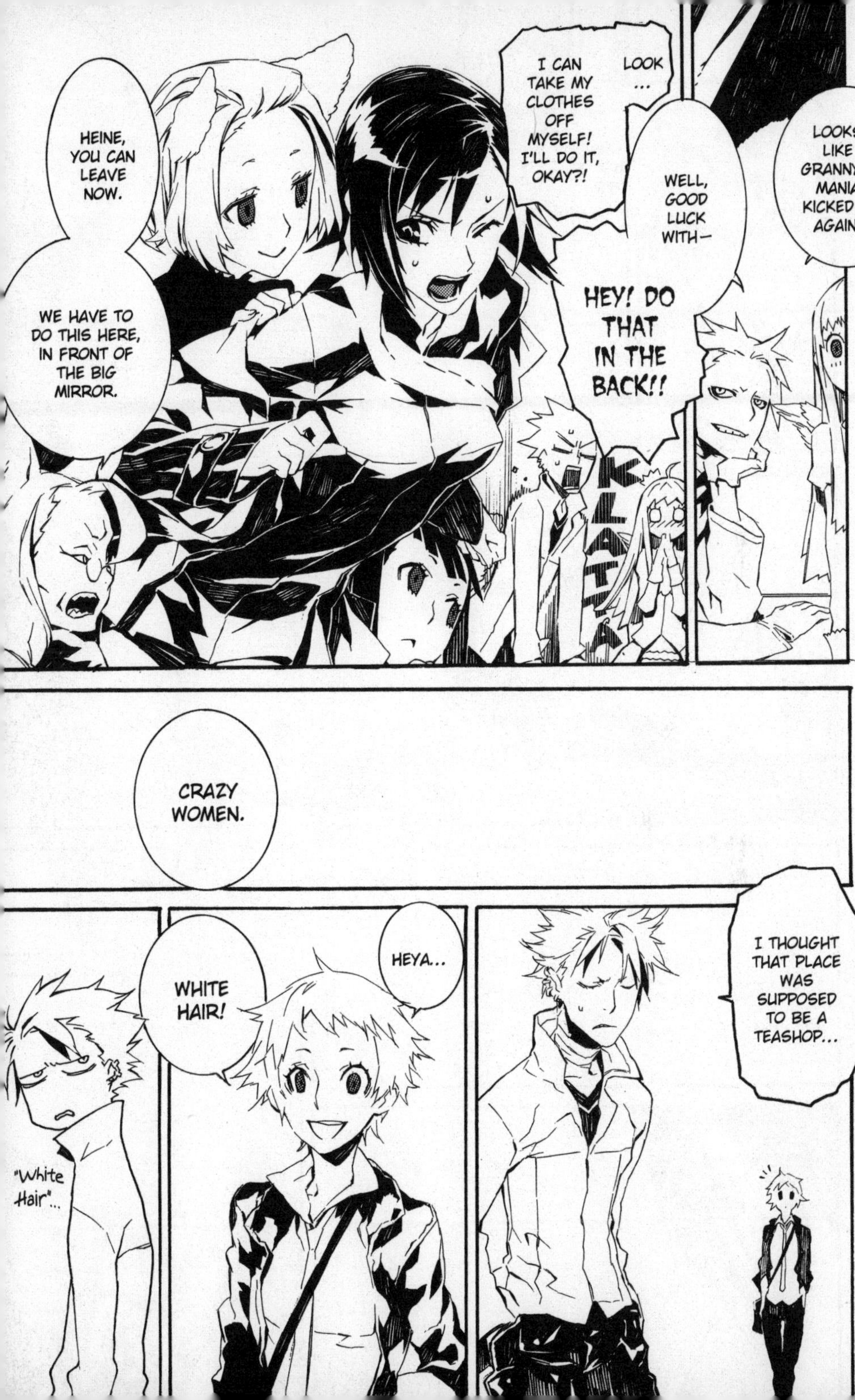
LOOKS LIKE GRANNY'S MANIA KICKED IN AGAIN.
WELL, GOOD LUCK WITH—
HEY! DO THAT IN THE BACK!!
LOOK ...
I CAN TAKE MY CLOTHES OFF MYSELF! I'LL DO IT, OKAY?!
HEINE, YOU CAN LEAVE NOW.
WE HAVE TO DO THIS HERE, IN FRONT OF THE BIG MIRROR.
KLATA
CRAZY WOMEN.
I THOUGHT THAT PLACE WAS SUPPOSED TO BE A TEASHOP...
HEYA...
WHITE HAIR!
"White Hair"...

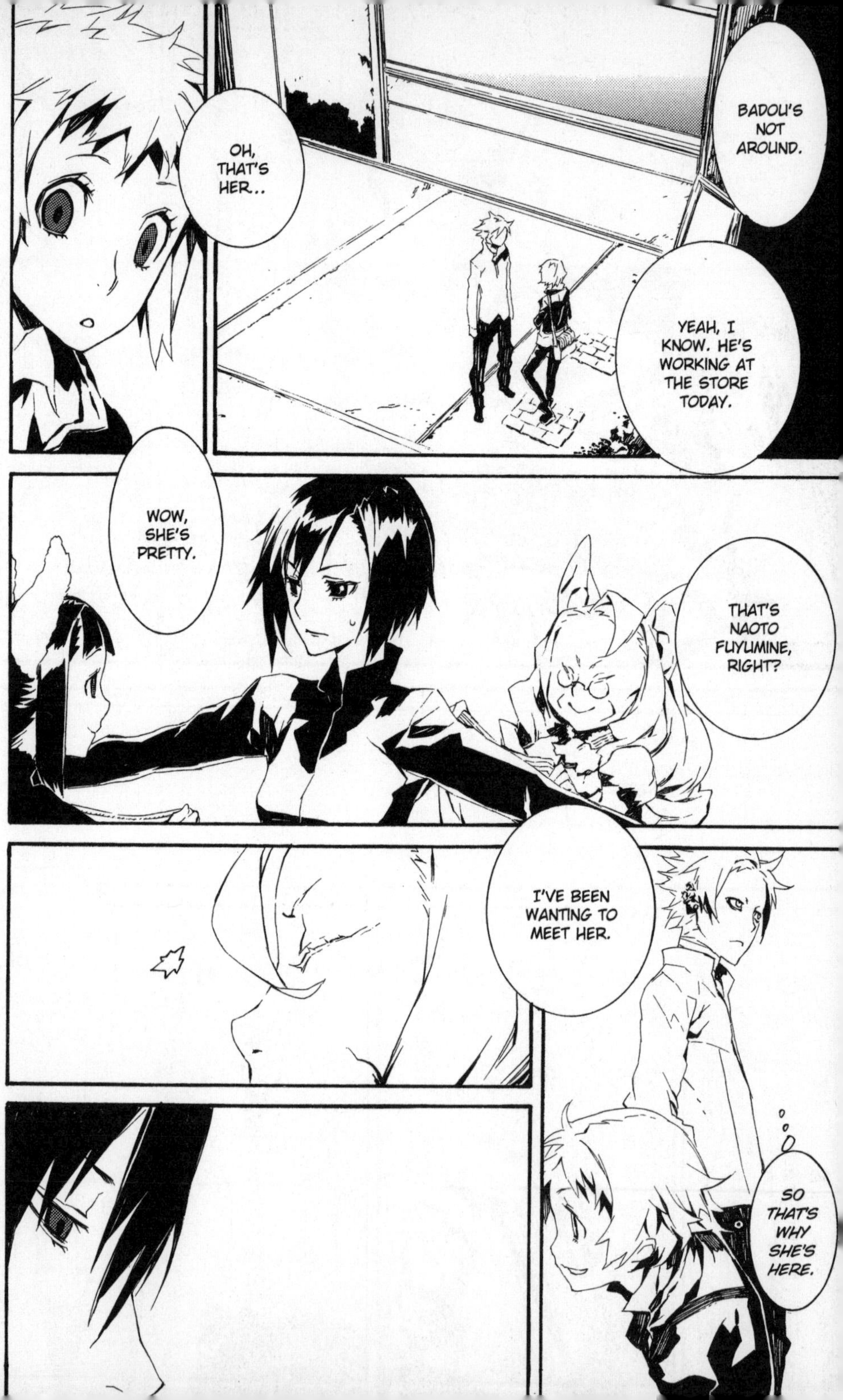
BADOU'S NOT AROUND.
YEAH, I KNOW. HE'S WORKING AT THE STORE TODAY.
OH, THAT'S HER...
THAT'S NAOTO FUYUMINE, RIGHT?
WOW, SHE'S PRETTY.
I'VE BEEN WANTING TO MEET HER.
SO THAT'S WHY SHE'S HERE.

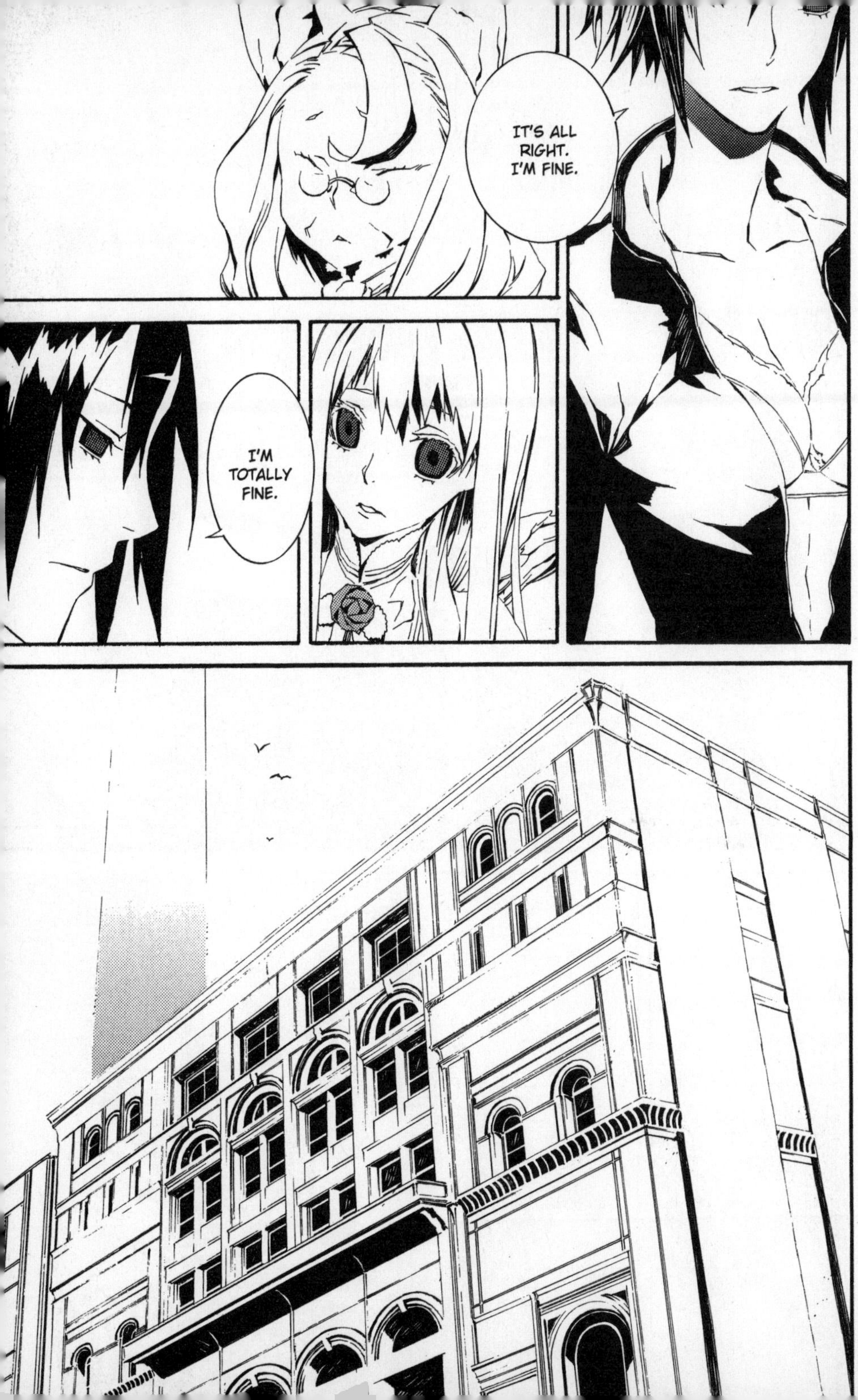
IT'S ALL RIGHT. I'M FINE.
I'M TOTALLY FINE.

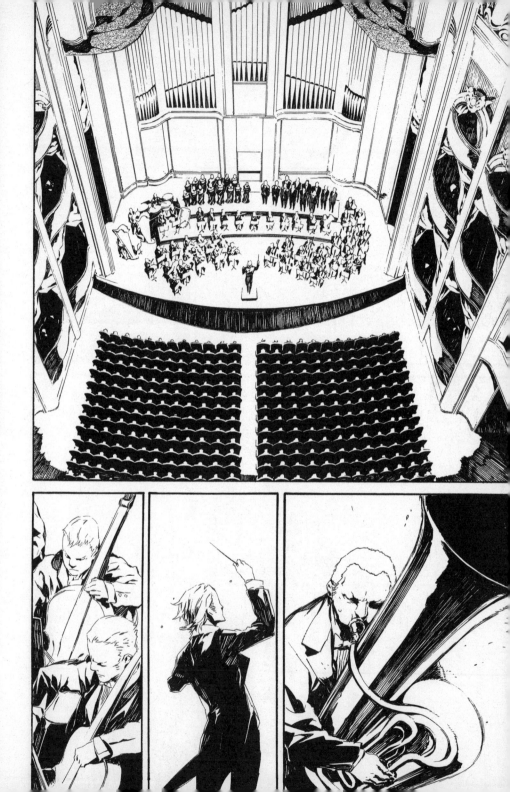

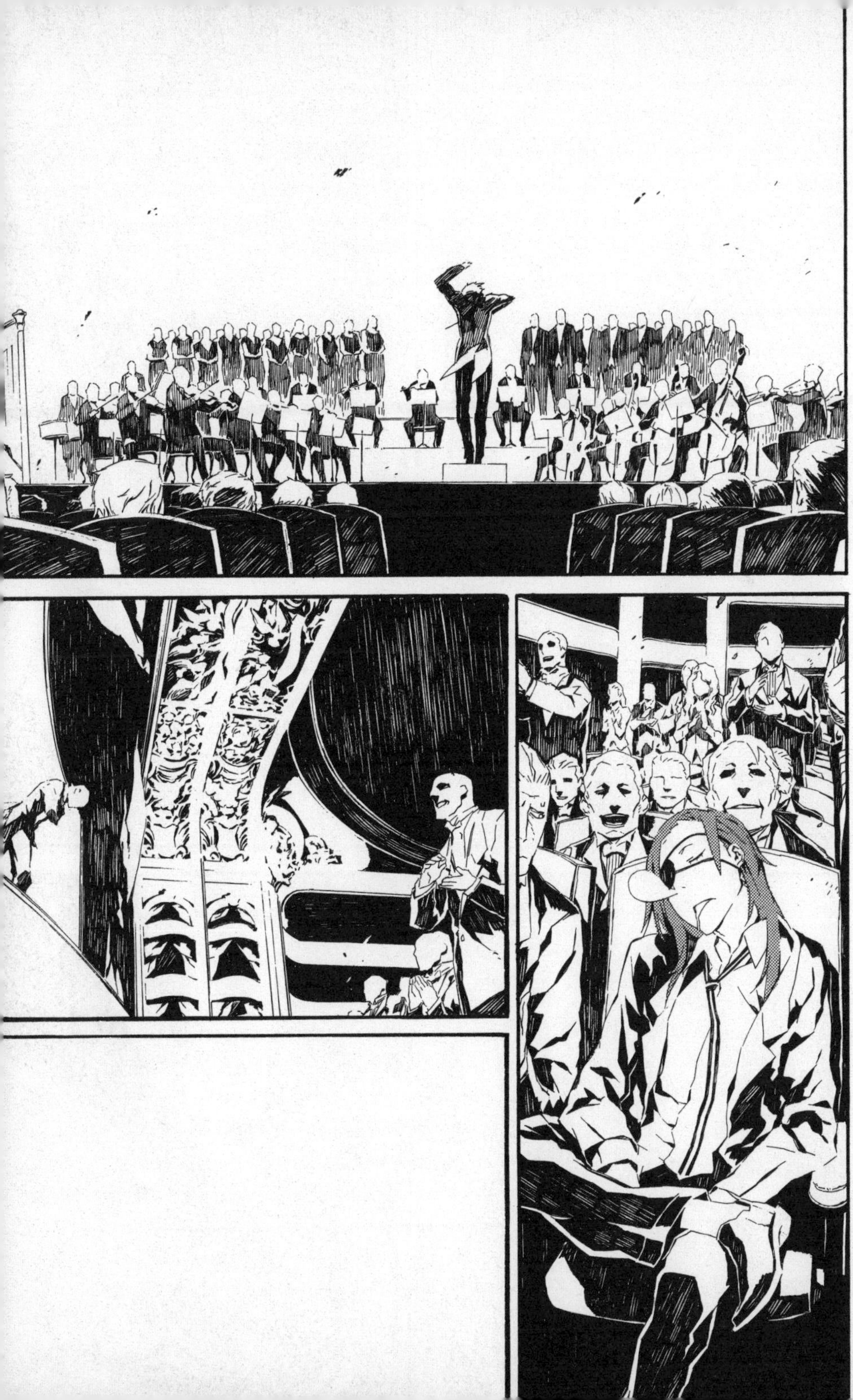

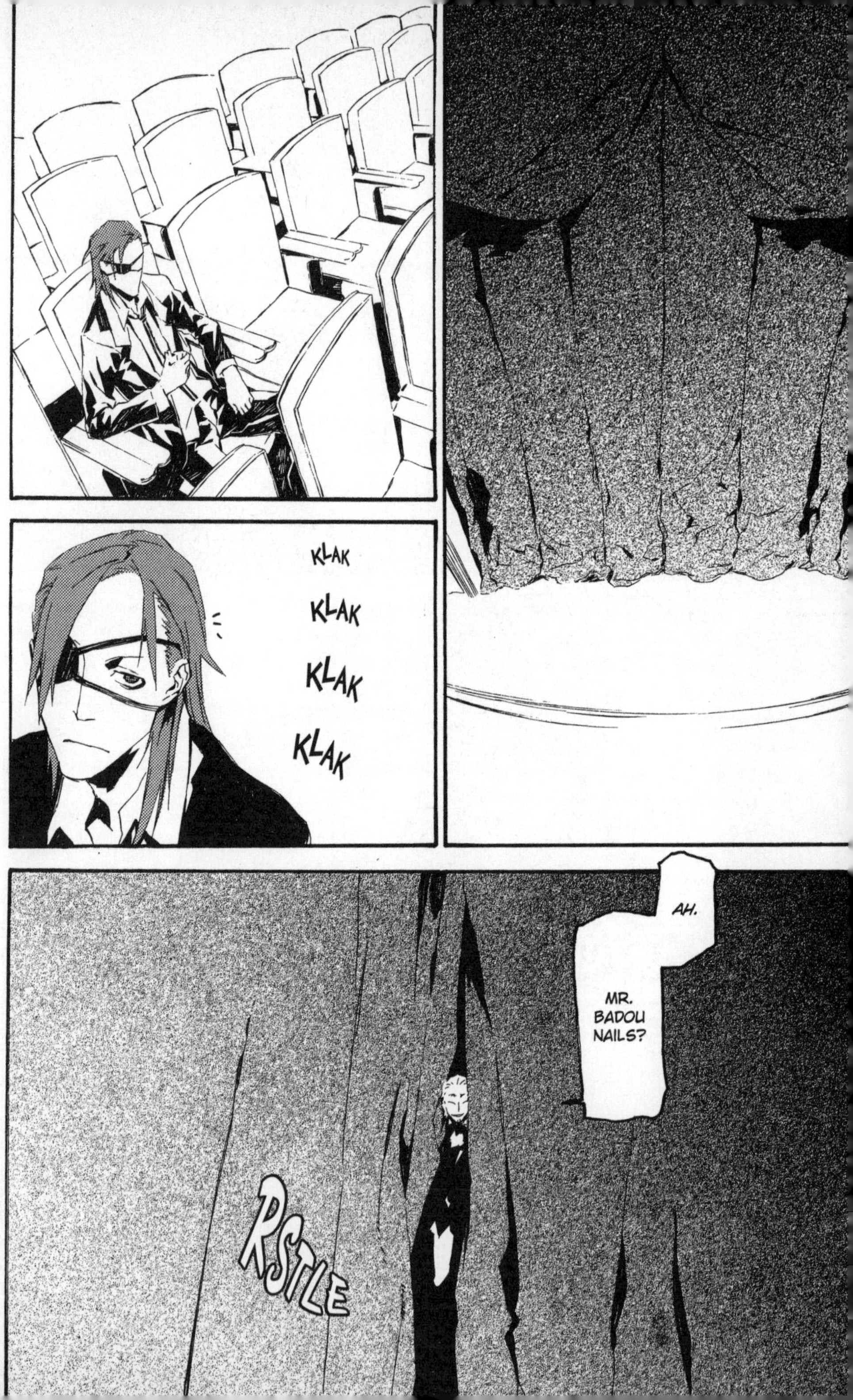
KLAK
KLAK
KLAK
KLAK
AH.
MR. BADOU NAILS?
RSTLE

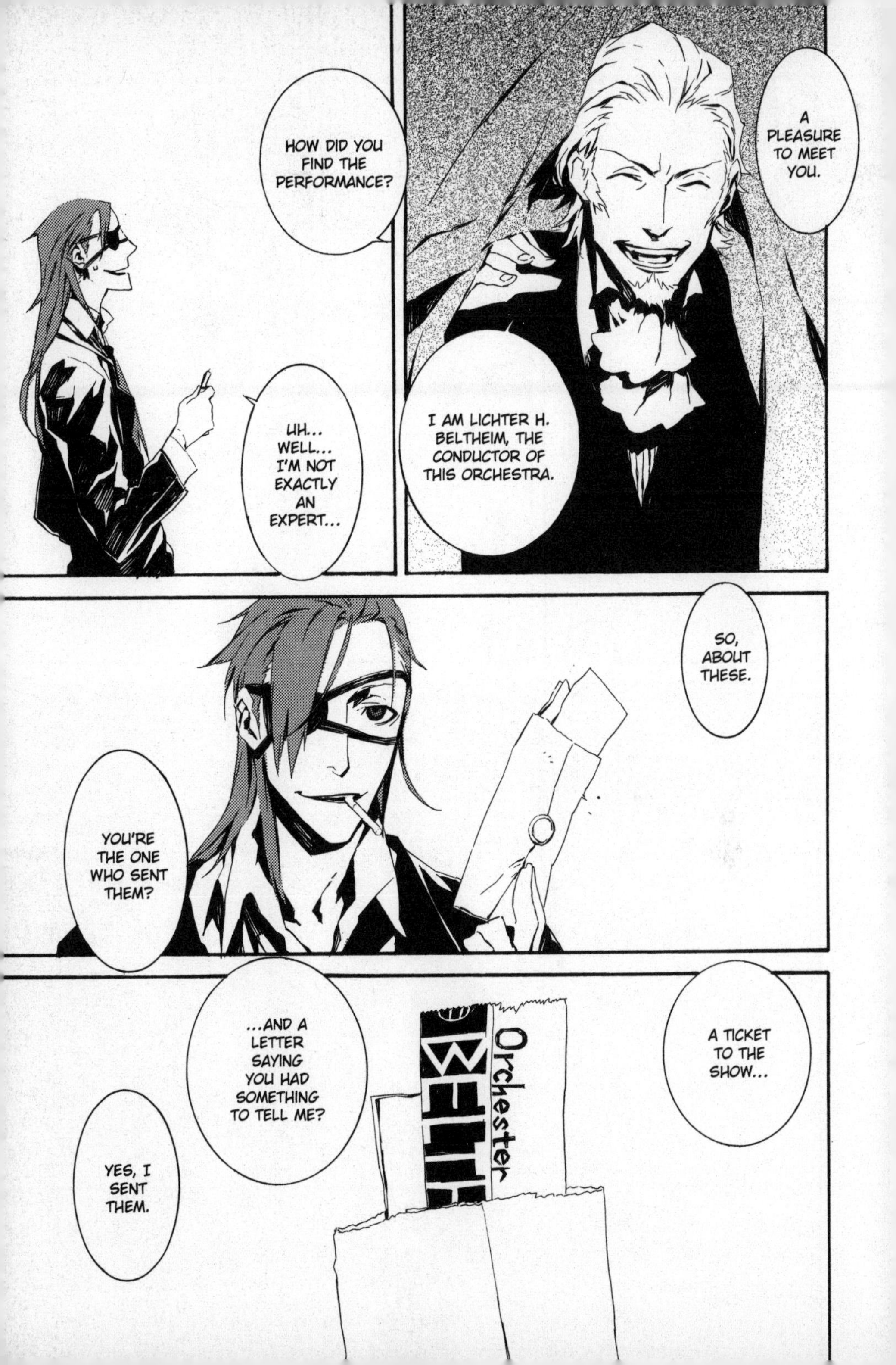
A PLEASURE TO MEET YOU.
I AM LICHTER H. BELTHEIM, THE CONDUCTOR OF THIS ORCHESTRA.
HOW DID YOU FIND THE PERFORMANCE?
UH... WELL... I'M NOT EXACTLY AN EXPERT...
SO, ABOUT THESE.
YOU'RE THE ONE WHO SENT THEM?
A TICKET TO THE SHOW...
...AND A LETTER SAYING YOU HAD SOMETHING TO TELL ME?
Orchester
YES, I SENT THEM.

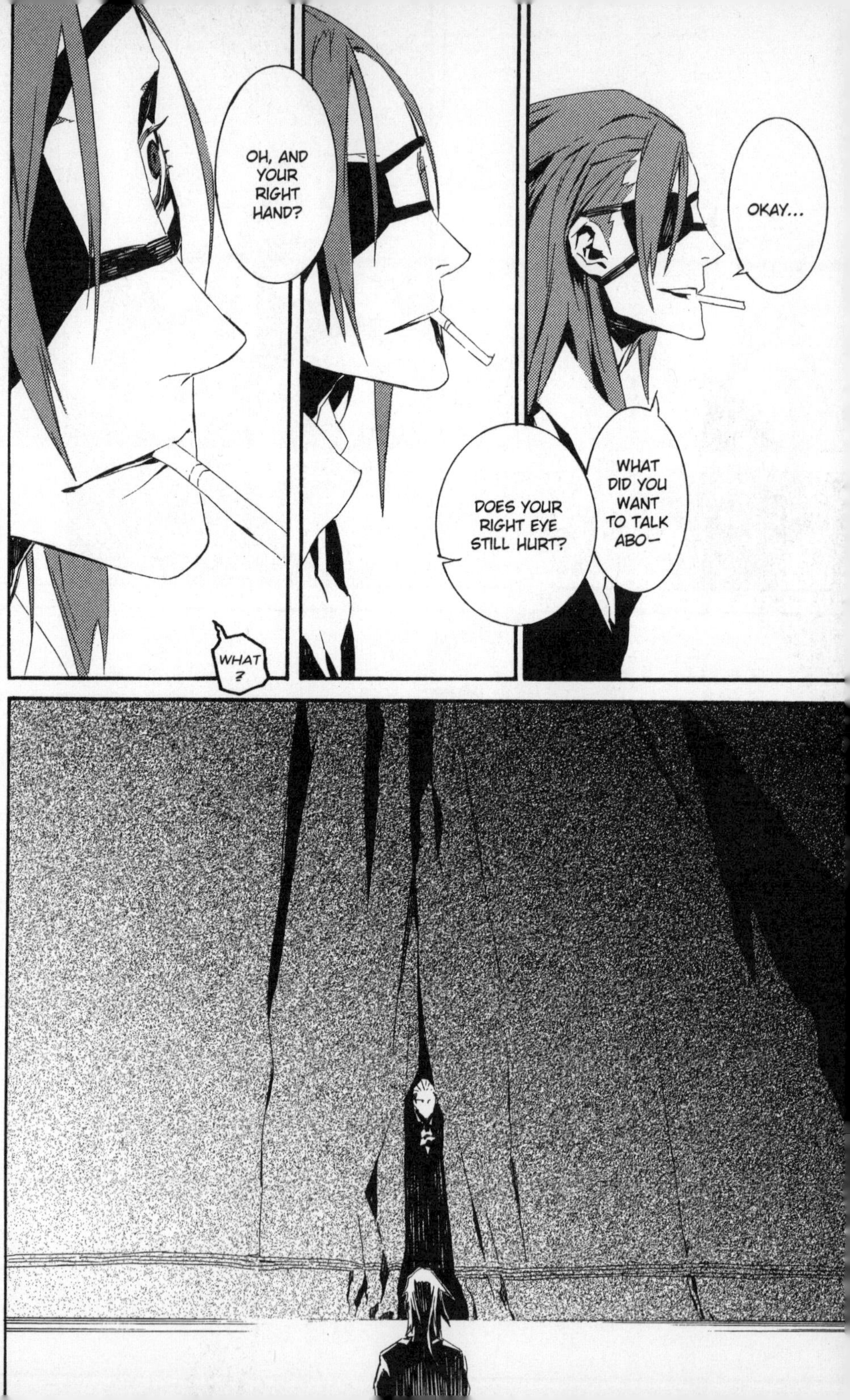
OKAY...
WHAT DID YOU WANT TO TALK ABO—
DOES YOUR RIGHT EYE STILL HURT?
OH, AND YOUR RIGHT HAND?
WHAT?

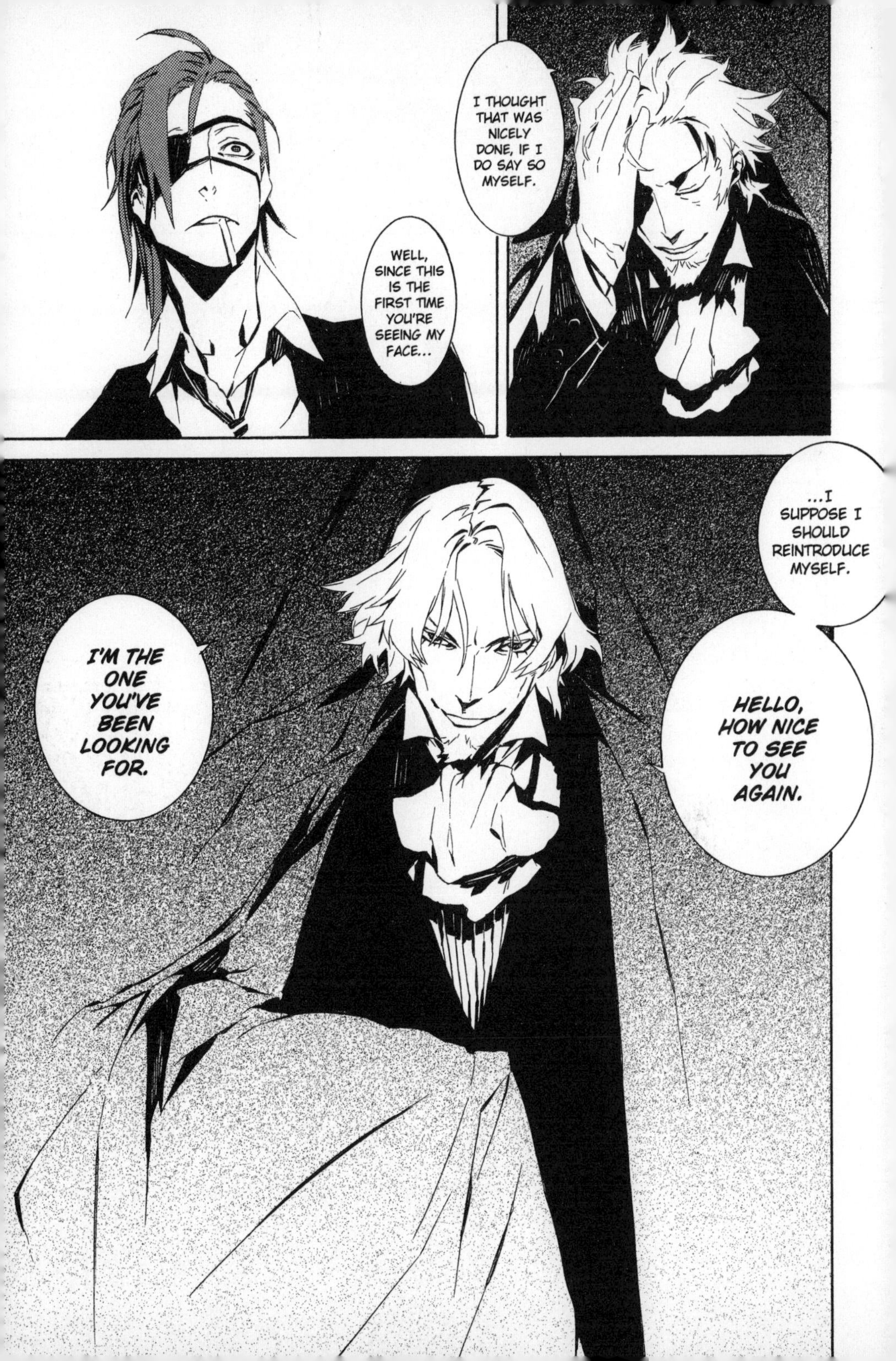
I THOUGHT THAT WAS NICELY DONE, IF I DO SAY SO MYSELF.
WELL, SINCE THIS IS THE FIRST TIME YOU'RE SEEING MY FACE...
...I SUPPOSE I SHOULD REINTRODUCE MYSELF.
HELLO, HOW NICE TO SEE YOU AGAIN.
I'M THE ONE YOU'VE BEEN LOOKING FOR.

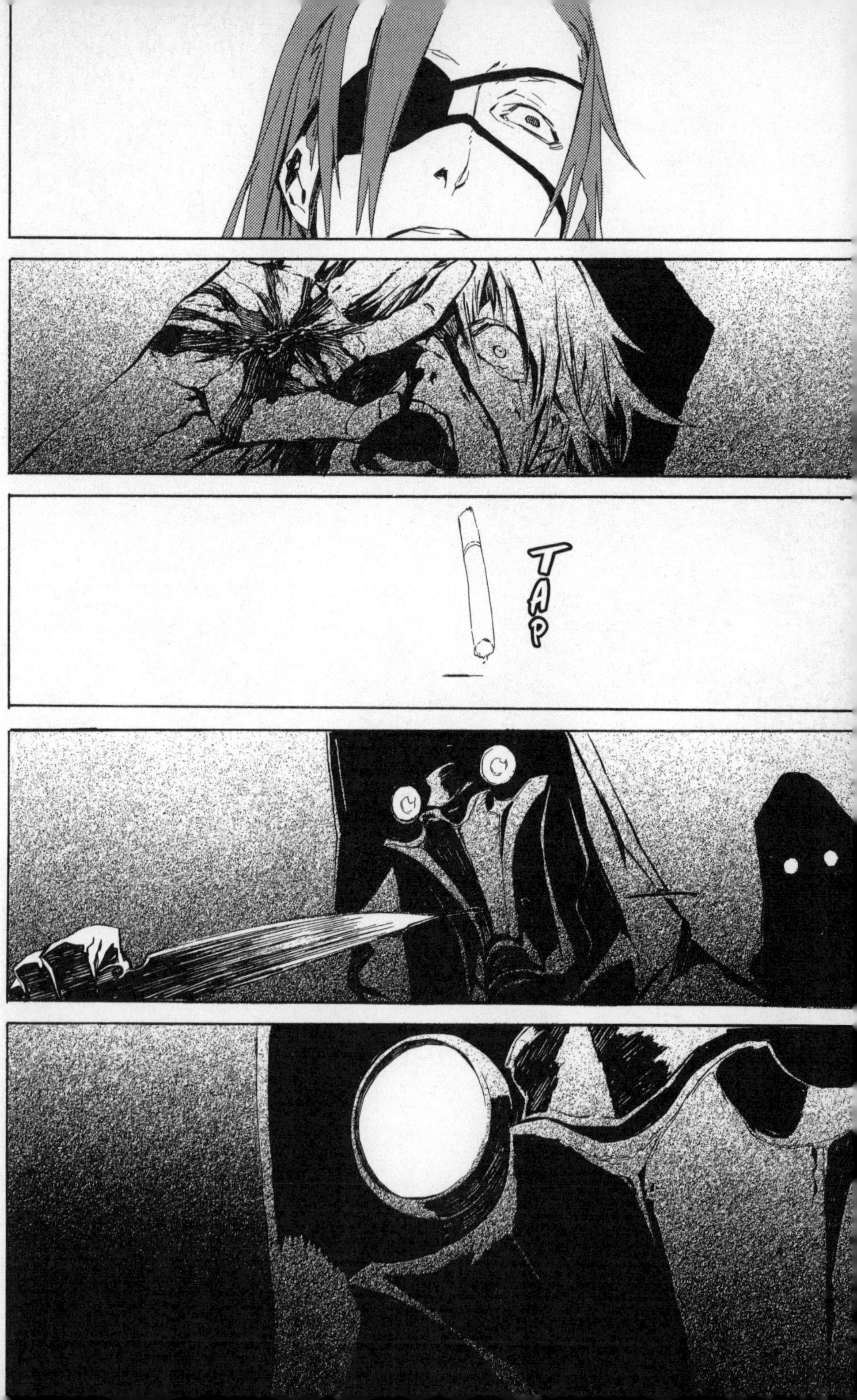
TAP

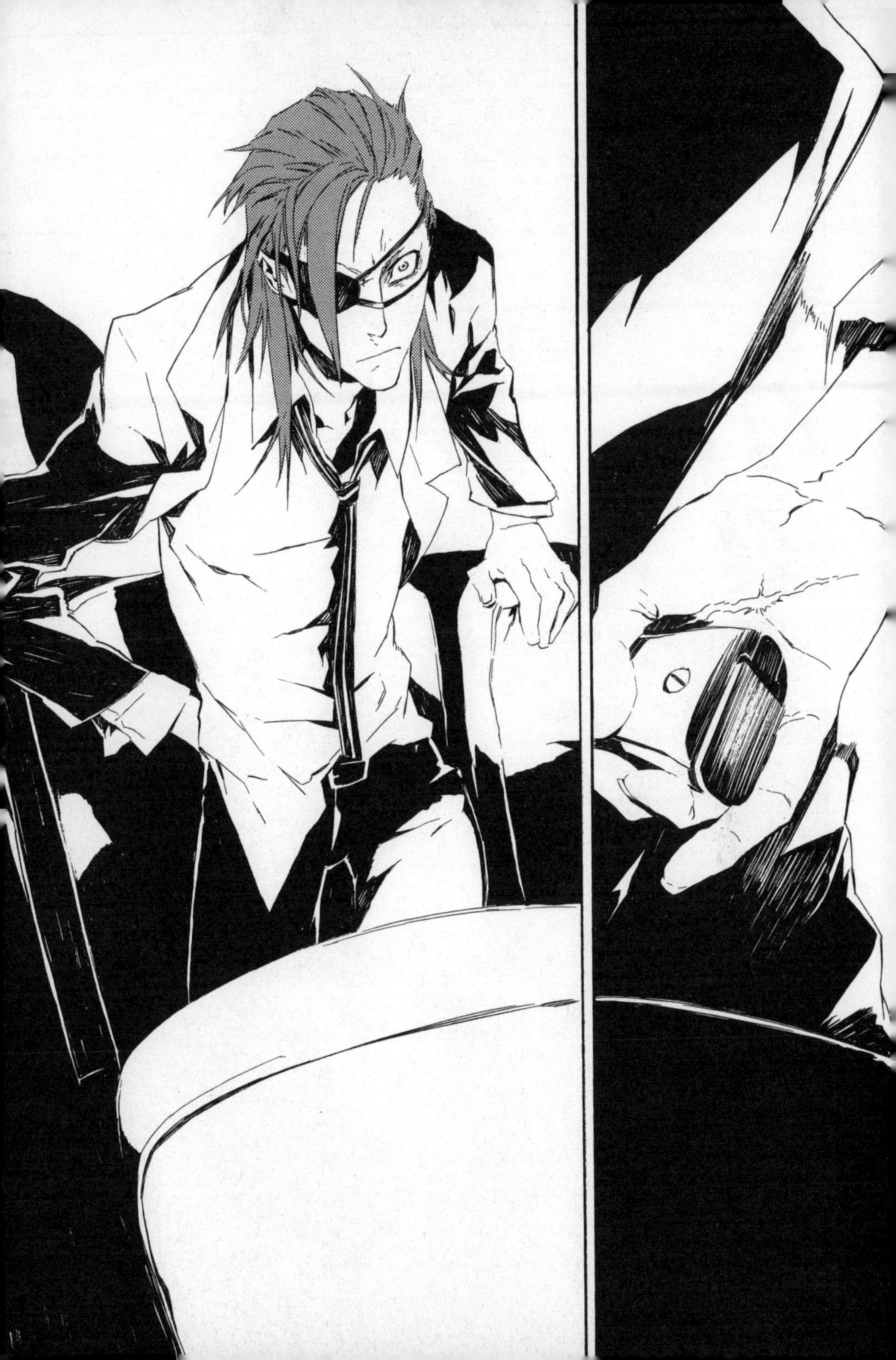

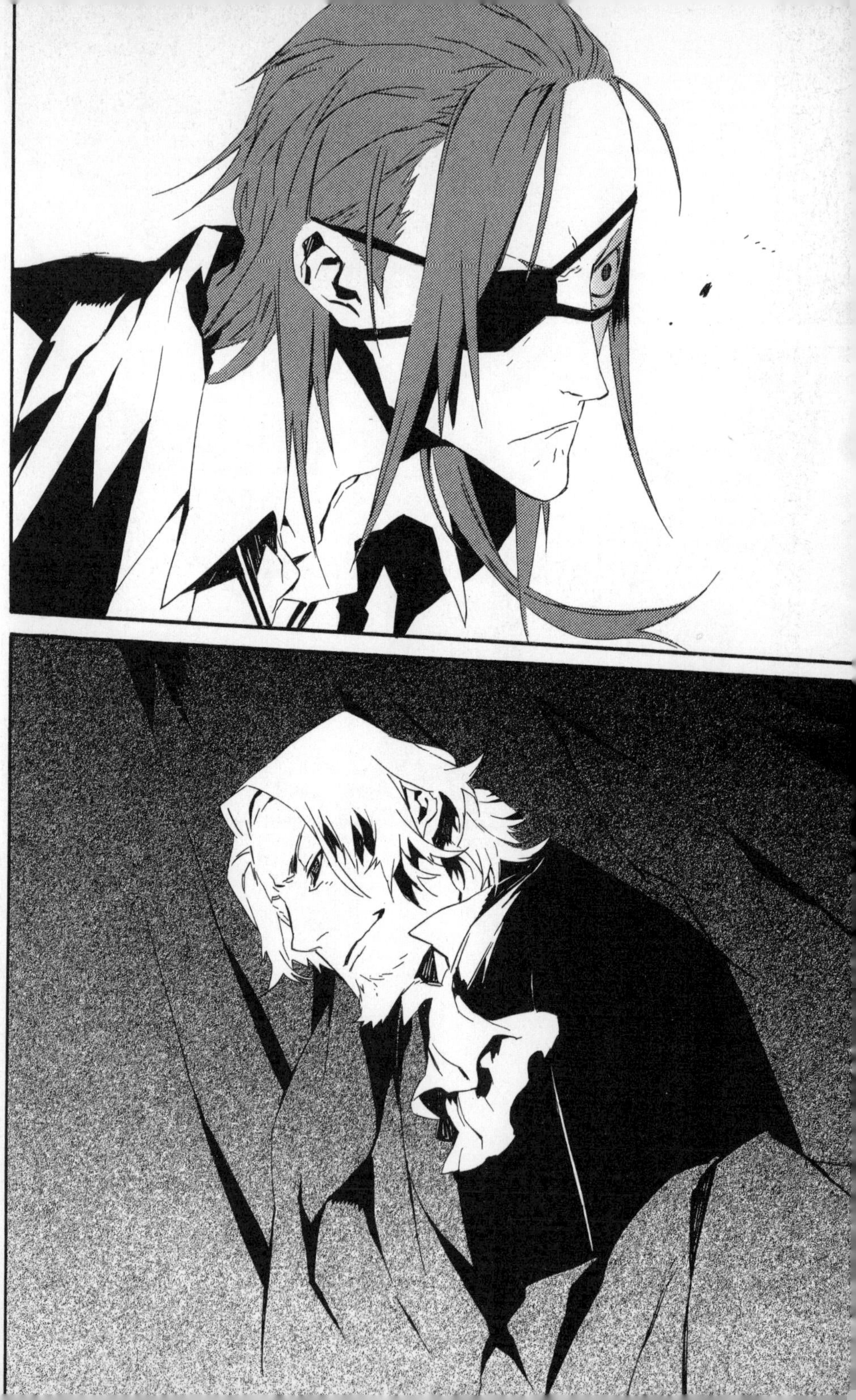

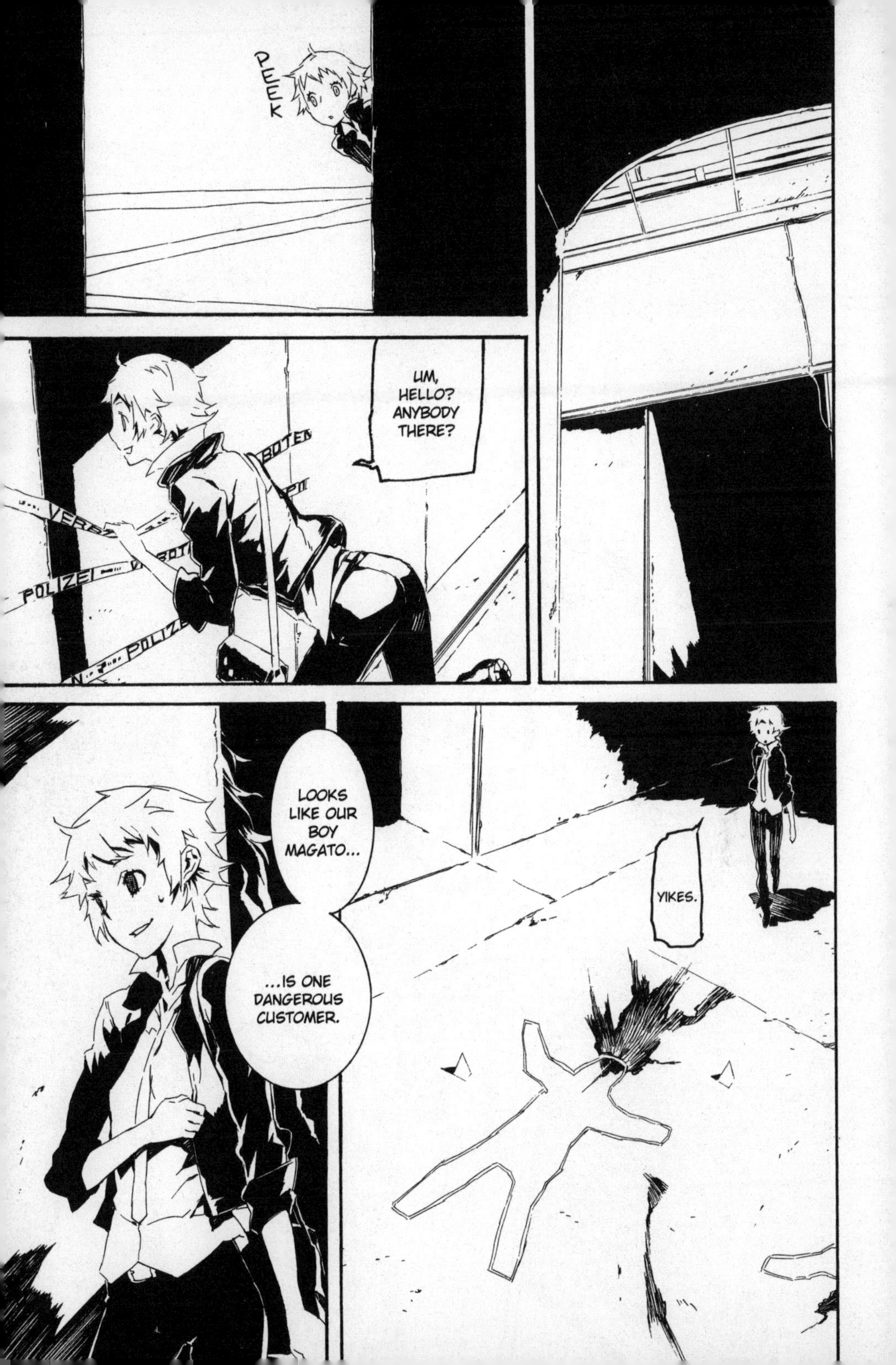
PEEK
UM, HELLO? ANYBODY THERE?
POLIZEI
YIKES.
LOOKS LIKE OUR BOY MAGATO...
...IS ONE DANGEROUS CUSTOMER.

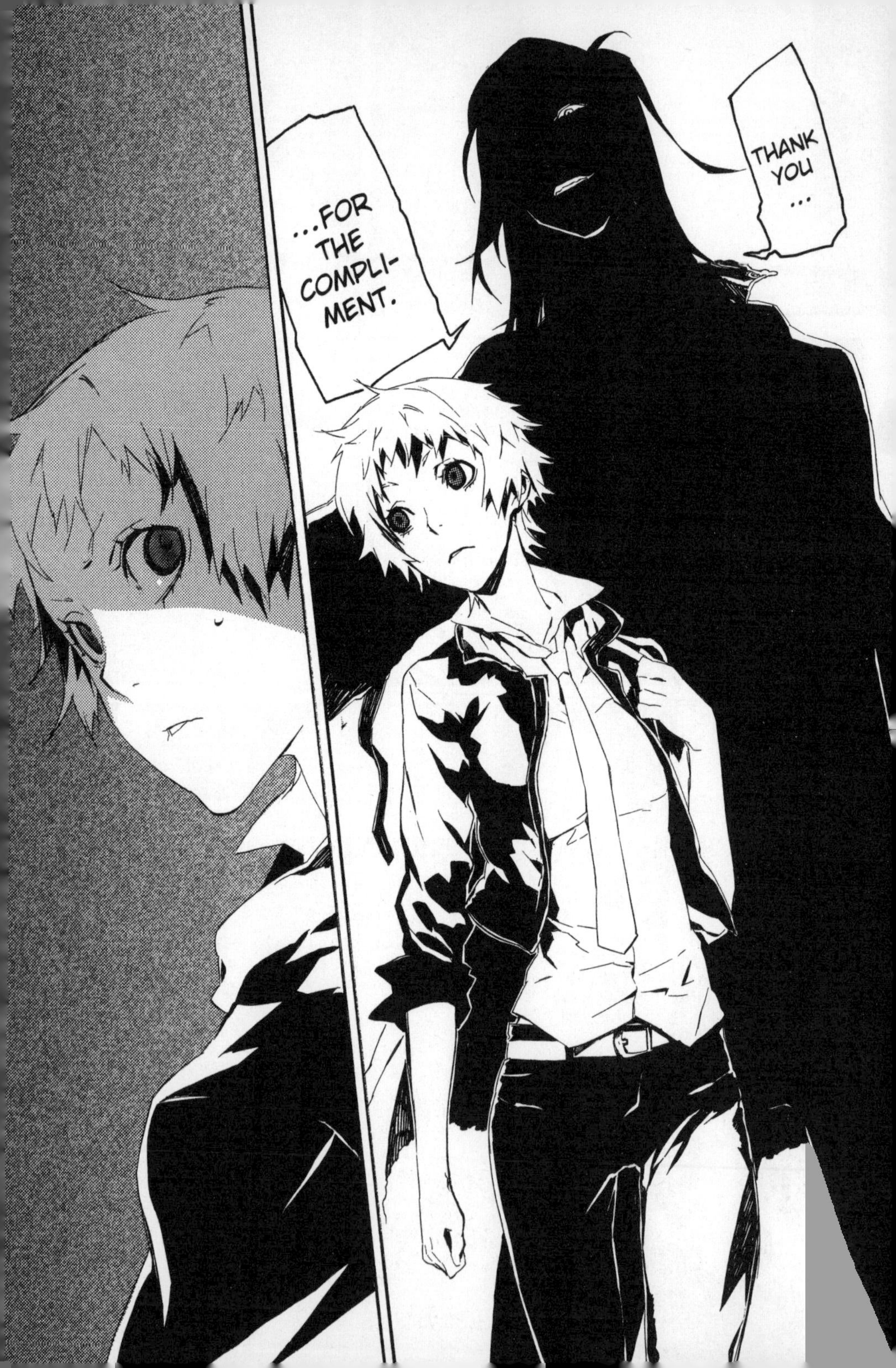
THANK YOU ...
...FOR THE COMPLI-MENT.

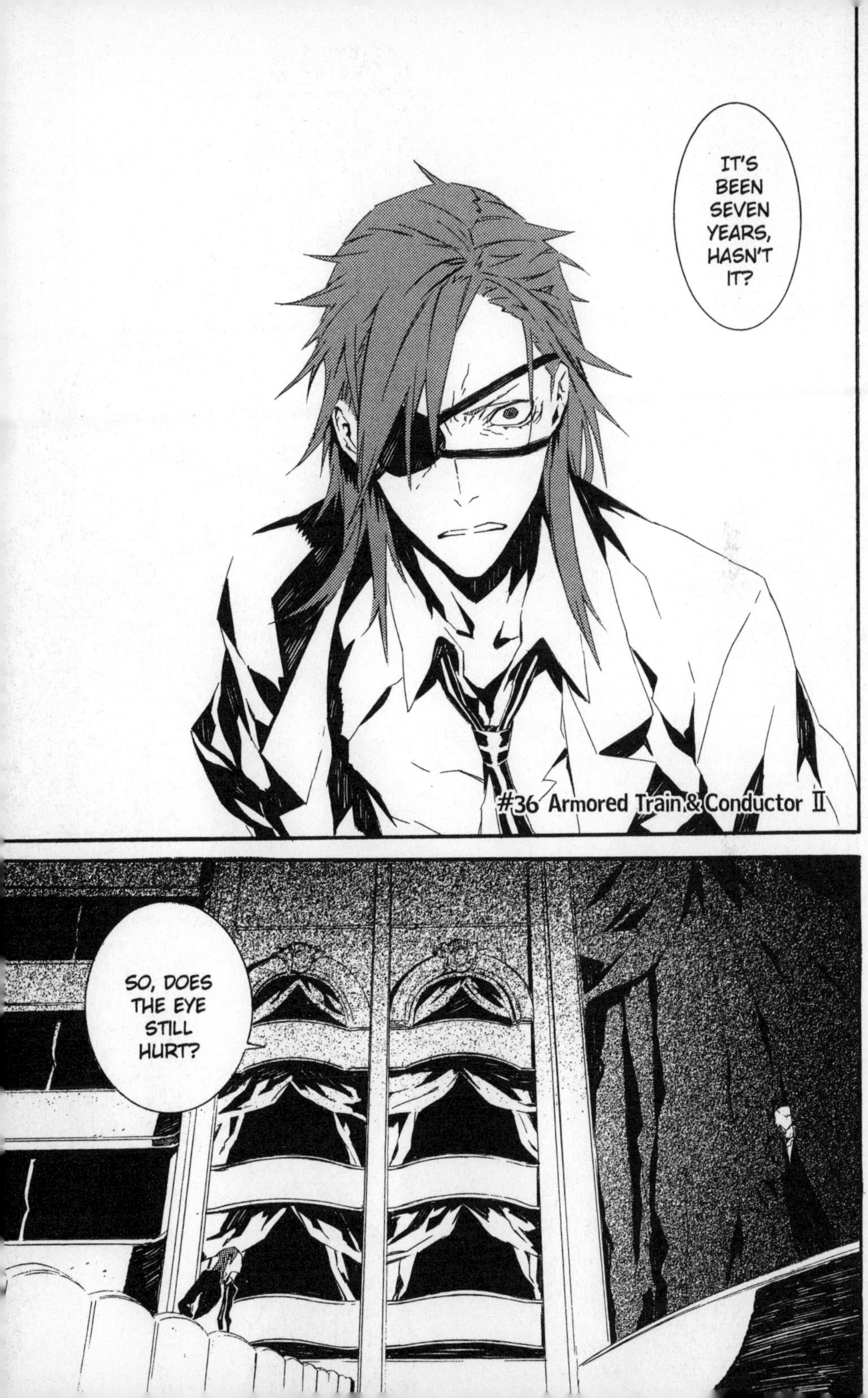
IT'S BEEN SEVEN YEARS, HASN'T IT?
#36 Armored Train & Conductor Ⅱ
SO, DOES THE EYE STILL HURT?

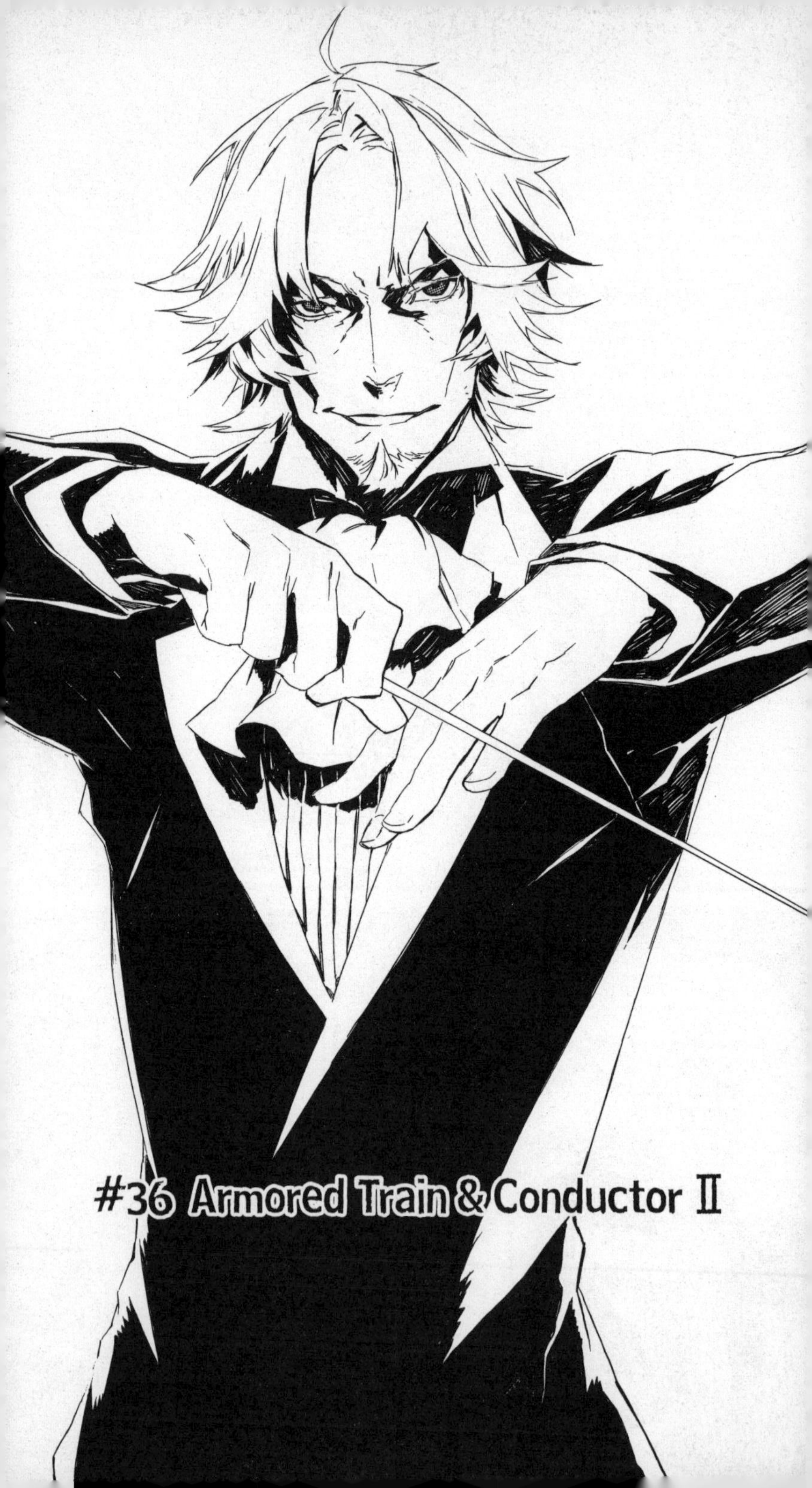

#36 Armored Train & Conductor Ⅱ

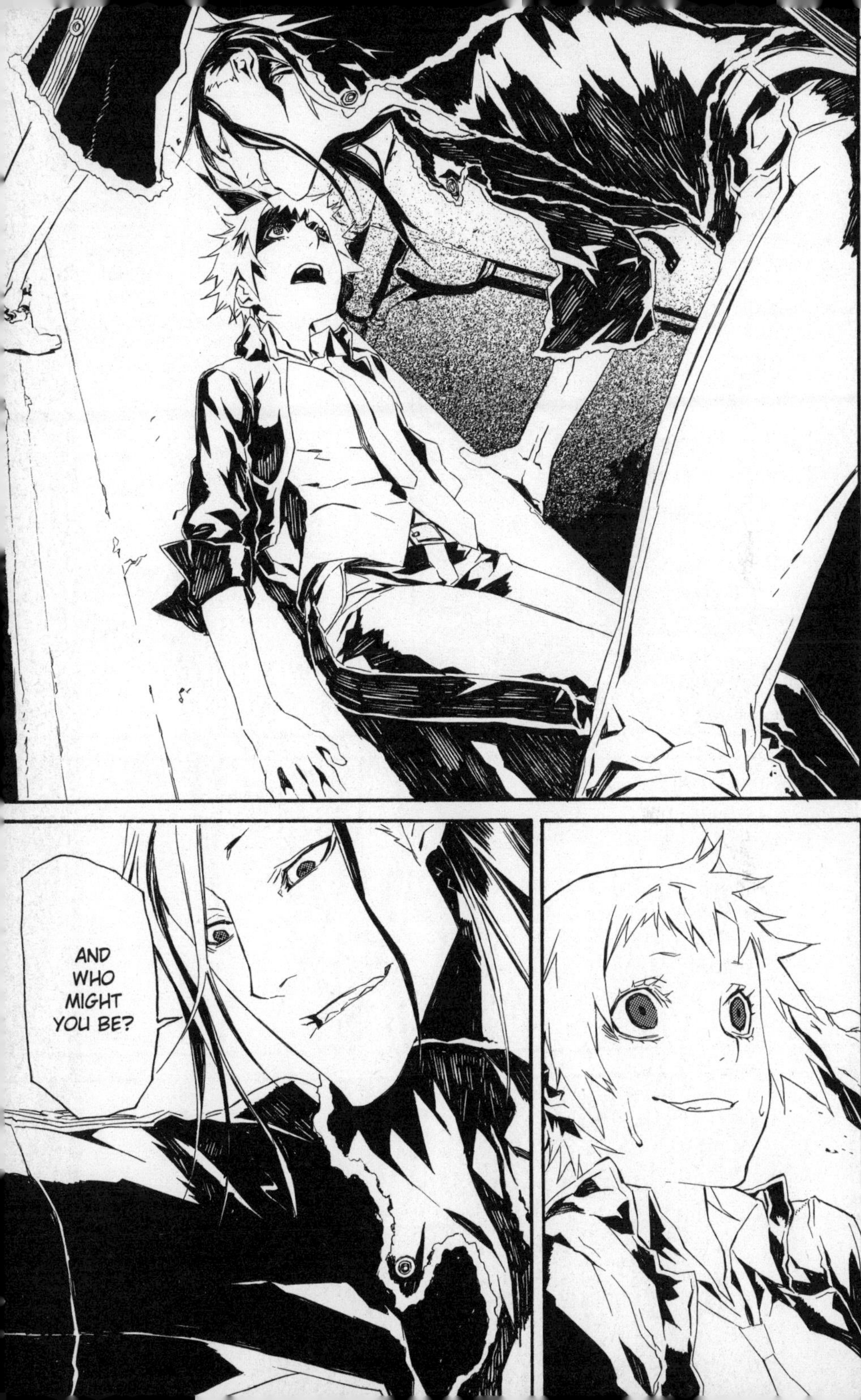
AND WHO MIGHT YOU BE?

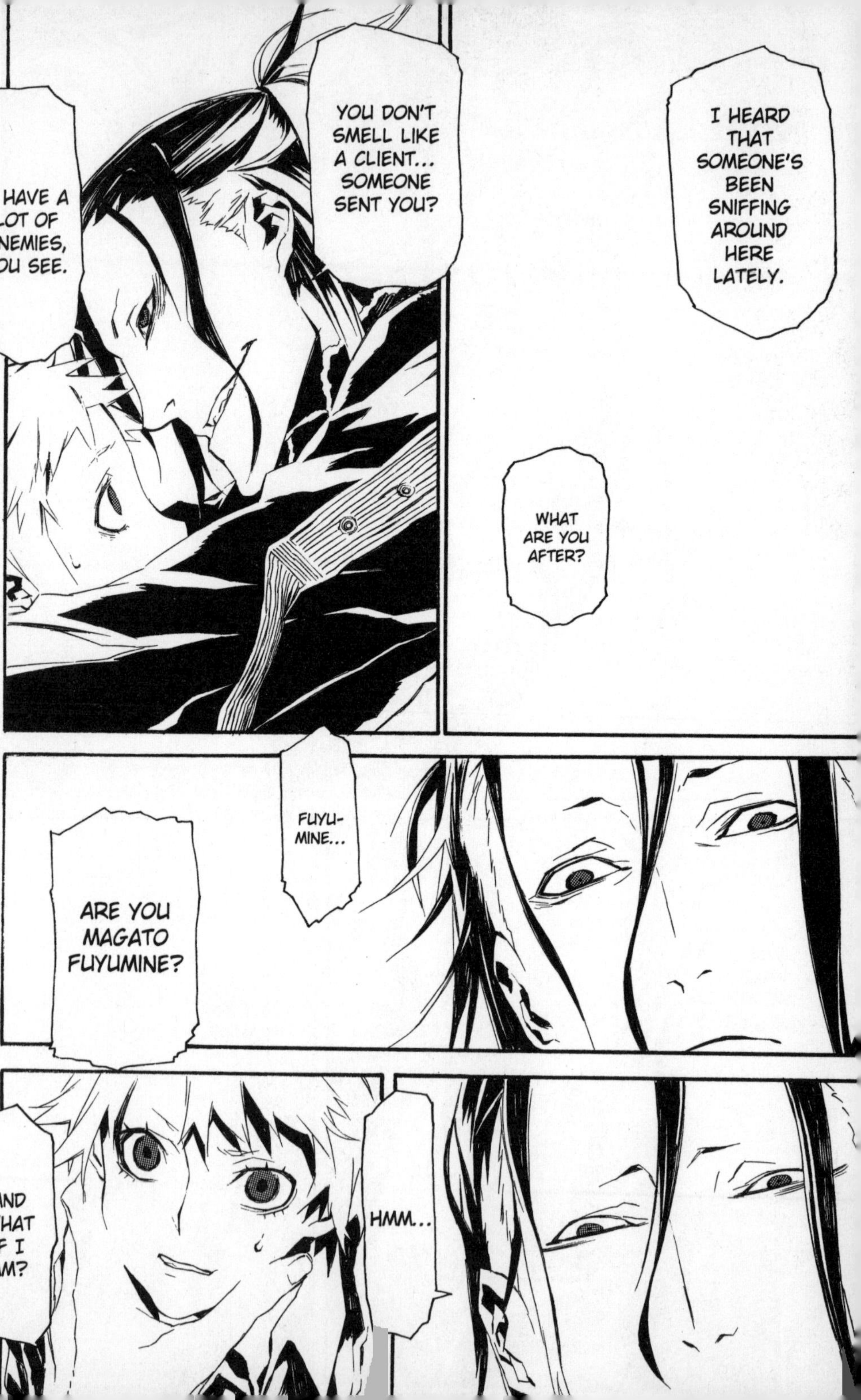

I HEARD THAT SOMEONE'S BEEN SNIFFING AROUND HERE LATELY.
WHAT ARE YOU AFTER?
YOU DON'T SMELL LIKE A CLIENT... SOMEONE SENT YOU?
I HAVE A LOT OF ENEMIES, YOU SEE.
FUYU-MINE...
ARE YOU MAGATO FUYUMINE?
HMM...
AND WHAT IF I AM?

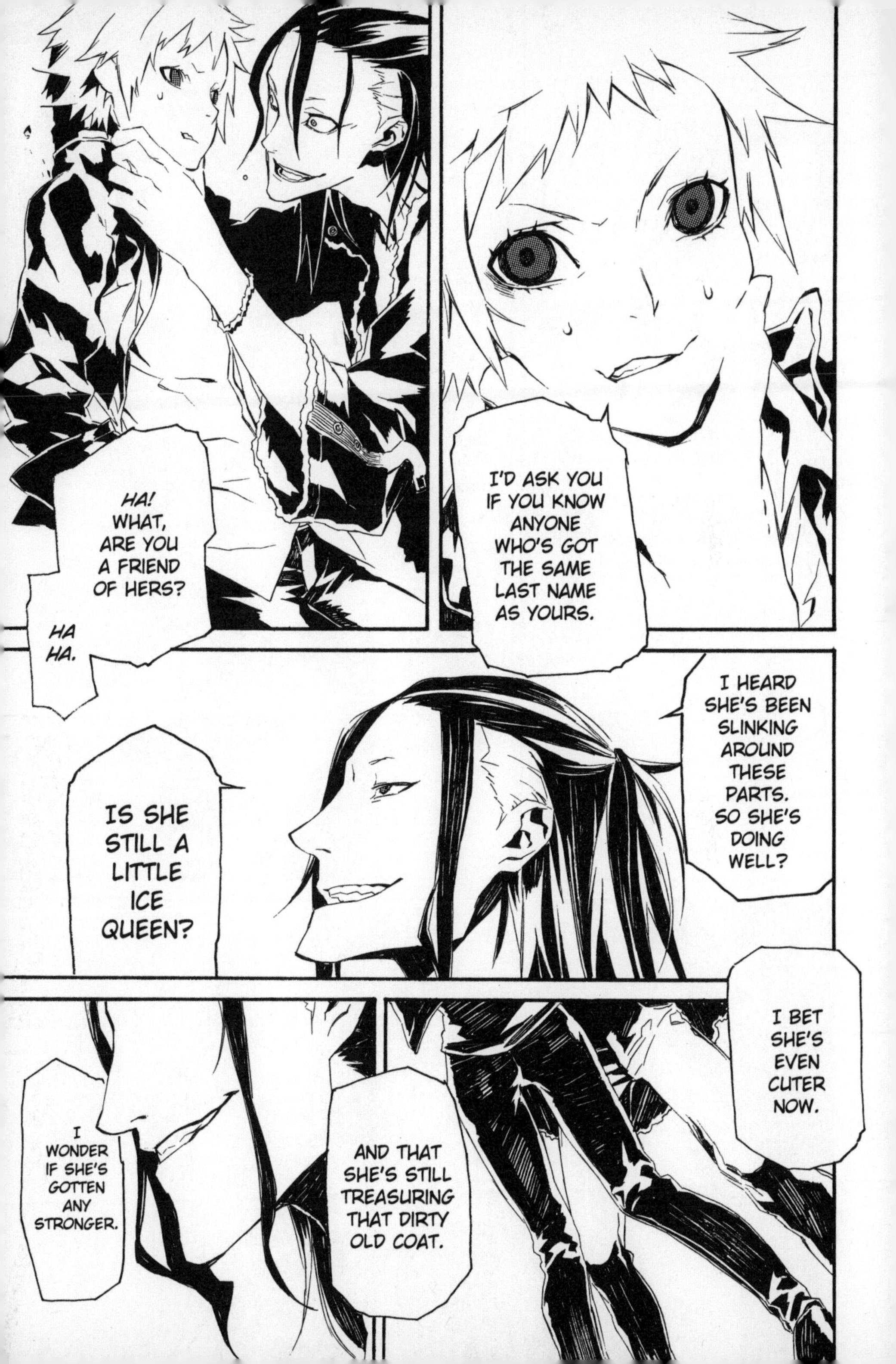
I'D ASK YOU IF YOU KNOW ANYONE WHO'S GOT THE SAME LAST NAME AS YOURS.
HA! WHAT, ARE YOU A FRIEND OF HERS?
HA HA.
I HEARD SHE'S BEEN SLINKING AROUND THESE PARTS. SO SHE'S DOING WELL?
IS SHE STILL A LITTLE ICE QUEEN?
I BET SHE'S EVEN CUTER NOW.
AND THAT SHE'S STILL TREASURING THAT DIRTY OLD COAT.
I WONDER IF SHE'S GOTTEN ANY STRONGER.

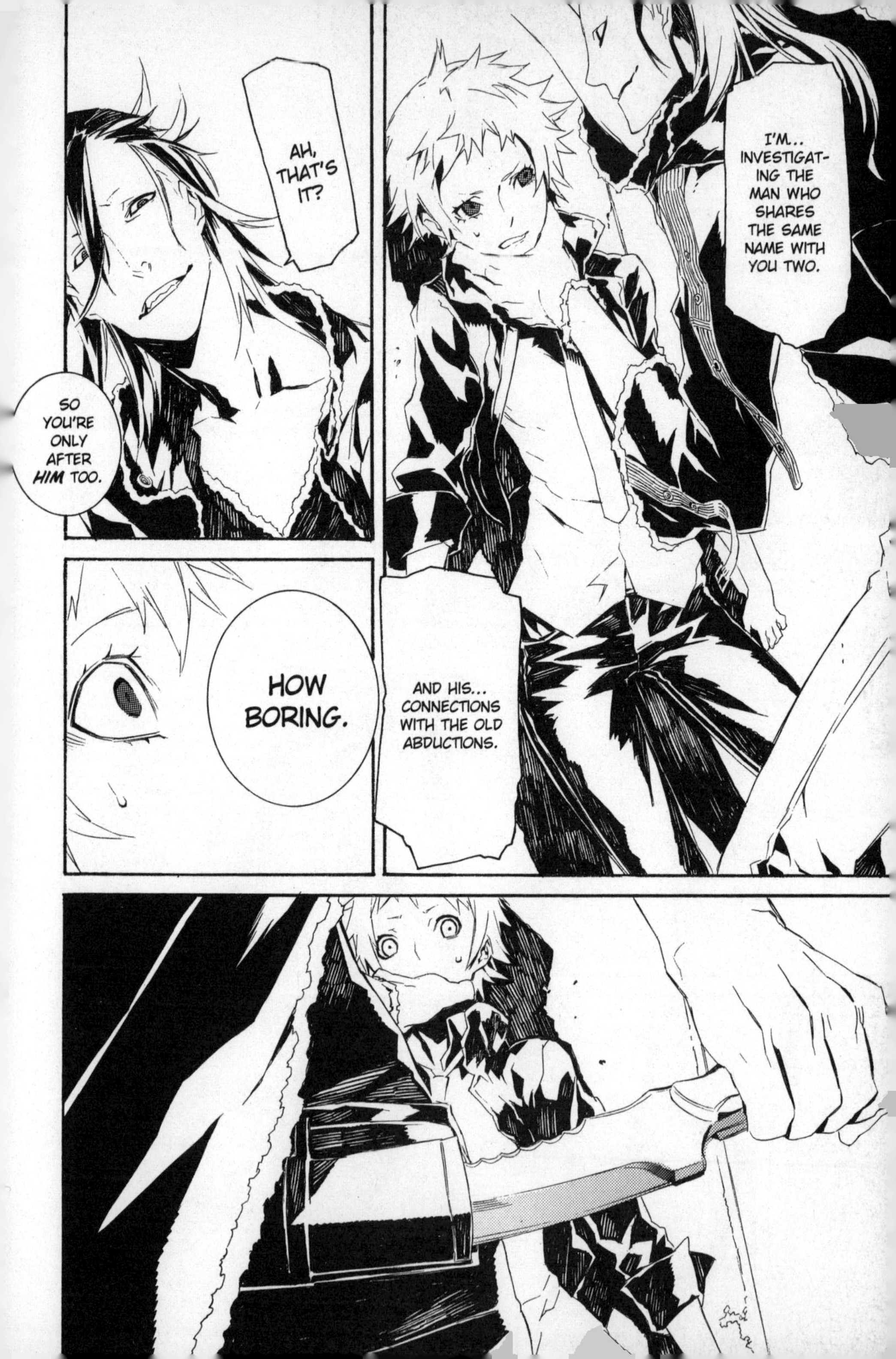
I'M... INVESTIGATING THE MAN WHO SHARES THE SAME NAME WITH YOU TWO.
AND HIS... CONNECTIONS WITH THE OLD ABDUCTIONS.
AH, THAT'S IT?
SO YOU'RE ONLY AFTER *HIM* TOO.
HOW BORING.

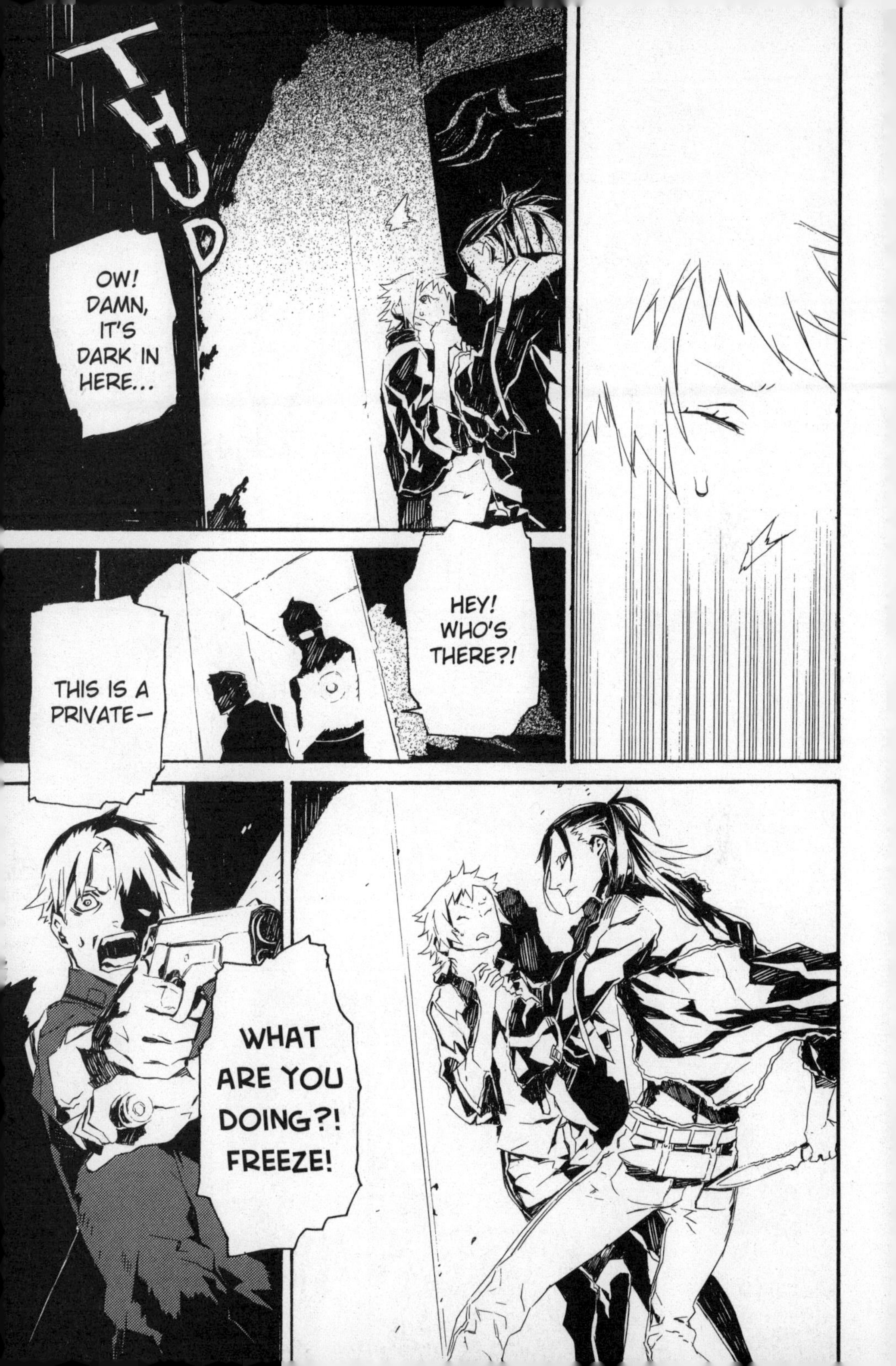
THUD
OW! DAMN, IT'S DARK IN HERE...
HEY! WHO'S THERE?!
THIS IS A PRIVATE—
WHAT ARE YOU DOING?! FREEZE!

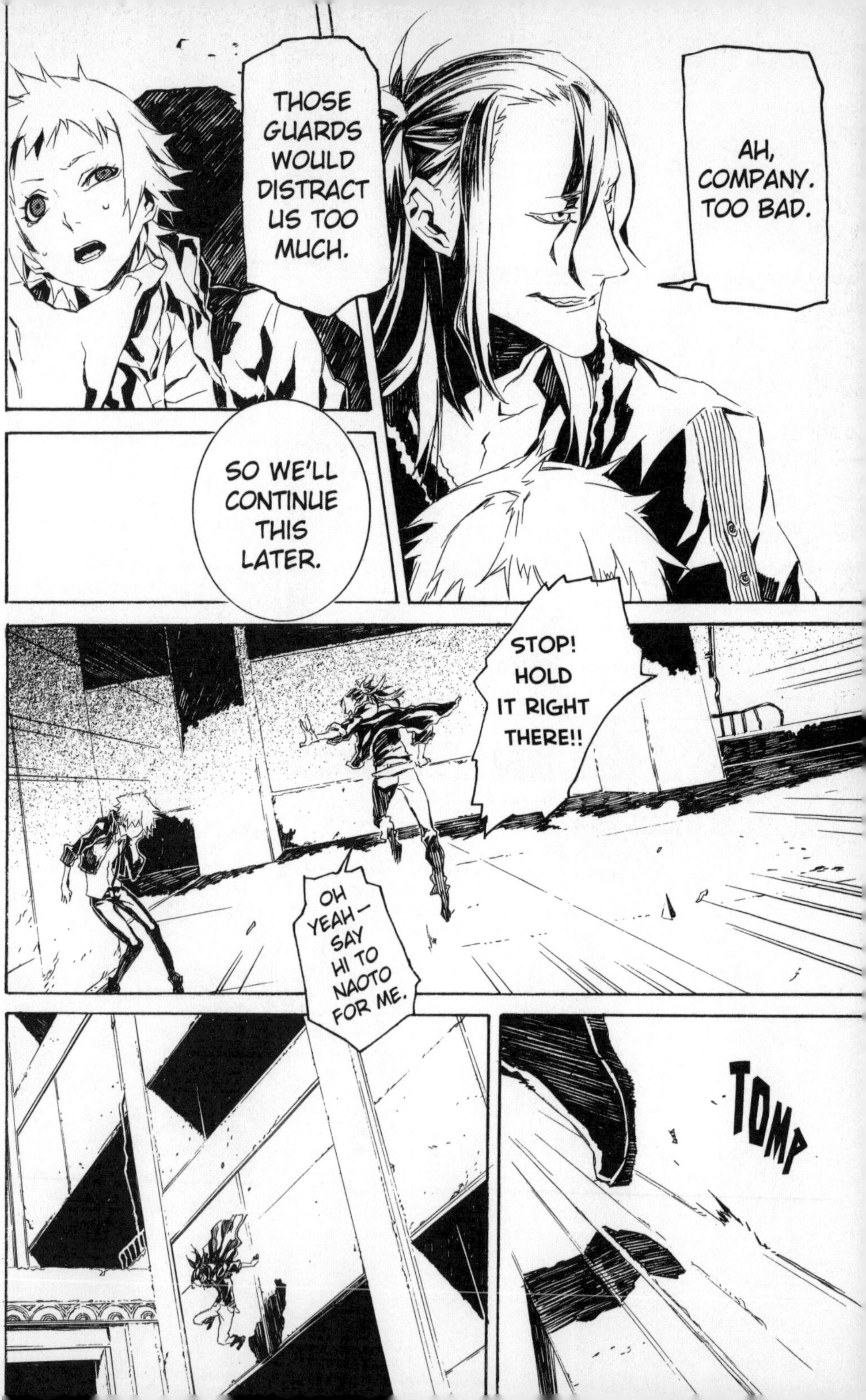
AH, COMPANY. TOO BAD.
THOSE GUARDS WOULD DISTRACT US TOO MUCH.
SO WE'LL CONTINUE THIS LATER.
STOP! HOLD IT RIGHT THERE!!
OH YEAH— SAY HI TO NAOTO FOR ME.
TOMP

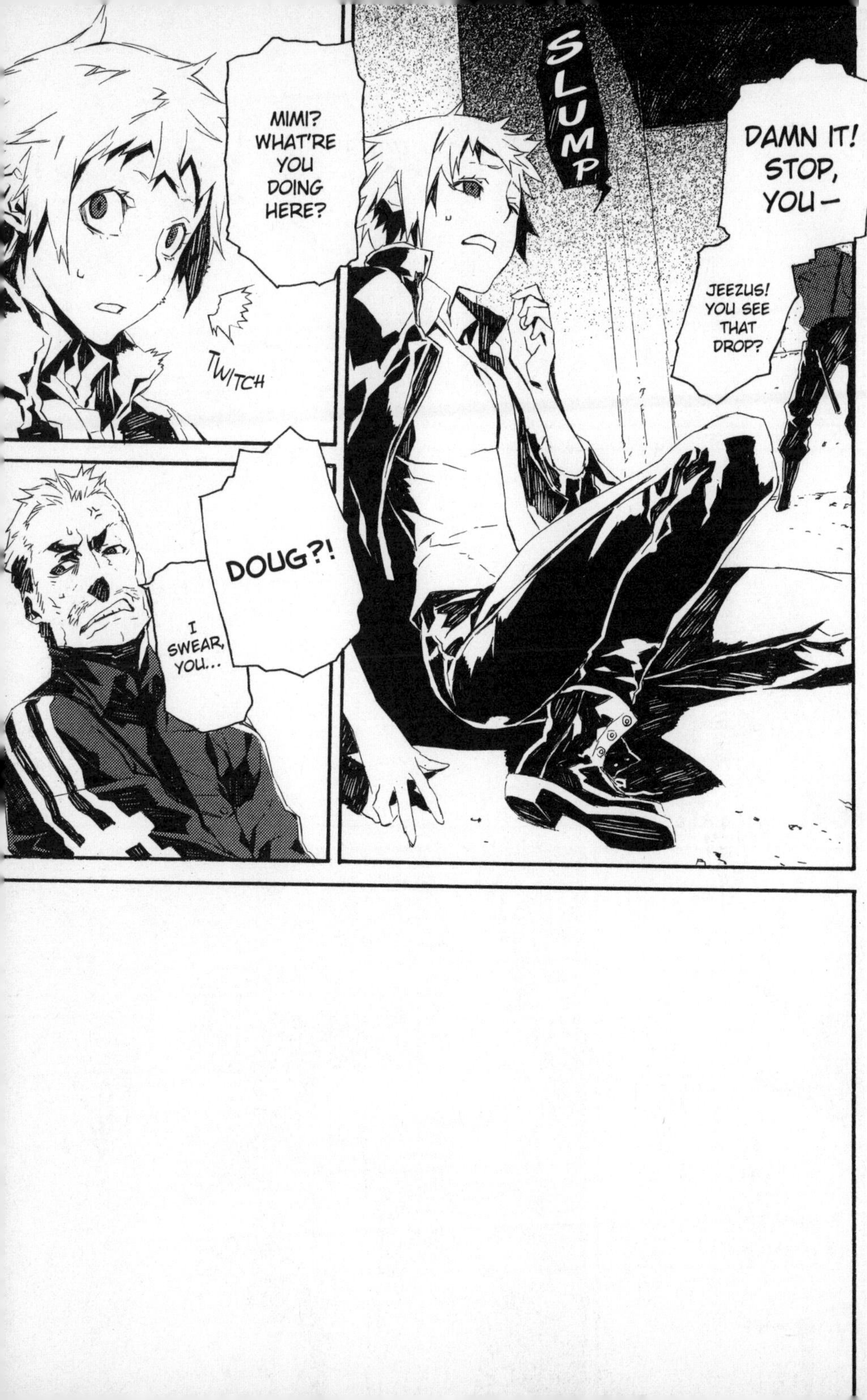
SLUMP
DAMN IT! STOP, YOU—
JEEZUS! YOU SEE THAT DROP?
MIMI? WHAT'RE YOU DOING HERE?
TWITCH
DOUG?!
I SWEAR, YOU...

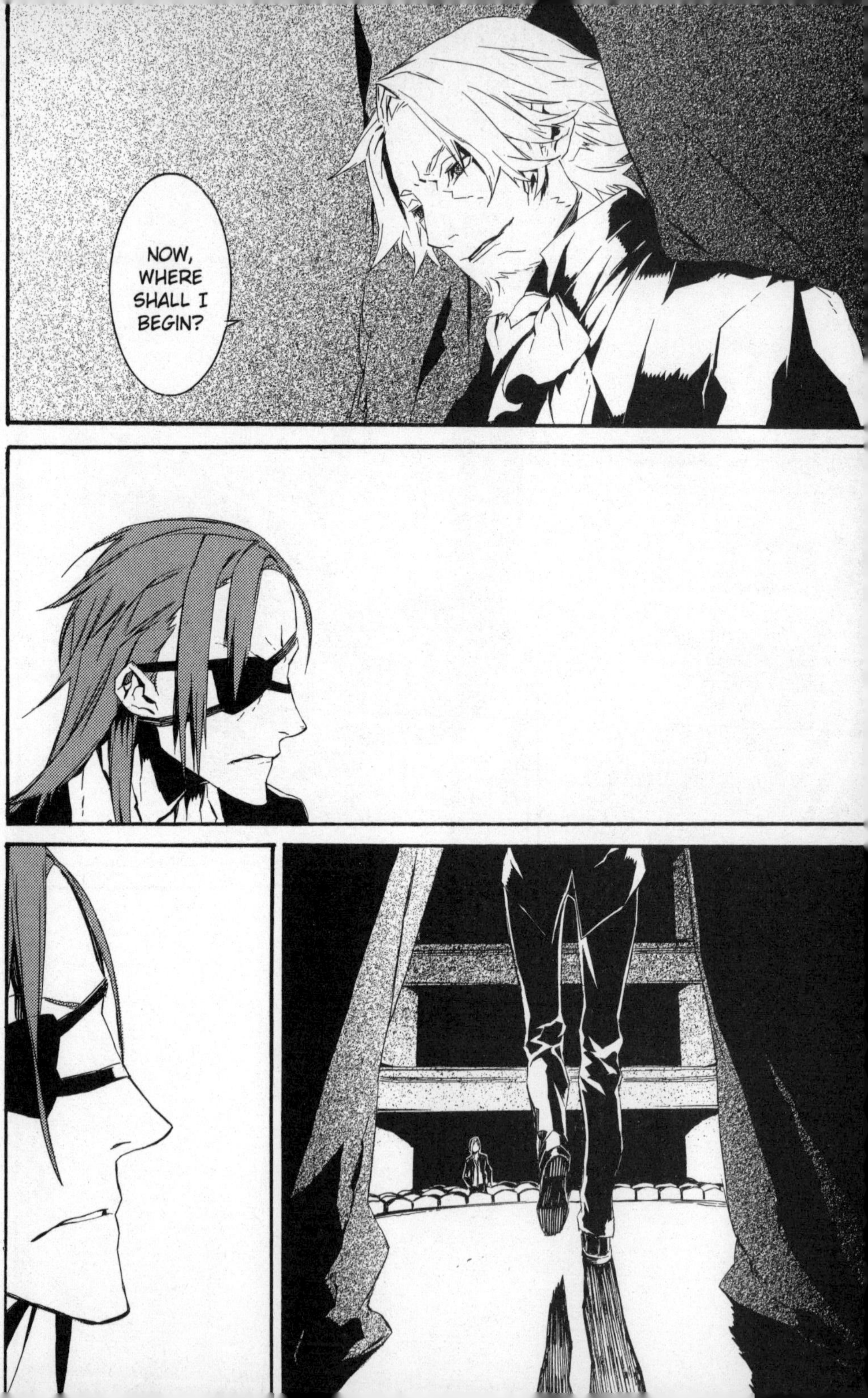
NOW, WHERE SHALL I BEGIN?

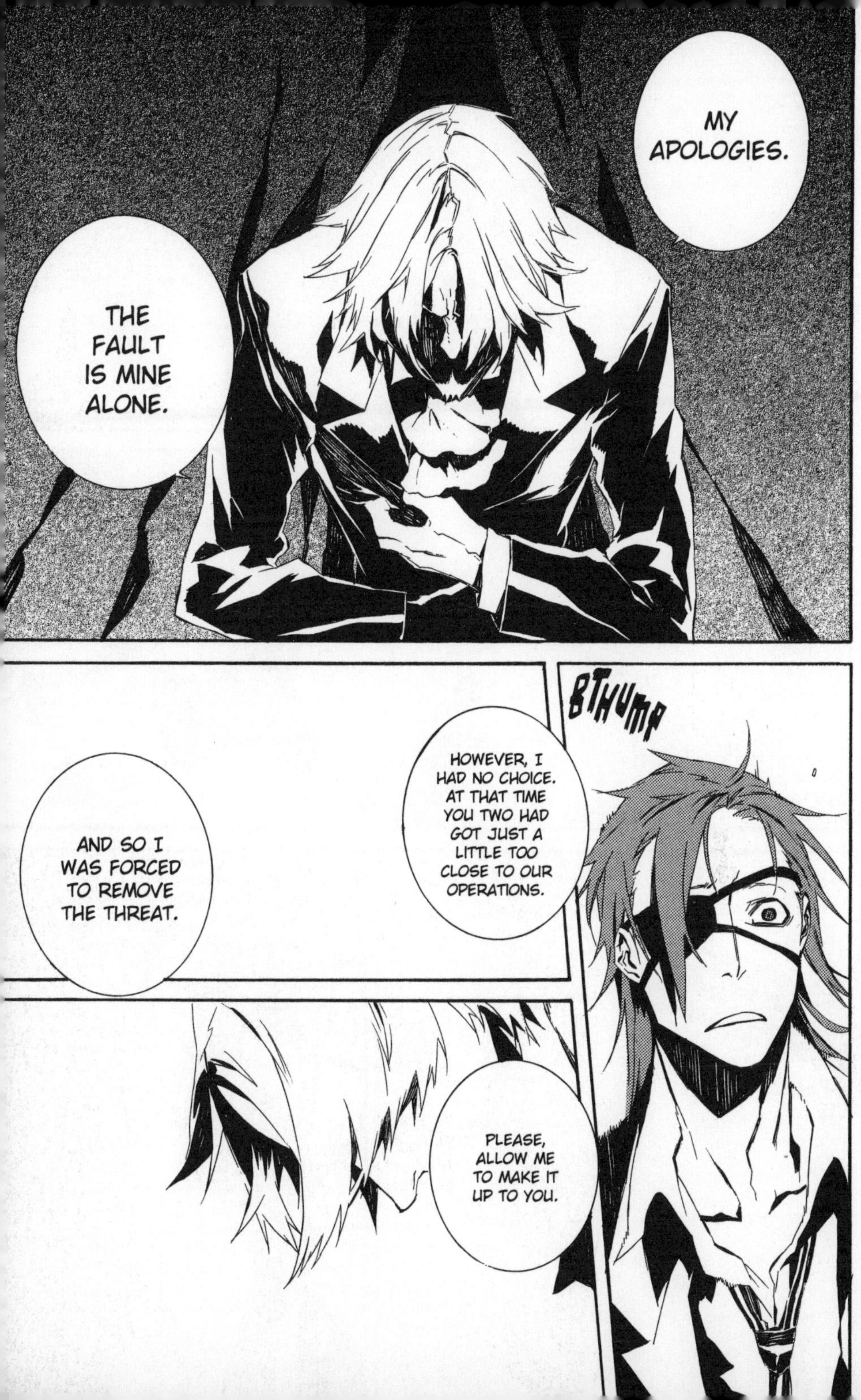
MY APOLOGIES.
THE FAULT IS MINE ALONE.
BTHUMP
HOWEVER, I HAD NO CHOICE. AT THAT TIME YOU TWO HAD GOT JUST A LITTLE TOO CLOSE TO OUR OPERATIONS.
AND SO I WAS FORCED TO REMOVE THE THREAT.
PLEASE, ALLOW ME TO MAKE IT UP TO YOU.

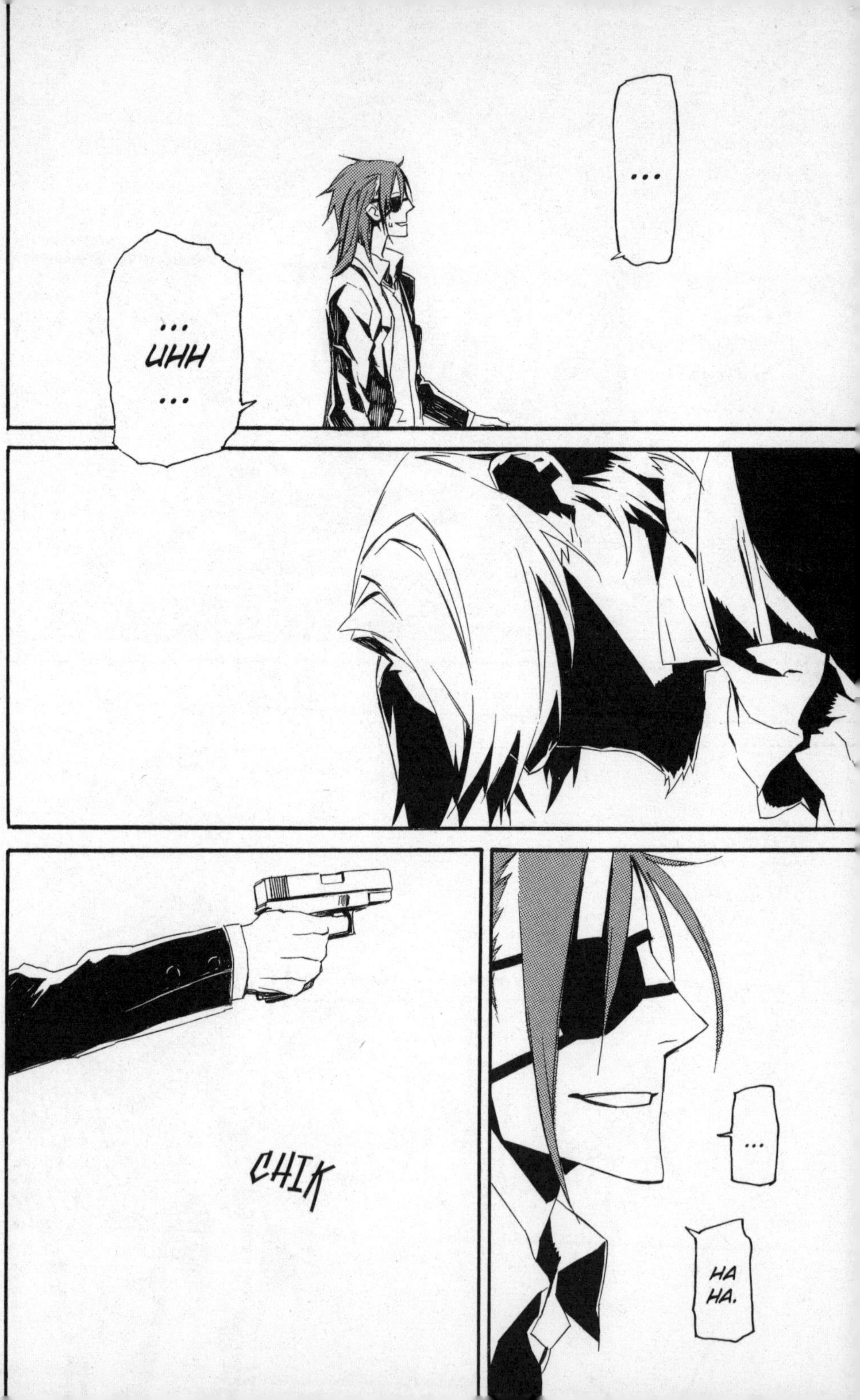
...
... UHH ...
...
HA HA.
CHIK

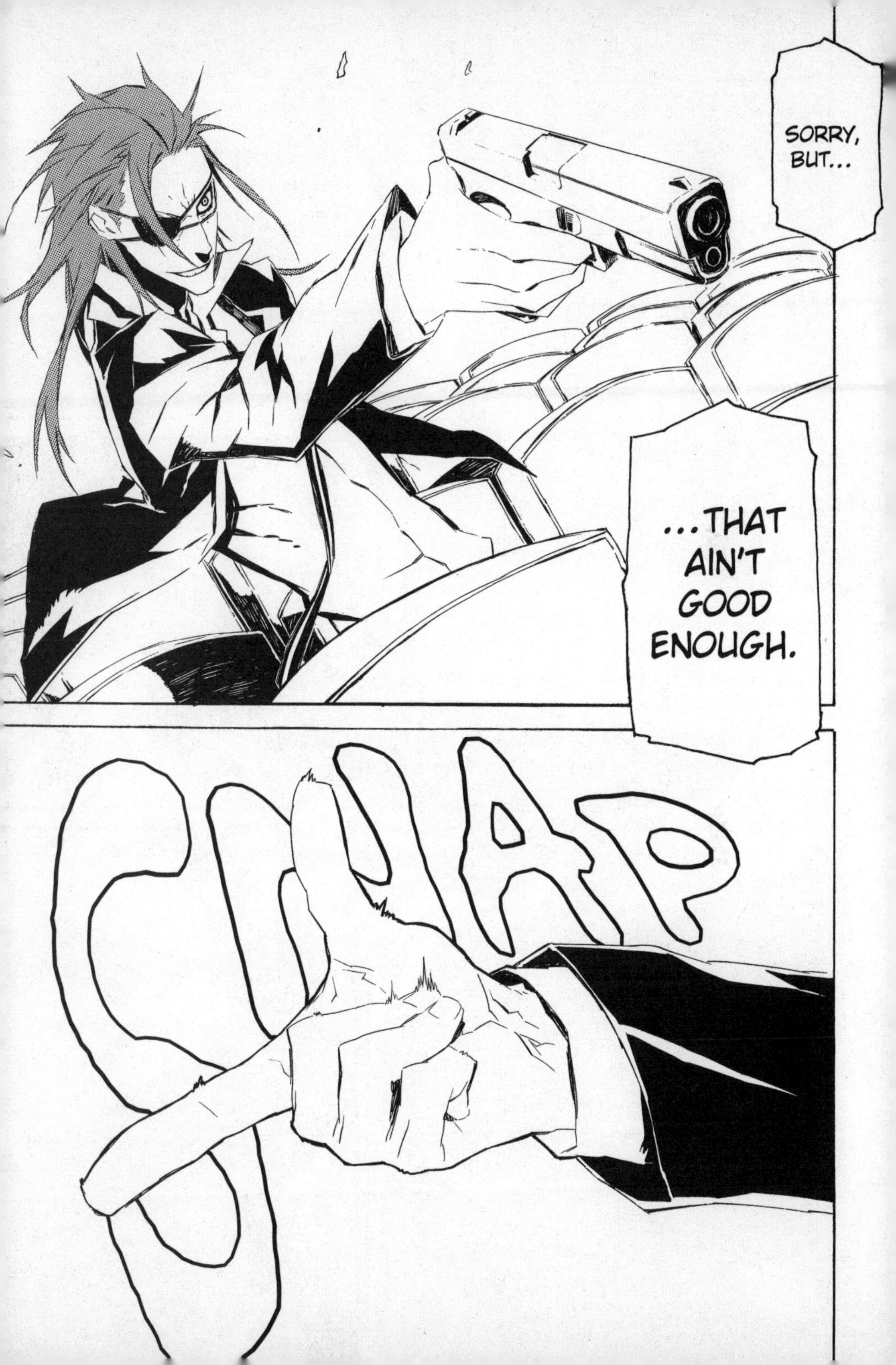
SORRY, BUT...
...THAT AIN'T GOOD ENOUGH.
CHAP

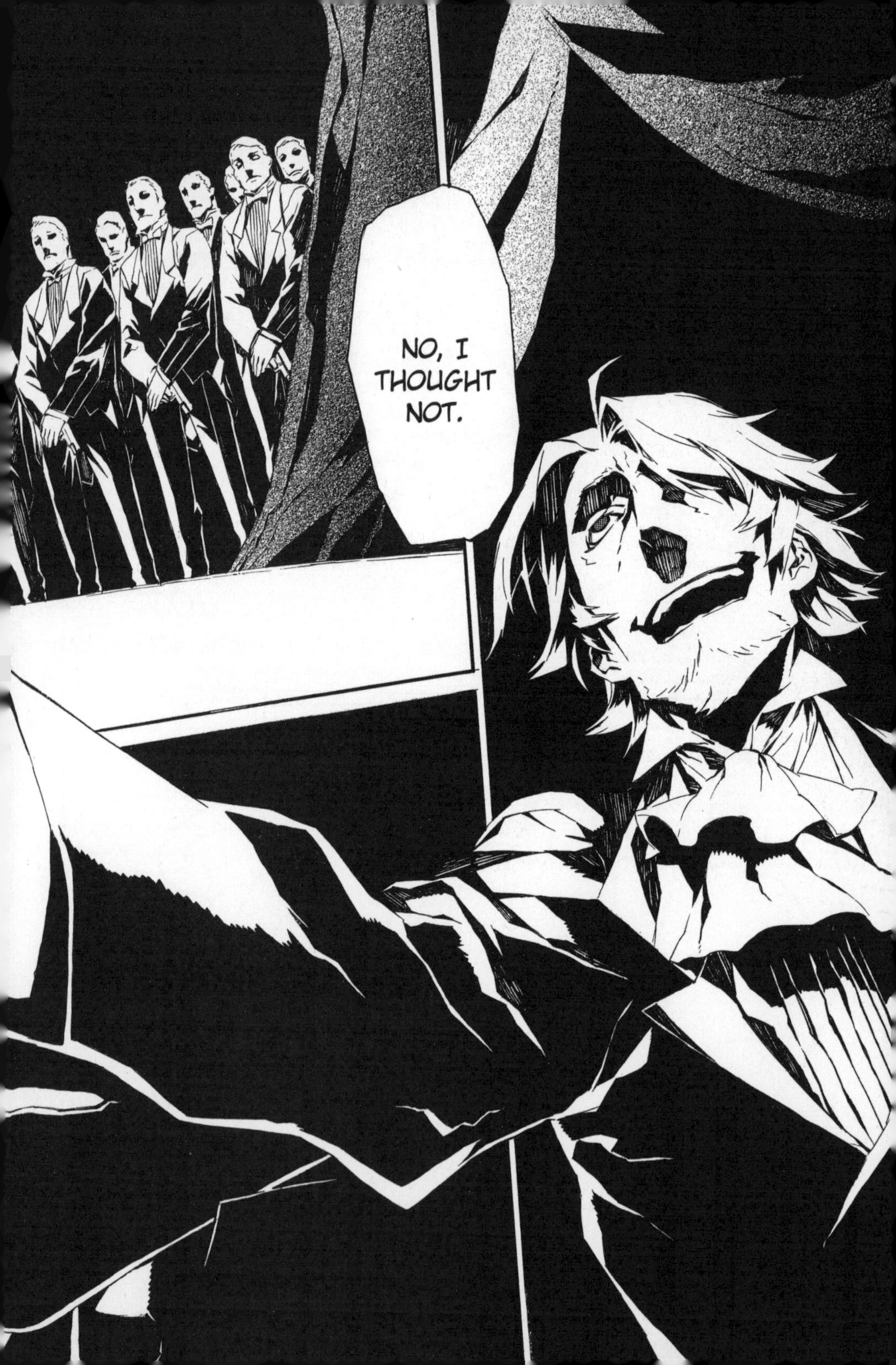
NO, I THOUGHT NOT.

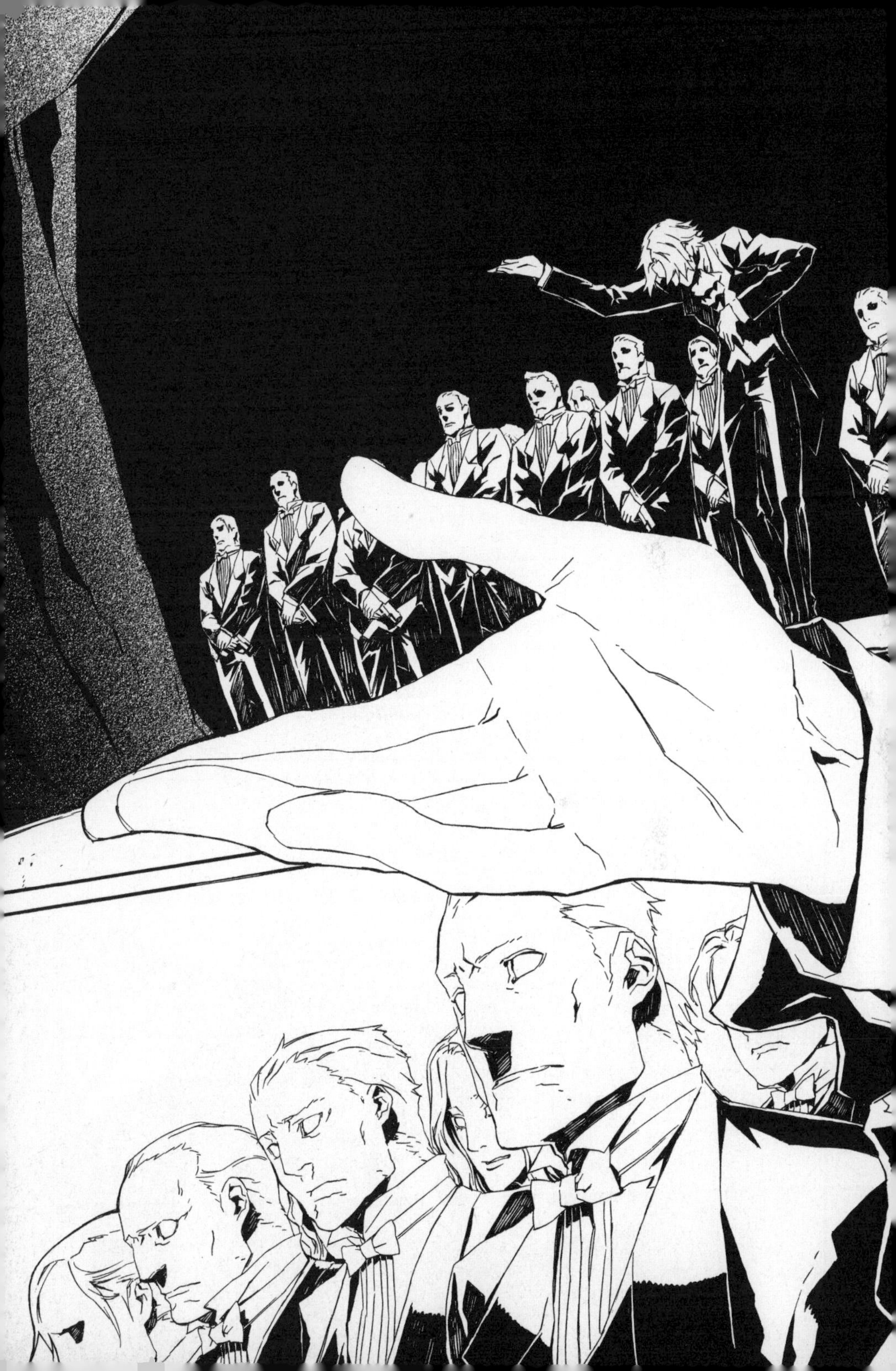

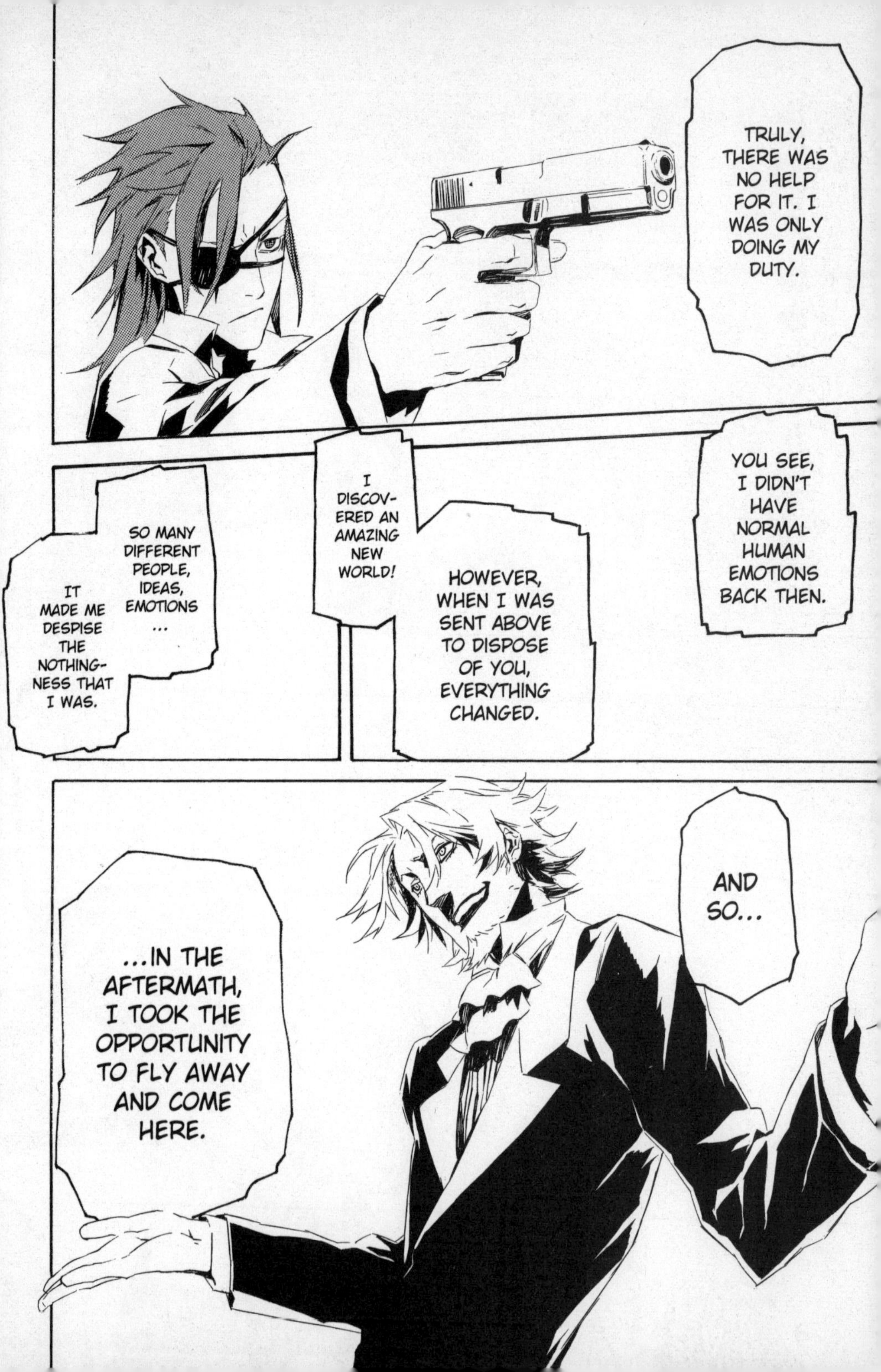
TRULY, THERE WAS NO HELP FOR IT. I WAS ONLY DOING MY DUTY.
YOU SEE, I DIDN'T HAVE NORMAL HUMAN EMOTIONS BACK THEN.
HOWEVER, WHEN I WAS SENT ABOVE TO DISPOSE OF YOU, EVERYTHING CHANGED.
I DISCOVERED AN AMAZING NEW WORLD!
SO MANY DIFFERENT PEOPLE, IDEAS, EMOTIONS...
IT MADE ME DESPISE THE NOTHINGNESS THAT I WAS.
AND SO...
...IN THE AFTERMATH, I TOOK THE OPPORTUNITY TO FLY AWAY AND COME HERE.

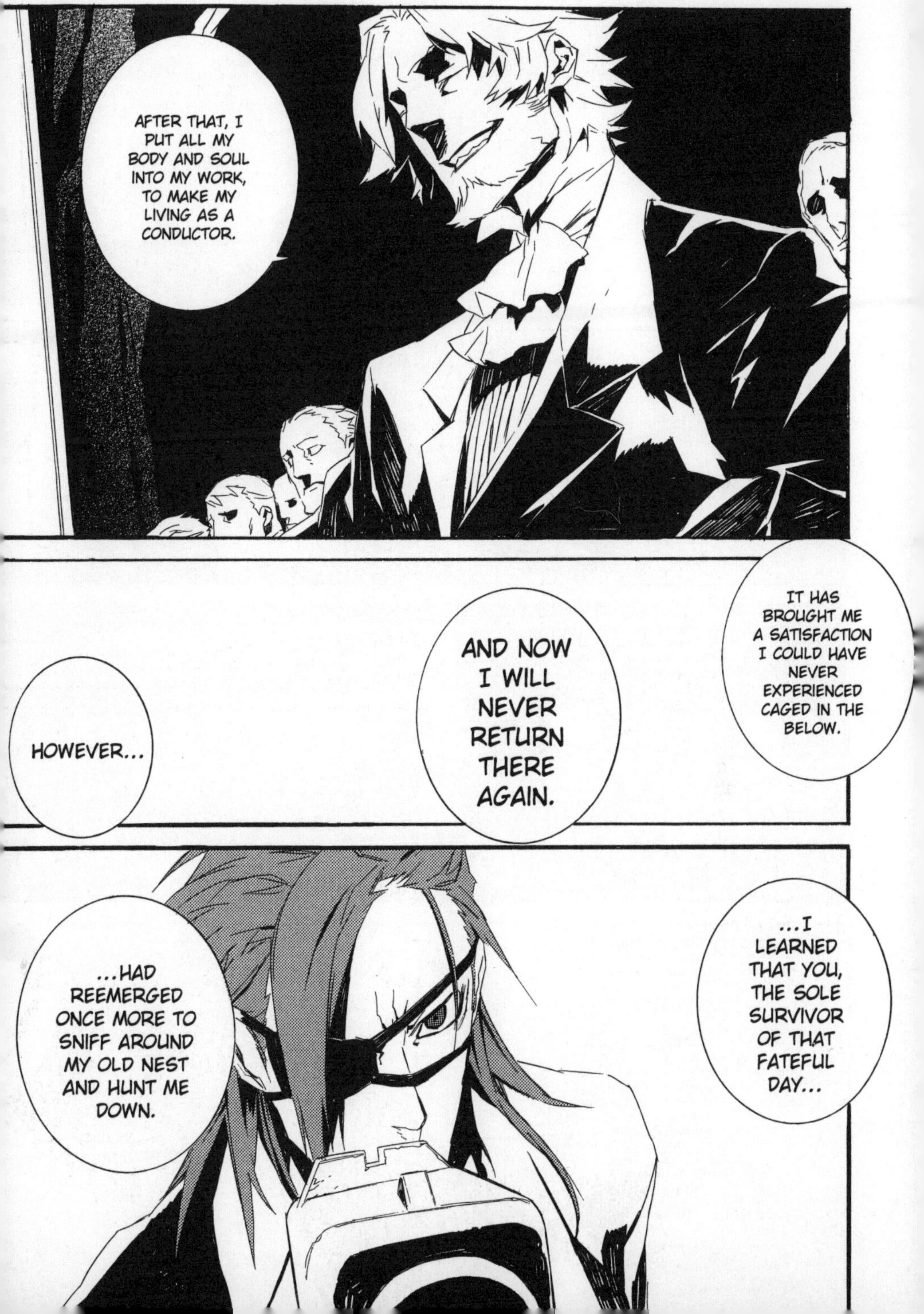
AFTER THAT, I PUT ALL MY BODY AND SOUL INTO MY WORK, TO MAKE MY LIVING AS A CONDUCTOR.
IT HAS BROUGHT ME A SATISFACTION I COULD HAVE NEVER EXPERIENCED CAGED IN THE BELOW.
AND NOW I WILL NEVER RETURN THERE AGAIN.
HOWEVER...
...I LEARNED THAT YOU, THE SOLE SURVIVOR OF THAT FATEFUL DAY...
...HAD REEMERGED ONCE MORE TO SNIFF AROUND MY OLD NEST AND HUNT ME DOWN.

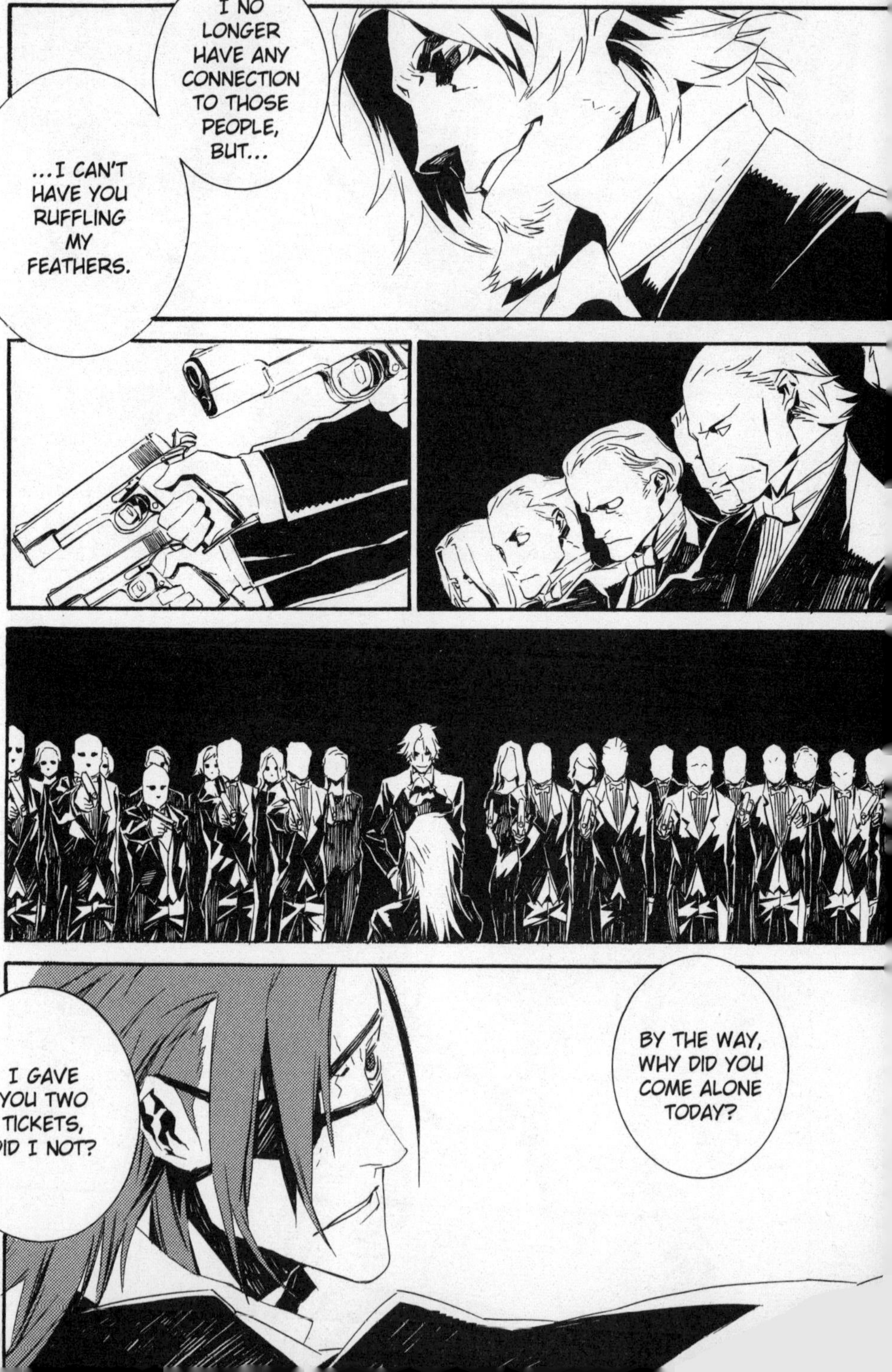
I NO LONGER HAVE ANY CONNECTION TO THOSE PEOPLE, BUT...
...I CAN'T HAVE YOU RUFFLING MY FEATHERS.
BY THE WAY, WHY DID YOU COME ALONE TODAY?
I GAVE YOU TWO TICKETS, DID I NOT?

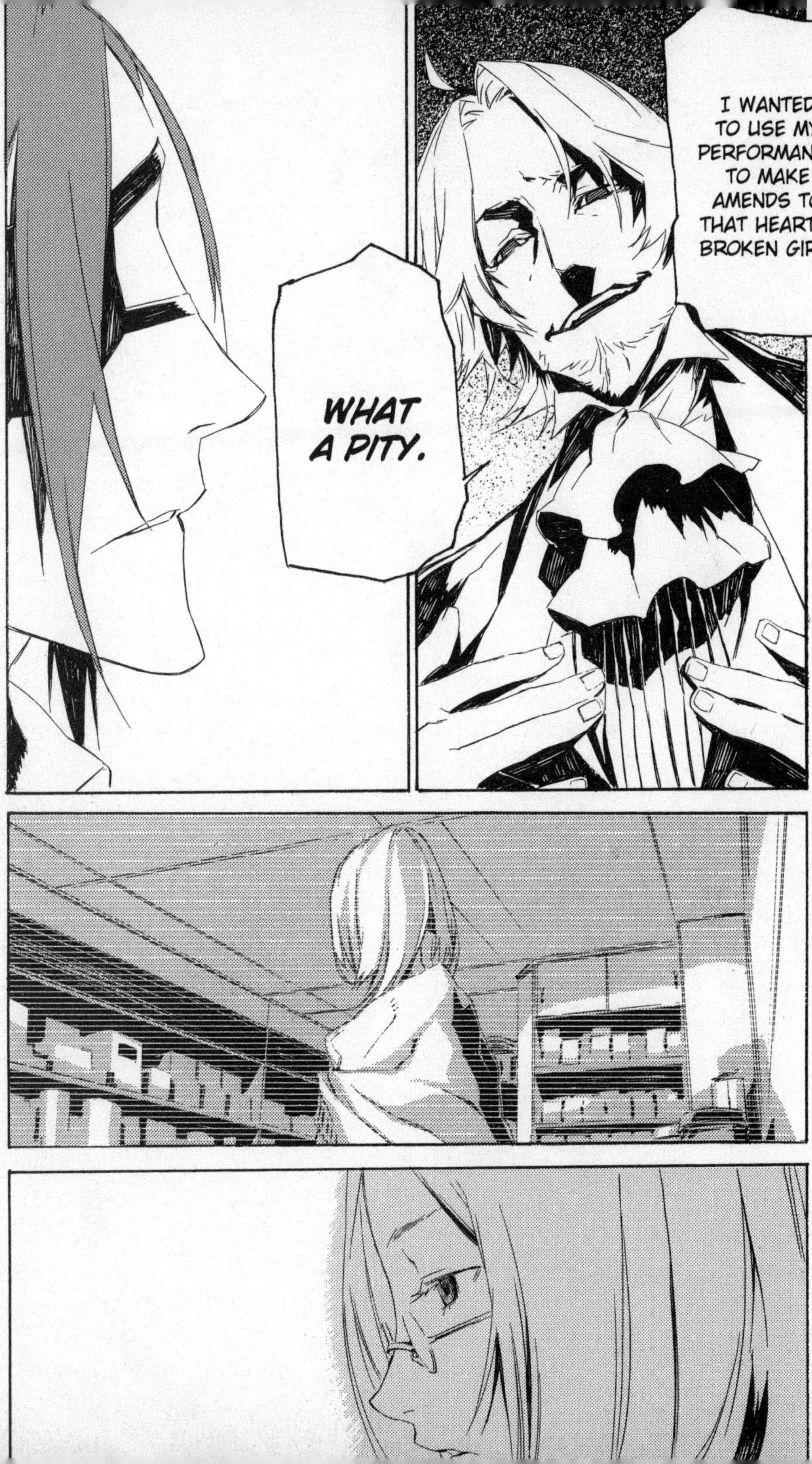
I WANTED TO USE MY PERFORMANCE TO MAKE AMENDS TO THAT HEART-BROKEN GIRL.
WHAT A PITY.

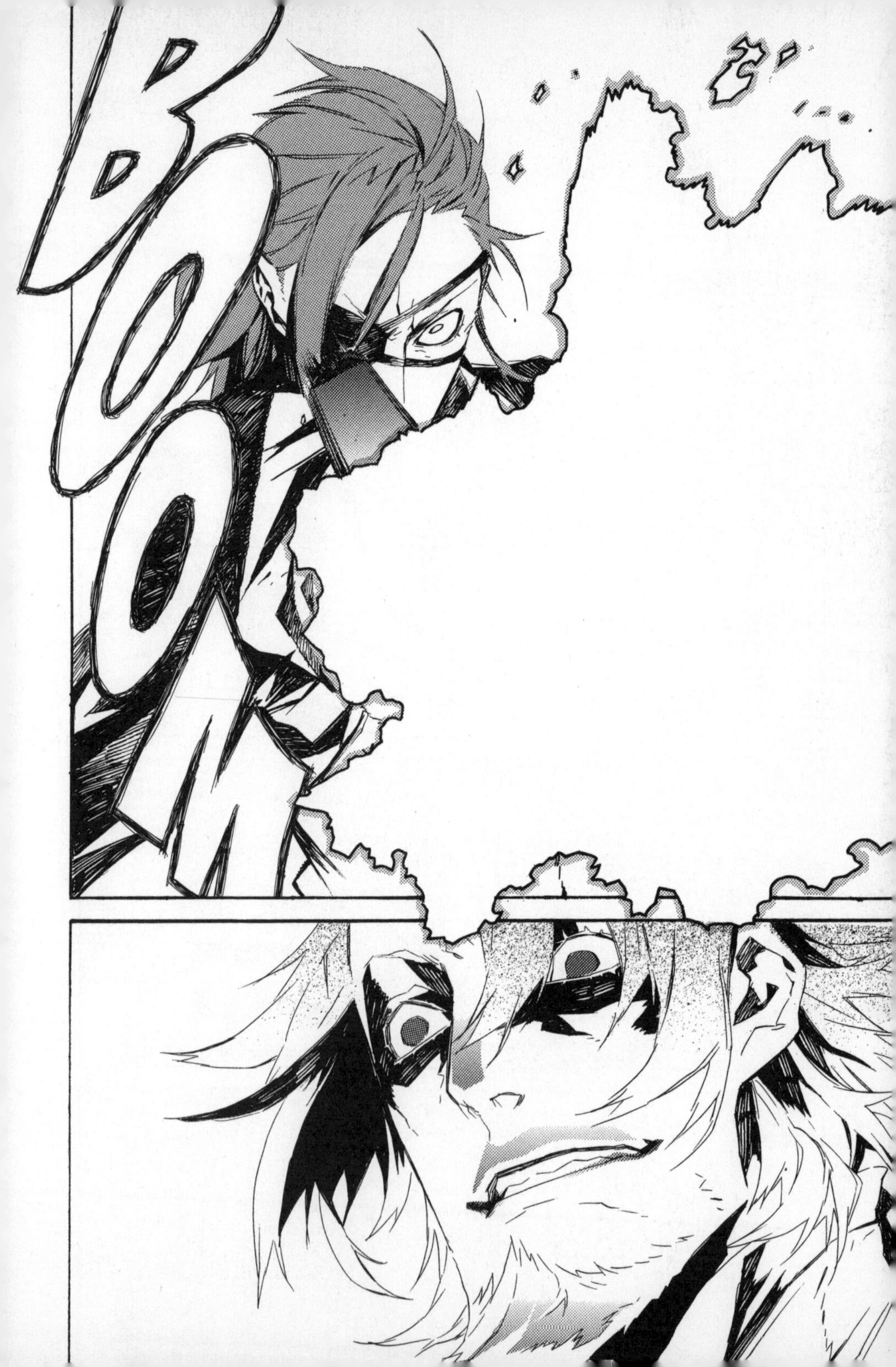
BOOM

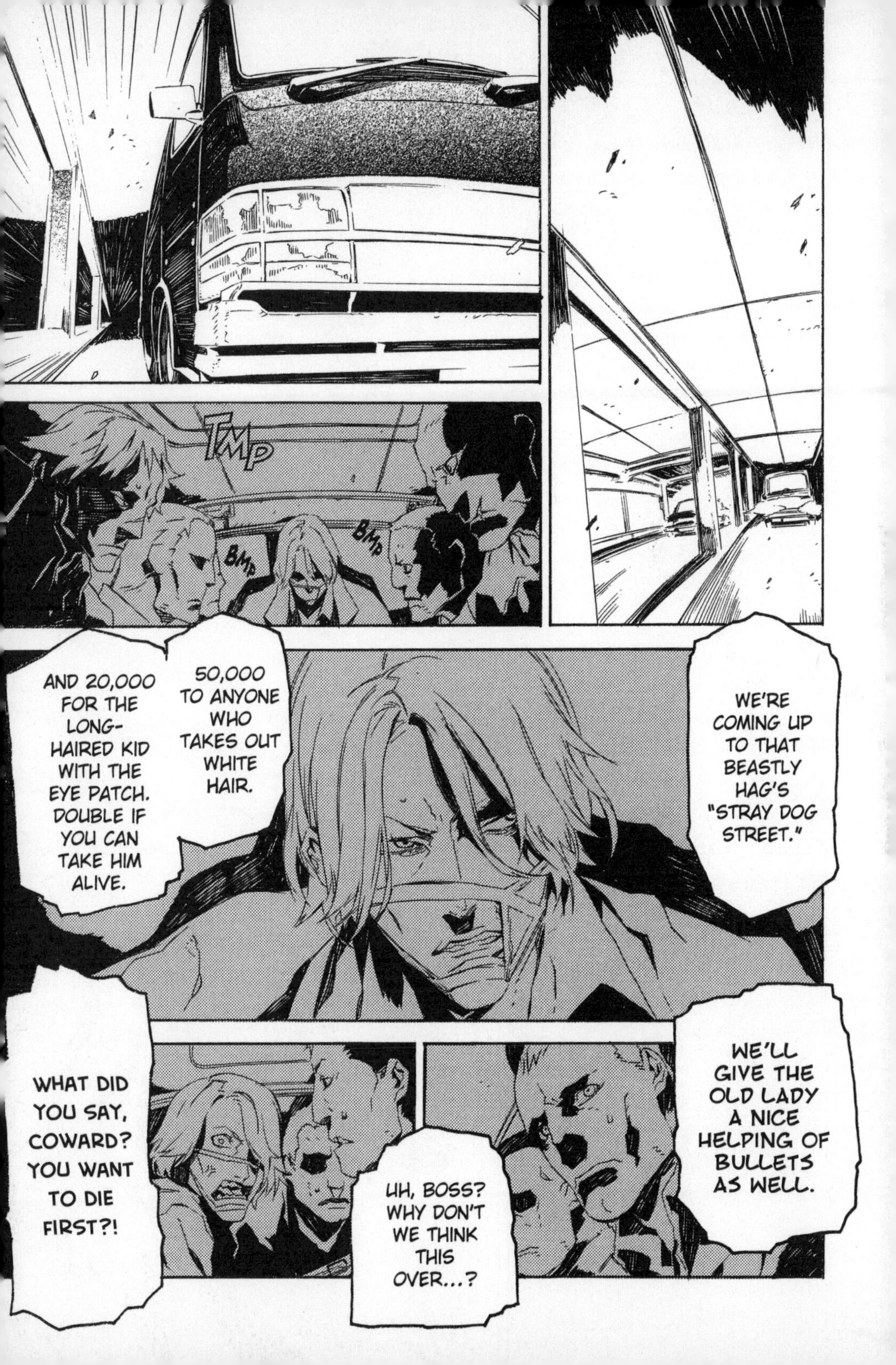
TMP
BMP
BMP
WE'RE COMING UP TO THAT BEASTLY HAG'S "STRAY DOG STREET."
50,000 TO ANYONE WHO TAKES OUT WHITE HAIR.
AND 20,000 FOR THE LONG-HAIRED KID WITH THE EYE PATCH. DOUBLE IF YOU CAN TAKE HIM ALIVE.
WE'LL GIVE THE OLD LADY A NICE HELPING OF BULLETS AS WELL.
UH, BOSS? WHY DON'T WE THINK THIS OVER...?
WHAT DID YOU SAY, COWARD? YOU WANT TO DIE FIRST?!

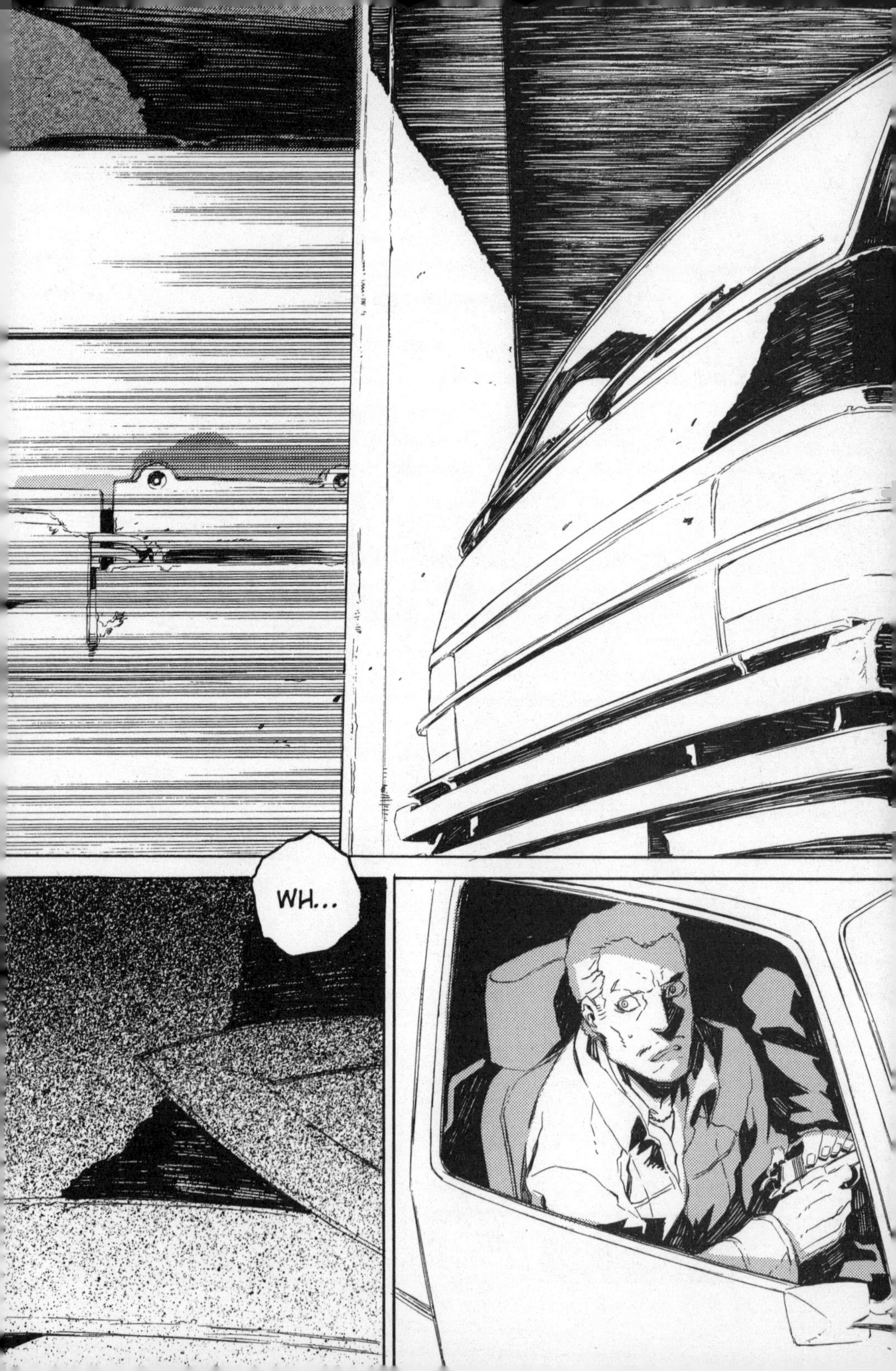
WH...

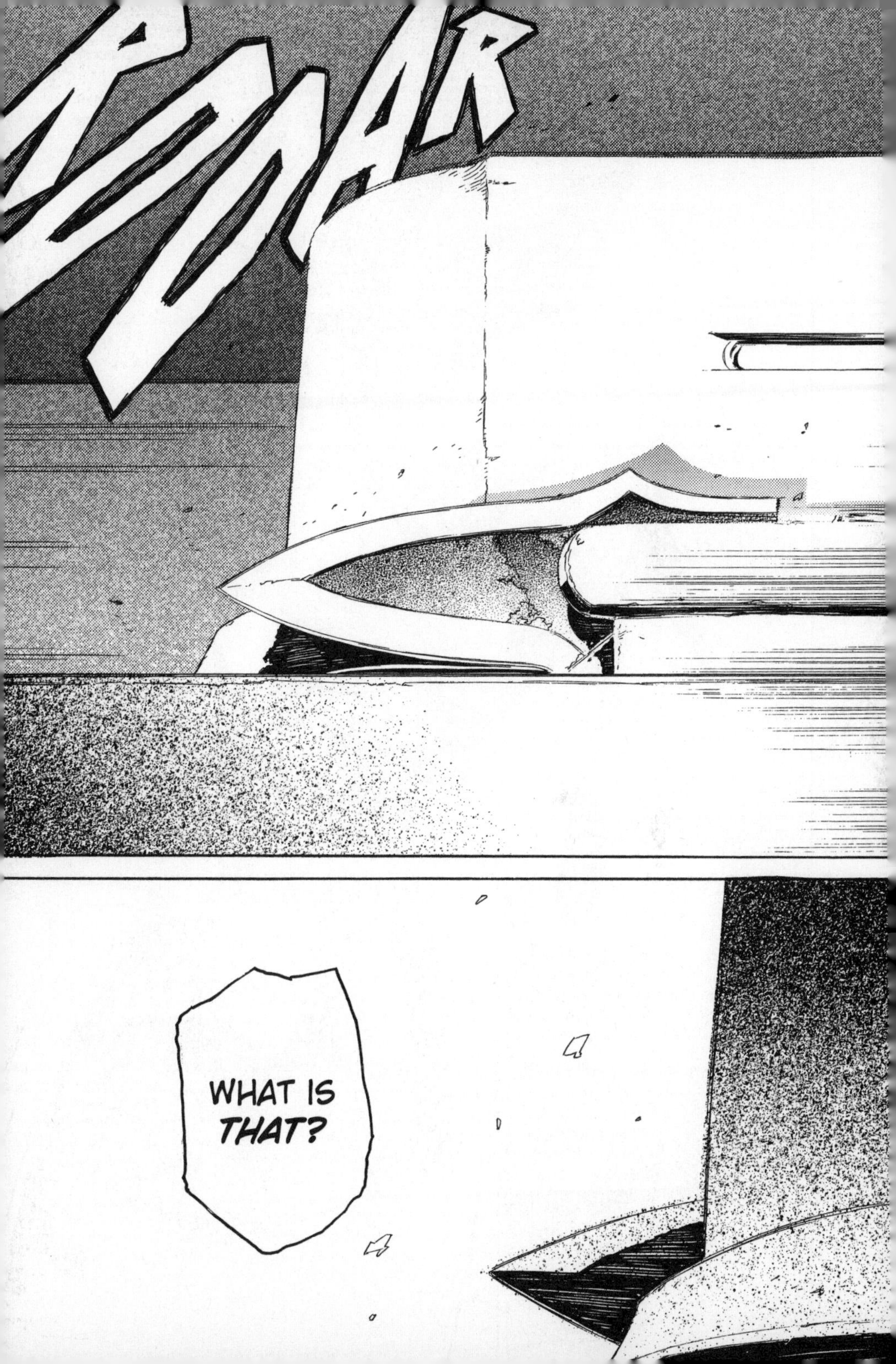
ROAR
WHAT IS THAT?

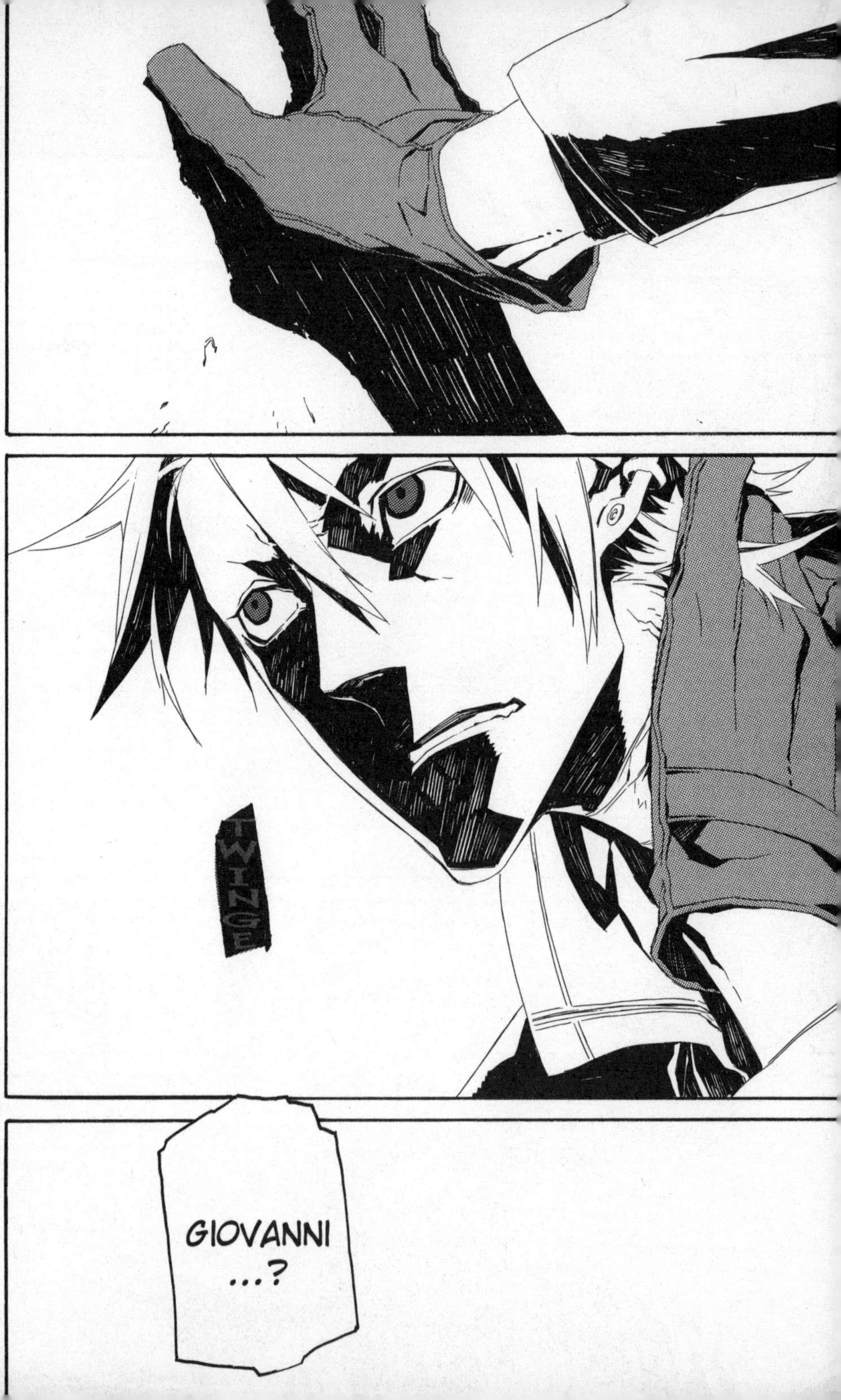
TWINGE
GIOVANNI ...?

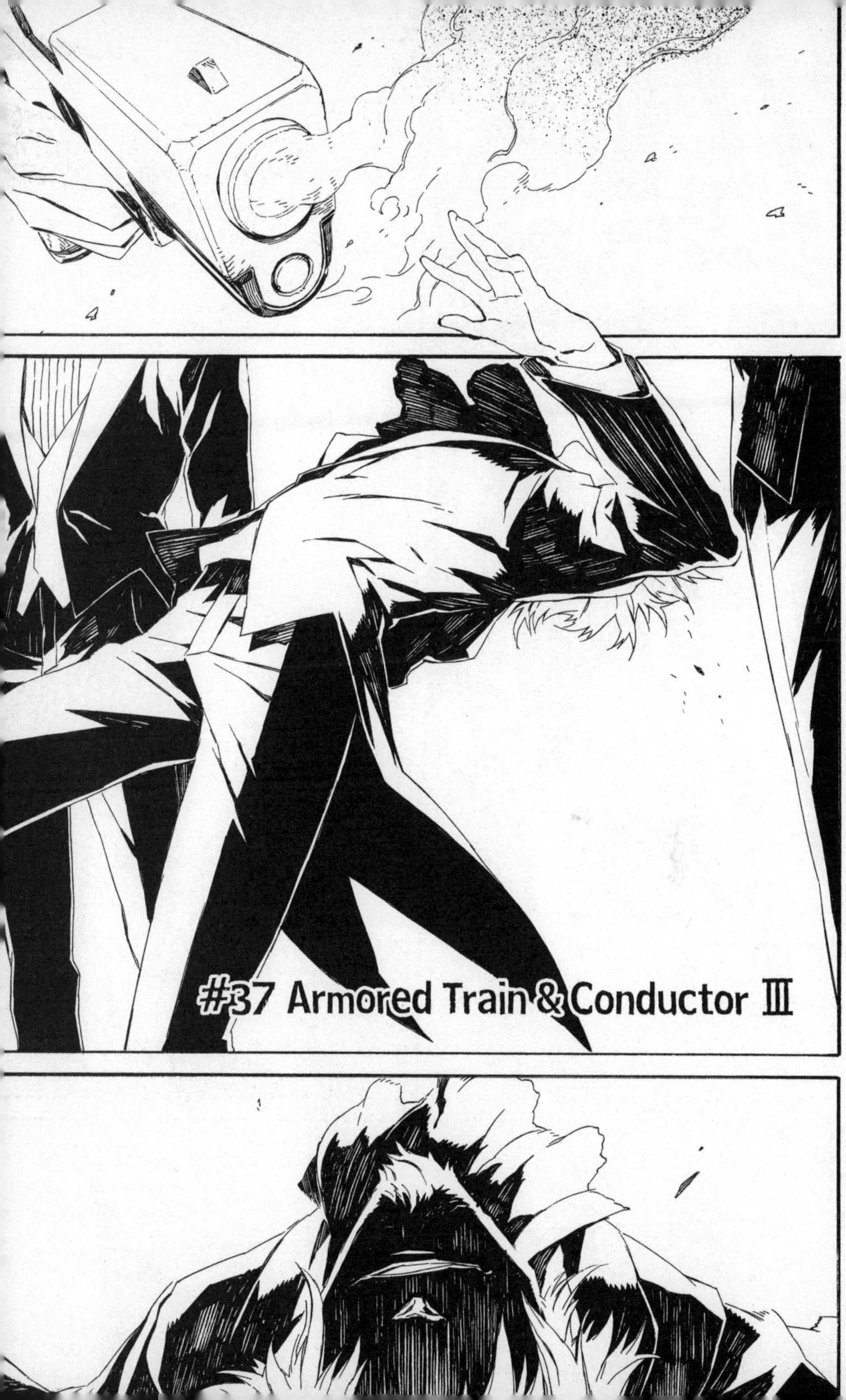
#37 Armored Train & Conductor III

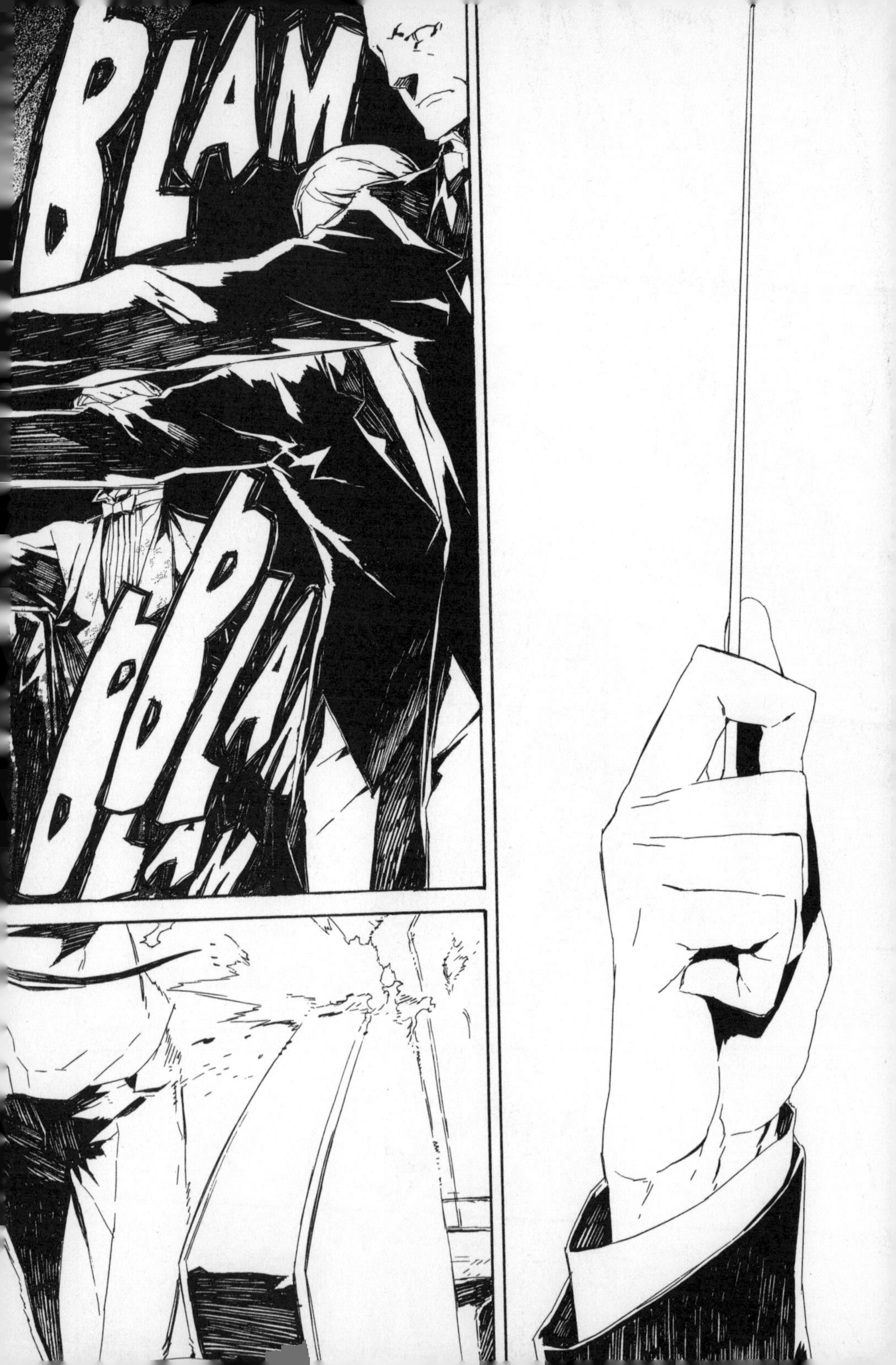
BLAM
BLAM
BLAM

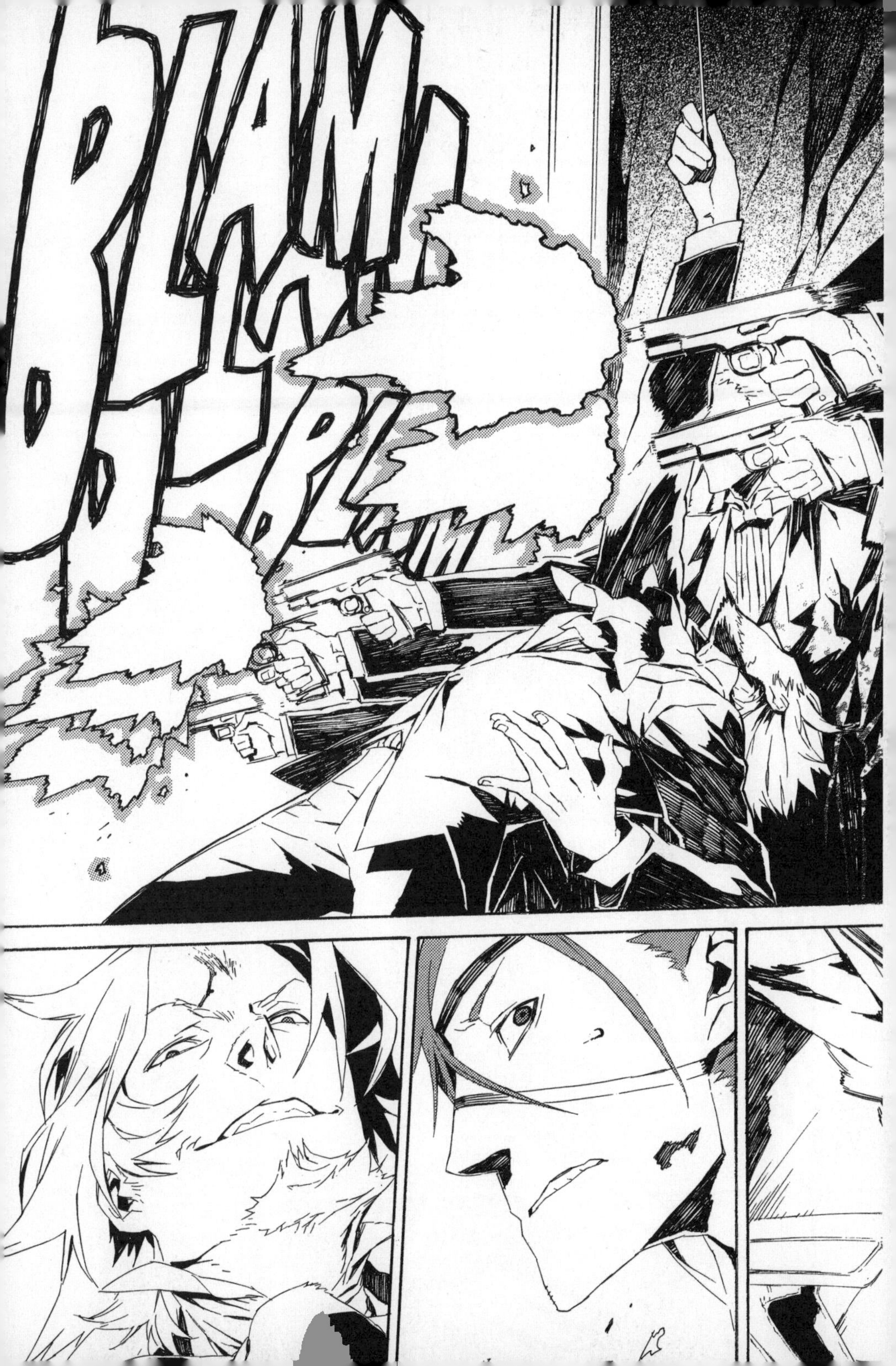
BLAM
BLAM

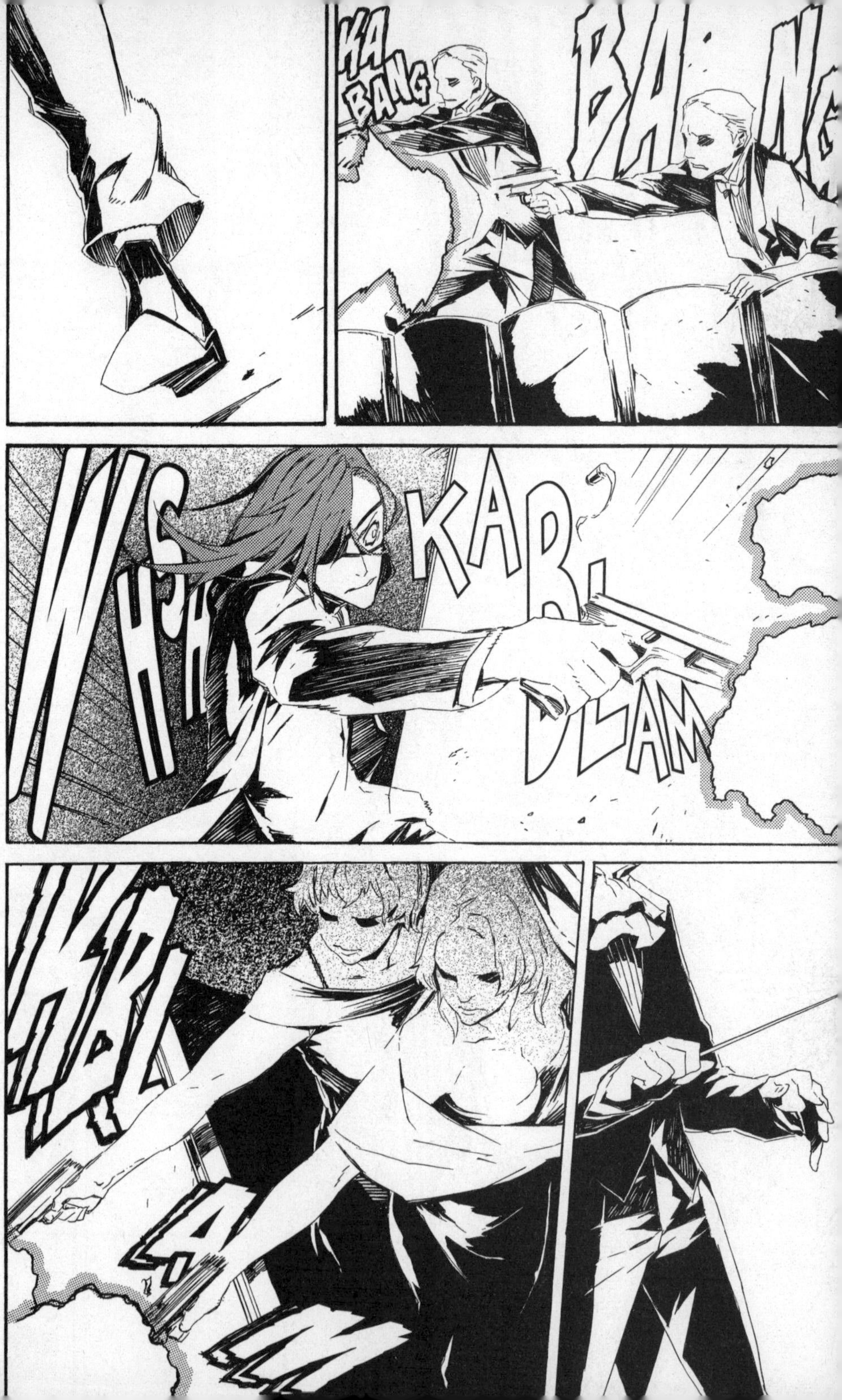
BANG
KA BANG
KA BLAM

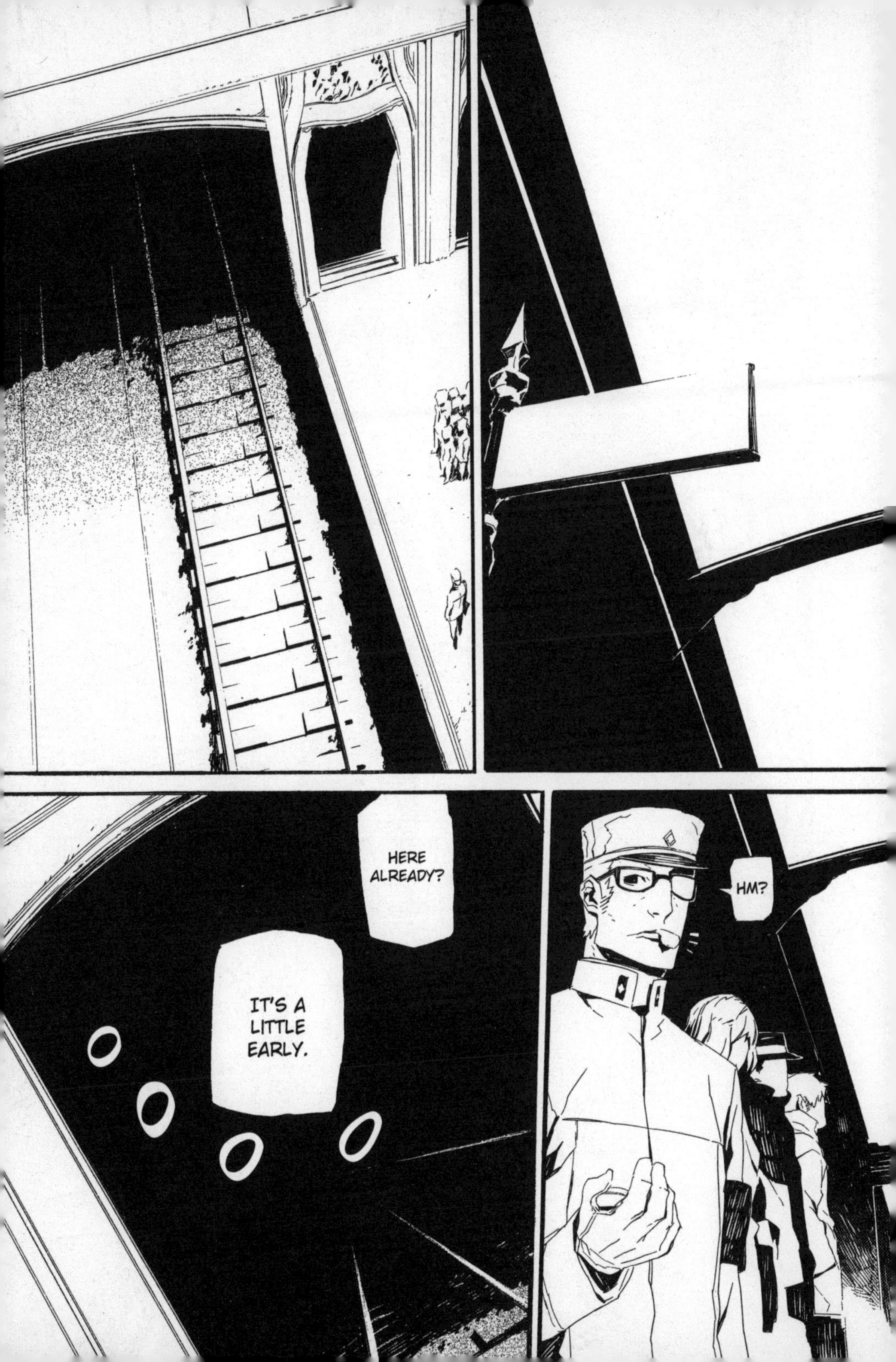
HM?
HERE ALREADY?
IT'S A LITTLE EARLY.

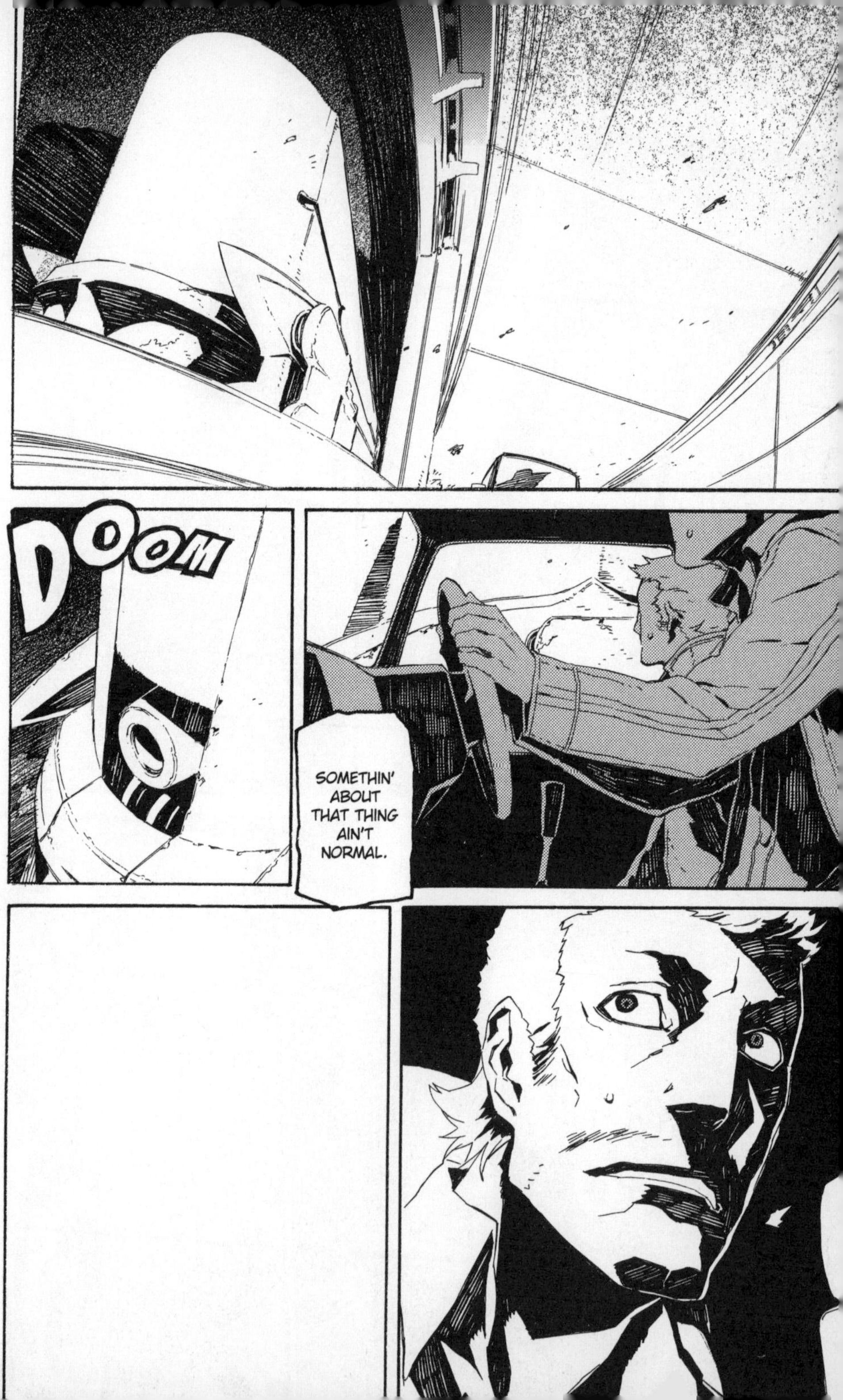
DOOM
SOMETHIN' ABOUT THAT THING AIN'T NORMAL.

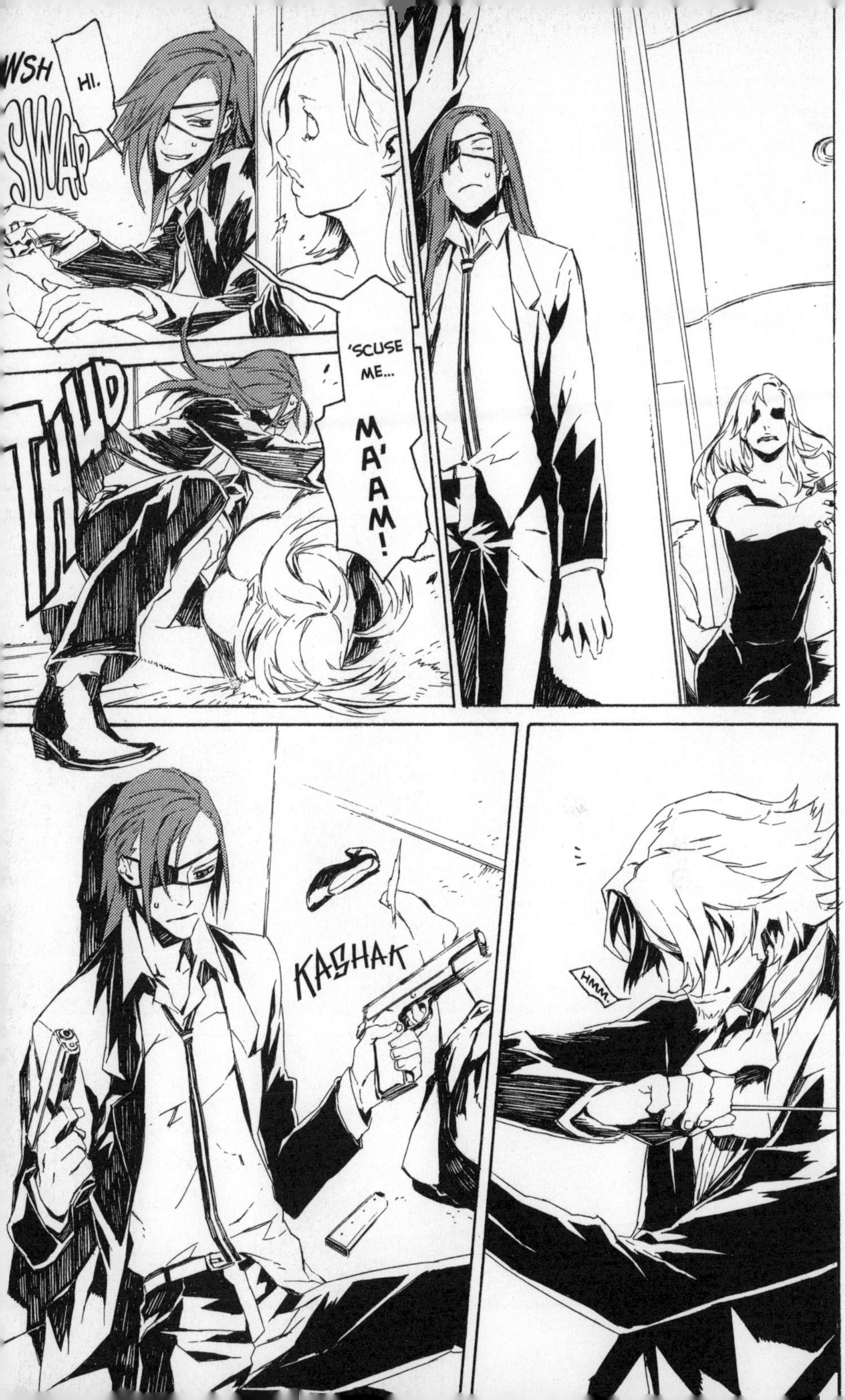
'SCUSE ME...
MA'AM!
WSH
SWAP
HI.
THUD
HMM.
KASHAK

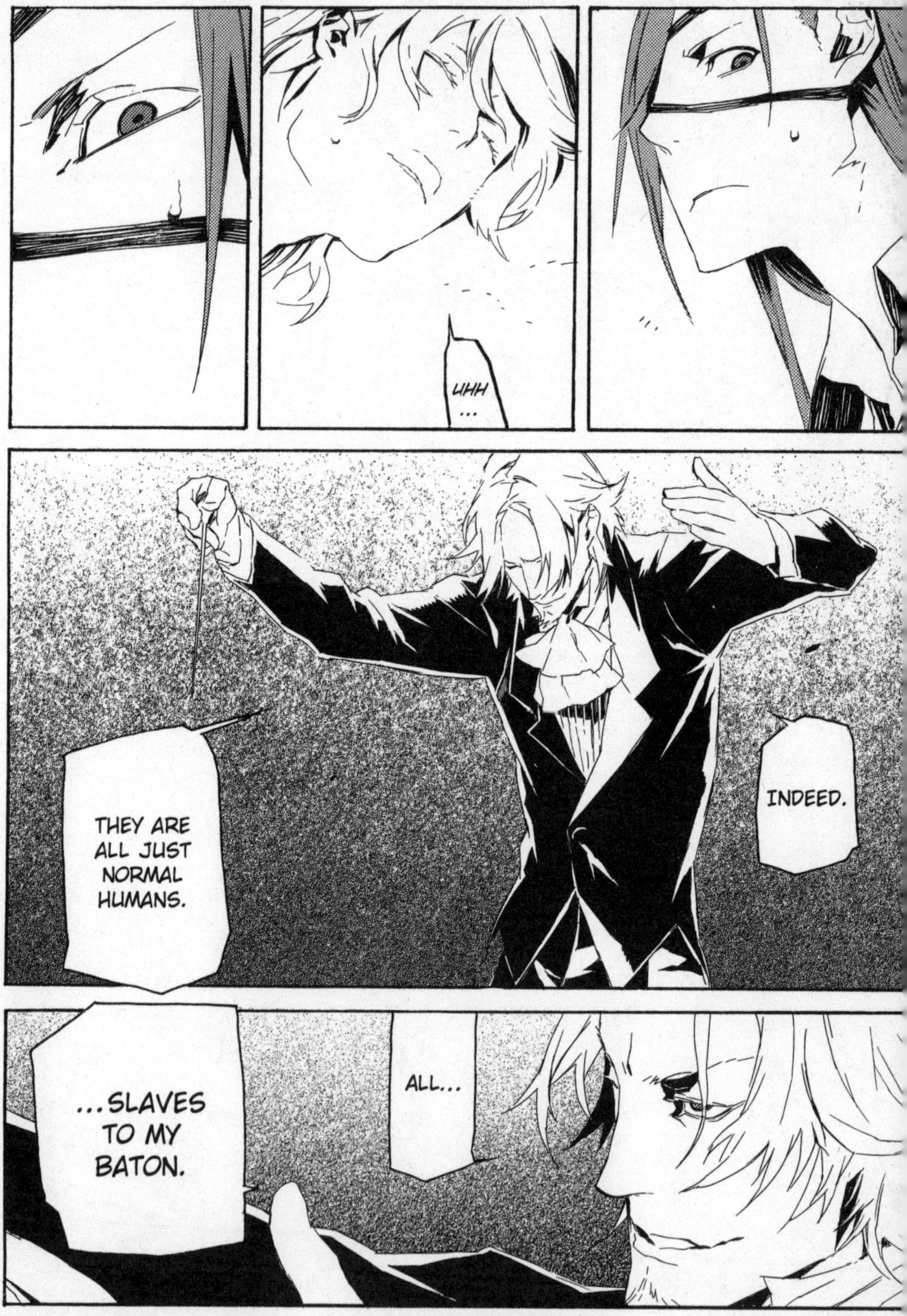
UHH ...
INDEED.
THEY ARE ALL JUST NORMAL HUMANS.
ALL...
...SLAVES TO MY BATON.

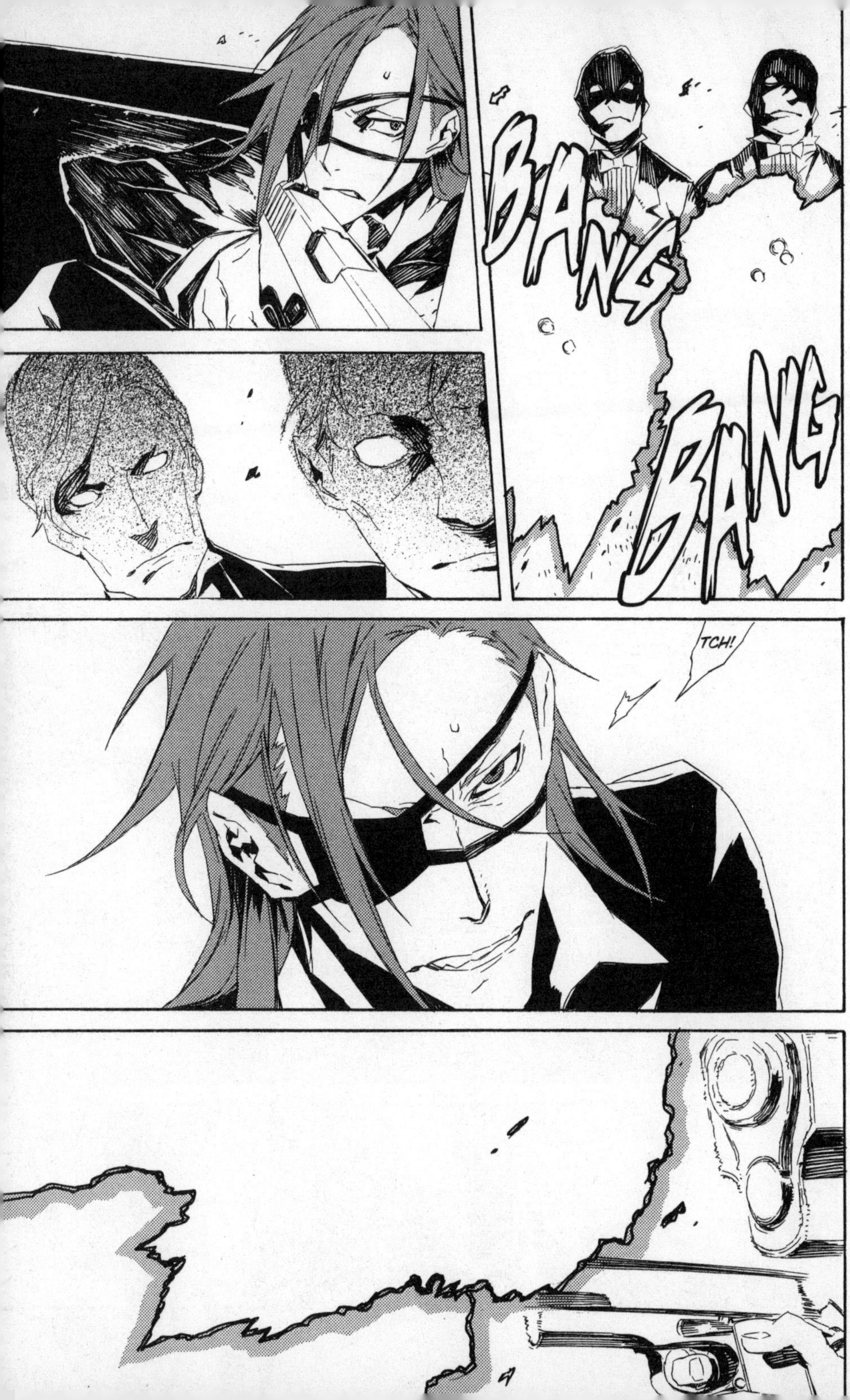
BANG
BANG
TCH!

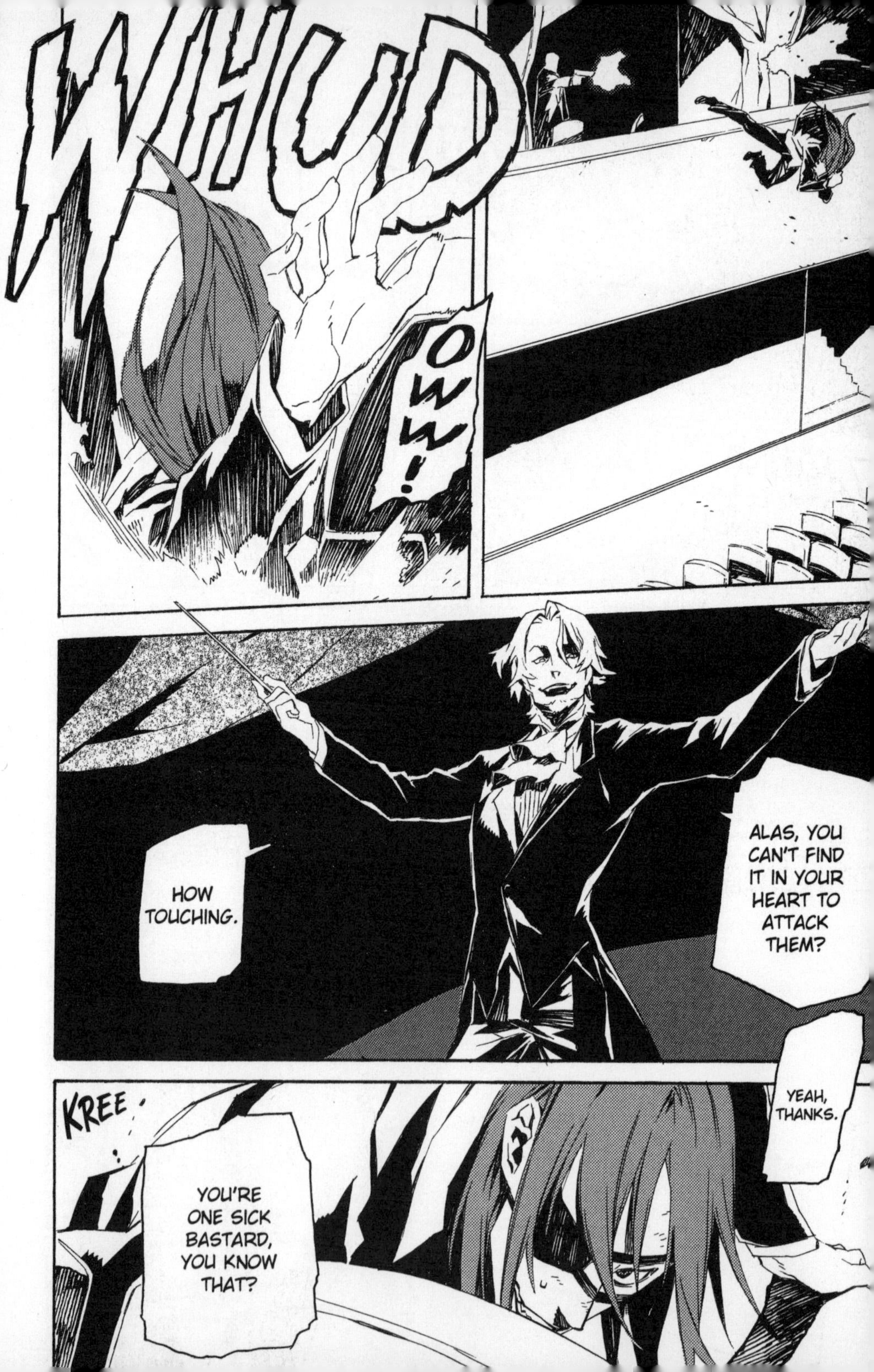
WHUD
OWW!
ALAS, YOU CAN'T FIND IT IN YOUR HEART TO ATTACK THEM?
HOW TOUCHING.
YEAH, THANKS.
KREE
YOU'RE ONE SICK BASTARD, YOU KNOW THAT?

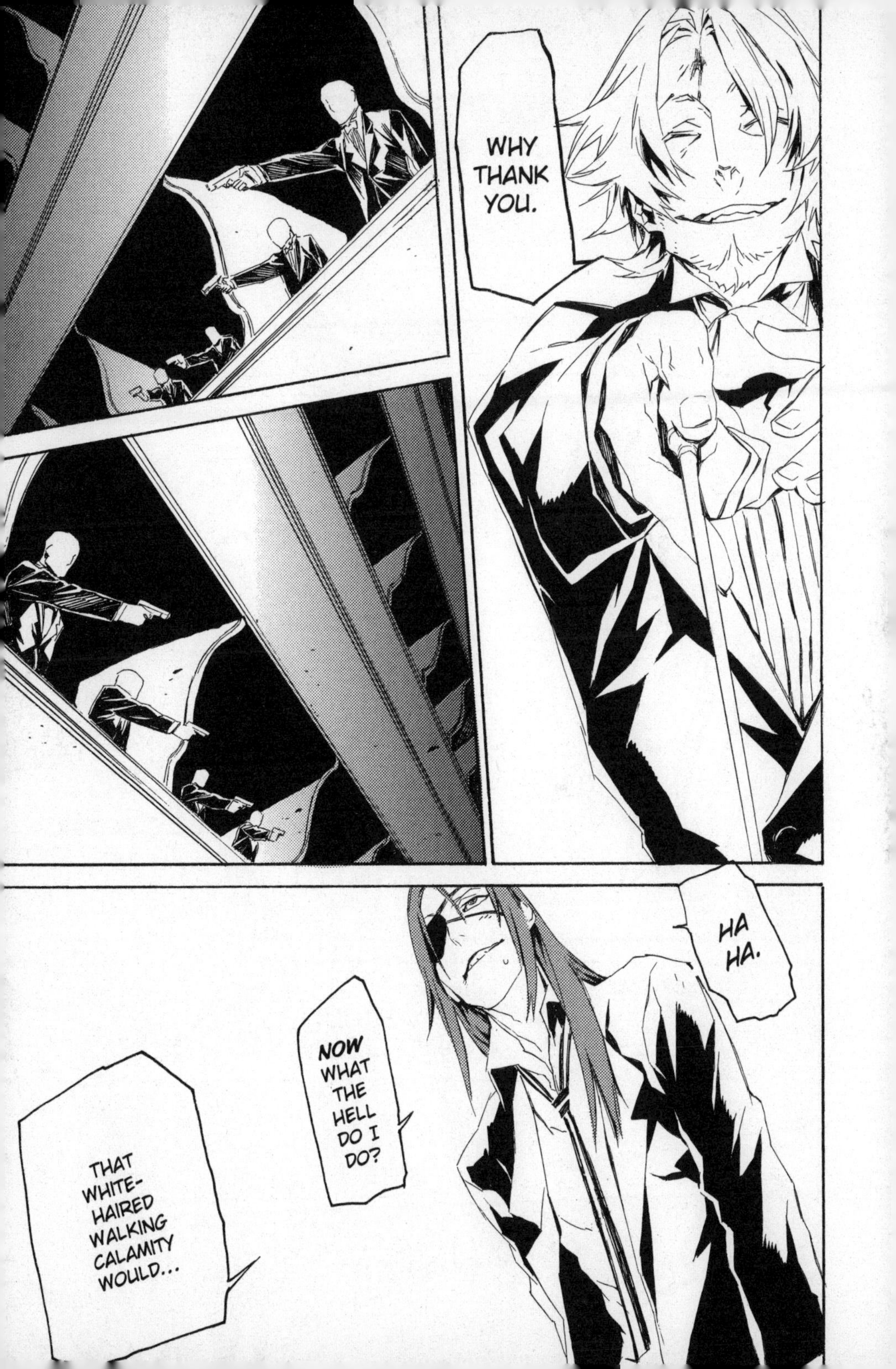
WHY THANK YOU.
HA HA.
NOW WHAT THE HELL DO I DO?
THAT WHITE-HAIRED WALKING CALAMITY WOULD...

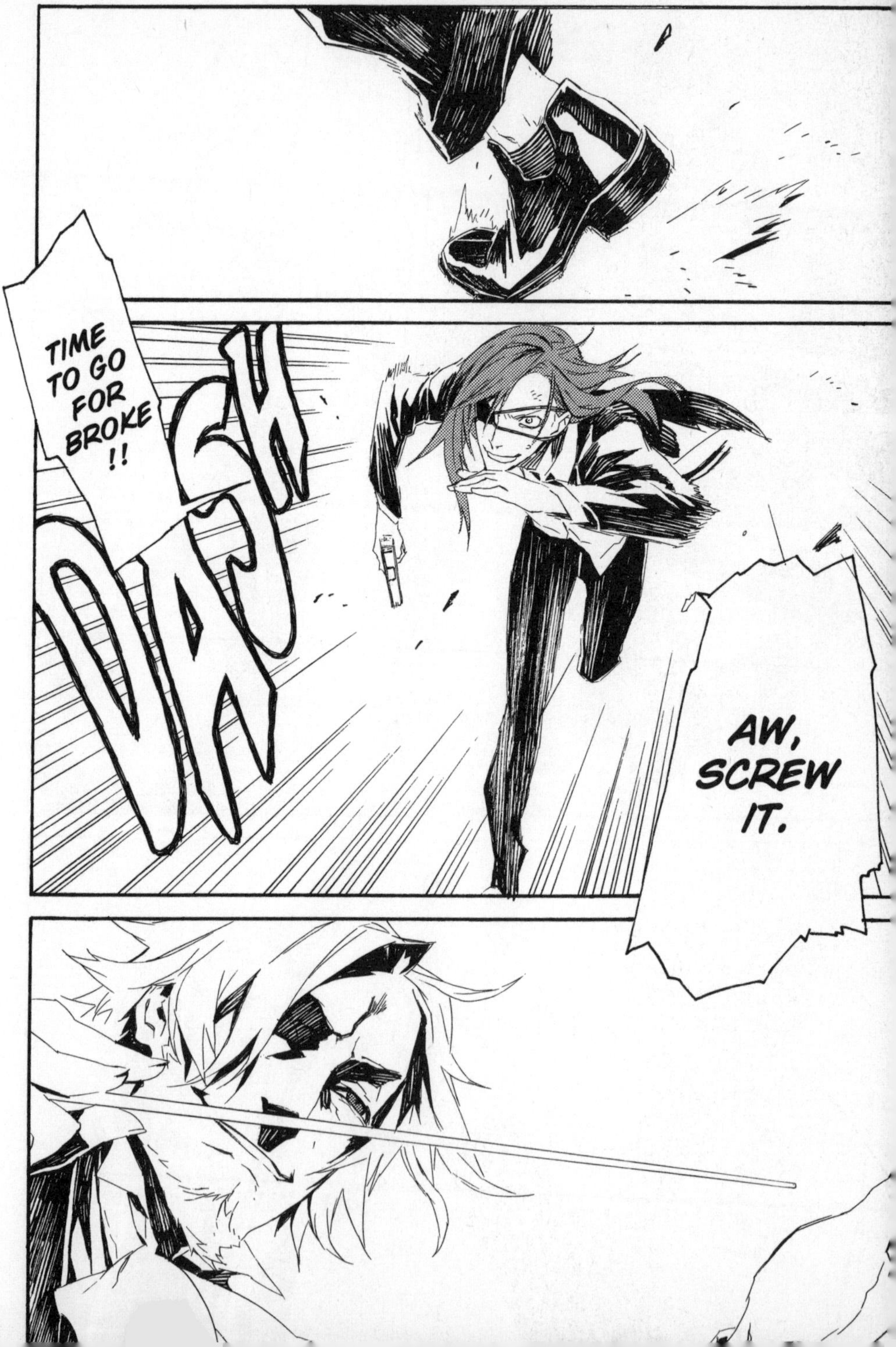
AW, SCREW IT.
TIME TO GO FOR BROKE!!
DASH

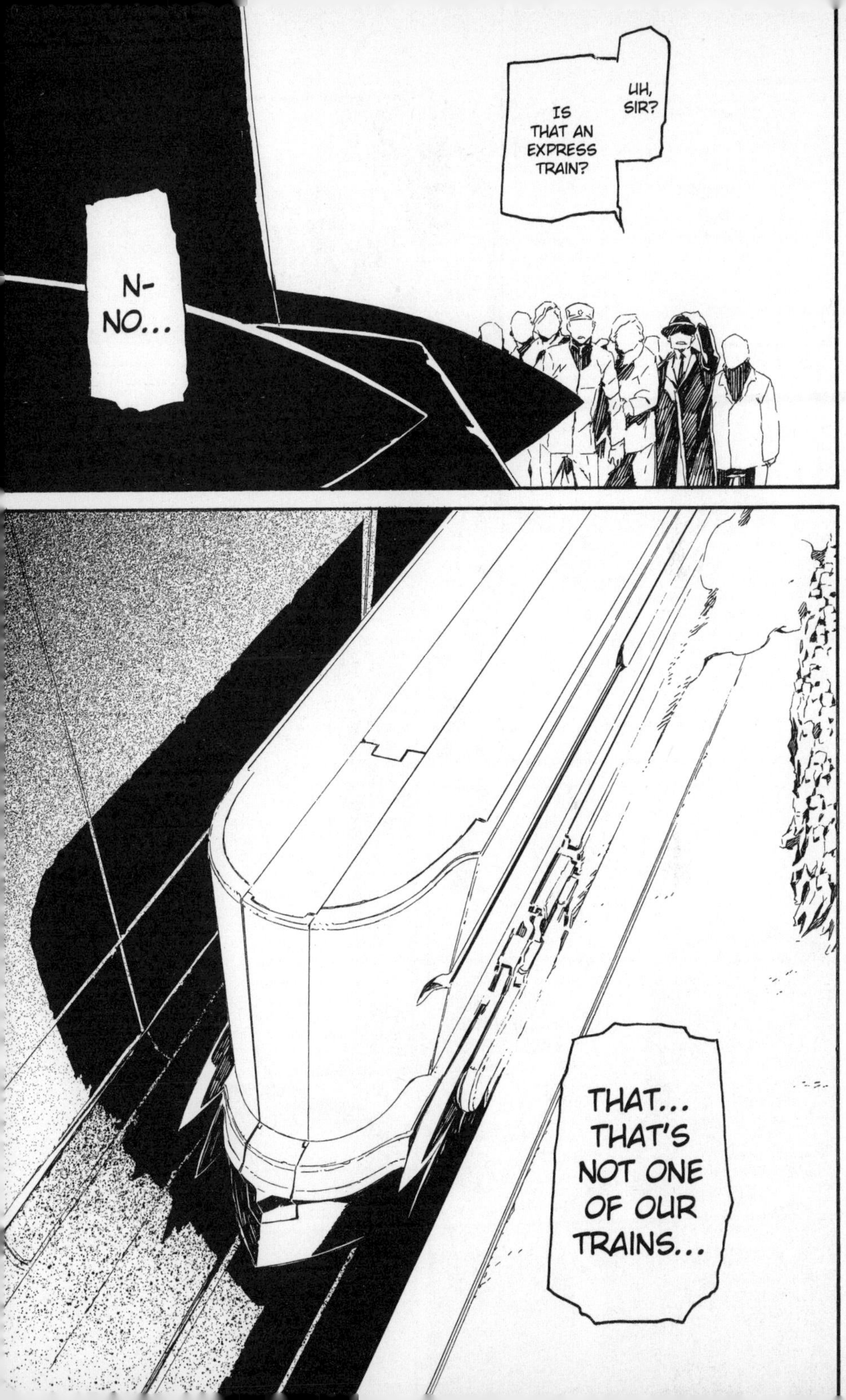
UH, SIR?
IS THAT AN EXPRESS TRAIN?
N-NO...
THAT... THAT'S NOT ONE OF OUR TRAINS...

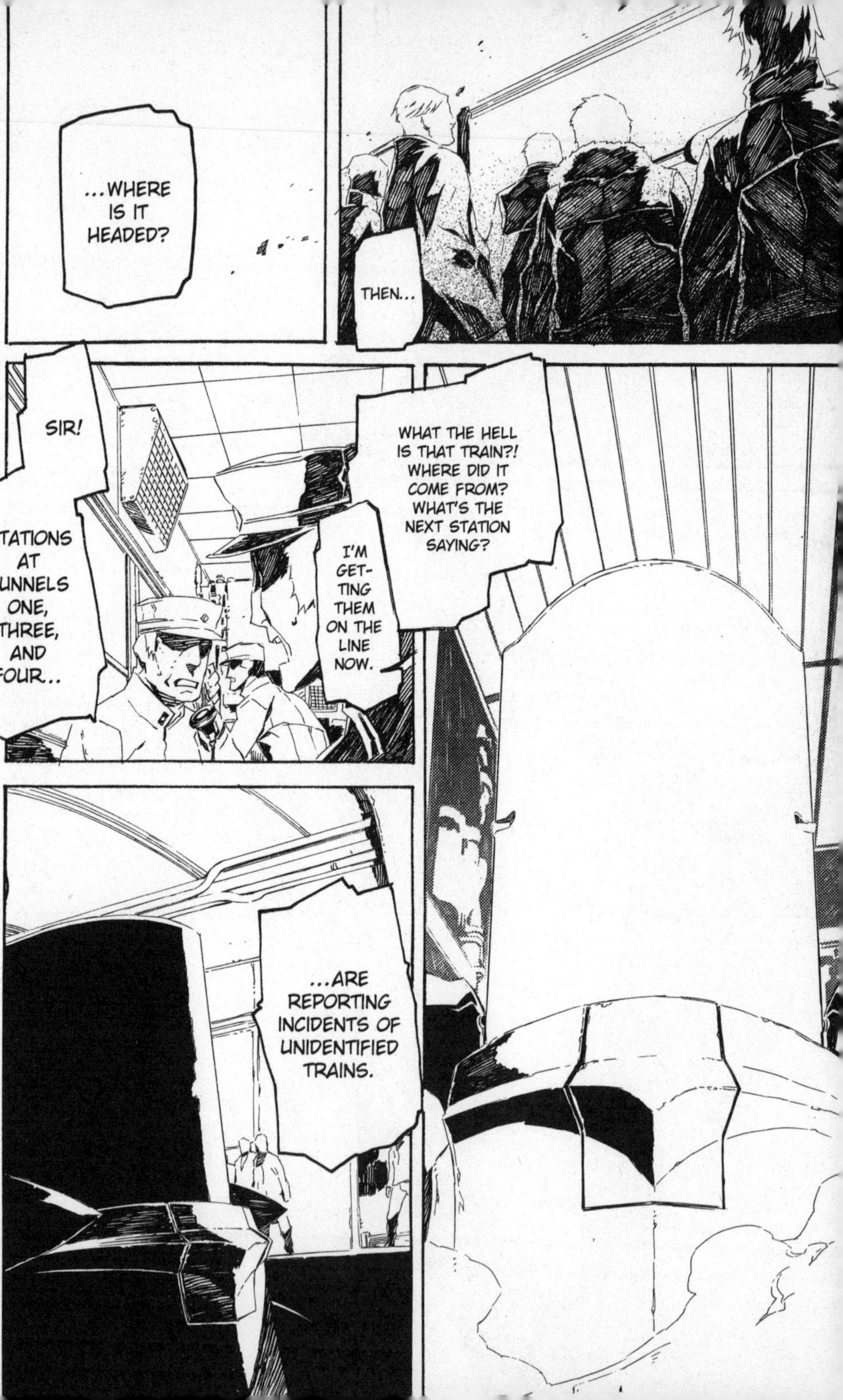
THEN...
...WHERE IS IT HEADED?
WHAT THE HELL IS THAT TRAIN?! WHERE DID IT COME FROM? WHAT'S THE NEXT STATION SAYING?
I'M GET- TING THEM ON THE LINE NOW.
SIR!
STATIONS AT TUNNELS ONE, THREE, AND FOUR...
...ARE REPORTING INCIDENTS OF UNIDENTIFIED TRAINS.

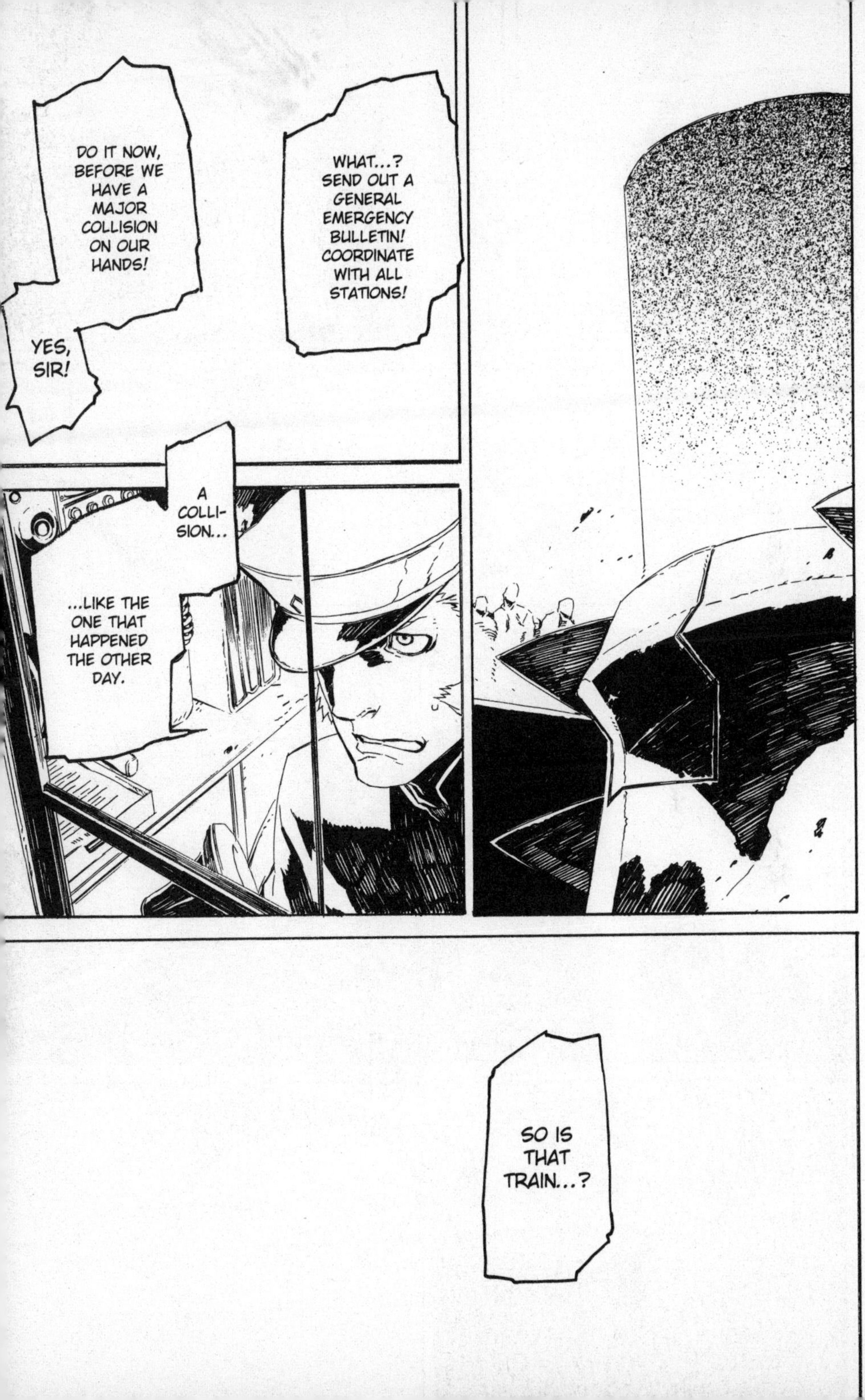
WHAT...? SEND OUT A GENERAL EMERGENCY BULLETIN! COORDINATE WITH ALL STATIONS!
DO IT NOW, BEFORE WE HAVE A MAJOR COLLISION ON OUR HANDS!
YES, SIR!
A COLLI-SION...
...LIKE THE ONE THAT HAPPENED THE OTHER DAY.
SO IS THAT TRAIN...?

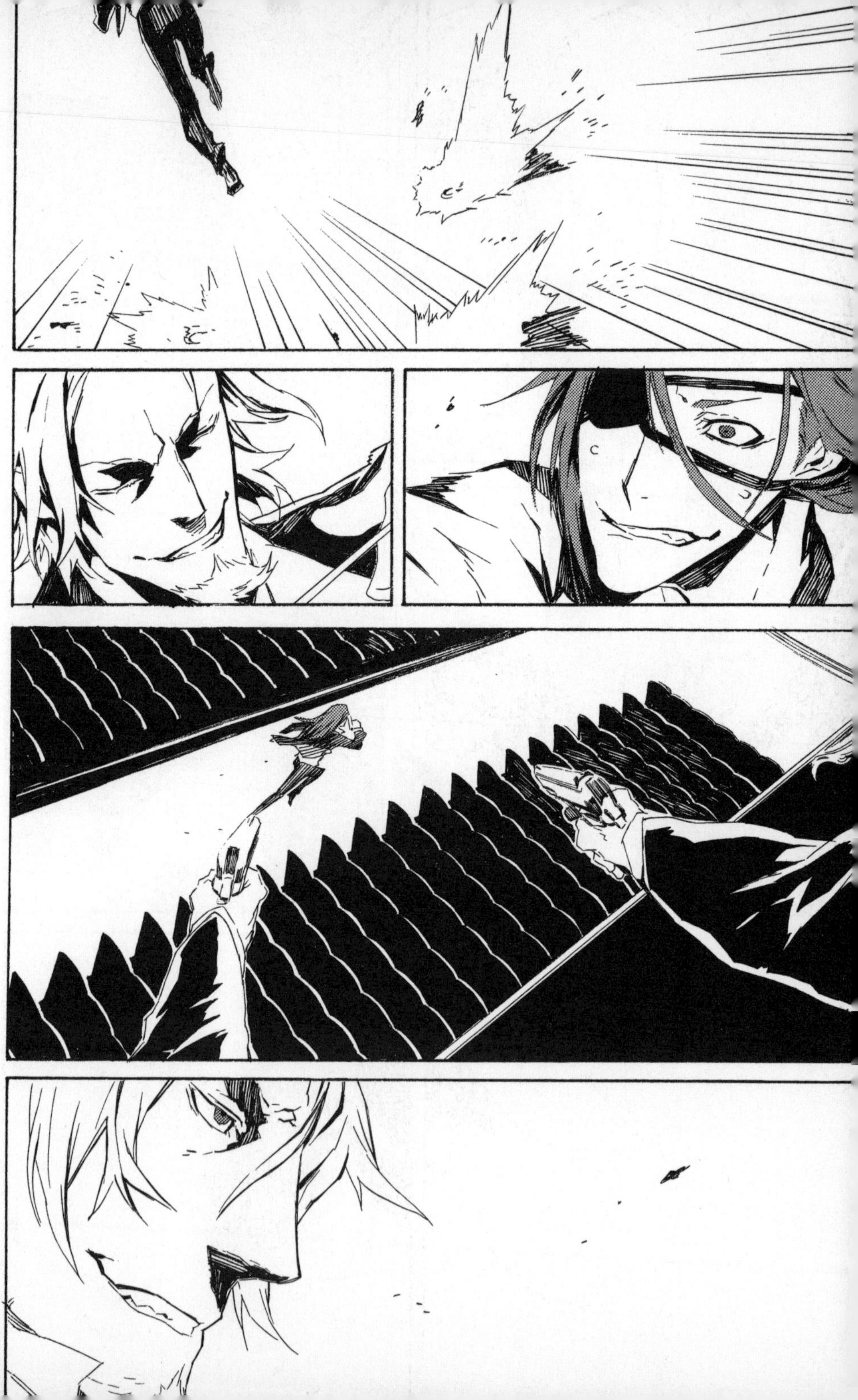

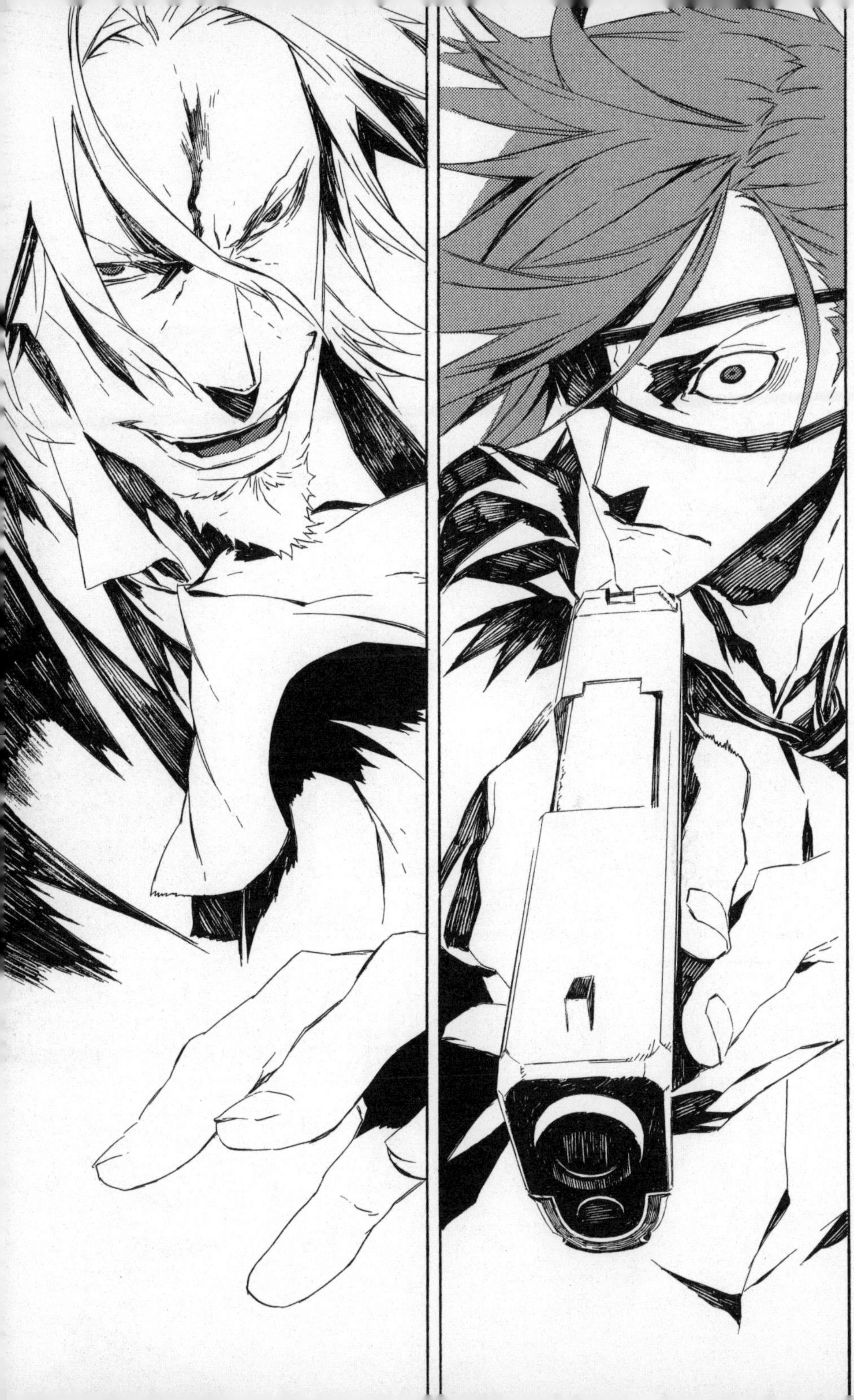

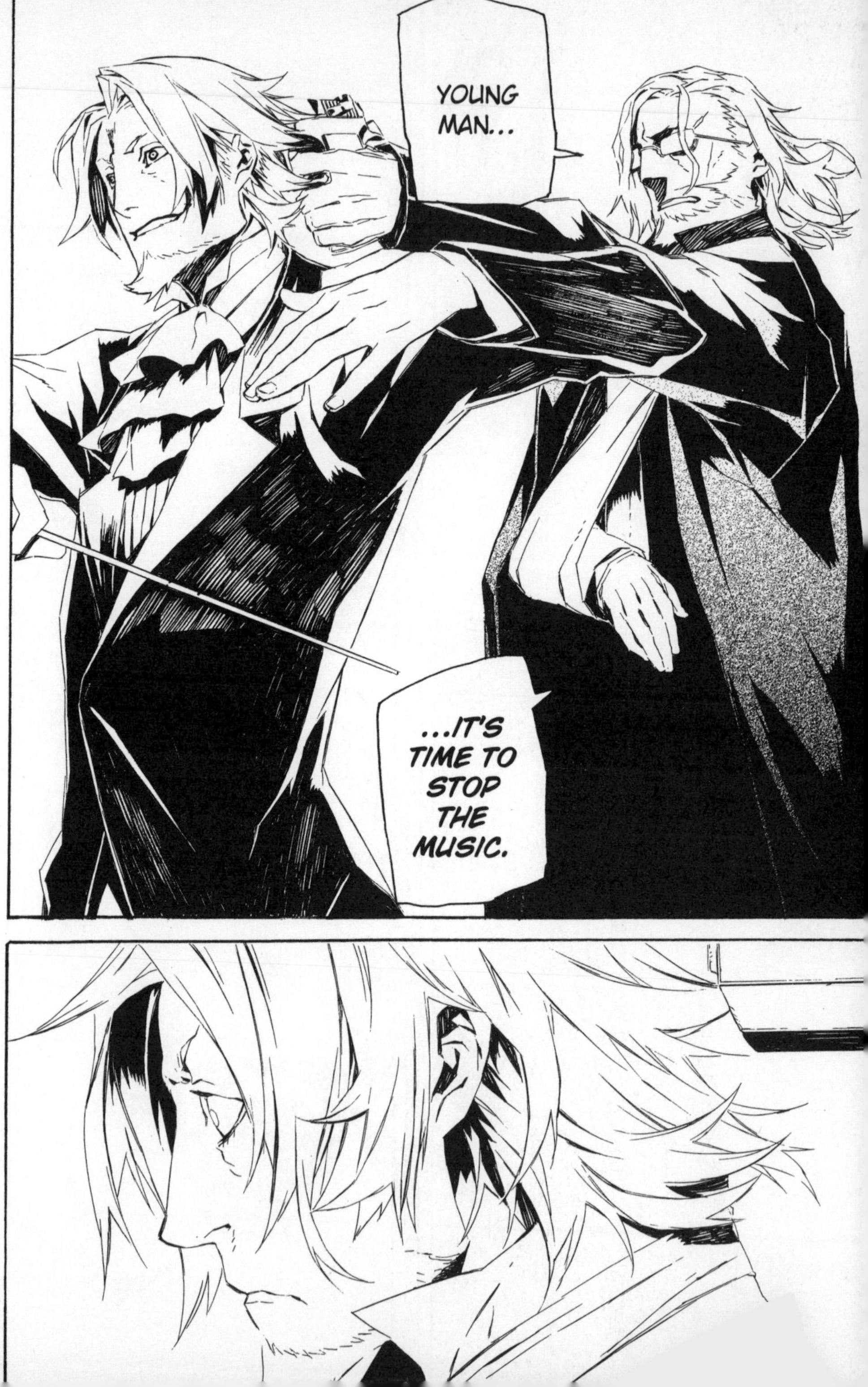
YOUNG MAN...
...IT'S TIME TO STOP THE MUSIC.

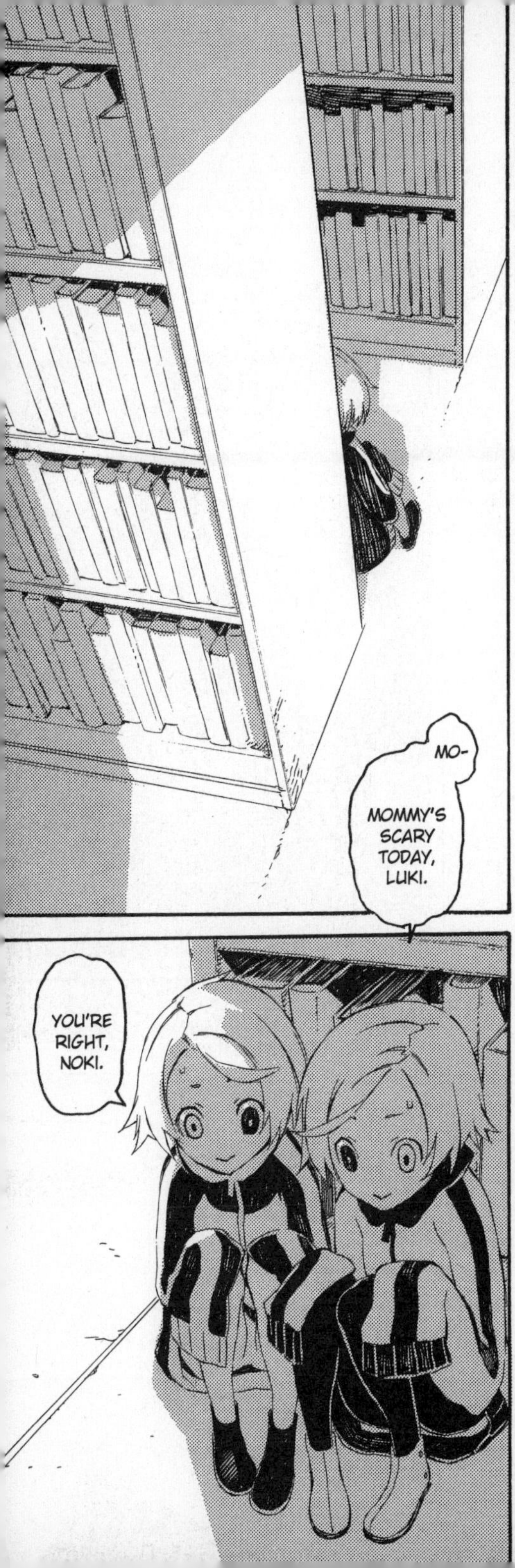
MO-
MOMMY'S SCARY TODAY, LUKI.
YOU'RE RIGHT, NOKI.

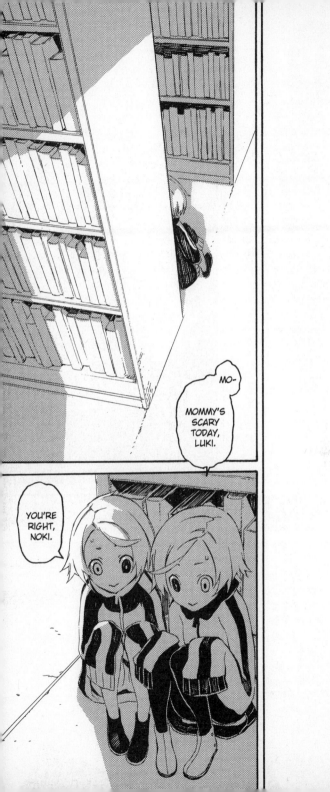

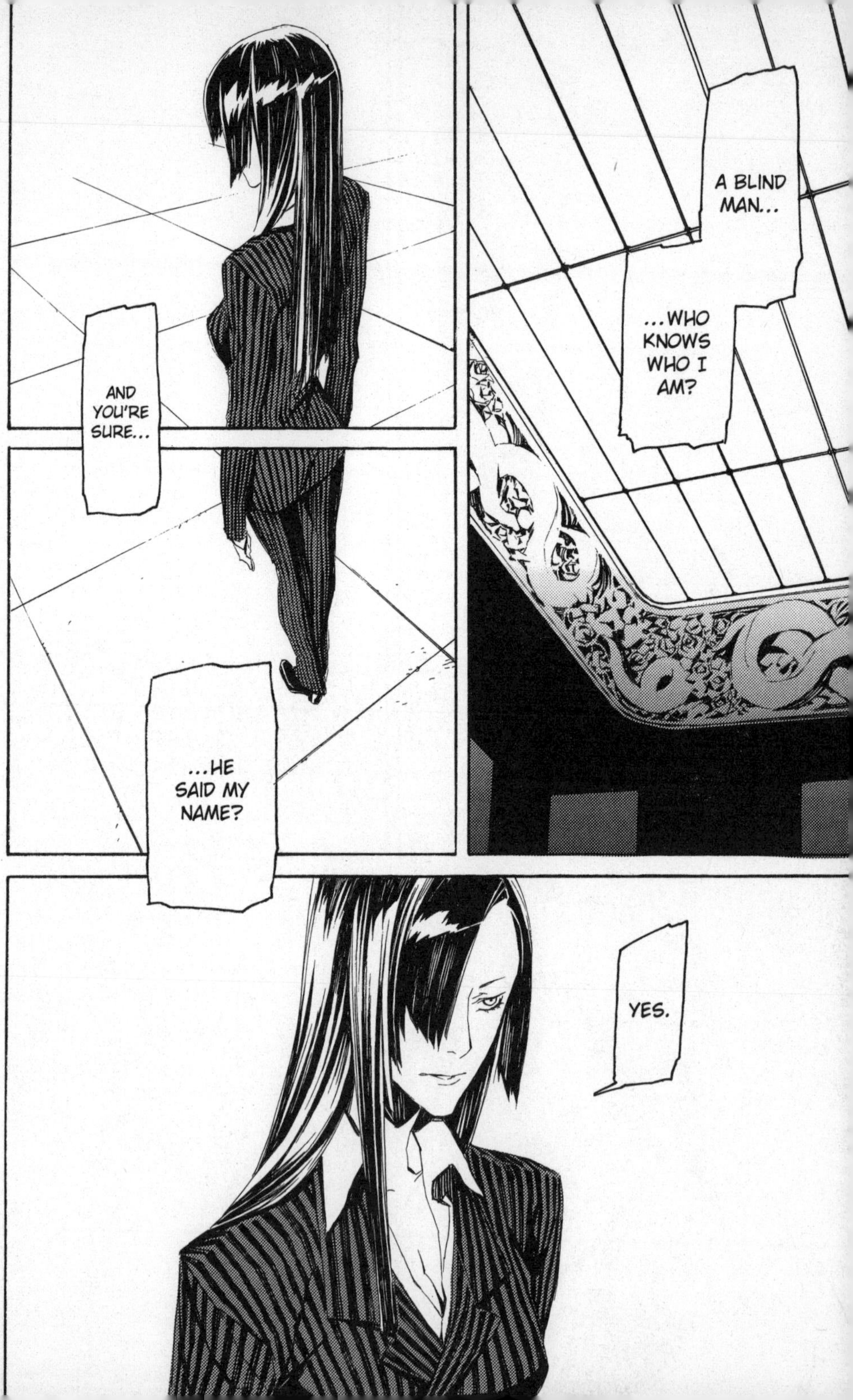
A BLIND MAN...
...WHO KNOWS WHO I AM?
AND YOU'RE SURE...
...HE SAID MY NAME?
YES.

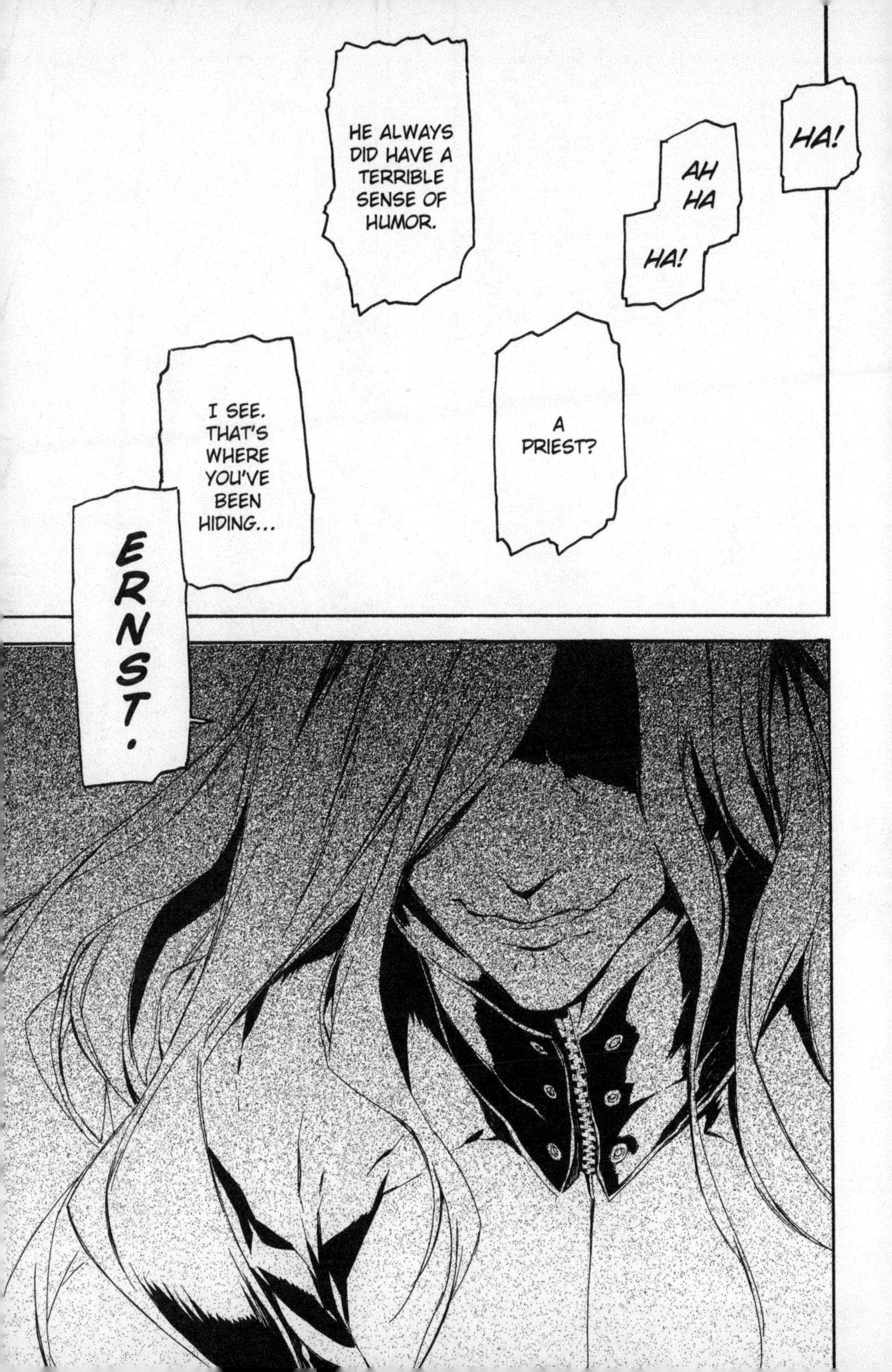
HA!
AH HA HA!
HE ALWAYS DID HAVE A TERRIBLE SENSE OF HUMOR.
A PRIEST?
I SEE. THAT'S WHERE YOU'VE BEEN HIDING...
ERNST.

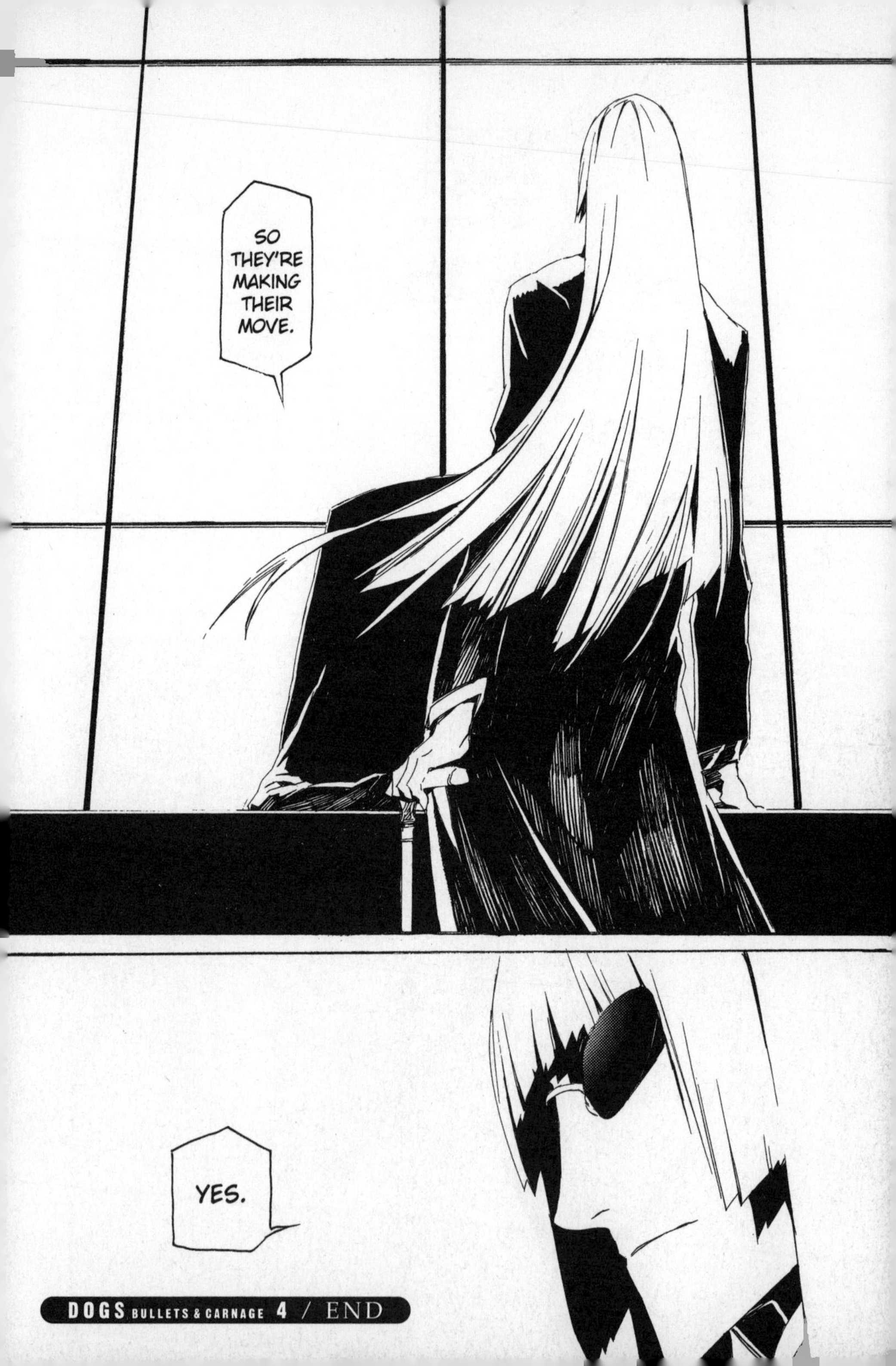
SO THEY'RE MAKING THEIR MOVE.
YES.
DOGS BULLETS & CARNAGE 4 / END

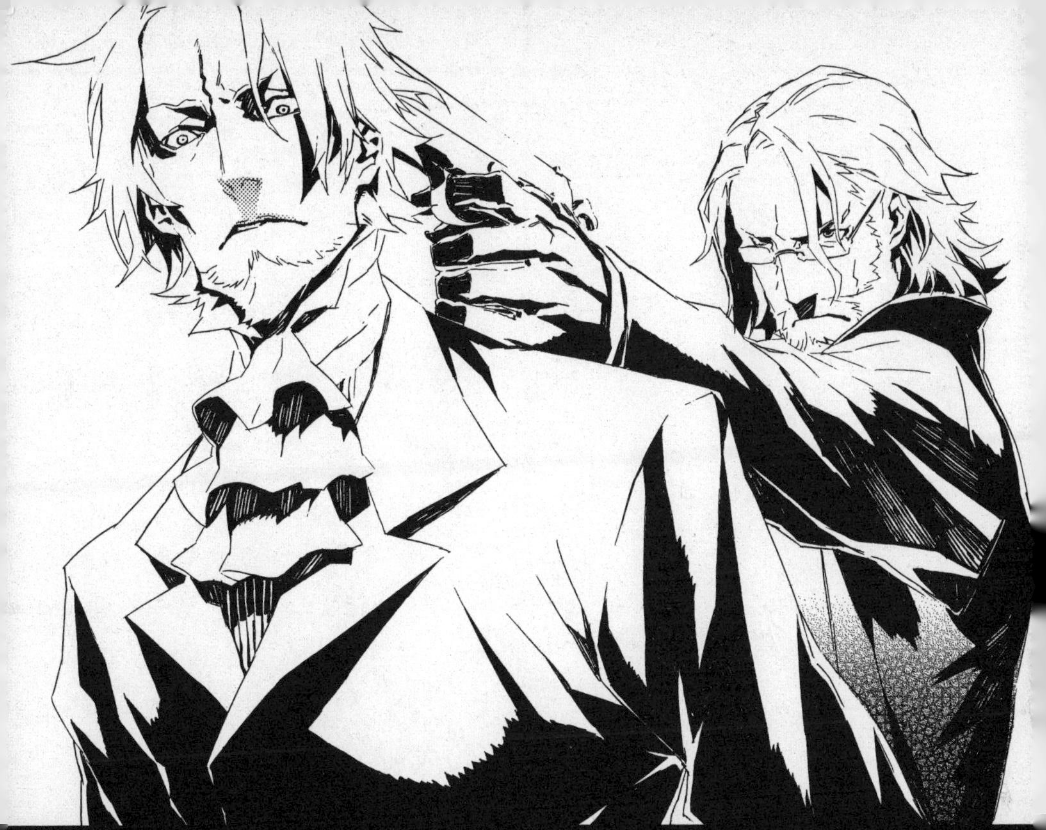

IN THE NEXT VOLUME

Mihai enters the stage just in time to save Badou from starring in his own death scene, but now the two of them are a captive audience to Beltheim's display of his lethal skills. As bad as things are in the Above though, they're even worse in the Below: under Giovanni's command, the dog soldiers have started their final assault against the underground city.

Available April 2011

SPECIAL THANKS

Iko Sasagawa

U

Suga

SERIES EDITOR

Satoshi Yamauchi

BOOK EDITOR

Rie Endou

ORIGINAL DESIGN

LIGHTNING

ABOUT THE AUTHOR

Shirow Miwa debuted in *UltraJump* magazine in 1999 with the short series *Black Mind*. His next series, *Dogs*, published in the magazine from 2000 to 2001, instantly became a popular success. He returned in 2005 with *Dogs: Bullets & Carnage*, which is currently running in *UltraJump*. Miwa also creates illustrations for books, music videos and magazines, and produces doujinshi (independent comics) under the circle name m.m.m.WORKS. His website is http://mmm-gee.net.

DOGS: BULLETS & CARNAGE
Volume 4

VIZ Signature Edition

Story & Art by
SHIROW MIWA

Translation & Adaptation/Katherine Schilling
Touch-up Art & Lettering/Eric Erbes
Cover & Graphic Design/Sam Elzway
Editor/Leyla Aker

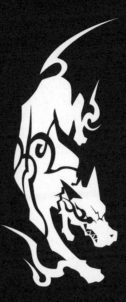

Printed in the U.S.A.

Published by VIZ Media, LLC
P.O. Box 77010
San Francisco, CA 94107

10 9 8 7 6 5 4 3 2
First printing, September 2010
Second printing, February 2014

RATED M FOR MATURE

PARENTAL ADVISORY
DOGS is rated M for Mature and is recommended for mature readers. This volume contains graphic violence and mature themes.

ratings.viz.com

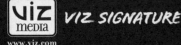

VIZ SIGNATURE

www.viz.com